Lee and His Generals in War and Memory

★ ★ ★

Lee and His Generals in War and Memory

GARY W. GALLAGHER

Louisiana State University Press   *Baton Rouge*

cloth
08   07   06   05   04   03   02   01   00   99   6   5   4   3   2

paper
13   12   11   10   09   08   07   06   05   04   5   4   3   2

Library of Congress Cataloging-in-Publication Data:

Gallagher, Gary W.
     Lee and his generals in war and memory / Gary W. Gallagher.
       p.   cm.
     Includes index.
     ISBN 0-8071-2286-6 (cloth); ISBN 0-8071-2958-5 (pbk.)
       1. Lee, Robert E. (Robert Edward), 1807–1870—Military leadership.
     2. Generals—Confederate States of America—History.   3. Confederate States
     of America. Army of Northern Virginia—History.   4. United States—
     History—Civil War, 1861–1865—Campaigns.   I. Title.
     E467.1.L4G3   1998
     973.7'3013—dc21   98-6215
                                                                            CIP

The paper in this book meets the guidelines for permanence and durability of the
Committee on Production Guidelines for Book Longevity of the Council on
Library Resources. ∞

Maps by George Skoch

In memory of Rose Pearl Gray,
whose understanding and enthusiasm helped
nourish a grandson's interest in Civil War history

Contents

Preface / xi

Credits for the Essays / xv

I LEE

1

The Idol of His Soldiers and the Hope of His Country:
Lee and the Confederate People / 3

2

The Best Possible Outcome One Could Hope For: Lee and the
Army of Northern Virginia in the 1862 Maryland Campaign / 21

3

If the Enemy Is There, We Must Attack Him:
Lee and the Second Day at Gettysburg / 47

4

The Army of Northern Virginia in May 1864:
Lee and a Crisis of High Command / 77

II LEE'S GENERALS

5

The Making of a Hero and the Persistence of a Legend: Stonewall
Jackson during the Civil War and in Popular History / 101

6

The Undoing of an Early Confederate Hero:
John Bankhead Magruder at the Seven Days / 118

7

Scapegoat in Victory:
James Longstreet and the Battle of Second Manassas / 139

8

Confederate Corps Leadership on the First Day at Gettysburg:
A. P. Hill and Richard S. Ewell in a Difficult Debut / 158

9

Revisiting the 1862 and 1864 Valley Campaigns: Stonewall
Jackson and Jubal Early in the Shenandoah / 182

III FIGHTING FOR HISTORICAL MEMORY

10

Jubal A. Early, the Lost Cause, and Civil War History:
A Persistent Legacy / 199

11

A Widow and Her Soldier: LaSalle Corbell Pickett
as the Author of
George E. Pickett's Civil War Letters / 227

IV DISTANT REVERBERATIONS

12

How Familiarity Bred Success: Military Campaigns
and Leaders in Ken Burns's *The Civil War* / 245

13

Battlefields, the Lost Cause, and the Legacy of the Civil War / 264

Index / 285

Maps

Theater of Operations, Army of Northern Virginia,
June 1862–April 1865 / 12

Lee's Movement into Maryland, September 3–13, 1862 / 31

Gettysburg, July 1–3, 1863 / 53

The Wilderness & Spotsylvania, May 5–12, 1864 / 86

Area of Operations, Seven Days Campaign, June 26–July 1, 1862 / 125

Preface

Robert E. Lee and his principal subordinates have inspired an enormous historical literature. Much of the framework within which they have been examined was created during the 1870s and 1880s by former Confederates, who in reminiscences and other writings constructed the Lost Cause interpretation of the conflict. According to their reading of events, the conflict was decided in the eastern theater, where Lee outshone all other generals and led his legendary army to a series of spectacular victories. Stonewall Jackson functioned as the perfect subordinate, his genius blossoming in the 1862 Shenandoah Valley campaign and ripening during subsequent collaborations with Lee. Inept or sulking lieutenants sometimes frustrated Lee's plans, but the Confederate chieftain's brilliance only loomed larger as he strove to compensate for failings in others. He and the Army of Northern Virginia provided the backbone of Confederate resistance for three long years before finally capitulating in the face of overwhelming Union manpower and resources. In defeat, Lee and his soldiers could look back on a record of selfless regard for duty and magnificent accomplishment.

This interpretation of Lee and his generals, in both its original Lost Cause form and in later variations, has captivated generations of readers. I have a long-standing interest in how Lost Cause authors and their writings have shaped popular ideas. I have tried to gauge the impact on subsequent historians—and, by extension, on the people who read their books—of Jubal A. Early, Walter H. Taylor, John B. Gordon, and others who wrote extensively about the Confederate war effort. Many of these authors sought above all else to mold posterity's views of the Confederacy and its leaders, and I believe they succeeded to a degree likely beyond their imagining. That success has led some historians to counter Lost Cause hyperbole by creating a revisionist literature that suffers from its own set of distortions.

All of the essays in this book explore in some fashion the effect of Lost Cause arguments on popular perceptions of Lee and several of his most famous lieutenants. Written over a period of twelve years, they fall into four groups.

In Part I, the first essay responds to scholars such as Thomas L. Connelly and Alan T. Nolan, who have mounted a heavy assault on the Lost Cause portrait of a nearly perfect warrior who performed miracles on the battlefield. I have no doubt that Lee made a number of mistakes. But, unlike these historians, I believe his generalship suited the Confederate people almost perfectly and yielded military results that sustained hopes for independence long past the point at which white southerners otherwise would have lost heart. The second essay examines the 1862 Maryland campaign, during which Lee made a number of questionable decisions. The third looks at the critical events of July 1, 1863, in the course of which Lee decided to pursue the tactical offensive at Gettysburg. The final essay in this section examines the initial month of the 1864 Overland campaign, which revealed Lee's ability to maintain an effective defense despite a series of crises affecting the army's high command.

Although Lee remains a major presence in Part II, the spotlight shifts to a half dozen of his subordinates. These five essays examine how Lost Cause writings enhanced or diminished Confederate military reputations and attempt to shed light on several specific questions. Did Stonewall Jackson's performances in the Shenandoah Valley and elsewhere justify his reputation as a peerless corps commander? Did John Bankhead Magruder's service at the Seven Days compare favorably to Jackson's? If so, why did the two men suffer such different fates in the aftermath of that campaign? Should modern readers judge James Longstreet's actions at Second Manassas harshly or favorably? Did A. P. Hill and Richard S. Ewell fail Lee on the first day at Gettysburg by precipitating a fight the commanding general did not want and then fumbling an opportunity to achieve a more decisive victory? And how did Jubal Early's leadership during the 1864 Valley campaign stack up against Jackson's in his Shenandoah operations in 1862?

Confederates wielding pens rather than swords assume center stage in Part III. The first essay analyzes Jubal Early's efforts to bequeath a written legacy favorable to Lee and Jackson and the nascent republic for which they fought. It finds abundant evidence in modern publishing, as well as in recent Civil War fiction and art, to suggest that "Old Jube" did his work well. Few Confederate generals enjoy a more romantic image than George E. Pickett, whose name is synonymous with the war's most famous infantry assault. The second essay looks at how LaSalle Corbell Pickett frustrated historical understanding of her husband by publishing what she claimed were his wartime letters to her. The letters were mostly clumsy fabrications, but even scholars who should know better have used them. Like Jubal Early, LaSalle Pickett succeeded in her major goal—portraying her husband as a gallant Lost Cause warrior utterly devoted to his wife. But in the process she also complicated the task of anyone hoping to comprehend Pickett as a man or a general.

The two essays in Part IV address Ken Burns's television documentary *The Civil War* and the issue of battlefield preservation. Both essays show that Lost Cause interpretations of Lee and his generals still abound, but they also address the wider issues of how the Civil War should be presented to the American people, and why academic and popular conceptions about the conflict are often so different. Did Burns devote too much attention to battles and generals, glorify Lee and his army, and slight the importance of slavery and emancipation? In a time when the Lost Cause and its symbols have come under increasing attack, do battlefields offer safe refuge to neo-Confederates seeking to pay homage to Lee and other rebels? Do the battlefields hinder rather than enhance understanding of the war? How should Americans approaching a new millennium view their nation's most riveting trial?

All but the first and last of these thirteen essays have been previously published, some for a scholarly audience and others with a general readership in mind. I have revised all of them with an eye toward contributing something useful to both specialists and lay readers. If this book does anything to bridge the gap between academic and popular history, I will consider it a success.

A number of people generously helped with this book. William A. Blair, William C. Davis, and Joseph T. Glatthaar provided valuable suggestions for shaping the material. Sylvia Frank lent an enthusiastic ear to my initial proposal and solid encouragement thereafter. Eileen Anne Gallagher persuaded me that the last essay belonged in the collection. The dedication offers long overdue thanks to my maternal grandmother, a native Californian who knew little about the Civil War but indulged my childhood interest by giving me books on birthdays and other special occasions. Her gifts of *Lee's Lieutenants* when I was eleven years old and *R. E. Lee* a year later helped convert youthful interest into lifelong passion. I still miss her.

Credits for the Essays

All but the first and last essays in this volume have been published elsewhere, some under slightly different titles. They have been revised, some more substantially than others, in order to provide a more integrated collection. I am indebted to the original publishers for permission to reprint the essays in their revised forms.

"The Best Possible Outcome One Could Hope For: Lee and the Army of Northern Virginia in the 1862 Maryland Campaign" is a heavily revised version of two essays originally published as "The Autumn of 1862: A Season of Opportunity" and "The Maryland Campaign in Perspective," in Gary W. Gallagher, ed., *Antietam: Essays on the 1862 Maryland Campaign* (Kent, Ohio: Kent State University Press, 1989), 1–13, 84–94. Reprinted by permission of The Kent State University Press.

"If the Enemy Is There, We Must Attack Him: Lee and the Second Day at Gettysburg" was originally published in Gary W. Gallagher, ed., *The Second Day at Gettysburg: Essays on Confederate and Union Leadership* (Kent, Ohio: Kent State University Press, 1993), 1–32, 173–78. Reprinted by permission of The Kent State University Press.

"The Army of Northern Virginia in May 1864: Lee and a Crisis of High Command" was originally published in *Civil War History* 36 (June 1990):101–18. Reprinted by permission of The Kent State University Press.

"The Making of a Hero and the Persistence of a Legend: Stonewall Jackson during the Civil War and in Popular History" was originally published in *Civil War: The Magazine of the Civil War Society* 56 (April 1996):20–24. Reprinted by permission of Outlook, Incorporated.

"The Undoing of an Early Confederate Hero: John Bankhead Magruder at the Seven Days" was originally published as "The Fall of 'Prince John' Magruder," in *Civil War: The Magazine of the Civil War Society* 19 (1989):8–15. Reprinted by permission of Outlook, Incorporated.

"Scapegoat in Victory: James Longstreet and the Battle of Second Manassas" was originally published in *Civil War History* 34 (December 1988):293–311. Reprinted by permission of The Kent State University Press.

"Confederate Corps Leadership on the First Day at Gettysburg: A. P. Hill and Richard S. Ewell in a Difficult Debut" was originally published in Gary W. Gallagher, ed., *The First Day at Gettysburg: Essays on Confederate and Union Leadership* (Kent, Ohio: Kent State University Press 1992), 30–56. Reprinted by permission of The Kent State University Press.

"Revisiting the 1862 and 1864 Valley Campaigns: Stonewall Jackson and Jubal Early in the Shenandoah" was originally published as "Stonewall Jackson vs. Jubal Early: A Comparison of the Two Confederate Campaigns in the Shenandoah Valley" in *Columbiad: A Quarterly Review of the War between the States* 1 (April 1997):20–33. Reprinted by permission of Cowles History Group.

"Jubal A. Early, the Lost Cause, and Civil War History: A Persistent Legacy" was originally published as the Frank L. Klement Lecture No. 4 (Milwaukee: Marquette University Press, 1995). Reprinted by permission of Marquette University Press.

"A Widow and Her Soldier: LaSalle Corbell Pickett as Author of George E. Pickett's Civil War Letters" was originally published in the *Virginia Magazine of History and Biography* 94 (July 1986):329–44. Reprinted by permission of the Virginia Historical Society.

"How Familiarity Bred Success: Military Campaigns and Leaders in Ken Burns's *The Civil War*" was originally published in Robert Brent Toplin, ed., *Ken Burns's "The Civil War": Historians Respond* (New York: Oxford University Press, 1996), 39–59. Reprinted by permission of Oxford University Press.

I

Lee

★ I ★

The Idol of His Soldiers
and the Hope of His Country

Lee and the Confederate People

James Longstreet's First Corps awaited an important review on the afternoon of April 29, 1864. Recently returned to the Army of Northern Virginia after several trying months in north Georgia and east Tennessee, Longstreet's soldiers stood in ranks extending across a broad field partially framed by oak woods. About one o'clock, under a bright spring sun that played off the burnished metal of thousands of muskets, music and an artillery salute announced the appearance of Robert E. Lee. The general guided Traveller between a pair of square gateposts and onto the crest of a knoll opposite the waiting infantry. "As he rode up to the colors, and the men caught sight of his well known figure," reported a witness two days later, "a wild and prolonged cheer, fraught with a feeling that thrilled all hearts, ran along the lines and rose to the heavens. Hats were thrown high, and many persons became almost frantic with emotion." Longstreet waved his hat enthusiastically, and Lee uncovered his head in restrained acknowledgment of the demonstration. Shouts mingled with tears among the veteran soldiers: "What a noble face and head!" "Our destiny is in his hands!" "He is the best and greatest man on this continent!" An artillerist described a "wave of sentiment . . . [that] seemed to sweep over the field. Each man seemed to feel the bond which held us all to Lee. . . . [T]he effect was that of a military sacrament, in which we pledged anew our lives."[1]

The soldiers at this memorable review—the last ever held by Lee—honored their unspoken pledge during bitter fighting over the next six weeks. They joined the rest of the Army of Northern Virginia to provide Lee with an instrument capable of blocking Ulysses S. Grant's powerful offensive blows. Taking heart from Lee's skillful leadership during the Overland campaign, Confederate civilians articulated their own bond with the general. Typical was Catherine Ann Devereux Edmondston, a North Carolinian who followed events in Virginia very closely. "This constant anxiety & watching must tell on our men!" she wrote on June 11, 1864. "How does Gen Lee support it? God's blessing only & God's strength enables him to bear up under [the strain]. What a position does he occupy—the idol, the point of trust, of confidence & repose of thousands! How nobly has he won the confidence, the admiration of the nation." Edmondston believed "'Marse Robert' can do any & all things. God grant that he may long be spared to us. He nullifies [Braxton] Bragg, [Robert] Ransom, & a host of other incapables."[2]

The emotional review and Edmondston's comments illuminate Lee's profound impact on the men in his army and on civilians behind the lines. Well before the midpoint of the Civil War, most Confederates looked to him as their greatest hope for winning independence. He and his army came to occupy a position in their fledgling nation much like that of George Washington and the Continental Army during the American Revolution. Repeated disasters in the western theater and along the Confederacy's coasts took a toll on southern morale throughout the war, but news from Virginia provided an effective counterbalance. Thousands of Confederates believed that their struggle for nationhood might succeed so long as Lee and the Army of Northern Virginia remained in the field, an attitude that persisted despite mounting evidence of northern superiority. As late as mid-March 1865, an astute foreign visitor commented about the degree to which Confederates drew strength

1. R to editor of the *Daily South Carolinian* (Columbia), May 1, 1864 (published in the May 10, 1864, issue); Edward Porter Alexander, *Fighting for the Confederacy: The Personal Recollections of General Edward Porter Alexander*, ed. Gary W. Gallagher (Chapel Hill: University of North Carolina Press, 1989), 346.

2. Catherine Ann Devereux Edmondston, *"Journal of a Secesh Lady": The Diary of Catherine Ann Devereux Edmondston, 1860–1866*, ed. Beth Gilbert Crabtree and James W. Patton (Raleigh: North Carolina Division of Archives and History, 1979), 576.

ROBERT EDMUND LEE,

COMMANDER-IN-CHIEF OF THE CONFEDERATE FORCES.

Robert E. Lee in the *Southern Illustrated News*, January 17, 1863. This engraving, based on a prewar photograph and giving an incorrect middle name, was the first portrait of Lee ever seen by many Confederates.

from Lee: *"Genl R. E. Lee* ... [is] the idol of his soldiers & the Hope of His Country," wrote Thomas Conolly, a member of the British Parliament: "[T]he prestige which surrounds his person & the almost fanatical belief in his judgement & capacity . . . is the one idea of an entire people."[3]

How did Lee become such a towering presence in the Confederacy? Part

3. Thomas Conolly, *An Irishman in Dixie: Thomas Conolly's Diary of the Fall of the Confederacy*, ed. Nelson D. Lankford (Columbia: University of South Carolina Press, 1988), 52 (entry for March 16, 1865).

of the answer lies in his background and personality. He had begun the war with a strong reputation. His service in the war with Mexico, as superintendent of West Point, and as a senior cavalry officer in the late 1850s had made him known in many circles. Winfield Scott's lavish praise of Lee's accomplishments in Mexico had been especially noteworthy. When it became known in April 1861 that Lee had resigned his United States commission and would take command of Virginia's state forces, the Richmond *Enquirer* gleefully reported Scott's sorrow at losing Lee's services for the Union cause. Another Virginia newspaper rejoiced that Lee, "the very Flower of the Army," had left his old flag to serve a new one. Confederate citizens emulated their newspapers in noting Scott's discomfort, as when South Carolina diarist Emma Holmes quoted the old general as saying "'that it was better for every officer in the army to die, himself included, than Robert Lee,' on account of his military genius."[4] It would be an exaggeration to say that all Confederates placed Lee first among southern officers in the spring of 1861, but he was an admired figure from whom much was expected.

Confederates also found many of Lee's personal qualities attractive. He seemed to embody all the virtues cherished by antebellum white southerners. His generosity toward others impressed countless observers, as did his modesty. "The General is affable, polite, and unassuming," remarked a man who traveled with Lee on a train in early 1864, "and shares the discomforts of a crowded railroad coach with ordinary travelers." Pronouncing Lee "as unostentatious and unassuming in dress as he is in manners," this individual noted that the Confederacy's greatest hero wore "a Colonel's coat (three stars without the wreath) a good deal faded, blue pantaloons, high top boots, blue cloth talma, and a high felt hat without adornment save a small cord around the crown." Surgeon Samuel Merrifield Bemiss had touched on similar qualities in describing Lee to his children in April 1863. "I wish you all could see him," wrote Bemiss. "He is so noble a specimen of men . . . always polite and agreeable, and thinking less of himself than he ought to, and thinking indeed of nothing, hoping and praying for nothing but the success of our cause and the return of blessed peace."[5]

4. Richmond *Enquirer*, April 27, 25, 1861; Emma Holmes, *The Diary of Miss Emma Holmes, 1861–1866*, ed. John F. Marszalek (Baton Rouge: Louisiana State University Press, 1979), 38 (entry for April 25, 1861).

5. Mobile *Advertiser and Register*, March 16, 1864; Samuel Merrifield Bemiss to My dear Children, April 10, 1863, Bemiss Family Papers, 1779–1921, Mss 1B4255d23, Virginia Historical Society, Richmond.

Lee's well-known Christian piety impressed many southerners. In this early postwar engraving by A. R. Waud, the general prays with a group of his soldiers.
John Esten Cooke, *A Life of Gen. Robert E. Lee* (New York: D. Appleton, 1871)

On the battlefield, Lee exhibited the unquestioned courage Confederates demanded from their most admired leaders. Francis Lawley of the *Times* of London noted this quality during the battle of Fredericksburg on December 13, 1862. Describing how Lee rode slowly along the southern lines, Lawley told his readers, "It would be presumptuous in me to say one word in commendation of the serenity, or, if I may so express it, the unconscious dignity of General Lee's courage, when he is under fire." The Englishman believed Lee's behavior in combat reflected his personality away from the fray: "No one who sees and knows his demeanour in ordinary life would expect anything else from one so calm, so undemonstrative and unassuming." It seemed to Lawley, who borrowed a phrase from a biographer of Britain's Lord Raglan, that Lee possessed an "antique heroism" that bespoke utter disregard for danger.[6]

Perhaps most reassuring to Confederates who believed themselves to be God's chosen people was Lee's deep Christian faith. The Richmond *Dispatch* developed this theme in late April 1861, asserting that a "more heroic Christian, noble soldier and gentleman could not be found." Lee seemed the perfect instrument to translate Confederate desires for independence into reality. "Of

6. *Times* (London), January 13, 1863.

him it was said before his appointment, and of him it may well be said," stated the *Dispatch,* "no man is superior in all that constitutes the soldier and the gentleman—no man more worthy to head our forces and lead our army. . . . His reputation, his acknowledged ability, his chivalric character, his probity, honor, and—may we add to his eternal praise—his Christian life and conduct make his very name a 'tower of strength.'"[7]

Lee also looked the part of a general. Mary Chesnut called him "the picture of a soldier." Lieutenant Colonel A. J. L. Fremantle, the British officer whose remarkable diary of his journey through the Confederacy has captivated generations of readers, confirmed Mrs. Chesnut's observation in a detailed description of Lee during the Gettysburg campaign. "General Lee is, almost without exception, the handsomest man of his age I ever saw," wrote Fremantle. "He is fifty-six years old, tall, broad-shouldered, very well made, well set up—a thorough soldier in appearance; and his manners are most courteous and full of dignity. He is a perfect gentleman in every respect." Fremantle also thought Traveller a handsome mount—man and horse together cut a striking figure. Beyond appearances, Fremantle noted that Lee had "none of the small vices, such as smoking, drinking, chewing, or swearing, and his bitterest enemy never accused him of any of the greater ones." The Britisher could imagine no man who had so few enemies or enjoyed such universal esteem: "Throughout the South, all agree in pronouncing him to be as near perfection as a man can be."[8]

Although Fremantle undoubtedly spoke the truth about Lee's standing in June 1863, he would have found a different popular attitude in late 1861 and early 1862. Lee's antebellum accomplishments, gentlemanly demeanor, and Christianity—all of which contributed to his later fame—counted for little at a time when many Confederates thought him timid on the battlefield. His reputation reached its nadir following a frustrating campaign in western Virginia during the fall of 1861, in the course of which forces under William S. Rosecrans and George B. McClellan solidified Union control over much of the area. Subsequent service along the South Atlantic coast added scant luster to

7. Richmond *Dispatch,* April 26, May 1, 1861.

8. Mary Chesnut, *The Private Mary Chesnut: The Unpublished Civil War Diaries,* ed. C. Vann Woodward and Elisabeth Muhlenfeld (New York: Oxford University Press, 1984), 87 (entry for July 3, 1861); Arthur James Lyon Fremantle, *Three Months in the Southern States: April–June, 1863* (1863; reprint, Lincoln: University of Nebraska Press, 1991), 248 (entry for June 30, 1863).

Lee's record. The press suggested, and whispers among soldiers and civilians agreed, that he preferred entrenching to fighting. By the spring of 1862, Lee was back in Richmond functioning as Jefferson Davis's chief military adviser, a bureaucratic post that offered little opportunity for accomplishments that would generate public acclaim.[9]

Armistead L. Long of Lee's staff recalled the winter of 1861–1862 as a period when "the press and the public were clamorous against" his chief. Prominent among the critics was influential newspaper editor Edward A. Pollard of the Richmond *Examiner,* who denigrated Lee in western Virginia as "a general who had never fought a battle . . . and whose extreme tenderness of blood induced him to depend exclusively upon the resources of strategy, to essay the achievement of victories without the cost of life." Pollard insisted that Lee's reluctance to press the Federals in western Virginia had frittered away the "opportunity of a decisive battle."[10] Word that Lee would take command of the Army of Northern Virginia after Joseph E. Johnston suffered a grievous wound at Seven Pines on May 31, 1862, disturbed many Confederates. Edward Porter Alexander, who served as Lee's chief of ordnance from the Seven Days through Antietam, recalled that when Lee replaced Johnston "some of the newspapers . . . pitched into him with extraordinary virulence." With Lee in charge, claimed unhappy editors, "our army would never be allowed to fight." Catherine Edmondston, whose opinion of Lee in mid-1864 was so high, castigated him in June 1862 as an officer who was "too timid, believes too much in masterly inactivity, finds 'his strength' too much in 'sitting still.'" Voicing thoughts shared by many others in the Confederacy, Edmondston stated that Lee had failed in western Virginia, retreated too often, and impressed few people with his efforts in South Carolina. "His nick name last summer was '*old-stick-in-the- mud,*'" she observed bitingly: "There is mud enough now in and about our lines, but pray God he may not fulfil the whole of his name."[11]

The Army of Northern Virginia's new commander confronted a daunting

9. For an in-depth recent treatment of Lee's unhappy experience in western Virginia, see Clayton R. Newell, *Lee vs. McClellan: The First Campaign* (Washington, D.C.: Regnery, 1996).

10. Armistead L. Long, *Memoirs of Robert E. Lee: His Military and Personal History Embracing a Large Amount of Information Hitherto Unpublished* (1886; reprint, Secaucus, N.J.: Blue and Grey Press, 1983), 130; Edward A. Pollard, *Southern History of the War: The First Year of the War* (1862; reprint, New York: Charles B. Richardson, 1864), 265.

11. Alexander, *Fighting for the Confederacy,* 90; Edmondston, *"Journal of a Secesh Lady,"* 169, 189 (entries for May 6, June 8, 1862).

military situation in June 1862. Unremitting defeat had stalked Confederate efforts in the western theater earlier that year. Forts Henry and Donelson had fallen, and a failed southern counteroffensive at Shiloh left Federals in control of much of middle Tennessee. The loss of New Orleans in late April and of Memphis in early June darkened an already grim picture. In the East, meanwhile, George B. McClellan had moved his Army of the Potomac to within a few miles of Richmond, fending off Johnston's inept offensive at Seven Pines and preparing to invest the Confederate capital. Although Stonewall Jackson's small victories in the Shenandoah Valley in May and early June lifted southern spirits, the loss of Richmond, coming on the heels of so much defeat west of the Appalachians, almost certainly would have doomed the Confederacy.

Apart from the purely military dimension of his challenge, Lee had to deal with a restive Confederate populace. No analysis of his generalship should overlook the importance of civilian expectations. He served in a democracy at war, and the key to success lay in providing the type of leadership that would generate continued popular support for the national military effort. Since the victory at First Manassas in July 1861, it seemed to many Confederate citizens that their armies had forged a record dominated by defeat and retreat. The result had been an erosion of public morale and an almost frantic yearning for offensive victories. During the winter of 1861–1862, a Richmond newspaper alluded to a "public mind . . . restless, and anxious to be relieved by some decisive action that shall have a positive influence in the progress of the war." In late June 1862, from his vantage point in the Confederate War Department, John B. Jones observed that "our people are beginning to *fear* there will be no more fighting around Richmond until McClellan *digs* his way to it." Whenever combat ceased, stated Jones, "our people have fits of gloom and despondency; but when they snuff battle in the breeze, they are animated with confidence."[12]

Lee certainly understood Confederate morale as he prepared to face McClellan outside Richmond. Aggressive by nature, he must have known that his preference for dictating the action rather than reacting to the enemy's moves suited his people's temperament. He used his first three weeks in field

12. Richmond *Dispatch*, January 3, 1862; John B. Jones, *A Rebel War Clerk's Diary at the Confederate Capital*, 2 vols. (1866; reprint, Alexandria, Va.: Time-Life Books, 1982), 1:135 (entry for June 24, 1862).

command to prepare his army and then launched an offensive against McClellan in the Seven Days battles, a decision that saved Richmond and laid the groundwork for his later fame.

When Lee ordered assaults at Mechanicsville on June 26, McClellan lay at Richmond's doorstep with more than 100,000 men and Irvin McDowell menaced the capital with another 30,000 Federals at Fredericksburg. Additional Union forces lurked in the Shenandoah Valley and northern Virginia. Three months later, Lee's bold strategic and tactical movements had won victories at the Seven Days and Second Manassas and pushed the military frontier in the eastern theater across the Potomac River into western Maryland. No Union force of substantial size remained anywhere on Virginia soil (although Fort Monroe and Norfolk remained in northern hands). The Civil War witnessed no other strategic reorientation of such magnitude in so short a time.

The battle of Antietam ended this spectacular run in mid-September, but Lee already had accomplished immense good in the crucial area of civilian morale. Confederates exulted at the thought of an aggressive posture that took the war to the enemy. A newspaper in Macon, Georgia, struck a familiar note in applauding Lee's decision to march north toward Maryland: "Having in this war exercised Christian forbearance to its utmost extent, by acting on the defensive, it will now be gratifying to all to see . . . the war carried upon the soil of those barbarians who have so long been robbing and murdering our quiet and unoffending citizens."[13]

Lee's offensive successes swept away doubts about his willingness to take chances and thrust his name into the front rank of southern generals. The Richmond *Dispatch* commented on how quickly the transformation had occurred. "The rise which this officer has suddenly taken in the public confidence is without precedent," noted the paper eight days after the conclusion of the Seven Days: "At the commencement of the war he enjoyed the highest reputation of any officer on the continent. But the fame was considerably damaged by the result of his campaign in the mountains." Formerly among Lee's critics, the *Dispatch* now suggested that Lee had lacked only a proper opportunity. Recent fighting around Richmond had permitted Lee to demonstrate his "great abilities." An officer writing as Lee's army prepared to cross the Potomac in September 1862 supported the *Dispatch*'s view. "We have the

13. Macon *Journal and Messenger*, September 10, 1862.

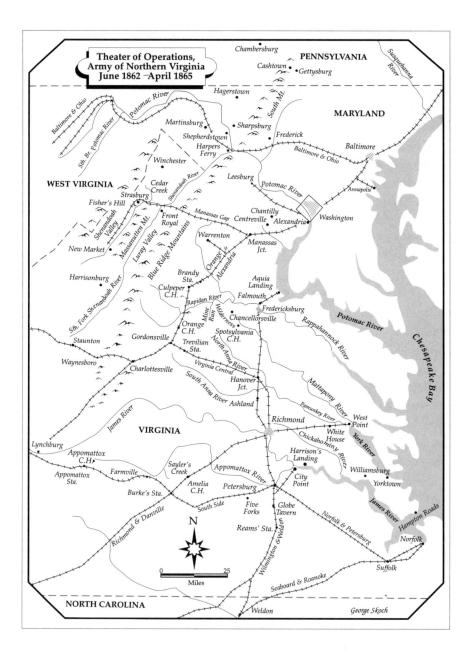

**Theater of Operations,
Army of Northern Virginia
June 1862 –April 1865**

PENNSYLVANIA

Chambersburg
Cashtown
Gettysburg

Susquehanna River

MARYLAND

Hagerstown
Martinsburg
Sharpsburg
Frederick
Baltimore

Baltimore & Ohio
Sth. Br. Potomac River
Potomac River
Shepherdstown
Harpers Ferry
Winchester

WEST VIRGINIA

Cedar Creek
Strasburg
Fisher's Hill
Front Royal
New Market
Harrisonburg

Shenandoah Valley
Massanutten Mt.
Luray Valley
Blue Ridge Mountains
Sth. Fork Shenandoah River

Leesburg

Potomac River
Annapolis
Washington

Chantilly
Centreville
Alexandria

Manassas Gap
Warrenton
Manassas Jct.

Orange & Alexandria

Brandy Sta.
Culpeper C.H.
Rapidan River
Aquia Landing
Falmouth

Staunton
Gordonsville
Orange C.H.
Mine Run
Wilderness
Chancellorsville
Fredericksburg

Waynesboro
Charlottesville
Trevilian Sta.
Spotsylvania C.H.
North Anna River

Virginia Central
South Anna River

Rappahannock River

Potomac River

Chesapeake Bay

Hanover Jct.
Ashland
Pamunkey River
West Point
White House
York River
Williamsburg
Yorktown

Mattapony River

James River

VIRGINIA

Lynchburg
Appomattox C.H.
Appomattox Sta.
Farmville
Sayler's Creek
Burke's Sta.
Amelia C.H.
Appomattox River
Petersburg
City Point
Harrison's Landing
Chickahominy River

Richmond

South Side
Five Forks
Globe Tavern
Reams' Sta.
Richmond & Danville
Wilmington & Weldon
Norfolk & Petersburg
James River
Hampton Roads
Norfolk
Suffolk

N

0   25
Miles

Seaboard & Roanoke

NORTH CAROLINA
Weldon

George Skoch

South Mt.

best leader in the Civilized world," affirmed Colonel Robert H. Jones of the 22nd Georgia Infantry. "Genl Lee stands now above all Genls in Modern History. Our men will follow him to the end."[14]

Shortly after the war, Edward Pollard accurately summed up the impact of the Seven Days on Lee's reputation. Among southerners hoping for offensive action in late 1861, stated the acerbic editor, Lee may have been "the most unpopular commander of equal rank in the Confederate service." But his aggressive performance during the Seven Days set him on a course where he "might have had the Dictatorship of the entire Southern Confederacy, if he had but crooked his finger to accept it."[15]

The stunning victory at Chancellorsville in May 1863 confirmed Lee as the leading military hero of the Confederacy. In the scrub forest of Spotsylvania County he wrested the initiative from Joseph Hooker and sent the far more powerful Federal army reeling back across the Rappahannock River. The manner in which Lee accomplished this latest triumph thrilled the Confederacy. Dividing his army no fewer than three times, he had marched rapidly, attacked furiously, and vanquished a posturing foe. "Thus ends the career of Gen. Hooker, who, a week ago, was at the head of an army of 150,000 men, perfect in drill, discipline, and all the muniments of war," wrote a Richmonder. "He came a confident invader against Gen. Lee at the head of 65,000 'butternuts,' as our honest poor-clad defenders were called, and we see the result! An active campaign of less than a week, and Hooker is hurled back in disgrace and irreparable disaster!"[16] Lee turned north after Chancellorsville and by the anniversary of his initial offensive at Mechanicsville had placed 75,000 Confederates on Pennsylvania soil.

The soldiers who marched toward Pennsylvania in June 1863 possessed an almost breathtaking confidence that Lee would lead them to victory no matter the odds. The preceding fall, straggling and desertion had plagued the Confederate invading force as it marched into Maryland. At that stage of the conflict, the army had not yet become *Lee's* army. By the summer of 1863 it had. Comments from Lieutenant Lewis Battle on the eve of the Pennsylvania

14. Richmond *Dispatch,* July 9, 1862; Robert Jones to My Dear Wife, September 5, 1862, typescript provided to the author by Keith S. Bohannon.

15. Edward A. Pollard, *Lee and His Lieutenants: Comprising the Early Life, Public Services, and Campaigns of General Robert E. Lee and His Companions in Arms, with a Record of Their Campaigns and Heroic Deeds* (New York: E. B. Treat, 1867), 65.

16. Jones, *Diary* 1:314 (entry for May 8, 1863).

invasion typified feeling toward Lee within the Army of Northern Virginia. Battle's 37th North Carolina Infantry gave three cheers for the general after he reviewed A. P. Hill's Light Division in the wake of Chancellorsville; Lee heard the cheering and turned his attention to the men. "It is impossible for me to describe the emotions of my heart as the old silver headed hero acknowledged the salute by taking off his hat [and] thereby exposing the most noble countenance I ever beheld," wrote Battle of the moment when Lee and the Carolinians faced each other. "I felt proud that the Southern Confederacy could boast of such a man," confessed the awestruck lieutenant. "In fact, I was almost too proud for the occasion for I could not open my mouth to give vent to the emotions that were struggling within." Two months later, as the army recrossed the Potomac after Gettysburg, a Georgian spoke of the familial bond between Lee and his men. "Gen. Lee (old grand pa, as the boys all call him,) was on his horse on the Virginia side, superintending the crossing of his army in person," observed J. H. Reinhardt of the 16th Georgia Infantry. "Most of the boys cheered him as they passed by him. He looked as cool and as calm as a frosty morning."[17]

The Army of Northern Virginia's second campaign across the Potomac ended in bloody defeat at Gettysburg, but that should not obscure the magnitude of what Lee had accomplished during just one year in field command. His fabled string of victories had won the hearts of his soldiers, inspirited the Confederate people, and transformed him and his army into the nascent republic's principal rallying point. As the war dragged on with increasing fury and Confederates inside and outside the army coped with escalating material hardship, Lee and his men functioned as the most important national institution.[18]

Even after Gettysburg (which was not perceived as a decisive defeat by most Confederates), faith in Lee among his soldiers and behind the lines remained largely unshaken. The victories in 1862–1863, though admittedly won at a horrific price in southern blood, had created an expectation of success in the Virginia theater that sustained Confederate morale for nearly two more years. Letters and diaries from the period 1864–1865 frequently described Lee as invincible and expressed faith in his ability to withstand any-

17. Lewis Battle to his brother, May 29, 1863, Battle Family Papers, Southern Historical Collection, Wilson Library, University of North Carolina, Chapel Hill; J. H. Reinhardt in the Athens (Ga.) *Southern Watchman*, August 5, 1863.

18. For a fuller discussion of Lee's army as a Confederate rallying point, see chap. 2 of Gary W. Gallagher, *The Confederate War* (Cambridge, Mass.: Harvard University Press, 1997).

thing the North could throw against him. Thus could a soldier serving in the western theater comment in May 1864—nearly a year after Gettysburg—that he had "complete faith in General Lee, who has never been known to suffer defeat, and probably never will."[19]

In early 1864, Brigadier General Clement A. Evans wrote an evaluation that captured succinctly the relationship between Lee and his soldiers. "General Robt. E. Lee is regarded by his army as nearest approaching the character of the great & good Washington than any man living," recorded Evans in his diary. "He is the only man living in whom they would unreservedly trust all power for the preservation of their independence." Although Stonewall Jackson had inspired enthusiastic support, added Evans, the "love and reverence for Lee is a far deeper and more general feeling." Echoing Fremantle's earlier assessment, Evans stated that Lee had no enemies and that "all his actions are so exalted that mirth at his expense is never known."[20]

It is important to reiterate that Lee frequently pursued the strategic and tactical offensive to achieve his victories in 1862–1863—an element of his leadership frequently questioned by modern historians because of the high number of southern casualties. Critics such as J. F. C. Fuller, Russell F. Weigley, Grady McWhiney, Thomas L. Connelly, and Alan T. Nolan have discussed at length how Lee's famous victories (as well as some of his defeats) drained Confederate manpower, suggesting that perhaps the South would have been better off with a less aggressive officer in charge of the Army of Northern Virginia. There can be no denying the butcher's bill. In 1862, more than twenty percent of Lee's soldiers became casualties during the Seven Days battles, and roughly the same proportion fell at both Second Manassas and Antietam. During the first half of 1863, the army lost twenty percent again at Chancellorsville and suffered even more at Gettysburg.[21]

19. Felix Pierre Poché, *A Louisiana Confederate: Diary of Felix Pierre Poché*, ed. Edwin C. Bearss (Natchitoches: Louisiana Studies Institute of Northwestern State University of Louisiana, 1972), 126 (entry for May 27, 1864). On the topic of how Confederates reacted to Gettysburg, see Gary W. Gallagher, "Lee's Army Has Not Lost Any of Its Prestige: The Impact of Gettysburg on the Army of Northern Virginia and the Confederate Home Front," in Gallagher, ed., *The Third Day at Gettysburg and Beyond* (Chapel Hill: University of North Carolina Press, 1994).

20. Robert Grier Stephens, Jr., ed., *Intrepid Warrior: Clement Anselm Evans, Confederate General from Georgia; Life, Letters, and Diaries of the War Years* (Dayton, Ohio: Morningside, 1992), 342–43.

21. For Lee's critics, see J. F. C. Fuller's *The Generalship of Ulysses S. Grant* (1929; reprint, Bloomington: Indiana University Press, 1958); Russell F. Weigley's *The American Way of War:*

Did Lee's results justify the horrible attrition? With the exception of his seemingly effortless repulse of Ambrose E. Burnside's clumsy assaults at Fredericksburg in December 1862, each of the campaigns conveyed to the Confederate people a sense that their most famous army was taking the war to the enemy rather than simply awaiting the next Federal move.[22] Confederates mourned the army's huge losses but directed remarkably little criticism toward Lee as the officer responsible for the effusion of blood. Even during the protracted defensive fighting of 1864–1865, Lee retained a reputation as an audacious commander who would seize any opportunity to smite the enemy.

Joseph E. Johnston presents an interesting contrast to Lee in this regard. Although respected by most of his soldiers and popular in some civilian quarters, Johnston suffered from a widespread belief that he too often adopted a passive defensive strategy and yielded too much ground without a major struggle. Johnston either misread Confederate expectations or ignored them; the result was sharp criticism of his generalship at crucial points in the war. During his retreat up the Peninsula in the spring of 1862, for example, a young Georgian complained that "General Joseph Johnston, from whom we were led to expect so much, has done little else than *evacuate*, until the very mention of the word sickens one." Two years later, after Johnston had withdrawn from northern Georgia into the works surrounding Atlanta, a soldier in the Army of Tennessee guessed that Jefferson Davis had removed the general in favor of John Bell Hood "for not fighting and [for] allowing the Yanks to penetrate so far into Georgia." Initially a supporter of Johnston, this man thought him "too cautious . . . not willing to risk a battle until he is satisfied he can whip it." Late in the war, when Johnston had returned to command in the Carolinas, a young South Carolina woman bitterly denounced him: "This arch-retreater

---

A History of United States Military Strategy and Policy (New York: Macmillan, 1973); Thomas L. Connelly's "Robert E. Lee and the Western Confederacy: A Criticism of Lee's Strategic Ability" (*Civil War History* 15 [June 1969]); Grady McWhiney and Perry D. Jamieson's *Attack and Die: Civil War Military Tactics and the Southern Heritage* (University: University of Alabama Press, 1982); and Alan T. Nolan's *Lee Considered: General Robert E. Lee and Civil War History* (Chapel Hill: University of North Carolina Press, 1991). For a selection of critical and appreciative evaluations of Lee's generalship, see Gary W. Gallagher, ed., *Lee the Soldier* (Lincoln: University of Nebraska Press, 1996).

22. For Confederate sentiment unhappy with Lee's defensive victory at Fredericksburg, see Gary W. Gallagher, "The Yanks Have Had a Terrible Whipping: Confederates Evaluate the Battle of Fredericksburg," in Gallagher, ed., *The Fredericksburg Campaign: Decision on the Rappahannock* (Chapel Hill: University of North Carolina Press, 1995).

will probably retreat till perhaps he retreats to Gen. Lee, who may put a stop to his retrograde movement."[23]

Confederates impatient with strictly defensive campaigns could argue that such operations had exposed vast stretches of territory to the Federals while yielding only the most meager long-term results. Albert Sidney Johnston's position-oriented defense of the Kentucky-Tennessee arena in 1861–1862 sacrificed much of Tennessee and witnessed the surrender of approximately 15,000 soldiers at Fort Donelson. The capitulation of 30,000 Confederates at Vicksburg in 1863 capped another defensive disaster, and Joseph Johnston's retreat to Atlanta in 1864 set up a siege that culminated in a landmark victory for William Tecumseh Sherman. Indeed, every major siege of the conflict occurred during campaigns marked by Confederate defensive strategies, and each of them ended in Union triumph. That roster included Petersburg, which concluded as Lee predicted it would in June 1864. "We must destroy this army of Grant's before he gets to [the] James River," Lee told Jubal Early just after the battle of Cold Harbor. "If he gets there, it will become a siege, and then it will be a mere question of time."[24]

Nor did defensive campaigns conserve Confederate manpower. Leaving aside surrendered troops (a factor that dramatically increased the defender's losses), strategically defensive campaigns often consumed manpower at a rate roughly equal to that experienced by the offensive side. Defenders almost always reached a point where they had to attack in order to avoid a siege, and these tactical counteroffensives often took place amid circumstances unfavorable for the attackers. Joseph Johnston's retreat toward Richmond in May 1862 illustrates this phenomenon. In the delaying action at Williamsburg and at Seven Pines, where he became the aggressor because the Army of the Potomac had nearly reached Richmond, Johnston's casualties approached 8,000

23. Charles C. Jones Jr. to Rev. C. C. Jones, May 12, 1862, in Robert Manson Myers, ed., *The Children of Pride: A True Story of Georgia and the Civil War* (New Haven, Conn.: Yale University Press, 1972), 893; Jack King to his wife, July 19, 1864, in Mills Lane, ed., *"Dear Mother: Don't grieve about me. If I get killed, I'll only be dead." Letters from Georgia Soldiers in the Civil War* (Savannah, Ga.: Beehive Press, 1977), 258; Emma LeConte, *When the World Ended: The Diary of Emma LeConte*, ed. Earl Schenck Miers (New York: Oxford University Press, 1957), 83 (entry for March 18, 1865).

24. Lee is quoted in Jubal A. Early, *The Campaigns of Gen. Robert E. Lee. An Address by Lieut. General Jubal A. Early, before Washington and Lee University, January 19th, 1872* (Baltimore: John Murphy, 1872), 42.

compared with fewer than 7,500 for the Federals. Similarly, during May 1864, as Johnston fell back across North Georgia toward Atlanta, the Confederates lost 10,000 men to Sherman's 11,768. Even during Lee's masterful defensive campaign from the Rapidan to the James River, throughout which Confederate soldiers usually fought from behind well-prepared breastworks, the Army of Northern Virginia suffered proportionately heavier losses than Grant's relentlessly aggressive Federals.[25]

Jefferson Davis understood that the Confederacy had received an excellent return on its investment of men and matériel in Lee's generalship. With the celebrated victories of 1862–1863 doubtless in mind, the southern president prophesied just after Gettysburg that Lee's achievements would make him and his army "the subject of history and object of the world's admiration for generations to come." At the time Davis wrote these words, Lee already was the object of his nation's admiration—so much so that his surrender at Appomattox signaled the end of the war to virtually all Confederates (as well as to their northern opponents). Thousands of Confederate soldiers remained under arms after April 9, 1865, but without Lee and his men in the field there seemed no reason to fight on. "Everybody feels ready to give up hope," was a Georgia woman's representative reaction to news of Lee's surrender. "'It is useless to struggle longer,' seems to be the common cry," she noted sadly, "and the poor wounded men go hobbling about the streets with despair on their faces."[26]

The week after Chancellorsville, the Lynchburg *Virginian* told its readers that "The central figure of this war is, beyond all question, that of Robert E. Lee."[27] Untold thousands of Confederates would have agreed with this statement. They saw in Lee the best qualities of a Christian gentleman, a quiet man who thought first of others and turned his surpassing military gifts to the task

25. Thomas L. Livermore, *Numbers and Losses in the Civil War in America: 1861–1865* (1900; reprint, Bloomington: Indiana University Press, 1957), 80–81, 119–20. At Kennesaw Mountain, where Sherman attacked Johnston's army on June 27, 1864, the Federals lost another 2,051 men and the Confederates 442.

26. Jefferson Davis to R. E. Lee, August 11, 1863, in Dunbar Rowland, ed., *Jefferson Davis, Constitutionalist: His Life and Letters*, 10 vols. (Jackson: Mississippi Department of Archives and History, 1923), 5:588–90; Eliza Frances Andrews, *The War-Time Journal of a Georgia Girl 1864–1865*, ed. Spencer Birdwell King (1908; reprint, Atlanta: Cherokee, 1976), 371 (entry for April 18, 1865).

27. Lynchburg *Virginian*, May 12, 1863.

General Lee Entering Richmond after the Surrender, a crude sketch by Adalbert J. Volck, conveys a sense of the emotional bond that had developed between Lee and the Confederate people by the end of the war.
Emily V. Mason, *Popular Life of Gen. Robert Edward Lee* (Baltimore: John Murphy, 1872)

of assuring southern independence. More important, they also saw in him their only reliable source for good news from the battlefield, a daring commander whose strategic and tactical skills wrought splendid offensive victories during his memorable first year in command of the Army of Northern Virginia. Because they believed in Lee so fervently, the Confederate people resisted long past the point at which they otherwise would have conceded their inability to overcome northern numbers and power.[28] More than once he brought them to the verge of independence, in the process creating a record of military accomplishment amid difficult circumstances to which Confederates looked with pride both during and after the war. That scores of thousands of their young men had perished to forge that record scarcely affected Lee's reputation. He had given Confederates hope during the war, and after Appomattox he and his army stood as their primary symbol of honorable striving in a cause that had suffered utter defeat.[29]

Jubal Early undoubtedly spoke for most former Confederates when, in an address delivered on the anniversary of Lee's birth in 1872, he spoke of Lee's importance to white southerners. Disdaining a comparison between Lee and Grant, Early sniffed that he might as well "compare the great pyramid which rears its majestic proportions in the valley of the Nile, to a pigmy perched on Mount Atlas." "No, my friends," continued Early, "it is a vain work for us to seek anywhere for a parallel to the great character which has won our admiration and love. Our beloved Chief stands, like some lofty column which rears its head among the highest, in grandeur, simple, pure and sublime, needing no borrowed lustre; and he is all our own."[30]

28. Recent scholarship has reached a quite firm consensus that the Confederacy failed because its people possessed insufficient will to endure the sacrifices necessary to achieve victory. In reaching this conclusion, historians point to internal dissension and disaffection related to fissures along class, race, and gender lines. This interpretation overlooks a mass of testimony to the contrary—a discussion of which is beyond the scope of this essay. For an argument that Confederates exhibited tenacious popular will, see chap. 1 of Gallagher, *Confederate War*.

29. On Lee as a postwar icon in the South, see Mark E. Neely Jr., Harold Holzer, and Gabor S. Boritt, *The Confederate Image: Prints of the Lost Cause* (Chapel Hill: University of North Carolina Press, 1987). The authors offer a perceptive analysis of artworks with a Confederate theme marketed in the southern states after the war.

30. Early, *Campaigns of Lee*, 50–51.

★ 2 ★

The Best Possible Outcome
One Could Hope For

Lee and the Army of Northern Virginia
in the 1862 Maryland Campaign

White's Ford on the Potomac River near Leesburg, Virginia, presented a memorable scene on September 4–7, 1862. The weather was brilliantly fine, with sunshine drenching the water of the historic river that symbolized the division between North and South. Wildflowers grew thick along the banks, their colors vivid against the dense foliage of towering trees that framed the Potomac. Long lines of veterans of the Confederate Army of Northern Virginia, victors in recent battles with the Army of the Potomac outside Richmond and on the rolling plains of Manassas, crossed the river into Maryland. Above the winding columns, the careless chatter of soldiers mixed with the strains of "Maryland, My Maryland" played by Confederate bands on the Virginia side of the Potomac. It was a grand panorama of an army in motion, only slightly flawed by the obviously ragged appearance of the Confederate soldiers.[1]

1. This description is based on Jedediah Hotchkiss, *Make Me a Map of the Valley: The Civil War Journal of Stonewall Jackson's Topographer*, ed. Archie P. McDonald (Dallas: Southern Methodist University Press, 1973), 78 (entry for September 5, 1862).

The Army of Northern Virginia crossing the Potomac River at White's Ford, September 1862.
Robert Underwood Johnson and Clarence Clough Buel, eds., *Battles and Leaders of the Civil War,* 4 vols. (New York: Century, 1887–88)

The Confederacy's leadership sensed opportunity in late summer and early autumn 1862. As Robert E. Lee's soldiers tramped into Maryland, southern fortunes on the battlefield rapidly approached a crest. Far to the west, forces under Braxton Bragg and Edmund Kirby Smith soon would move into the bluegrass region of Kentucky. Between them, the incursions into Maryland and Kentucky would mark the geographical high point of the Confederacy's military effort. Lee and the Army of Northern Virginia shouldered the principal burden of making this southern counteroffensive a success. In a strictly military sense, the war would be won in the western theater, where Ulysses S. Grant, William Tecumseh Sherman, and George H. Thomas eventually outmatched their Confederate opponents. But many people perceived the eastern theater to be the critical arena. Much of the northern and southern public, important politicians on both sides, and foreign observers looked to the well-traveled one-hundred-mile strip of disputed land between Washington and Richmond for signs of victory. The opposing capitals were there, the most famous armies were there—the war must be decided there.

A combination of diplomatic, political, and military factors created a potential opportunity for the Confederacy in the fall of 1862. Political leaders in England and France watched events with special interest. The *Times* of London set the tone for many in Britain when it observed that the Seven Days, which it called a severe Union defeat, had been one of the epochal battles of the century. "After pouring forth blood like water and fertilizing the fields of Virginia with thousands of corpses," stated the *Times* in late July, "the North finds itself obliged to begin all over again, with credit destroyed, a ruined revenue, a depreciated currency, and an enormous debt." A firm believer that the South must demonstrate its independence before Britain intervened as an arbitrator, Prime Minister Viscount Palmerston overlooked Federal triumphs west of the Appalachians and interpreted the Seven Days as a turning point. He suggested to the Queen on August 6 that England should propose an armistice in October, when the results of the fall campaigning in Virginia presumably would be known (and presumably would favor the Confederacy).[2]

Lee's victory at Second Manassas on August 29–30 added to the expectation of probable northern failure. Palmerston thought General John Pope's Army of Virginia had gotten a "very complete smashing" that placed at risk Washington and Baltimore, while Lord John Russell, who as head of the Foreign Office had resisted British interference in the American upheaval, concluded that Lee's movement north presaged an end to the war. By mid-September (it took news several days to travel from America to England), Palmerston spoke of Britain and France proffering "an arrangement upon the basis of separation" between the warring sections. Chancellor of the Exchequer William Gladstone favored outright recognition of the Confederacy. In these three men, the Confederacy had powerful supporters who might sway a cabinet that contained several members devoted to strict neutrality. The English people were divided on the question. Historians have long thought that class governed British attitudes toward the American war—working-class per-

2. *Times* (London), July 22, 1862; D. P. Crook, *The North, the South, and the Powers: 1861–1865* (New York: John Wiley and Sons, 1974), 219. On the subject of British views of the situation in the summer and fall of 1862, see Brian Jenkins, *Britain and the War for the Union*, 2 vols. (Montreal: McGill-Queen's University Press, 1974, 1980), 2, chaps. 5–6; and Howard Jones, *Union in Peril: The Crisis over British Intervention in the Civil War* (Chapel Hill: University of North Carolina Press, 1992), chaps. 6–9.

sons held an antislavery sentiment for the Union, while aristocratic, privileged classes were for the slaveholding Confederacy. But, in fact, economic self-interest blurred class lines. As long as the North did not declare emancipation a war aim, the pervasive abolitionist impulse in England would not coalesce behind the Lincoln government.[3]

Emperor Louis Napoleon of France waited for England to make the first move. Confederate independence would abet his scheme to create a vassal state in Mexico and bring more cotton to French ports, but after the Russians declined a French suggestion for Anglo-French-Russian mediation in late July 1862 the emperor decided that British action was vital. French Foreign Minister Antoine Edouard Thouvenel wrote in early September that "the undertaking of conquering the South is almost superhuman . . . to me the undertaking seems impossible." French minister to the United States Baron Henri Mercier advised his superiors in Paris on September 2 that Union setbacks during the Seven Days and at Second Manassas had created an atmosphere conducive to mediation in the North. On September 17, the day of the battle of Antietam, Lord Russell agreed with Palmerston that Britain should offer to mediate "with a view to the recognition of the independence of the Confederates." Should such mediation fail, added Russell, "we ought ourselves to recognize the Southern States as an independent State." He concluded with the observation that a Federal defeat in Maryland would prepare the North to receive Britain's proposal.[4]

Diplomatic officials from the warring American parties agreed that the climate looked favorable for the Confederacy during the summer of 1862. Southern representatives in Europe predicted as early as the end of July that recognition was imminent. In Liverpool, United States Consul Thomas Dudley seconded this reading of events when he stated on July 19 that all of Europe was against the North and "would rejoice at our downfall."[5]

3. Crook, *North, South, and Powers*, 222–24. On the question of class-based support for the Union and Confederacy, see Mary Ellison, *Support for Secession: Lancashire and the American Civil War* (Chicago: University of Chicago Press, 1972), which argues that British labor was divided; and Philip S. Foner, *British Labor and the American Civil War* (New York: Holmes & Meier, 1981), which insists that British workers staunchly supported emancipation and the Union.

4. Crook, *North, South, and Powers*, 212, 222–23; Lynn M. Case and Warren F. Spencer, *The United States and France: Civil War Diplomacy* (Philadelphia: University of Pennsylvania Press, 1970), 336; Daniel B. Carroll, *Henri Mercier and the American Civil War* (Princeton: Princeton University Press, 1971), 210–11.

5. Jones, *Union in Peril*, 147.

Lee and his army held the key to diplomatic movement on the continent. Another victory for the Army of Northern Virginia might bring recognition for the Confederacy. In their optimism, southerners thought back to the alliance with France in 1778 and the French ships and soldiers that tipped the scales in favor of George Washington's army at Yorktown. But parallels between 1778 and 1862 were flawed. European military intervention on the side of the Confederacy was highly unlikely; moreover, the Lincoln administration left no doubt that despite any setback on the battlefield, it would rebuff mediation. In sum, a diplomatic opportunity of unknown magnitude hung tantalizingly before the Confederacy in September 1862.

It seemed also within reach of Confederate arms to influence northern politics. The Lincoln administration anticipated determined opposition from Democrats on a range of issues in the summer and fall of 1862. Unless Federal armies produced victories in the autumn campaigning, the Republicans stood to suffer in November's off-year elections. Apart from their long-standing differences with the Republicans over economic issues, Democrats argued that draconian measures such as Lincoln's selective suspension of the writ of habeas corpus mocked individual rights. They resented the Militia Act of July 17, 1862, which gave the president broad powers to coerce service in Federal militia units. They blanched when Lincoln, facing a severe shortage of men, issued a call for three hundred thousand nine-month militiamen in the first week of August, and the War Department sent instructions on enrollment and draft procedures to the states.

Perhaps most galling to Democrats was increasing pressure from many Republicans to add emancipation as a northern objective. The war had changed, insisted outraged Democrats. They supported a war to preserve the Union and its constitutional safeguards for citizens' rights, but the conflict had become a gross distortion of that original crusade. Unbridled federal power had grown arrogant and oppressive, threatening to compel whites to die for the freedom of blacks. Northern Democrats expressed their unhappiness and frustration in words and, increasingly, with acts of violence.[6]

The extent of antiwar sentiment north of the Potomac was well known but imperfectly understood in the Confederacy. Jefferson Davis and Robert E.

6. For an overview of Democratic unhappiness with the Lincoln administration's policies during the summer of 1862, see chap. 16 of James M. McPherson, *Battle Cry of Freedom: The Civil War Era* (New York: Oxford University Press, 1988).

Lee read newspaper accounts of a developing peace party. Lee thought the presence of his army north of the Potomac for several weeks in the fall of 1862 would galvanize northern opposition to the war. Four days after the first of his infantry had crossed the Potomac at White's Ford, he wrote to Davis that the time seemed appropriate for the Confederacy to suggest that the United States recognize its independence. More than a year of fighting had brought intense suffering "without advancing the objects which our enemies proposed to themselves in beginning the contest." "The rejection of this offer would prove to the country that the responsibility of the continuance of the war does not rest upon us," reasoned Lee, "but that the party in power in the United States elect to prosecute it for purposes of their own." In offering peace, the Confederacy would "enable the people of the United States to determine at their coming elections whether they will support those who favor a prolongation of the war, or those who wish to bring it to a termination, which can but be productive of good to both parties without affecting the honor of either."[7]

Lee and Davis held high hopes for the state of Maryland. Had not Federal bayonets kept that slave state in the Union against the wishes of its residents? Citizens of Baltimore had rioted against the 6th Massachusetts Regiment in April 1861. Marylanders had been arrested and incarcerated without benefit of the writ of habeas corpus. Thirty-one secessionist members of the state legislature, together with the mayor of Baltimore, had been imprisoned for several weeks during the fall of 1861. Similarly heavy-handed measures had ensured a Unionist majority in the legislature elected in November 1861. Some Marylanders arrested on political grounds still languished in prison when the Army of Northern Virginia entered the state; neither they nor those released earlier had seen any evidence against them. Thousands of other Marylanders wondered if their liberties would stand in abeyance for the duration of the war. Lee believed the influence of his victorious army might embolden citizens of Maryland to step forward in active support of the Confederacy, after which they could once again "enjoy the inalienable rights of freemen, and restore independence and sovereignty to your State."[8]

Lee and Davis were correct in assuming that a Confederate victory or a protracted stay north of the Potomac would hurt the Republicans in Novem-

7. Lee to Jefferson Davis, September 8, 1862, in R. E. Lee, *The Wartime Papers of R. E. Lee*, ed. Clifford Dowdey and Louis H. Manarin (Boston: Little, Brown, 1961), 301.

8. Lee to the People of Maryland, September 8, 1862, *ibid.*, 299. McPherson, *Battle Cry of Freedom*, 284–90, examines unrest in Maryland during the first eighteen months of the war.

Lee in 1862
Francis Trevelyan Miller, ed., *The Photographic History of the Civil War*, 10 vols. (New York: Review of Reviews, 1911)

ber. They went too far, however, in thinking that even a resounding Democratic victory would bring northern acceptance of an independent Confederacy. They confused Democratic unhappiness over the direction of the war with sentiment receptive to disunion. Only extreme Democrats countenanced the notion of a sovereign Confederacy; most were devoted to a conservative prosecution of the conflict embodied in the slogan "The Constitution as it is, the Union as it was." Lee and Davis similarly misread Maryland (Bragg and Kirby Smith made the same mistake in Kentucky), for the western part of the state, through which the Army of Northern Virginia passed, was staunchly Unionist. The eastern shore and Baltimore held most of Maryland's secessionists, who were far from the liberating influence of Lee's forces. Success on any battlefield in western Maryland probably would have earned few recruits for Lee's army. More important, Democratic political gains triggered by such a victory almost certainly would not have led to mediation of the question of southern independence. Confederate opportunity to affect northern politics through military success thus was limited to influencing how, rather than if, the North would continue to wage the war for the Union.[9]

The resolution of one momentous issue did depend largely on the outcome of Lee's operations in Maryland. Lincoln had decided by midsummer to issue a proclamation of emancipation. Pressed by elements of his party to move more quickly, and weary of obstinate refusals by the Border States to consider any type of emancipation, Lincoln had announced his intention to the cabinet on July 22. Debate among his advisers convinced him to hold off until the North won a military victory. Because of widespread perceptions that the war would be settled in the East, that victory ideally should come against Lee's army. Once issued, Lincoln's proclamation would alter the nature of the war, making it a struggle for freedom as well as for restoration of the Union. By extension, northern victory in Maryland would cost the Confederacy its slaves, thereby shattering its social and economic fabric. The proclamation also would render it nearly impossible for Britain, which had abolished slavery in the 1830s, to support a slave-based Confederacy against a North fighting for emancipation. Lee probably knew nothing of his chance to influence Lincoln's course on emancipation, though it was potentially the most profound opportunity present in the autumn of 1862.[10]

Although politics and diplomacy figured in Lee's conception of what his army might accomplish across the Potomac, his principal goals were military. John Pope's Army of Virginia and George B. McClellan's Army of the Potomac lay "much weakened and demoralized" in the vicinity of Washington. That presented an opportunity to flank the Federal capital by marching into Maryland. This would be a strategic offensive during which the Confederates would maintain a flanking posture northwest of Washington for most if not all of the autumn. Such a course offered diverse potential. The Federals would have to position themselves above the Potomac to guard Washington, thereby

9. On Democratic sentiment during this period, see Joel H. Silbey, *A Respectable Minority: The Democratic Party in the Civil War Era, 1860–1868* (New York: W. W. Norton, 1977), chaps. 2–3.

10. Lee denounced the proclamation as "savage and brutal" in a letter to James A. Seddon dated January 6, 1863. Lee, *Wartime Papers*, 390.

freeing northern Virginia of contending armies and allowing the Confederates to strengthen the defenses of Richmond. Lee would hold the initiative in Maryland, whereas in Virginia he could do little more than await the next Union effort to turn his position and strike at the Confederate capital. The operation would bring desperately needed supplies from Maryland and perhaps Pennsylvania to the Army of Northern Virginia. At the same time, the fall harvest in the Shenandoah Valley and elsewhere in Virginia might be gathered in safety. When the approach of winter exhausted supplies in Maryland, Lee would withdraw to Virginia.[11]

Lee expressed no fear of aggressive Union reaction to his movement. Reports through the first week of September indicated that the enemy was concentrating in the fortifications at Washington and Alexandria. Should a northern force stir itself to press Lee, he would have the advantage of fighting on the tactical defensive in a place of his choosing. "The only two subjects that give me any uneasiness," Lee wrote to Davis on September 4, "are my supplies of ammunition and subsistence." The former was not an immediate problem. "I have enough for present use, and must await results before deciding to what point I will have additional supplies forwarded." The farms of western Maryland would answer needs for food and fodder. Lee summed up his analysis of the military, political, and diplomatic opportunities of early autumn 1862 in the opening sentence of a letter to Davis on September 3: "The present seems to be the most propitious time since the commencement of the war for the Confederate Army to enter Maryland."[12]

Lee manifestly believed he could take advantage of at least some of the opportunities that beckoned. But was his army equipped to carry out a major campaign across the Potomac in early September 1862? If not, the glimmering possibilities at home and abroad were but so many dancing mirages. Many writers have proceeded from the assumption that Lee could have attained more if only certain crucial episodes had gone differently—if, for example, his orders for the campaign had not fallen into McClellan's hands on September 13. A close look at the Army of Northern Virginia as it entered and maneuvered in Maryland during the first ten days of the campaign—before any fighting took place—suggests otherwise.

The numerical strength of the Army of Northern Virginia on the eve of

11. Lee to Jefferson Davis, September 3, 1862, in Lee, *Wartime Papers*, 292–94.
12. Lee, *Wartime Papers*, 294, 292.

the campaign was at best marginally adequate to undertake an operation that might result in battle against Federal forces approaching one hundred thousand soldiers. Two months of hard fighting and marching had extracted a grievous toll. One careful observer wrote that when the army was at Frederick, Maryland, on September 7 its "divisions had sunk to little more than brigades, & brigades nearly to regiments." Though impossible to estimate with precision, Lee's effectives at the time he crossed the river probably stood at 40,000 to 45,000 infantry, 5,500 cavalry, and 4,000 artillery, for a total of 50,000 to 55,000 men.[13]

Critical shortages of clothing and equipment exacerbated a grim situation. Lee admitted to Davis on September 3 that "the army is not properly equipped for an invasion of an enemy's territory. It lacks much of the material of war, is feeble in transportation, the animals being much reduced, and the men are poorly provided with clothes, and in thousands of instances are destitute of shoes." This sobering information appeared in the same letter wherein Lee told Davis it was "the most propitious time since the commencement of the war" to carry the war northward. With scarcely half the men and but a fraction of the material resources of his foe, Lee could expect very little margin for error in Maryland.[14]

He could look with assurance to his principal subordinates. James Longstreet and Stonewall Jackson had matured in the crucible of fighting on the Peninsula and during the campaign of Second Manassas. Together with Lee, they would make the Army of Northern Virginia into a formidable instrument that in time would become one of the legendary field commands. Although each of the three men was injured in early September, they could be relied upon for solid direction at the top. No less an asset was cavalry chief Jeb

13. Edward Porter Alexander, *Fighting for the Confederacy: The Personal Recollections of General Edward Porter Alexander*, ed. Gary W. Gallagher (Chapel Hill: University of North Carolina Press, 1989), 139; Stephen W. Sears, *Landscape Turned Red: The Battle of Antietam* (New York: Ticknor & Fields, 1983), 69. Sears estimated that on September 3 "Lee could count perhaps 50,000 troops with which to undertake his expedition beyond the Confederacy's northern frontier." In *The Gleam of Bayonets: The Battle of Antietam and Robert E. Lee's Maryland Campaign, September 1862* (New York: Thomas Yoseloff, 1965), 104, James V. Murfin also concluded that at the time Lee crossed the Potomac he "could count only 50,000 [soldiers in his army], a disappointing figure for what he had in mind." In *Military Memoirs of a Confederate: A Critical Narrative* (New York: Charles Scribner's Sons, 1907), 243, Edward Porter Alexander stated that Lee had "about 55,000" men at the beginning of the campaign.

14. Lee, *Wartime Papers*, 293.

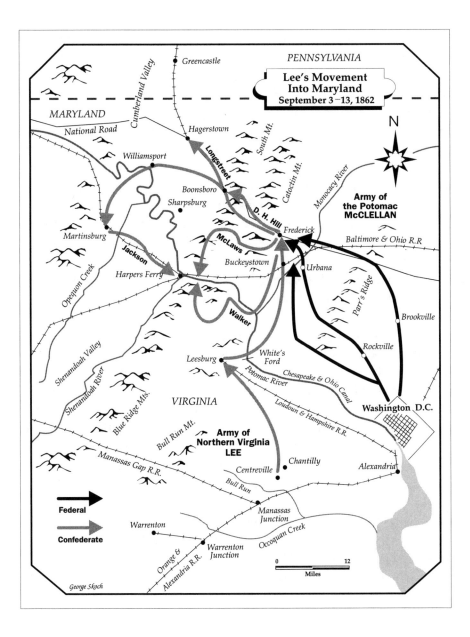

Lee's Movement
Into Maryland
September 3–13, 1862

Stuart, whose skill in screening and reconnaissance, and whose presence of mind on the battlefield, assured Lee of superlative support from his mounted arm. William Nelson Pendleton provided indifferent direction to the artillery, although able young subordinates substantially offset his ineptitude.

Lower levels of command presented a more problematic picture. Attrition among generals had been frightful since late June. In Jackson's wing of the army, colonels rather than brigadier generals led several brigades. With Richard S. Ewell out of action because of his wound at Groveton and A. P. Hill under arrest owing to a dispute with Jackson, not one of the wing's division commanders held the appropriate rank of major general. Longstreet's wing was in better shape, although John Bell Hood, Longstreet's fiercest fighter, was under arrest as a result of a silly quarrel with Brigadier General Nathan "Shanks" Evans over some ambulances captured at Second Manassas. Losses among field and company-grade officers in both Jackson's and Longstreet's wings had been so high since June that efficiency and discipline had suffered serious declines.[15]

Lee's emphasis on the need to gather provisions in Maryland told the story of food and fodder in the Army of Northern Virginia. Men and animals alike suffered cruel shortages. Testimony on this point is so overwhelming and well known that a single example will suffice to convey the gravity of Lee's plight. A soldier in James L. Kemper's brigade of D. R. Jones's division remembered that as the army turned north on September 2 after the battle of Chantilly, "[our] haversacks were all turned wrong side out, and the very dust of the crackers were scraped out and devoured." The next day there were "no signs of our commissary wagons, and not a mouthful of food did we have all day." September 4 brought some green corn, and for three days the soldiers relied on that bowel-churning fare. On September 8 this soldier wrote simply, "We were hungry, for six days not a morsel of bread or meat had gone in our stomachs—and our *menu* consisted of apples and corn." Horses and mules were in a similar state. The lack of shoes among Lee's men posed another barrier to effective maneuver. A soldier from Georgia put this crisis very succinctly: "I had no shoes. I tried it barefoot, but somehow my feet wouldn't callous. They

15. For an incisive analysis of the army's command structure during the Maryland campaign, see Robert K. Krick, "The Army of Northern Virginia in September 1862: Its Circumstances, Its Opportunities, and Why It Should Not Have Been at Sharpsburg," in Gary W. Gallagher, ed., *Antietam: Essays on the 1862 Maryland Campaign* (Kent, Ohio: Kent State University Press, 1989).

just kept bleeding." Strive as he might, this man could not keep up with his unit.[16]

In ragged clothing, poorly shod, and inadequately nourished, the men of the Army of Northern Virginia, as well as the animals that toiled alongside them, were not physically prepared for an active march into Maryland and Pennsylvania. Lee's admission of as much on September 3 did not portend a successful campaign.

Morale in the army as it embarked on its invasion deserves closer scrutiny than it has received from historians. Nearly every writer dwells on the massive straggling. The army that crossed the Potomac with 50,000 to 55,000 men mustered only about 30,000 bayonets at Sharpsburg on September 17. The loss of so many men chastened Lee. "Our great embarrassment," he wrote Davis on September 13, "is the reduction in our ranks by straggling, which it seems impossible to prevent with our present regimental officers. Our ranks are very much diminished, I fear from a third to a half of the original numbers." Alexander Cheves Haskell, member of a South Carolina family that sent several brothers into the Confederate army, wrote home just after Antietam, "Our army is small, but fights gloriously. . . . Great numbers of the men have straggled off, until none but heroes are left." Brigadier General William Dorsey Pender of A. P. Hill's Light Division recorded in exasperation on September 19: "In one of my Regts. the other day when they thought they were going to get into a fight, six out [of] ten officers skulked out and did not come up until they thought all danger over. More than half my Brigade went off the same day. Oh dear, oh dear, our army is coming to a pretty pass." Stern warnings and harsh measures failed to stop the flood of soldiers dropping away from their units.[17]

What had happened? Why did the army, following two resounding victories, hemorrhage at such an alarming rate? The traditional explanations are familiar: thousands of men fell out of the ranks because their unshod feet gave

---

16. Alexander Hunter, "A High Private's Account of the Battle of Sharpsburg. Paper No. 1," in J. William Jones *et al.*, eds., *Southern Historical Society Papers*, 52 vols. (1876–1959; reprint, with 3-vol. index, Wilmington, N.C.: Broadfoot, 1990–92), 10:507; Murfin, *Gleam of Bayonets*, 95.

17. Lee, *Wartime Papers*, 307; Louise Haskell Daly, *Alexander Cheves Haskell: The Portrait of a Man* (1934; reprint, Wilmington, N.C.: Broadfoot, 1989), 84; William Dorsey Pender, *The General to His Lady: The Civil War Letters of William Dorsey Pender to Fanny Pender*, ed. William W. Hassler (Chapel Hill: University of North Carolina Press, 1965), 175.

out; malnourishment and diarrhea left others too weak to carry on; others still, especially those from western North Carolina, felt uncomfortable moving north to fight on enemy soil (they had enlisted to defend their homes). All of these men, the usual argument goes, rejoined their units as soon as the army returned to Virginia.

Taken as a group, these factors undoubtedly account for a large percentage of the men who were not present at Antietam. They do not, however, explain Lee's losing fully one-third of his army. Lee himself informed Davis on September 21 (when the army was back in Virginia) that his force remained "greatly paralyzed by the loss to its ranks of the numerous stragglers. I have taken every means in my power from the beginning to correct this evil, which has increased instead of diminished." Many soldiers had never entered Maryland, stated Lee, while others who did move north "kept aloof." "The stream has not lessened since crossing the Potomac [recrossing the river back into Virginia]," Lee concluded, "though the cavalry has been constantly employed in endeavoring to arrest it." What Lee described was more than straggling; it was straggling in tandem with large-scale desertion. Desertion is an ugly word that few who have studied the Maryland campaign have been willing to use, but desertion it was that kept men away from their units during and after the campaign.[18]

Lee also acknowledged that his soldiers were plundering beyond the control of their officers. Although he devoted considerable time to trying to stop this wanton destruction of private property, he confessed to Davis that he was having little success. General John R. Jones, who was assigned to round up those absent from their commands, reported ten days after Antietam that he had sent approximately six thousand men back to the army, but that the area around Winchester was still "full of stragglers." Jones stated in disgust that the "number of officers back here was most astonishing." There were about 1,200 barefoot men as well, many of whom, believed Jones, "threw away their shoes in order to remain."[19] This shocking situation indicated more than a lack of sufficient food and shoes. An unprecedented percentage of the Army of

18. U.S. War Department, *The War of the Rebellion: A Compilation of the Official Records of the Union and Confederate Armies*, 128 vols. (Washington, D.C.: GPO, 1880–1901), ser. 1, vol. 19, pt. 1:143 [hereinafter cited as OR; all references are to series 1]. For a review of the traditional explanations for this loss of manpower, see Douglas Southall Freeman, *Lee's Lieutenants: A Study in Command*, 3 vols. (New York: Charles Scribner's Sons, 1942–44), 2:149–52.

19. J. R. Jones to Major Paxton, September 27, 1862, in OR 19 (2):629–30.

Northern Virginia suffered from low morale and lax discipline and simply refused to fight in Maryland. Alexander Haskell's comment was most revealing:
the steadfast soldiers fought magnificently at Antietam, but they fought without the help of thousands of their compatriots.

The loss of veteran company- and field-grade officers doubtless contributed to poor discipline and low morale during the Maryland campaign. The
toll of more than two months of strenuous marching punctuated by heavy
combat also played a role. William Garrett Piston has suggested that the shift
from Joseph E. Johnston's to Lee's leadership may have been a third factor.
Many soldiers in the army considered Lee a stand-in for the popular Johnston,
who, they believed, would return following his recuperation. By the first of
September, some of these men may have seen all they wanted of Lee's style of
generalship. In three months under Lee's direction prior to the battle of Antietam, the army had suffered more than thirty-five thousand battle casualties.
This was bloodshed on an unimaginable scale. It might have fostered feelings
among some of the men that if they survived until Johnston resumed command they had a better chance of living a full life.[20]

Whatever the complete story of straggling and desertion in the Army of
Northern Virginia, it seems incontrovertible that morale and discipline were
uneven. Lee's army lacked the self-confidence, devotion to its commander,
and profound willingness to do anything he asked of it that would be its trade-
mark by the time it set out for Gettysburg in June 1863.

Because of these problems and the material odds against them, Lee and
his army probably lacked the capacity to achieve a decisive victory or maintain a protracted presence in the North. Edward Porter Alexander, the most
sagacious of all the Confederates who wrote about Lee's army, argued that in
light of inferior southern strength and supplies, "a drawn battle, such as we did
actually fight, was the best *possible* outcome one could hope for." Only
McClellan's unbelievable timidity and failure to commit his entire army,
added Alexander, permitted even that unsatisfactory result.[21] Barring egre-
gious errors or criminal sloth on the part of his opponent, Lee's army reasonably stood scant chance of seizing the political, diplomatic, and military opportunities that have fascinated students of the Maryland campaign. Yet the

20. William Garrett Piston, *Lee's Tarnished Lieutenant: James Longstreet and His Place in
Southern History* (Athens: University of Georgia Press, 1987), 27–28.

21. Alexander, *Fighting for the Confederacy*, 146.

movement north probably represented Lee's best strategic option. If he remained in Virginia, the North certainly would mount another offensive, which he would be obliged to resist in the same exhausted section of Virginia that already had witnessed so much destructive campaigning. Defensive maneuvering also would offer less potential to score gains in the political and diplomatic arenas, and southern civilians likely would respond more favorably to a successful march into the North than to a defensive operation. In sum, Lee faced a dilemma in early September 1862: he almost had to decide to follow up his victory at Second Manassas, but unless the Union collapsed in fear, he would not be able to sustain a long-term offensive and his return to Virginia would look like a retreat.

The real opportunity that autumn lay in Federal hands. Confronted with a range of potential rewards, the audacious Lee had calculated the risks and chosen to go north. He relied on a period of Federal confusion and inaction after Second Manassas to permit his establishment of a good position in Maryland before having to confront any menace from the Army of the Potomac. But Lee underestimated George B. McClellan's brilliance in rallying Pope's dispirited troops. Within days McClellan had restored morale and built confidence among the ranks of his combined force, and Lincoln discerned that a beautiful opening lay before the Federals. Lee's army was vulnerable once it had crossed into Maryland, its safe passage to Virginia dependent on the Potomac's fords. The farther north Lee went, thought Lincoln, the more tenuous his position. Unaffected by the hysteria that gripped much of the North following news of the Confederate invasion, Lincoln concentrated on offensive operations. Receiving reports on September 12 that the enemy was crossing back into Virginia, he urged McClellan, "Please do not let him get off without being hurt." Three days later the president implored his general to "Destroy the rebel army, if possible."[22]

Lincoln's hopes were not fanciful. The autumn of 1862 was the only time in the war that one major army in the East had an opportunity to destroy another major army. Many generals loved to talk about fashioning Cannae-type victories, but McClellan actually had such an opportunity in mid-September 1862 when Lee's badly outnumbered army stood backed against the Potomac at Sharpsburg. In deciding to stay north of the Potomac and fight, Lee gave

---

22. Abraham Lincoln, *The Collected Works of Abraham Lincoln*, ed. Roy P. Basler *et al.*, eds., 9 vols. (New Brunswick, N.J.: Rutgers University Press, 1953), 5:418, 426.

McClellan the most incredible military opportunity of the conflict. Porter Alexander termed Lee's action the greatest blunder he ever committed and marveled at McClellan's good fortune: "Not twice in a life time does such a chance come to any general. Lee for once has made a mistake, & given you a chance to ruin him if you can break his lines, & such game is worth great risks."[23]

Great risks and great opportunities were the leitmotifs of the 1862 Maryland campaign. Willing to risk all in pursuit of the opportunities he and his government saw before them, Lee misjudged the resources of his army. He crossed the Potomac, divided his infantry into five components, and sent three of the five under Jackson to capture Harpers Ferry. After losing control of the gaps in South Mountain during fighting on September 14, Lee reconcentrated his force just in time to face the Federals on September 16–18 along Antietam Creek. His daring maneuvering thrust before the Federals a dazzling opening that McClellan, despite Lincoln's prodding and the fortuitous capture of Lee's plans, declined to exploit. The upshot was that Lee remained on the battlefield at Antietam on September 18 before escaping to Virginia, his army battered but intact.

The ferocious fighting on September 17 at Sharpsburg felled more than 10,000 Confederates—roughly a third of those present on the field. "Great God," wrote a Georgian to his wife the day after the battle, "what awful things I have to chronicle this morning! One of the most awful battles that was ever fought was fought yesterday[.] [It] commenced at daylight and continued all day until dark." This man wondered how long the Confederate army would "follow up the Yankees and how much more we will fight." Obviously shaken, he observed that "it looks like they are going to kill all the men in battle before they stop. This war will have to stop before long, as all the men will be killed off. God grant that it may close and close soon!" Similar statements from other men appalled by the savagery of the battle abound in the literature on Antietam.[24]

The overall military result of the campaign was open to dispute. Almost from the moment the guns fell silent in the gathering dusk of September 17, 1862, Confederates expressed contradictory reactions about what had tran-

23. Alexander, *Fighting for the Confederacy*, 146.

24. William Stillwell to his wife, September 18, 1862, in Mills Lane, ed., *"Dear Mother: Don't grieve about me. If I get killed, I'll only be dead." Letters from Georgia Soldiers in the Civil War* (Savannah, Ga.: Beehive Press, 1977), 184–85.

spired. Lee's official report and congratulatory order to his troops understandably emphasized the positive aspects of the expedition. His army had cleared Federals from northern Virginia, captured 12,000 Federals and several dozen cannon at Harpers Ferry, provisioned itself from western Maryland, and maintained a position near the south bank of the Potomac after Antietam. As for his soldiers' conduct in the battle, Lee told Davis with obvious pride that "History records but few examples of a greater amount of labor and fighting than has been done by this army during the present campaign." To the Army of Northern Virginia, Lee expressed "admiration of the indomitable courage it has displayed in battle and its cheerful endurance of privation and hardship on the march." The army's "valor and patriotism" had been fully equal to their tasks. No hint of the straggling and desertion that had plagued Lee's movements intruded on this analysis; however, Lee admitted to Davis on September 25 that the army did not "exhibit its former temper and condition." James Longstreet, who doubtless was privy to Lee's thinking in the aftermath of the invasion, recorded after the war that "General Lee was not satisfied with the result of the Maryland campaign."[25]

Opinion from the Confederate ranks generally spoke of success. Letters, diaries, and postwar accounts mentioned the prisoners and guns taken at Harpers Ferry, the steadfast courage of the men at Antietam, and McClellan's failure to drive the Army of Northern Virginia from the battlefield on September 18. "At night we lay down on our arms," remembered a Virginian of September 17. "The next morning, expecting a renewal of the battle, we were up bright and early. But the enemy was badly whipped and did not make a demonstration during the day." Chaplain Nicholas A. Davis of Hood's Texas Brigade stated shortly after the campaign that "Harper's Ferry had fallen, and its rich prizes were ours." Davis emphasized that the Confederate "march to and across the river was undisturbed.—This, of itself, will show to the world the nature of McClellan's victory. And if he had beaten and driven us, . . . why did he allow us to pass quietly away, after holding the field a whole day and night?"[26]

25. Lee, *Wartime Papers*, 312–24; Lee to Jefferson Davis, September 25, 28, 1862, *OR* 19 (2):627, 633; General Orders No. 116, October 2, 1862, *ibid.*, 644–45; James Longstreet, "The Invasion of Maryland," in Robert Underwood Johnson and Clarence Clough Buel, eds., *Battles and Leaders of the Civil War*, 4 vols. (New York: Century, 1887), 2:674.

26. John Worsham, *One of Jackson's Foot Cavalry* (1912; reprint, Jackson, Tenn.: McCowat-Mercer Press, 1964), 89; Nicholas A. Davis, *The Campaign from Texas to Maryland, with the Battle of Fredericksburg* (1863; reprint, Austin, Tex.: Steck, 1961), 92–93.

John Hampden Chamberlayne, a Virginia artillerist, cautioned his sister not "to suppose we were driven out of Maryland; no such thing; our campaign is almost unexampled for quickness & completeness of success." "We have done much more," Chamberlayne insisted, "than a sane man could have expected." In *The Lost Cause*, published in 1866, Edward A. Pollard suggested that the campaign had "few parallels in history for active operations and brilliant results." The wartime editor of Richmond's *Examiner*, Pollard noted sarcastically that if "McClellan was under the impression that he had won a victory, he showed but little disposition to improve it, or to gather its fruits." Not only had the Union commander "attempted no pursuit" after the eighteenth, but he also had asked Lincoln for reinforcements later in the month because he feared Lee might recross the Potomac.[27]

Confederate General Jubal A. Early enumerated the positive facets of the Maryland raid in his postwar autobiography. After forcing Union armies away from Richmond and out of northern Virginia, Lee "had crossed the Potomac, captured an important stronghold defended by a strong force, securing a large amount of artillery, small arms, and stores of all kinds, and had fought a great battle with the newly reorganized and heavily reinforced and recruited army of the enemy, which later was so badly crippled that it was not able to resume the offensive for nearly two months." Lee then stood "defiantly on the banks of the Potomac, the extreme northern limit of the Confederacy," and from that position menaced Washington while at the same time freeing Richmond from direct threat. When the Federals finally moved into Virginia again, stated Early, Lee was in perfect position "to interpose his army, and inflict a new defeat on the enemy."[28]

A few Confederates confessed doubts about their accomplishments in Maryland. Four days after Antietam, Walter H. Taylor of Lee's staff somewhat bitterly counseled his sister not to "let any of your friends sing 'My Maryland,' not 'my West[er]n' Md anyhow." Taylor insisted that the campaign had not been "without happy results. The capture of H[arpers] Ferry was sufficiently

27. John Hampden Chamberlayne to Lucy Parke Chamberlayne, September 22, 1862, in John Hampden Chamberlayne, *Ham Chamberlayne—Virginian: Letters and Papers of an Artillery Officer in the War for Southern Independence, 1861–1865*, ed. C. G. Chamberlayne (Richmond, Va.: Dietz Printing, 1932), 110; Edward A. Pollard, *The Lost Cause: A New Southern History of the War of the Confederates* (New York: E. B. Treat, 1866), 318.

28. Jubal A. Early, *Lieutenant General Jubal Anderson Early C.S.A.: Autobiographical Sketch and Narrative of the War between the States* (1912; reprint, Wilmington, N.C.: Broadfoot, 1989), 160–61.

important to compensate for all the trouble experienced," and the fighting at Antietam demonstrated that Lee's soldiers could "contend with and resist three times their own number." But Taylor conceded that "we do not boast a victory—it was not sufficiently decisive enough for that." The young staff officer added bravely that if either side had an edge at Antietam, "it certainly was with us." Dorsey Pender informed his wife Fanny that he had heard but one feeling expressed about the raid into Maryland, "and that is a regret at our having gone there. Our Army has shown itself incapable of invasion and we had better stick to the defensive." A Georgia captain told his wife that the "heavyest fight of the war was fought in Md., near & at Sharpsburg [on] Wednesday the 17th. . . . The war is becomeing more desperate dayly, I think, which makes me have some hopes that it will end this winter." "I fear this Md. trip has rather injured us more than good done," he continued. "Wee lost more than wee gained in it, I think." South Carolinian Alexander Cheves Haskell praised the fighting qualities of the Confederates at Antietam but stressed that huge numbers of their comrades had abandoned the army. "We are in far better condition in every respect," he affirmed from the Virginia side of the Potomac on October 2, "than when we first invaded the cold, treacherous soil of Maryland."[29]

What is a fair evaluation of the military ledger sheet for Lee and his army in the 1862 Maryland campaign? It is a fascinating blend of accomplishment and useless loss, of questionable strategic decisions after September 15 and brilliant tactical leadership on the battlefield. Lee's movement north represented an effort to take the war out of Virginia, gather food and fodder, threaten Washington from the west, and prevent another Union incursion south of the Potomac before the onset of winter. He accomplished the first three of these, and managed also to postpone the next Federal drive toward Richmond until Ambrose E. Burnside's unusual winter campaign that ended ignominiously for the Union at Fredericksburg in mid-December. Lee knew when he crossed the Potomac that he would have to fall back to Virginia at

29. Walter Taylor to his sister, September 21, 1862, in Walter Taylor, *Lee's Adjutant: The Wartime Letters of Colonel Walter Herron Taylor, 1862–1865*, ed. R. Lockwood Tower (Columbia: University of South Carolina Press, 1995), 44; William Dorsey Pender to Fanny Pender, September 22, 1862, in Pender, *General to His Lady*, 176; Shepherd Green Pryor to Penelope Pryor, September 23, 1862, in Shepherd Pryor, *A Post of Honor: The Pryor Letters, 1861–63, Letters from Capt. S. G. Pryor, Twelfth Georgia Regiment and His Wife, Penelope Tyson Pryor*, ed. Charles R. Adams Jr. (Fort Valley, Ga.: Garret, 1989), 262; Haskell, ed., *Alexander Cheves Haskell*, 85.

some point, preferably in late fall. The battle of Antietam compelled him to withdraw sooner than he wished. Yet because McClellan allowed him to maintain a position immediately south of the Potomac, Lee accomplished from northern Virginia what he had planned to accomplish in western Maryland or southern Pennsylvania. Stonewall Jackson's capture of the garrison at Harpers Ferry was a bonus that Lee could not envision at the outset.

Against these positive results must be reckoned the loss of more than a quarter of the Army of Northern Virginia. The vast majority of those casualties came at Antietam, where Lee stood to gain not a single military advantage. After the fighting in the gaps of South Mountain on September 14, Lee retained no viable offensive options. Harpers Ferry had fallen. No hope of surprise remained as an overwhelmingly more powerful foe closed in from the east. With the Potomac at his rear, only Boteler's Ford offered escape should a crisis arise, and the disparity in numbers virtually guaranteed that the army would face a bitter contest. Porter Alexander subsequently observed that on September 15 "our whole army was back on the Va. side of the Potomac except Longstreet's & Hill's divisions. These could have been easily retired across the river, & we would, indeed, have left Maryland without a great battle, but we would nevertheless have come off with good prestige & a very fair lot of prisoners & guns, & lucky on the whole to do this, considering the accident of the 'lost order.'" Lee had erred badly in choosing to fight at Sharpsburg. It was, thought Alexander, his "greatest military blunder."[30]

Ironically, this battle that Lee should not have fought proved a showcase for the Confederate high command. Lee, Jackson, and Longstreet directed a tactical masterpiece, and their soldiers added heroic luster to a reputation already high. Not until disaster threatened at the Widow Tapp field in the Wilderness and in the Mule Shoe at Spotsylvania in May 1864 would Lee again take so direct a hand in the tactical affairs of his army.

If fighting at Antietam must be reckoned a mistake, Lee's decision to stay on the field another day and contemplate a counterattack amounted to sheer folly. The usual explanations are well known: Lee wanted the men to stand their ground lest morale drop; he knew the cautious McClellan would risk no further assaults; he had confidence in his army's ability to repulse the enemy.

These rationalizations wither under even the slightest scrutiny. Lee realized all too well that morale already had sagged among thousands of his sol-

---

30. Alexander, *Fighting for the Confederacy*, 145.

diers. How would a potentially catastrophic defeat along the river improve it? The second argument is equally flimsy. McClellan had attacked for twelve hours on September 17. How could Lee possibly know his opponent would fail to resume those efforts on the eighteenth? As for the contention that Lee's army could repulse the enemy, the seventeenth had consisted of a series of near calamities and no factor had changed in his favor. Another round of equally heavy Federal assaults on September 18 almost certainly would have broken the Army of Northern Virginia. In *R. E. Lee: A Biography*, Douglas Southall Freeman stepped back in awe of Lee's resolute stand at Sharpsburg on the eighteenth: "What manner of man was he who would elect after that doubtful battle against vast odds to stand for another day with his back to the river?" The answer is, a man who placed his entire army in peril.[31]

Lee's gravest error was in striving to do too much with a limited force, but the salient feature of the Maryland campaign was McClellan's failure to exploit the Confederate army's weakness. Following receipt of Lee's Special Orders No. 191, McClellan dawdled while the Army of Northern Virginia lay scattered across western Maryland. On September 15–16, he allowed Lee to concentrate his far-flung units near Sharpsburg. Artillerist Alexander's critique of McClellan at Antietam conveys a proper sense of disbelief. Lee managed a tactical standoff that day only "by the Good Lord's putting it into McClellan's heart to keep Fitz John Porter's corps entirely out to the battle, & Franklin's nearly all out." "I doubt whether many hearts but McClellan's would have accepted the suggestions, even from a Divine source," noted Alexander wryly. "For Common Sense was just shouting, 'Your adversary is backed against a river, with no bridge & only one ford, & that the worst one on the whole river. If you whip him now, you destroy him utterly, root & branch & bag & baggage. . . . & such game is worth great risks. Every man must fight & keep on fighting for all he is worth.'" "No military genius," concluded Alexander, "but only the commonest kind of every day common sense, was necessary to appreciate that."[32]

Lee's determination to maintain his lines on September 18 created McClellan's ultimate opportunity. Reinforced during the night, he outnumbered Lee nearly three to one. Thousands of his men were fresh, while the enemy was fatigued beyond telling. But once again McClellan lacked the forti-

31. Douglas Southall Freeman, *R. E. Lee: A Biography*, 4 vols. (New York: Charles Scribner's Sons, 1934–36), 2:404.

32. Alexander, *Fighting for the Confederacy*, 146.

tude to seek complete victory. The Union army waited and watched through a long, tense day on September 18, and then it was over. The Army of Northern Virginia marched away that night to execute an undisputed crossing at Boteler's Ford. The northern army had wasted the opportunity to deliver a fatal blow. Destruction of Lee's force would have uncovered Richmond and crippled Confederate morale; it might have ended the war.

Confederate civilian reaction to the Maryland campaign has not received enough attention from scholars to permit confident generalizations about sentiment south of the Potomac. It is fair to say that many people were pessimistic or at best subdued. Robert Garlick Hill Kean of the Confederate Bureau of War characterized Jefferson Davis as being "very low down after the battle of Sharpsburg." Davis confessed to Secretary of War George Wythe Randolph that the Confederacy's "maximum strength had been laid out, while the enemy was but beginning to put forth his." A young woman in Front Royal, Virginia, recorded with apprehension that "reports concerning the Sharpsburg battle are confirmed . . . our army are certainly recrossing the river. It looks rather gloomy for our prospects in Md. and I cannot possibly understand it all." The government did not at first disclose official figures for casualties—"a bad sign for us," thought Catherine Edmondston in Halifax County, North Carolina. "The possession of Harpers Ferry was claimed by us as worth the advance into Maryland," wrote Edmondston, "& yet we cannot hold it. God be with us! Turn not away Thy face, O God, but be with our army a help in time of need." Despite early stories in the Richmond *Enquirer* and elsewhere that Antietam was a stunning Confederate victory, many southerners wondered whether the Maryland campaign had been more than a bloody stalemate at best.[33]

Judged by its nonmilitary results, Lee's campaign into Maryland failed. The most telling consequence came on September 22, 1862, when Lincoln told his cabinet that he would issue a preliminary proclamation of emancipa-

33. Robert Garlick Hill Kean, *Inside the Confederate Government: The Diary of Robert Garlick Hill Kean*, ed. Edward Younger (New York: Oxford University Press, 1957), 86 (entry for July 27, 1863); Lucy Rebecca Buck, *Sad Earth, Sweet Heaven: The Diary of Lucy Rebecca Buck during the War between the States, Front Royal, Virginia, December 25, 1861–April 15, 1865*, ed. William P. Buck (Birmingham, Ala.: Cornerstone, 1973), 144 (entry for September 20, 1862); Catherine Ann Devereux Edmondston, *"Journal of a Secesh Lady": The Diary of Catherine Ann Devereux Edmondston, 1860–1866*, ed. Beth Gilbert Crabtree and James W. Patton (Raleigh: North Carolina Division of Archives and History, 1979), 267 (entry for September 29, 1862).

tion. Should the states in rebellion refuse to return to the Union by January 1, 1863, said the president, their chattels "shall be then, thenceforward, and forever free." Envisioned by Lincoln as a war measure designed to undermine the Confederacy's ability to resist, the proclamation helped open the way for nearly two hundred thousand black men to fight in Federal armies. It also foreclosed the option of reunion on the basis of the status quo ante bellum. The South's social and economic structure was doomed unless Confederate armies won independence on the battlefield.[34]

Both Lee's retreat from Maryland and the Emancipation Proclamation influenced events in Europe. At flood tide in early September, Confederate hopes for assistance from Europe receded quickly. Prime Minister Palmerston believed that events in Maryland had blunted the momentum generated by Lee's victories at the Seven Days and Second Manassas. "The whole matter is full of difficulty," he thought, "and can only be cleared up by some more decided events between the contending armies." In a letter to Lord Russell on October 2, Palmerston suggested that "ten days or a fortnight more may throw a clearer light upon future prospects." William Gladstone and Russell continued their agitation for recognition through October. On the seventh of that month, Gladstone delivered his memorable paean to the Confederacy in a speech at Tyneside: "Jefferson Davis and other leaders of the South have made an army; they are making, it appears, a navy; and they have made what is more than either, they have made a nation."[35]

The loud cheers that greeted those strident phrases had no impact on a British government that backed away from any type of intervention during the second half of October. With Palmerston made cautious by Antietam, the Cabinet declined to adopt Gladstone's position and rejected a French plan calling for Britain, France, and Russia to suggest a six-month armistice and suspension of the blockade. News of the Emancipation Proclamation further undercut friends of the Confederacy. Neither Lee's withdrawal from Maryland nor the proclamation guaranteed that Europe would stay aloof, but together they helped persuade the British to wait until military developments favored the Confederates. Southern arms ultimately proved unequal to the daunting task of compiling enough victories to bring European intercession.[36]

34. Lincoln, *Collected Works* 5:433–38, prints the text of the preliminary proclamation.

35. Jones, *Union in Peril,* 177–78, 182–83; Ephraim Douglass Adams, *Great Britain and the American Civil War,* 2 vols. (1925; reprint, 2 vols. in 1, New York: Russell & Russell, [1958]), 2:43–44.

36. Adams, *Great Britain and the Civil War* 2:46–66.

Lee's expectation of gathering recruits in Maryland came to little. Indeed, illusions about pro-Confederate Marylanders waiting to break free of Union oppression disappeared even before the battle of Antietam. As early as September 7, Lee had cautioned Davis that despite "individual expressions of kindness that have been given," he did not "anticipate any general rising of the people in our behalf." The next day, September 8, Lee issued a proclamation informing Marylanders that "our army has come among you, and is prepared to assist you with the power of its arms in regaining the rights of which you have been despoiled." The numerous Germans in western Maryland turned a distinctly cold shoulder to the intruders. The ragged clothing and gaunt frames of the Confederates, as well as their lice and pungent odor, put off even sympathetic civilians. No more than a few hundred Marylanders stepped forward to join the thin ranks of the Army of Northern Virginia.[37]

As Lee's soldiers crossed the Potomac into Virginia on the night of September 18, John H. Lewis of the 9th Virginia Infantry noted a changed attitude toward Maryland. "When going over the river the boys were singing 'Maryland, my Maryland,'" he observed, "But all was quiet on that point when we came back. Occasionally some fellow would strike that tune, and you would then hear the echo, 'Damn My Maryland.' All seemed to be disgusted with that part of Maryland." An artillerist had anticipated this revised opinion in a letter penned at Frederick on September 6. Alluding to the western counties of the state, he said, "This part of Md. does not welcome us warmly; I have long thought the state was a humbug."[38]

Lee experienced a final failure relating to the northern elections that fall. He had hoped to strengthen the peace interests, but the Army of Northern Virginia's two-week stay north of the Potomac supplied poor aid to those who opposed the Republican administration. Union half-victories at Antietam and Perryville spawned little if any rejoicing in the North, but they at least avoided the sort of dramatic defeat that might have sent Republican fortunes spiraling downward. Ironically, the Emancipation Proclamation, made possible by Lee's retreat, did provoke an angry reaction that helped the Democrats. Results of the canvass of 1862 nonetheless showed only modest Democratic gains for an off-year election—thirty-four seats in the House of Repre-

37. Lee, *Wartime Papers*, 298–99.

38. John H. Lewis, *Recollections from 1860 to 1865: With Incidents of Camp Life, Descriptions of Battles, the Life of the Southern Soldier, His Hardships and Sufferings, and the Life of a Prisoner of War in the Northern Prisons* (1895; reprint, Dayton, Ohio: Morningside, 1983), 56; Chamberlayne, ed., *Ham Chamberlayne*, 103.

sentatives, gubernatorial victories in New York and New Jersey, and control of the Illinois and Indiana legislatures. The Republicans managed to gain five seats in the Senate and retain control of the House (their net loss in the House was the smallest in the last ten elections for the majority party). The war would continue under Republican direction.[39]

The Maryland campaign holds a unique position in the galaxy of Lee's military operations. Hoping to maintain the momentum generated by his victories at the Seven Days and Second Manassas, he marched north and fought a horrific battle, avoided a series of lurking disasters, and eventually found refuge along the southern bank of the Potomac River. He pressed his worn army to the edge of ruin in pursuit of beckoning opportunity, absorbing awful losses in the process. Because he maintained a strong position along the Potomac frontier after Antietam, the operation was not a complete strategic failure. Diplomatically and politically, however, the invasion of Maryland yielded bitter fruit for the Confederacy. It allowed Lincoln to issue his preliminary proclamation of emancipation, which helped change the nature of the conflict. With freedom for millions of slaves and the entire social and economic fabric of the Confederacy now at stake, the war would admit of no easy reconciliation. Lee and his army would form the bulwark of Confederate hopes for independence throughout the rest of the war, but realization of those hopes would prove a more daunting task because of what transpired in Maryland in September 1862.

39. McPherson, *Battle Cry of Freedom*, 561–62.

★ 3 ★

If the Enemy Is There, We Must Attack Him

Lee and the Second Day at Gettysburg

No aspect of Robert E. Lee's military career has sparked more controversy than his decision to pursue the tactical offensive at Gettysburg. Lee's contemporaries and subsequent writers produced a literature on the subject notable for its size and discordancy. Unwary students can fall victim to the hyperbole, dissembling, and self-interest characteristic of many accounts by participants. The massive printed legacy of the "Gettysburg Controversy," with its blistering critiques of James Longstreet and "Old Pete's" clumsy rejoinders, demands special care. Even many modern writers unfurl partisan banners when they approach the topic. Despite the size of the existing literature, Lee's decision to resume offensive combat on July 2 remains a topic worthy of study. Before passing judgment on his actions, however, it is necessary to assess the merits of earlier works—an exercise that underscores the contradictory nature of the evidence and the lack of interpretive consensus among previous writers.

The Army of Northern Virginia went into Pennsylvania at its physical apogee, supremely confident that under Lee's direction it could triumph on any battlefield. LeRoy Summerfield Edwards of the 12th Virginia Infantry struck a common note in a letter written near Shepherdstown on June 23: "The health of the troops was never better and above all the morale of the army was never more favorable for offensive or defensive operations . . . victory will inevitably attend our arms in any collision with the enemy." British observer A. J. L. Fremantle detected a similar outlook when he spoke to a pair of officers from Louisiana on that same day. Recuperating from wounds suffered in fighting at Winchester during the march northward, these men gave Fremantle "an animated account of the spirits and feeling of the army. At no period of the war, they say, have the men been so well equipped, so well clothed, so eager for a fight, or so confident of success."[1]

Two weeks and more than 25,000 casualties later, the picture had changed. The soldiers still believed in Lee, but some of them had lost their almost mystical faith in certain victory. Randolph H. McKim, a young Marylander in Richard S. Ewell's Second Corps, betrayed such sentiment in his diary shortly after Gettysburg: "I went into the last battle feeling that victory must be ours—that such an army could not be foiled, and that God would certainly declare himself on our side. Now I feel that unless He sees fit to bless our arms, our valor will not avail." Stephen Dodson Ramseur, a brigadier in Robert E. Rodes's division, reacted similarly to the shock of Gettysburg. "Our great campaign," wrote Ramseur a month after the battle, "admirably planned & more admirably executed up to the fatal days at Gettysburg, has failed. Which I was not prepared to anticipate." Although insisting that Gettysburg did not spell the doom of the Confederacy, he believed it foreshadowed other crises the South must overcome to gain independence. Ramseur looked "the thing square in the face" and stood ready "to undergo dangers and hardships and trials to the end."[2]

Staggering losses and a shift in morale thus grew out of Lee's decision to

1. Joan K. Walton and Terry A. Walton, eds., *Letters of LeRoy S. Edwards Written during the War between the States* (N.p.: n.p., [1985]), [57]; Arthur James Lyon Fremantle, *Three Months in the Southern States: April–June, 1863* (1863; reprint, Lincoln: University of Nebraska Press, 1991), 231–32.

2. Randolph H. McKim, *A Soldier's Recollections: Leaves from the Diary of a Young Confederate* (1910; reprint, Washington, D.C.: Zenger, 1983), 182; Stephen Dodson Ramseur to Ellen Richmond, August 3, 1863, folder 7, Stephen Dodson Ramseur Papers, Southern Historical Collection, Wilson Library, University of North Carolina, Chapel Hill [repository hereinafter cited as SHC]. On Confederate morale in the wake of Gettysburg, see Gary W. Gallagher, "Lee's Army Has Not Lost Any of Its Prestige: The Impact of Gettysburg on the Army of Northern Virginia and the Confederate Home Front," in Gallagher, ed., *The Third Day at Gettysburg and Beyond* (Chapel Hill: University of North Carolina Press, 1994).

press for a decisive result on the field at Gettysburg. Some Confederates immediately questioned his tactics. "Gettysburg has shaken my faith in Lee as a general," Robert Garlick Hill Kean of the War Department wrote in his diary on July 26, 1863. "To fight an enemy superior in numbers at such terrible disadvantage of position in the heart of his own territory, when the freedom of movement gave him the advantage of selecting his own time and place for accepting battle, seems to have been a great military blunder . . . and the result was the worst disaster which has ever befallen our arms." Brigadier General Wade Hampton used comparably strong language in a letter to Joseph E. Johnston less than a month after the battle. The Pennsylvania campaign was a "complete failure," stated Hampton, during which Lee resorted to unimaginative offensive tactics. "The position of the Yankees there was the strongest I ever saw & it was in vain to attack it." Hampton had expected the Confederates to "choose our own points at which to fight" during the expedition, but "we let Meade choose his position and then we attacked."[3]

More restrained in his disapproval was James Longstreet, who informed his uncle Augustus Baldwin Longstreet confidentially in late July 1863 that the "battle was not made as I would have made it. My idea was to throw ourselves between the enemy and Washington, select a strong position, and force the enemy to attack us." Through such a defensive stance, thought Longstreet, the Confederates might have "destroyed the Federal army, marched into Washington, and dictated our terms, or, at least, held Washington and marched over as much of Pennsylvania as we cared to, had we drawn the enemy into attack upon our carefully chosen position in his rear."[4]

The early postwar years witnessed a rapid escalation of the debate over

3. Robert Garlick Hill Kean, *Inside the Confederate Government: The Diary of Robert Garlick Hill Kean*, ed. Edward Younger (New York: Oxford University Press, 1957), 84; Wade Hampton to Joseph E. Johnston, July 30, 1863, quoted in Herman Hattaway and Archer Jones, *How the North Won: A Military History of the Civil War* (Urbana: University of Illinois Press, 1983), 414.

4. James Longstreet to Augustus Baldwin Longstreet, July 24, 1863, reproduced in part in J. William Jones *et al.*, eds., *Southern Historical Society Papers*, 52 vols. (1876–1959; reprint, with 3-vol. index, Wilmington, N.C.: Broadfoot, 1990–92), 5:54–55 [hereinafter cited as *SHSP*]). This letter also appeared in the New Orleans *Republican* on January 25, 1876, in the New York *Times* four days later, and in Longstreet's article "The Campaign of Gettysburg" in the Philadelphia *Weekly Times*, November 3, 1877 (the *Weekly Times* article also appeared under the title "Lee in Pennsylvania," in [A. K. McClure], ed., *The Annals of the War, Written by Leading Participants North and South* [Philadelphia, 1879], 414–46 [the last work hereinafter cited as *Annals of the War*]).

Lee's generalship at Gettysburg. Longstreet served as a catalyst for an out-pouring of writing, the opening salvo of which appeared the year after Appomattox in William Swinton's *Campaigns of the Army of the Potomac*. A northern journalist, Swinton interviewed Longstreet and drew heavily on his opinions to portray Lee's tactics at Gettysburg as misguided and contrary to a precampaign pledge to "his corps-commanders that *he would not assume a tactical offensive*, but force his antagonist to attack him." Lee's assaults on the second day were a "grave error" explained by overconfidence in the prowess of his soldiers, fear that withdrawal without battle would harm morale in the Army of Northern Virginia and among southern civilians, and contempt for the Army of the Potomac. Having "gotten a taste of blood in the considerable success of the first day," suggested Swinton in language similar to that used elsewhere by Longstreet, "the Confederate commander seems to have lost that equipoise in which his faculties commonly moved, and he determined to give battle."[5]

Other early postwar accounts also highlighted questions about Lee's aggressive tactics. Edward A. Pollard, the staunchly pro-Confederate editor of the Richmond *Examiner* during the war, alluded in 1866 to "a persistent popular opinion in the South that Gen. Lee, having failed to improve the advantage of the first day, did wrong thereafter to fight at Gettysburg." Granting the "extraordinary strength" of the Federal position, Pollard nonetheless asserted that the superlative morale of Lee's army might have justified the attempt to drive Meade's army from the field.[6] James D. McCabe Jr.'s generally appreciative *Life and Campaigns of General Robert E. Lee*, also published in 1866, ar-

5. William Swinton, *Campaigns of the Army of the Potomac: A Critical History of Operations in Virginia, Maryland, and Pennsylvania, from the Commencement to the Close of the War, 1861–1865* (1866; revised ed., New York: Charles Scribner's Sons, 1882), 340–41. Swinton credited "a full and free conversation" with Longstreet as his source for "revelations of the purposes and sentiments of Lee." In "Lee in Pennsylvania," 433, Longstreet used almost precisely the same language as Swinton when he observed: "There is no doubt that General Lee, during the crisis of that campaign, lost the matchless equipoise that usually characterized him, and that whatever mistakes were made were not so much matters of deliberate judgment as the impulses of a great mind disturbed by unparalleled conditions."

6. Edward A. Pollard, *The Lost Cause: A New Southern History of the War of the Confederates* (New York: E. B. Treat, 1866), 406–407. Pollard's assessment of Lee is a bit harsher in his *Lee and His Lieutenants: Comprising the Early Life, Public Services, and Campaigns of General Robert E. Lee and His Companions in Arms, with a Record of Their Campaigns and Heroic Deeds* (New York: E. B. Treat, 1867).

gued that after July 1 the Confederate army "had before it the task of storming a rocky fortress stronger than that against which Burnside had dashed his army so madly at Fredericksburg, and every chance of success lay with the Federals." Citing Swinton's work as corroboration, McCabe endorsed Longstreet's proposal to shift around the Federal left and invite attack from a position between the Union army and Washington. "There are those who assert that General Lee himself was not free from the contempt entertained by his men for the army they had so frequently vanquished, and that he was influenced by it in his decision upon this occasion," added McCabe in reference to Lee's resumption of assaults on July 2. "This may or may not be true. It is certain that the decision was an error."[7]

The interpretive tide turned in Lee's favor shortly after the general's death. Led by Jubal A. Early, a number of former Confederates eventually mounted a concerted effort in the Southern Historical Society's *Papers* and elsewhere to discredit Longstreet (whose Republicanism made him an especially inviting target) and prove Lee innocent of all responsibility for the debacle at Gettysburg. Speaking at Washington and Lee University on the anniversary of Lee's birth in 1872, Early disputed the notion that the Confederates should have refrained from attacking after July 1. "Some have thought that General Lee did wrong in fighting at Gettysburg," remarked Early in obvious reference to Longstreet's views, "and it has been said that he ought to have moved around Meade's left, so as to get between him and Washington. . . . I then thought, and still think, that it was right to fight the battle of Gettysburg, and I am firmly convinced that if General Lee's plans had been carried out in the spirit in which they were conceived, a decisive victory would have been obtained, which perhaps would have secured our independence."

As the most prominent member of the Lost Cause school of interpretation, Early won a deserved reputation as Lee's most indefatigable defender and Longstreet's harshest critic. He blamed defeat on Longstreet's sulking sloth in mounting the assaults on July 2. Lee expected the attacks to begin at dawn, insisted Early (a charge Longstreet easily proved to be literally untrue—though Lee certainly wanted the attacks to start as early as possible); Longstreet began the offensive about 4:00 P.M., by which time Meade's entire army was in place. "The position which Longstreet attacked at four, was not occu-

7. James D. McCabe Jr., *Life and Campaigns of General Robert E. Lee* (St. Louis: National, 1866), 393–95.

pied by the enemy until late in the afternoon," concluded Early, "and Round Top Hill, which commanded the enemy's position, could have been taken in the morning without a struggle."[8]

Although few veterans of the Army of Northern Virginia spoke publicly against Lee during the postwar years, many did not share Early's views. Benjamin G. Humphreys, who commanded the 21st Mississippi Infantry in William Barksdale's brigade on the second day at Gettysburg, revealed sharp disagreement with the Lost Cause writers in comments he scribbled in the margins of his copy of Walter H. Taylor's *Four Years with General Lee*. Humphreys deplored the "necessity of hunting out for a 'scapegoat'" to guarantee that the "'infallibility' of Lee must not be called into question." The commanding general "took upon himself all the blame for Gettysburg," observed Humphreys mockingly; "was that not an evidence of his infallibility?"[9]

Lee himself said little publicly beyond his official report. The fighting on July 1 had escalated from a meeting engagement to a bitter contest involving two corps on each side, during which the serendipitous arrival of Ewell's leading divisions had compelled the Federals to withdraw through Gettysburg to high ground below the town. "It had not been intended to deliver a general battle so far from our base unless attacked," wrote Lee in apparent confirmation of Longstreet's assertion that he had envisioned acting on the tactical defensive in Pennsylvania, "but coming unexpectedly upon the whole Federal Army, to withdraw through the mountains with our extensive trains would have been difficult and dangerous." Nor could the Confederates wait for Meade to counterattack, "as the country was unfavorable for collecting supplies in the presence of the enemy, who could restrain our foraging parties by holding the mountain passes with local troops." "A battle had, therefore,

---

8. Jubal A. Early, *The Campaigns of Gen. Robert E. Lee. An Address by Lieut. General Jubal A. Early, before Washington and Lee University, January 19th, 1872* (Baltimore: John Murphy, 1872), 30–32. Fitzhugh Lee, J. William Jones, and William Nelson Pendleton were among Longstreet's chief critics. For the early arguments in the Gettysburg controversy, see vols. 4–6 of the *SHSP*. Useful modern treatments include Thomas L. Connelly, *The Marble Man: Robert E. Lee and His Image in American Society* (New York: Alfred A. Knopf, 1977); William Garrett Piston, *Lee's Tarnished Lieutenant: James Longstreet and His Place in Southern History* (Athens: University of Georgia Press, 1987); and Glenn Tucker, *Lee and Longstreet at Gettysburg* (Indianapolis: Bobbs-Merrill, 1968).

9. Frank E. Everett Jr., "Delayed Report of an Important Eyewitness to Gettysburg—Benjamin G. Humphreys," *Journal of Mississippi History* 46 (November 1984):318.

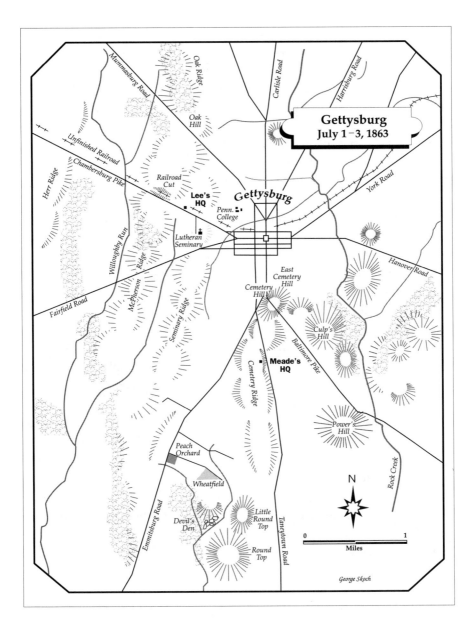

Gettysburg
July 1–3, 1863

Mummasburg Road

Oak Ridge

Carlisle Road

Harrisburg Road

Oak Hill

Unfinished Railroad

Chambersburg Pike

Herr Ridge

Railroad Cut

Lee's HQ

Gettysburg

York Road

Penn. College

Willoughby Run

McPherson Ridge

Lutheran Seminary

Hanover Road

Seminary Ridge

East Cemetery Hill

Fairfield Road

Cemetery Hill

Culp's Hill

Cemetery Ridge

Meade's HQ

Baltimore Pike

Power's Hill

Peach Orchard

Rock Creek

Wheatfield

N

Emmitsburg Road

Devil's Den

Little Round Top

Taneytown Road

Round Top

0   1
Miles

George Skoch

become in a measure unavoidable," concluded Lee, "and the success already gained gave hope of a favorable issue."[10]

Lee offered the last hopeful statement despite a firm understanding of the terrain. "The enemy occupied a strong position," he conceded, "with his right upon two commanding elevations adjacent to each other, one southeast and the other, known as Cemetery Hill, immediately south of the town. . . . His line extended thence upon the high ground along the Emmitsburg Road, with a steep ridge in rear, which was also occupied. This ridge was difficult of ascent, particularly the two hills above mentioned as forming its northern extremity, and a third at the other end, on which the enemy's left rested." Stone and rail fences affording protection to defenders, together with generally open approaches three-quarters of a mile wide, complicated any plan of assault. Yet offensive thoughts dominated Lee's thinking. When Ewell declined to strike at Cemetery Hill late on the afternoon of July 1, the commanding general opted to await the arrival of Longstreet's two leading divisions: "It was determined to make the principal attack upon the enemy's left. . . . Longstreet was directed to place the divisions of McLaws and Hood on the right of Hill, partially enveloping the enemy's left, which he was to drive in." A. P. Hill would engage the Union center with a demonstration, while Ewell's troops would do the same on the enemy's right with an eye toward exploiting any opening.[11]

Almost matter-of-fact in its explication of the reasons for resuming attacks on July 2, Lee's report contains no hint that he considered the decision a bad one. Five years after the battle, he responded to a query about Gettysburg in a similar vein: "I must again refer you to the official accounts. Its loss was occasioned by a combination of circumstances. It was commenced in the absence of correct intelligence. It was continued in the effort to overcome the difficulties by which we were surrounded, and it would have been gained could one determined and united blow have been delivered by our whole line."[12]

---

10. U.S. War Department, *The War of the Rebellion: A Compilation of the Official Records of the Union and Confederate Armies,* 128 vols. (Washington, D.C.: GPO, 1880–1901), ser. 1, vol. 27, pt. 2:318 [hereinafter cited as *OR*; all references are to ser. 1].

11. *Ibid.,* 318–19.

12. Robert E. Lee Jr., *Recollections and Letters of General Robert E. Lee* (1904; reprint, Wilmington, N.C.: Broadfoot, 1988), 102. Lee wrote to Major William M. McDonald of Berryville, Virginia.

Several secondhand accounts also suggest that Lee never deviated from the tenor of his report. Colonel William Allan, former chief of ordnance in the Second Corps, made notes of a conversation with Lee on April 15, 1868, wherein Lee talked passionately about Gettysburg. Lee had hoped to avoid a general battle in Pennsylvania, recorded Allan, but "Jeb" Stuart's absence caused the opposing forces to stumble into one another on July 1. The commanding general "found himself engaged with the Federal army therefore, unexpectedly, and had to fight. This being determined on, victory w[oul]d have been won if he could have gotten one decided simultaneous attack on the whole line." Lee also observed that his critics "talked much of that they knew little about" and, in a likely reference to William Swinton's book, stated that he doubted Longstreet ever said Lee "was under a promise to the Leut. Generals not to fight a general battle in Pa. . . . He had never made any such promise, and had never thought of doing any such thing."[13]

Nearly two years later, Lee again "spoke feelingly" about Gettysburg with Allan. "Much was said about risky movements," noted Allan. Lee believed that "everything was risky in our war. He knew oftentimes that he was playing a very bold game, but it was the only *possible* one." This justification of risk, though not specifically tied to any phase of the campaign, certainly could apply to Lee's pursuing assaults after the first day. As in his earlier pronouncements on the subject, Lee seemed content with his principal decisions. He still maintained that Stuart's failure had precipitated the fighting, and the fact that he "never c[oul]d get a simultaneous attack on the enemy's position" sealed the result.[14]

Accounts by Brigadier General John D. Imboden and Major John Seddon further buttress an image of Lee as comfortable with his tactical conduct at Gettysburg. Early on the morning of July 4, wrote Imboden in the 1880s, he met with Lee at army headquarters outside Gettysburg. The conversation turned to the failed assaults on July 3: "I never saw troops behave more magnificently than Pickett's division of Virginians did to-day in that grand charge upon the enemy," said Lee. "And if they had been supported as they were to

13. William Allan, "Memoranda of Conversations with General Robert E. Lee," in Gary W. Gallagher, ed., *Lee the Soldier* (Lincoln: University of Nebraska Press, 1996), 13–14. Lee apparently misconstrued Longstreet's comment about an agreement not to fight an offensive battle, interpreting it as a claim that Lee had agreed to fight no battle at all.

14. Allan, "Conversations with Lee," in Gallagher, ed., *Lee the Soldier*, 17 (the conversation took place on February 19, 1870).

have been . . . we would have held the position and the day would have been ours." It is reasonable to infer from this passage that Lee also viewed the resumption of the offensive on July 2 as correct. Major Seddon, a brother of the Confederate secretary of war, met with Lee shortly after Gettysburg and subsequently related his conversation to Major General Henry Heth. Heth quoted Seddon as stating that Lee acknowledged a heavy loss at Gettysburg but pronounced it "no greater than it would have been from the series of battles I would have been compelled to fight had I remained in Virginia." After making this observation, Lee rose from his seat and with an "emphatic gesture said, 'and sir, we did whip them at Gettysburg, and it will be seen for the next six months that that army will be as quiet as a sucking dove.' "[15]

A smaller body of evidence portrays Lee as subject to doubts about his tactical moves at Gettysburg. Perhaps best known is Fremantle's description of Lee's response to Brigadier General Cadmus M. Wilcox as the latter brought his brigade out of the fight on July 3: "Never mind, General, *all this has been* MY *fault*—it is I that have lost this fight, and you must help me out of it in the best way you can."[16] Whether or not Lee meant the entire battle when he spoke of "this fight," his comment can be extended to the decision to keep attacking after July 1. In early August 1863, he informed President Davis that he was aware of public criticisms of his generalship at Gettysburg. "I do not know how far this feeling extends in the army," wrote Lee. "My brother officers have been too kind to report it, and so far the troops have been too generous to exhibit it. It is fair, however, to suppose that it does exist, and success is so necessary to us that nothing should be risked to secure it." Offering to step down as commander of the army, Lee implicitly recognized that he had erred in Pennsylva-

15. John D. Imboden, "The Confederate Retreat from Gettysburg," in Robert Underwood Johnson and Clarence Clough Buel, eds., *Battles and Leaders of the Civil War,* 4 vols. (New York: Century, 1887), 3:421 [hereinafter cited as *B&L*]; Henry Heth, "Letter from Major-General Henry Heth, of A. P. Hill's Corps, A.N.V.," in *SHSP* 4:154–55.

16. Fremantle, *Three Months,* 269. For other eyewitness versions of Lee's accepting full responsibility for the defeat while greeting survivors of the Pickett-Pettigrew assault, see Charles T. Loehr, *War History of the Old First Virginia Infantry Regiment, Army of Northern Virginia* (1884; reprint, Dayton, Ohio: Morningside, 1978), 38. (Loehr quotes Lee as saying to Pickett, "General, your men have done all that men could do, the fault is entirely my own."); and Robert A. Bright, "Pickett's Charge: The Story of It As Told by a Member of His Staff," in *SHSP* 31:234. (Bright has Lee comment, "Come, General Pickett, this has been my fight and upon my shoulders rests the blame.")

nia: "I cannot even accomplish what I myself desire. How can I fulfill the expectations of others?"[17]

Two additional vignettes, though both hearsay, merit mention. Henry Heth remembered after the war that he and Lee discussed Gettysburg at Orange Court House during the winter of 1863–1864. "After it is all over, as stupid a fellow as I am can see the mistakes that were made," said the commanding general somewhat defensively. "I notice, however, my mistakes are never told me until it is too late, and you, and all my officers, know that I am always ready and anxious to have their suggestions." Captain Thomas J. Goree of Longstreet's staff recalled in an 1875 letter to his old chief a similar episode at Orange Court House in the winter of 1864. Summoned to Lee's tent, Goree found that the general had been looking through northern newspapers. Lee "remarked that he had just been reading the Northern official reports of the Battle of Gettysburg, that he had become satisfied from reading those reports that if he had permitted you to carry out your plans on the 3d day, instead of making the attack on Cemetery Hill, we would have been successful."[18] Because Longstreet first argued for a movement around the Federal flank on July 2, it is possible that in retrospect Lee also considered the assaults of the second day to have been unwise.

Many later writings about Gettysburg by Confederate participants followed furrows first plowed by Jubal Early and his cohorts in their savaging of James Longstreet. They insisted that Longstreet had disobeyed Lee's orders to attack early on July 2, dragged his feet throughout that crucial day, and was

17. Lee to Jefferson Davis, August 8, 1863, in *OR* 51 (2):752. Lee also alluded to public disapproval in his talk with John Seddon: "Major Seddon, from what you have observed, are the people as much depressed at the battle of Gettysburg as the newspapers appear to indicate?" Seddon answered in the affirmative, whereupon Lee stated forcefully that popular sentiment misconstrued events on the battlefield—Fredericksburg and Chancellorsville were hollow victories yet lifted morale, whereas Gettysburg accomplished more militarily but lowered morale. Heth, "Letter from Major-General Henry Heth," 53–54.

18. Heth, "Letter from Major-General Henry Heth," 159–60; Thomas Jewett Goree to James Longstreet, May 17, 1875, in Thomas Jewett Goree, *Longstreet's Aide: The Civil War Letters of Major Thomas J. Goree*, ed. Thomas W. Cutrer (Charlottesville: University Press of Virginia, 1995), 158–59. Longstreet asked Goree for his recollections of Gettysburg in a letter of May 12, 1875. A portion of Goree's reply of May 17 (with several errors of transcription) appeared in Longstreet's *From Manassas to Appomattox: A Memoir of the Civil War in America* (Philadelphia: J. B. Lippincott, 1896), 400.

slow again on July 3. Had Old Pete moved with dispatch, the Confederates would have won the battle and perhaps the war. No questioning of Lee's commitment to bloody offensive action after July 1 clouded the simplistic reasoning of these authors, typical of whom was former Second Corps staff officer James Power Smith. In a paper read before the Military Historical Society of Massachusetts in 1905, Smith recounted the conference among Lee and his Second Corps subordinates on the evening of July 1. Events of that day dictated further attacks, stated Smith. "There was no retreat without an engagement," he affirmed. "Instead of the defensive, as he had planned, General Lee was compelled to take the offensive, and himself endeavor to force the enemy away. It was not by the choice of Lee nor by the foresight of Meade that the Federal army found itself placed on lines of magnificent defence." Persuaded that Ewell's corps lacked the power to capture high ground on the Union right, Lee concluded that Longstreet would spearhead an effort against the enemy's left on July 1. "Then with bowed head he added, 'Longstreet is a very good fighter when he gets in position, but he is *so slow.*'" This last comment, which almost certainly was based on Jubal A. Early's postwar account of the meeting, anticipated the further argument that Lee's sound planning ran aground on the rock of Longstreet's lethargic movements.[19]

Longstreet defended himself against his tormentors ineptly, launching indiscreet counterattacks that often strayed widely from the truth and provoked further onslaughts against his character and military ability. One notorious example of his poor judgment will suffice: "That [Lee] was excited and off his

19. James Power Smith, "General Lee at Gettysburg," in *Papers of the Military Historical Society of Massachusetts*, 15 vols. (1895–1918; reprint, Wilmington, N.C.: Broadfoot, 1989–90), 5:393. For Early's 1877 charge that Longstreet was slow, see p. 68 below. This charge was widely repeated in Lost Cause literature. For example, Fitzhugh Lee's "A Review of the First Two Days' Operations at Gettysburg and a Reply to General Longstreet by Fitzhugh Lee," in *SHSP* 5:193, quotes an unnamed officer who stated that Lee called Longstreet "the hardest man to move I had in my army," and Douglas Southall Freeman, *R. E. Lee: A Biography*, 4 vols. (New York: Charles Scribner's Sons, 1934–36), 3:80, cites W. Gordon McCabe, who in old age remarked to Freeman that Lee had told his son Custis that Longstreet was slow. No letter from Lee's hand supports this contention; however, William Preston Johnston made a memorandum of a conversation with Lee on May 7, 1868, in which he claimed that Lee, in the context of a discussion of the second day of the battle of the Wilderness, observed that "Longstreet was often slow." William Preston Johnston, "Memoranda of Conversations with General R. E. Lee," in Gallagher, ed., *Lee the Soldier*, 29. Because it is impossible to confirm when Johnston reconstructed his conversations with Lee, his undated memorandum should be used with care.

Lee in 1863, photographed by Julian Vannerson
Library of Congress

balance was evident on the afternoon of the 1st," claimed Longstreet in his memoirs, "and he labored under that oppression until enough blood was shed to appease him." Such statements provoked a massive response from Longstreet's critics, creating a body of evidence that would damn him in the eyes of many subsequent historians.[20]

The writings of Brigadier General Edward Porter Alexander stood in notable contrast to the emotional approach of many former Confederates. Easily the most astute military analyst among Lee's lieutenants, Alexander sometimes is perceived as an apologist for Longstreet because he served for much of the war as chief of artillery in the First Corps. In fact, he probed in brilliantly dispassionate fashion Lee's generalship at Gettysburg. He thought a casual reading of Lee's report "suggests that the aggressive on [the] second day seemed forced upon him, yet the statement is very much qualified by the expression 'in a measure,' & also by the reference to the hopes inspired by our partial success." Alexander bluntly declared that "no real difficulty" prevented Lee's shifting to the defensive on July 2 and maneuvering in such a manner as to force Meade to attack. Lee's reference to his trains failed to impress Alexander, who as the army's former chief of ordnance had an excellent grasp of the difficulties of moving large numbers of wagons.

With an engineer's love of precision, Alexander reckoned "it a reasonable estimate to say that 60 per cent of our chances for a great victory were lost by our continuing the aggressive. And we may easily imagine the boon it was to Gen. Meade . . . to be relieved from the burden of making any difficult decision, such as what he would have had to do if Lee had been satisfied with his victory of the first day; & then taken a strong position & stood on the defensive." Expressing astonishment that "the strength of the enemy's position seems to have cut no figure in the consideration [of] the question of the aggressive," Alexander labeled Meade's good fortune "more than impudence itself could have dared to pray for—a position unique among all the battlefields of the war, certainly adding fifty per cent to his already superior force, and an adversary stimulated by success to an utter disregard of all physical disadvantages."

These opinions aside, Alexander believed that victory eluded the Con-

---

20. Longstreet, *From Manassas to Appomattox*, 384. The best analysis of Longstreet's part in the Gettysburg controversy is Piston, *Lee's Tarnished Lieutenant*, esp. chaps. 7–9. Piston concluded that "Longstreet's efforts to defend his military reputation had been futile" (p. 150).

federates on July 2 only because Longstreet's assaults began so late. Professing no doubt that the offensive could have started sooner, he expressed equal certainty that "Gen. Lee much desired it to be made very much earlier." Longstreet's preference to await the arrival of Evander M. Law's brigade, to which Lee acceded, and the delay occasioned by Confederate infantry near Black Horse Tavern coming into view of Federal signalmen on Little Round Top slowed the flanking march. Present on the field the entire time and "apparently consenting to the situation from hour to hour," Lee bore a major portion of responsibility for the late opening of the attacks by Alexander's reading of the evidence.[21]

Modern writers have continued to explore Lee's choice to resume offensive operations on July 1. Easily the most influential of Lee's biographers is Douglas Southall Freeman. After discussing Lee's conferences with Ewell and Longstreet on the evening of July 1, Freeman asked, "But was it wise to attack at all? What alternatives were there?" Freeman listed four available courses of action: Lee could take up a defensive position on the field and invite attack from Meade; he could retreat to the western side of South Mountain; he could move around the Union left as Longstreet urged, placing the army between the Federals and Washington; or he could mount another series of attacks in the hope of achieving a complete victory. The first two alternatives Freeman dismissed quickly with a paraphrase of Lee's official report. The third he termed impractical, citing the opinions of "nearly all military critics"—including Jubal Early, William Allan, Armistead L. Long, and other stalwart members of the Lost Cause school of interpretation. With unintended irony, Freeman admitted in a footnote that George G. Meade "was the only critic who agreed with Longstreet. He said that Longstreet's proposal was ... the step he feared Lee would take."[22]

Freeman thus brought himself to the fourth option. Once again paraphrasing Lee, he concluded: "Strategically, then, Lee saw no alternative to attacking the enemy before Meade concentrated, much as he disliked to force a general engagement so early in the campaign and at such a distance from Virginia." Tactically, Freeman approved of Lee's plan to use the divisions of

21. Edward Porter Alexander, *Fighting for the Confederacy: The Personal Recollections of General Edward Porter Alexander*, ed. Gary W. Gallagher (Chapel Hill: University of North Carolina Press, 1989), 277–78. See also Alexander's *Military Memoirs of a Confederate: A Critical Narrative* (New York: Charles Scribner's Sons, 1907), 387–89.

22. Freeman, *R. E. Lee* 3:81–82.

McLaws and Hood to deliver the heaviest blow on the Union left, with Ewell's corps doing what it could against the enemy's far right. Little did Lee know, contended Freeman, that as he anticipated another day's combat his plans already were being undone. With a statement worthy of Jubal Early, Lee's great biographer closed his chapter on July 1: "The battle was being decided at that very hour in the mind of Longstreet, who at his camp, a few miles away, was eating his heart away in sullen resentment that Lee had rejected his long-cherished plan of a strategic offensive and a tactical defensive." That sullenness manifested itself in a performance on July 2 so sluggish "it has often been asked why Lee did not arrest him for insubordination or order him before a court-martial." Freeman answered that an absence of qualified officers forced Lee to make do with Longstreet, warts and all, even as he lamented the absence of Stonewall Jackson.[23]

Other historians offer a mixture of praise and censure for Lee's decision to attack on July 2. Clifford Dowdey, whom one reviewer aptly called "the last *Confederate* historian," endorsed Lee's offensive inclination, observing that the southern commander apparently never thought of shifting to the defensive. Dowdey emphasized the need for a quick triumph: "[Lee's] thinking was shaped by the background of the South's waning strength, by the present illustration of the attrition in high command, and by the need for a decisive victory away from home. . . . His men were driving the enemy, and, though Ewell had kept them from clinching the victory today, Lee thought only of how to complete it the next day." Poor execution robbed the army of success on July 2, but the decision to seek that success had been correct.[24] Frank E. Vandiver echoed Dowdey, with the twist that a spell of ill health in Pennsylvania had made Lee edgy and more inclined to seek a quick resolution. His physical ailments and Longstreet's stubbornness left Lee "generally irritated and he's determined that he is going to attack." "He has every reason for wanting to do that," judged Vandiver, "he has his army in Pennsylvania, it's at its finest strength and gear and this is the time to cast the die. Across the field is a

<hr />

23. *Ibid.*, 82–84, 159–60. Freeman offered a significantly different analysis in *Lee's Lieutenants: A Study in Command*, 3 vols. (New York: Charles Scribner's Sons, 1942–44), 3:173–74, finding that Longstreet's "attitude was wrong but his instinct was correct. He should have obeyed orders, but the orders should not have been given."

24. Clifford Dowdey, *Death of a Nation: The Story of Lee and His Men at Gettysburg* (New York: Alfred A. Knopf, 1958), 155, 239–40. The reviewer was Richard B. Harwell, whose blurb appeared on the dust jacket of Dowdey's *Lee* (Boston: Little, Brown, 1965).

Union general, George G. Meade, who has been in command of the Army of the Potomac only two weeks [sic], doesn't know much about his army and might be unready to fight a major engagement."[25]

Even the British historian J. F. C. Fuller, widely known as a severe critic of Lee, essentially accepted the rationale in the general's official report of the campaign. The "defective supply arrangements and the absence of his cavalry (to disengage himself) compelled him to fight," wrote Fuller, "and to fight an offensive action in place of a defensive one; for, as he had to live on the country, it was impossible for him to stand still for any length of time." Fuller believed that an inability to move and forage simultaneously ruled out Longstreet's option. This approval of the decision to attack on July 2 contrasted sharply with Fuller's estimate of Lee's tactical blueprint, which he considered "a thoroughly bad plan" with little prospect of success.[26]

H. J. Eckenrode and Bryan Conrad generally treated Lee favorably in their harsh biography of Longstreet (their real hero was Stonewall Jackson), but at Gettysburg these authors deviated from their usual pattern. They found that the commanding general "blundered into battle" and once committed "showed no genius in the manner in which he conducted it, making no feints and relying on frontal attacks on a formidable position."[27]

Few historians have probed the questions of Gettysburg more judiciously than Edwin B. Coddington, Harry W. Pfanz, and Alan T. Nolan—yet their careful examinations produced differing conclusions. Coddington weighed Lee's options for July 2, took into account the explanations in his official report, and resolved that although Lee's expressed concern about his trains and living off the countryside had some validity, the general had perhaps over-

25. Frank E. Vandiver, "Lee during the War," in *1984 Confederate History Symposium*, ed. D. B. Patterson (Hillsboro, Tex.: Hill Junior College Press, 1984), 17. Vandiver listed a series of physical factors: "Lee at Gettysburg was infirm, had been thrown from his horse a couple of weeks before and had sprained his hands; he may have been suffering from infectious myocarditis, did have diarrhea and stayed mainly in his tent." There is slim evidence to support such a catalog of ailments.

26. J. F. C. Fuller, *Grant and Lee: A Study in Personality and Generalship* (1933; reprint, Bloomington: Indiana University Press, 1957), 197. Fuller disliked Lee's tactical plan because it "depended on the earliest possible attack and the most careful timing to effect co-operation; further, Lee's troops were by no means concentrated, and to make things worse he issued no written orders."

27. H. J. Eckenrode and Bryan Conrad, *James Longstreet: Lee's War Horse* (1936; reprint, Chapel Hill: University of North Carolina Press, 1986), 213.

stated the dangers of withdrawal. The key to Lee's action was psychological—he and his army would not retreat unless pushed. "They had just achieved a smashing success against a part of the Union army," wrote Coddington, "and now was the time for them to finish the job. The stakes were high, and they might never again have as good an opportunity." Coddington viewed the decision as perfectly in keeping with the record of offensive combat forged by Lee and his army in previous campaigns.[28]

Pfanz agreed that Lee's decision to keep attacking was reasonable. Longstreet's proposed flanking movement posed logistical problems, Stuart was unavailable to screen the march, and the whereabouts of much of the Union army remained unknown; moreover, a "shift to the left and away from the valley that sheltered the Confederate line of communications was virtually out of the question." A defensive stand would transfer the initiative to Meade, who might circumscribe southern foraging while calling up Union reinforcements, and thus "did not seem a practical course of action." "In General Lee's words," Pfanz stated in summary, " 'a battle had, therefore, become in a measure unavoidable.' " Nolan disagreed strongly, attributing rationales for Lee's aggressive behavior after July 1 to an unpersuasive school of apologists for the southern chief. "When all is said and done, the commentators' rationalizations of Lee's most daring offensive thrusts seem contrived," insisted Nolan. "Although these commentators are aware that Lee's efforts were unsuccessful, costly, and destructive to the South's chances of victory in the war, they are committed to the Lee tradition and seem to strain to absolve him."[29]

Lee's decision to pursue the offensive on July 2 manifestly has produced such cacophonous opinions as to confuse the most earnest student. But despite the contradictory shadow cast by this imposing mass of material—and accepting the fact that definitive answers are impossible at a distance of more than a century and a quarter—it remains worthwhile to train a close lens on the crucial questions: Was it reasonable for Lee to renew assaults on July 2? On the basis of his knowledge at the time, did aggressive tactics offer the best chance for the type of sweeping success on northern soil that might propel the Confederacy toward independence?

28. Edwin B. Coddington, *The Gettysburg Campaign: A Study in Command* (New York: Charles Scribner's Sons, 1968), 362.

29. Harry W. Pfanz, *Gettysburg: The Second Day* (Chapel Hill: University of North Carolina Press, 1987), 16–27; Alan T. Nolan, *Lee Considered: General Robert E. Lee and Civil War History* (Chapel Hill: University of North Carolina Press, 1991), 98.

The situation at the end of the first day of fighting is well known. Lee had arrived on the field early in the afternoon and, in the words of Walter H. Taylor of his staff, "ascertained that the enemy's infantry and artillery were present in considerable force. Heth's division was already hotly engaged, and it was soon evident that a serious engagement could not be avoided."[30] Only two of Heth's brigades actually had experienced serious fighting at that point, however, and Lee found himself witness to a meeting engagement rather than a general battle. It soon became apparent that the positioning of units from Richard S. Ewell's Second Corps, which were arriving on the northern end of the field, afforded the Confederates a tactical edge that Lee promptly exploited to good advantage. By 4:30 P.M., Confederate attackers had driven the Federals to defensive lines along the high ground south of Gettysburg. Lee watched the action from atop Seminary Ridge, sensed the makings of a striking victory, and shortly after 5:00 P.M. instructed Ewell to seize the heights below town if practicable. For a variety of reasons, Ewell decided not to do so. Why Lee refused to commit some of A. P. Hill's troops—especially the fresh division of Richard H. Anderson—to a final joint assault with Ewell's brigades remains a mystery; the upshot was that daylight expired with Union troops firmly entrenched on Cemetery Hill.[31]

About 5:00 P.M., James Longstreet found Lee on Seminary Ridge. Dismounting and taking out his field glasses, Longstreet scanned the high ground that eventually would constitute the famous Union fish hook. Impressed by the strength of the enemy's position, Old Pete soon engaged Lee in an increasingly tense conversation. The only eyewitness testimony about this exchange comes from Longstreet, who left three versions that agree in substance but differ in detail. Longstreet suggested to Lee that the Confederates move around the Federal left and take up a defensive position between the Army of the Potomac and Washington; once situated, they could force Meade to attack them and then seek an opening for a counterstroke. This proposed movement, claimed Longstreet in all of his later writings, conformed to an agreement between himself and Lee to pursue a strategic offensive but remain on the tactical defensive in Pennsylvania. He therefore was surprised at Lee's response: "If

30. Walter H. Taylor, *Four Years with General Lee* (1877; reprint, Bloomington: Indiana University Press, 1962), 93.

31. For a disapproving discussion of Lee on the first day at Gettysburg, see Alan T. Nolan, "R. E. Lee and July 1 at Gettysburg," in Gary W. Gallagher, ed., *The First Day at Gettysburg: Essays on Confederate and Union Leadership* (Kent, Ohio: Kent State University Press, 1992).

the enemy is there to-morrow, we must attack him." Loath to embrace aggressive tactics, Longstreet persisted in his arguments. But Lee did not "seem to
abandon the idea of attack on the next day. He seemed under a subdued excitement, which occasionally took possession of him when 'the hunt was
up.'. . . The sharp battle fought by Hill and Ewell on that day had given him a
taste of victory."[32]

James Power Smith of Ewell's staff presently joined Lee and Longstreet
with news that Jubal Early and Robert Rodes believed they could take the high
ground south of Gettysburg if supported on their right. Thinking Hill's troops
too exhausted for such duty, Lee asked Longstreet if the leading elements of
the First Corps were near enough to assist. According to Smith, Longstreet
"replied that his front division, McLaws, was about six miles away, and then
was indefinite and noncommital."[33] Disappointed with Longstreet's response,
Lee instructed Smith to tell Ewell "he regretted that his people were not up to
support him on the right, but he wished him to take the Cemetery Hill if it
were possible; and that he would ride over and see him very soon."[34]

Lest Smith's reading be deemed suspect because of his well-known antipa-
thy toward Longstreet, it is important to note that a trio of witnesses friendly
to the First Corps chief also sketched a man deeply upset about the prospect of
attacking on July 2. G. Moxley Sorrel of Longstreet's staff remembered that his
commander "did not want to fight on the ground or on the plan adopted by
the General-in-Chief. As Longstreet was not to be made willing and Lee refused to change or could not change, the former failed to conceal some anger."
Raphael J. Moses, commissary officer of the First Corps, wrote in his autobiog-

---

32. The quotations are from the first of Longstreet's three accounts, in "Lee in Pennsylvania," *Annals of the War*, 411. See also James Longstreet, "Lee's Right Wing at Gettysburg," in
B&L 3:339–40, and Longstreet, *Manassas to Appomattox*, 358–59. Douglas Southall Freeman,
among others who sought to discredit Longstreet, made much of the fact that each of the three
narratives employed somewhat different language in recounting this episode (Freeman, *R. E. Lee*
3:74–75). The most important point, however, is that all three versions concur in juxtaposing
Longstreet's defensive and Lee's offensive inclinations.

33. Smith, "General Lee at Gettysburg," 391. This account was reprinted under the same
title in *SHSP* 33:135–60.

34. James Power Smith, "With Stonewall Jackson in the Army of Northern Virginia," in
SHSP 43:57–58. Smith presented a slightly different version of the discussion between Lee and
Longstreet here, adding: "I was the only other person present at this interview between Lee and
Longstreet on the afternoon of the first day of the Battle of Gettysburg." The version cited in the
preceding note does not mention's Lee's disappointment at Longstreet's reply.

raphy that later in the evening Longstreet expounded at length to Fremantle about the enemy's position, insisting that "the Union army would have greater advantages at Gettysburg than we had at Fredericksburg." Fremantle himself noted that over supper on July 1, "General Longstreet spoke of the enemy's position as being 'very formidable.' He also said that they would doubtless intrench themselves strongly during the night."[35] Of Longstreet's deep misgivings there can be no doubt; nor is it likely that his words and gestures failed to convey his feelings to Lee.

Sometime after 5:30 P.M., Longstreet departed and Lee rode toward Ewell's end of the line. Lee must have worried about the attitude of his senior lieutenant, whose friendship he valued and upon whom he had relied heavily since calling him "the staff of my right hand" in the wake of the Seven Days.[36] Although he knew from a reconnaissance by Armistead L. Long of his staff that Federals held Cemetery Hill in strength, Lee also wondered why firing had slackened along the Second Corps front. He had instructed Ewell to take that high ground if possible, and his postwar conversations with William Allan clearly indicated deep dissatisfaction at Ewell's failure to press his assaults. Walter Taylor's memoirs confirm that Lee was unhappy: "The prevailing idea with General Lee was, to press forward without delay; to follow up promptly and vigorously the advantage already gained. Having failed to reap the full fruit of the victory before night, his mind was evidently occupied with the idea of renewing the assaults upon the enemy's right with the dawn of day on the second."[37]

Lee thus reached Second Corps headquarters north of Gettysburg in a testy mood. He and the principal commanders of Stonewall Jackson's old corps gathered after dusk in the arbor of a small house near the Carlisle road.

---

35. G. Moxley Sorrel, *Recollections of a Confederate Staff Officer* (1905; reprint, Wilmington, N.C.: Broadfoot, 1987), 157; Raphael J. Moses, "Autobiography," 60–61, No. 529, SHC; Fremantle, *Three Months*, 156.

36. The quotation is from Thomas J. Goree to My Dear Mother, July 21, 1862, in Goree, *Longstreet's Aide*, 98. In *Lee and His Lieutenants*, 410, Edward A. Pollard described the relationship between Lee and Longstreet as "not only pleasant and cordial, but affectionate to an almost brotherly degree; an example of beautiful friendship in the war that was frequently remarked by the public."

37. Armistead L. Long to Jubal A. Early, April 5, 1876, printed in "Causes of the Defeat of Gen. Lee's Army at the Battle of Gettysburg—Opinions of Leading Confederate Soldiers," in *SHSP* 4:66; Allan, "Conversations with Lee," in Gallagher, ed., *Lee the Soldier*, 15 (the conversation took place on April 15, 1868); Taylor, *Four Years with General Lee*, 96.

The ensuing conversation deepened Lee's frustration with his lieutenants. "It was evident from the first," recalled Jubal Early in the fullest eyewitness account of the meeting, "that it was his purpose to attack the enemy as early as possible the next day." Early maintained that "there was not the slightest . . . difference of opinion" about Lee's idea of continuing the offensive; however, all three Second Corps leaders argued against their troops' spearheading the assaults. They had been impressed with the strength of Cemetery Hill, which Ewell's official report characterized as "a commanding position." Early took the lead in pointing to the Union left as the most vulnerable target.[38] Because Lee believed two of A. P. Hill's divisions had been fought out on July 1, the response of Ewell and his subordinates meant that the First Corps, headed by a suddenly peevish Longstreet, would perform the hardest work the following day.

Early stated in a controversial part of his account that Lee exhibited distress at the thought of relying on Longstreet: "When General Lee had heard our views . . . he said, in these very words, which are indelibly impressed on my memory: 'Well, if I attack from my right, Longstreet will have to make the attack;' and after a moment's pause, during which he held his head down in deep thought, he raised it and added: 'Longstreet is a very good fighter when he gets in position and gets everything ready, but he is *so slow.*'" This assertion, with its claim of precise accuracy nearly fifteen years after the alleged quotation was uttered, reeks of Lost Cause special pleading and lacks support from evidence closer to the event.[39] It is quite simply beyond belief that Lee would criticize his senior lieutenant in front of junior officers. Still, it is reasonable to assume that Lee did not relish the prospect of entrusting his assaults on July 2 to a man obviously opposed to resuming the offensive, and his facial expression may well have indicated as much to Early and the others.

Lee spent a long night working out details for the next day's fighting. Lack of enthusiasm among his subordinates for continuing the tactical offensive must have grated on him. The Army of Northern Virginia had built its formidable reputation on a series of impressive victories that with few exceptions included a large aggressive component. Had not the odds at the Seven Days or Second Manassas been less favorable for southern success? And what of

38. Jubal A. Early, "Leading Confederates on the Battle of Gettysburg. A Review by General Early," in *SHSP* 4:271–75. For descriptions of the ground in the official reports of Second Corps officers, see OR 27 (1):445 (Ewell), 469–70 (Early), and 555 (Rodes).

39. Early, "Leading Confederates on the Battle of Gettysburg," 273–74.

Chancellorsville? On all of those fields the army's offensive spirit had made the difference. Now Lee faced the prospect of planning a battle with substantive doubts regarding key Confederate commanders.

Although he strongly favored retaining the initiative, those doubts kept other options open. Longstreet's desire to flank the Federals remained on his mind. George Campbell Brown of Ewell's staff recalled in 1870 that Lee instructed him on the night of July 1 to tell Ewell "not to become so much involved as to be unable readily to extricate his troops." "I have not decided to fight here," stated Lee, "and may probably draw off by my right flank . . . so as to get between the enemy & Washington & Baltimore, & force them to attack us in position."[40] During his meeting with the officers of the Second Corps, Lee had proposed moving their troops to the right but dropped the idea when Early argued, among other things, that it would hurt morale to give up ground won through hard combat. Lee returned to this idea later, however, sending Ewell orders "to draw [his] corps to the right." A second conference with Ewell, during which the corps chief expressed a willingness to attack Culp's Hill, persuaded Lee to leave the Second Corps in position on the left.[41] As stated before, the commanding general's final plan for July 2 called for Longstreet to make the principal attack against the Union left while Hill and Ewell supported him with secondary assaults against the enemy's center and right. Lee admonished Ewell to exploit any opportunity to convert his offensive into a full-blown attack.[42]

Few episodes in Lee's career reveal more starkly his natural aggressiveness. He had examined closely the imposing Federal position later described so graphically in his official report. Even the most optimistic scenario would project heavy casualties in an attempt to seize that ground. Jedediah Hotchkiss's journal records that on the morning of July 2, Lee discussed the upcoming assault at Second Corps headquarters and was not "very sanguine of its success. He feared . . . a great sacrifice of life." Lee knew from prisoners that two Union

40. George Campbell Brown Memoir, 70–71, Brown-Ewell Papers, Tennessee State Library and Archives, Nashville. Brown admitted that he could not fix precisely the time of his meeting with Lee, suggesting that it might even have taken place on the night of July 2. His "strong impression" was that it was on the night of the first, however, and it seems far more likely that Lee was considering a flanking movement then—with Longstreet's arguments fresh in his mind—rather than after the second day's fighting.

41. Early, "Leading Confederates on the Battle of Gettysburg," 272–73; OR 27 (2):446.

42. OR 27 (2):318–19.

corps had been defeated on July 1, but he lacked information about the location of the bulk of the enemy's forces. In the absence of sound intelligence from his cavalry, he surmised only that the balance of Meade's army "was approaching Gettysburg."[43] His senior subordinate had disagreed sharply with the suggestion that offensive operations be resumed on July 2. Officers in the Second Corps were willing enough for Longstreet's soldiers to mount assaults but preferred a supporting role for their own men. In sum, powerful arguments could be raised against continuing the offensive.

Why did Lee choose to overlook all of them? His own explanations are unconvincing. Raphael Moses mentioned that Lee objected to Longstreet's flanking maneuver "on account of our long wagon and artillery trains"; as noted above, Lee also asserted in his official report that "to withdraw through the mountains with our extensive trains would have been difficult and dangerous." Lee further postulated a logistical crisis should he take a defensive position and await Meade's attack. His men had stripped the immediate region clean of supplies, and the enemy might use local troops to frustrate Confederate efforts to forage on a large scale.[44]

Porter Alexander countered both of these points in one telling passage. "Now when it is remembered that we stayed for three days longer on that very ground, two of them days of desperate battle, ending in the discouragement of a bloody repulse," wrote the artillerist in the 1890s, "& then successfully withdrew all our trains & most of the wounded through the mountains; and finding the Potomac too high to ford, protected them all & foraged successfully for over a week in a very restricted territory along the river . . . it does not seem improbable that we could have faced Meade safely on the 2nd at Gettysburg without assaulting him in his wonderfully strong position." David Gregg McIntosh, like Alexander an artillerist who held Lee in the highest esteem, similarly dismissed the obstacles to Lee's pulling back on July 2: "The fact that he was able to do so after the battle, justifies the belief that Longstreet was right in his opinion that an attack in front was not advisable, and that General Lee committed an error in determining upon that course."[45]

43. Jedediah Hotchkiss, *Make Me a Map of the Valley: The Civil War Journal of Stonewall Jackson's Topographer*, ed. Archie P. McDonald (Dallas, Tex.: Southern Methodist University Press, 1973), 157; OR 27 (2):317.

44. Moses, "Autobiography," p. 61; OR 27 (2):318.

45. Alexander, *Fighting for the Confederacy*, 233; David Gregg McIntosh, "Review of the Gettysburg Campaign. By One Who Participated Therein," in *SHSP* 37:140.

Lee's notion that local units posed a serious threat to his army strains credulity. Jubal Early's memoirs captured the attitude of Confederates in the Army of Northern Virginia toward such troops. Describing a clash with soldiers of the 26th Pennsylvania Militia several days before the battle of Gettysburg, "Old Jube" identified them as "part of Governor Curtin's contingent for the defence of the State . . . [who] seemed to belong to that class of men who regard 'discretion as the better part of valor.'" It was a good thing the regiment fled quickly, added Early sarcastically, "or some of its members might have been hurt, and all would have been captured." Those who did fall into Confederate hands received paroles the next day and were "sent about their business, rejoicing at this termination of their campaign." George Templeton Strong of the United States Sanitary Commission took an equally derisive view of the Pennsylvania militia. On learning that they were mustering in strength, Strong wrote an acidic entry in his diary on June 30: "Much good they would do, to be sure, in combat with Lee's desperadoes, cunning sharpshooters, and stark, hard-riding moss troopers."[46] Furthermore, correspondence on July 2–3 among Secretary of War Edwin M. Stanton and various Union commanders involved with local troops leaves no doubt about the ineffectiveness of the latter.[47] Had Lee decided to forage on either side of the South Mountain range, it is almost certain that his soldiers could have handled local Federal troops with impunity.

Even offensive moves by a combination of local forces and units from the Army of the Potomac—a remote possibility owing to problems of transportation and morale among the former—should not have given Lee undue pause. His decision to attack on July 2 reflected confidence that his soldiers could take a strong position from the enemy. It makes no sense to assert that those men would fail to hold a position against attacks from the same foe. Porter Alexander turned to a quotation from Stonewall Jackson in emphasizing this point: "We did sometimes fail to drive them out of position, but they *always* failed to drive us."[48]

What of Lee's dismissal of Longstreet's proposed flanking movement?

46. Jubal A. Early, *Lieutenant General Jubal Anderson Early, C.S.A.: Autobiographical Sketch and Narrative of the War between the States* (1912; reprint, Wilmington, N.C.: Broadfoot, 1989), 257–58; George Templeton Strong, *Diary of the Civil War, 1860–1865*, ed. Allan Nevins (New York: Macmillan, 1962), 327.

47. For a sampling of this correspondence, see OR 27 (3):494–508.

48. Alexander, *Fighting for the Confederacy*, 234.

Possible weaknesses in the plan must be given consideration (though Lee did not mention any in his report). If Longstreet envisioned a strategic rather than a tactical shift around Meade's left, the Army of Northern Virginia might have opened its own left flank to the Federals. Moreover, lines of supply and communication west of South Mountain might have been somewhat vulnerable.

But no such dangers would have obtained had Lee remained on the victorious field of July 1. As Porter Alexander put it, "We had a fine defensive position on Seminary Ridge ready at our hand to occupy. It was not such a really wonderful position as the enemy happened to fall into, but it was no bad one, & it could never have been successfully assaulted." To the west lay even stronger ground in the passes of South Mountain. A fragment of Lee's army had been driven from such gaps on September 14, 1862; however, the Army of Northern Virginia in July 1863 possessed the numbers and morale to hold the eastern face of the mountain indefinitely, all the while foraging in the lush Cumberland Valley. Had Lee fallen back to South Mountain "with all the prestige of victory," thought Alexander, "popular sentiment would have forced Meade to take the aggressive."[49] The likely result of northern assaults would have been a bloody repulse followed by some type of Confederate counterattack. Readily at hand was the example of Second Manassas, where Jackson had fixed the Federals with assaults on August 28, 1862, gone on the defensive the next day, and set the stage for Longstreet's smashing counterattack on August 30.

The difficulty of Meade's situation after July 1 should be kept always in mind. Abraham Lincoln and the Republicans could not tolerate for long the presence of the most famous rebel army on northern soil. As early as June 14, a day before the first elements of the Army of Northern Virginia crossed the Potomac at Williamsport, Secretary of the Navy Gideon Welles sketched a very uneasy Union leadership. Noting "scary rumors abroad of army operations and a threatened movement of Lee upon Pennsylvania," Welles described Secretary of War Stanton as "uneasy" and Lincoln as fearful that thousands of Federal troops in the Shenandoah Valley would be lost—"Harper's Ferry over again." The next day Welles mentioned a "panic telegraph" from Pennsylvania's governor, Andrew G. Curtin, and rumors of rebels in Chambersburg, Pennsylvania: "I can get nothing satisfactory from the War Depart-

49. *Ibid.*

ment. . . . There is trouble, confusion, uncertainty, where there should be calm intelligence."[50]

The onus was on the Federals to force Lee away from Pennsylvania. Meade's initial orders underscored his responsibility as head of "the covering army of Washington as well as the army of operation against the invading forces of the rebels." Should Lee menace either Washington or Baltimore, stated General in Chief Henry W. Halleck in a telegram to Meade on June 28, "it is expected that you will either anticipate him or arrive with him so as to give him battle."[51] The crucial part of this order is that Meade was to give battle rather than simply await the enemy's moves. Lee's comment that a battle had become "in a measure unavoidable" after July 1 applied far more realistically to Meade than to himself.

Clearly a number of factors militated against Lee's attacking on July 2. Just as clearly, a defensive posture might have opened the way for a decisive counterattack. The prudent decision would have been to shift to the defensive following the tactical victory on July 1. From such a posture, Lee would retain great freedom of action following a likely Union attempt to defeat the Army of Northern Virginia through offensive tactics. The Confederates could have stayed north of the Potomac for a protracted period of time, thus adding logistical and political accomplishment to any military success. Finally, had Lee gone over to the tactical defensive after the first day's battle, thousands of men shot down in assaults on July 2–3 would have been in the ranks for further service.

But acceptance of these statements does not prove that Lee made a foolish decision. A victory on northern soil might aggravate internal dissension in the North and thus weaken Union resolve. Within the context of dwindling Confederate manpower (a state of affairs Lee's aggressive generalship had helped to produce), there was reason to believe the Army of Northern Virginia would never again face the Army of the Potomac on such relatively equal terms. Lee had seen his men perform prodigious feats on a number of battlefields—most recently against intimidating odds at Chancellorsville. The overriding influence in his choosing to resume the offensive on July 2 might have been a belief that the splendid Confederate infantry could overcome the recalcitrance of

---

50. Gideon Welles, *Diary of Gideon Welles, Secretary of the Navy under Lincoln and Johnson*, ed. Howard K. Beale, 3 vols. (New York: W. W. Norton, 1960), 1:328, 330.

51. OR 27 (1):61.

his lieutenants, the difficulties of terrain, and everything else to achieve great results. Lee's subsequent comments that failures of coordination brought defeat suggest that he never doubted his soldiers might have won the fight. Fourteen years after the campaign, Henry Heth said simply, "The fact is, General Lee believed the Army of Northern Virginia, as it then existed, could accomplish anything."[52]

Ample testimony about soaring confidence in the Army of Northern Virginia lends credence to Lee's opinion, none more dramatically than Fremantle's description of morale on the night of July 1. Over supper that evening, recorded Fremantle, Longstreet discussed the reasons attacks might fail; however, in the ranks "the universal feeling in the army was one of profound contempt for an enemy whom they have beaten so constantly, and under so many disadvantages." Lee's great faith in his own men implied a degree of scorn for the Federals, an attitude noted by Fremantle's fellow foreign observer, Captain Justus Scheibert of the Prussian army: "Excessive disdain for the enemy . . . caused the simplest plan of a direct attack upon the position at Gettysburg to prevail and deprived the army of victory."[53]

If Lee did experience any regret about his decision to remain on the offensive after the first day's victory, perhaps it stemmed from a sense that he had asked the men to do so much despite obvious signs of trouble among his top lieutenants. Two of Lee's statements at the time illustrate this point. He wrote to Mrs. Lee on July 26, 1863, that the army had "accomplished all that could reasonably be expected." "It ought not to have been expected to perform impossibilities, or to have fulfilled the anticipations of the thoughtless and unreasonable," admitted the general in a sentence that could well be taken as self-criticism. Five days later Lee wrote a preliminary report for Adjutant General Samuel Cooper in which he praised the "heroic valor and fortitude" of his troops. "More may have been required of them than they were able to perform," he acknowledged, "but my admiration of their noble qualities and confidence in their ability . . . has suffered no abatement."[54]

Robert E. Lee confronted a crucial choice on the evening of July 1, 1863. His selection of the tactical offensive for July 2 reflected his predilection for aggressive action. Porter Alexander thought even Napoleon failed to surpass

52. Heth, "Letter from Major-General Henry Heth," 160.

53. Fremantle, *Three Months*, 256; Justus Scheibert, *Seven Months in the Rebel States during the North American War, 1863*, ed. William Stanley Hoole (Tuscaloosa, Ala.: Confederate, 1958), 118.

54. Lee, *Recollections and Letters*, 109; OR 27 (2):309.

Three Confederate soldiers at Gettysburg, photographed as prisoners of war on Seminary Ridge shortly after the battle. Lee's faith in such men was a crucial factor in his decision to press the tactical offensive on July 2.
Miller, ed., *Photographic History of the Civil War*

"some of the deeds of audacity to which Gen. Lee committed himself," and saw Gettysburg as an example of Lee's unnecessarily taking "the most desperate chances & the bloodiest road."[55] Without question Lee did gamble a very great deal on the throw of his offensive dice after July 1. He ruled out defensive maneuvers that might have opened breathtaking possibilities, and in the pro-

55. Alexander, *Fighting for the Confederacy*, 91–92.

cess he compromised the future offensive edge of his magnificent army. It is not unfair to state from the safe confines of historical perspective that Lee erred in his decision. Many of his own contemporaries realized as much at the time. But it is unfair to look at the grisly result and argue that his actions were entirely unreasonable. Momentum and morale count heavily in warfare, and it was probably those two factors that motivated Lee to a significant degree. Had Confederate infantry solidified the first day's victory through successful assaults on July 2, as they almost did, many of Lee's critics would have been silenced.

★ 4 ★

The Army of Northern Virginia
in May 1864

Lee and a Crisis of High Command

Robert E. Lee and the Army of Northern Virginia anticipated a third season of campaigning as they kept a watchful eye along the Rapidan-Rappahannock River frontier in late April 1864. Morale was generally high. One brigadier reflected a common attitude when he observed: "I feel so hopeful about the coming campaign. I have never felt so encouraged before." A Georgian of similar temperament informed his wife that he believed "the campaign will not open in several weeks, yet, and then Lee will attack Grant and go on to Pennsylvania."[1] Despite such thinking, three factors promised great difficulty for the

1. Stephen Dodson Ramseur to Ellen Richmond Ramseur, April 15, 1864, folder 9, Stephen Dodson Ramseur Papers, Southern Historical Collection, University of North Carolina, Chapel Hill [collection hereinafter cited as SHC]; Marion Hill Fitzpatrick, *Letters to Amanda, from Sergeant Major Marion Hill Fitzpatrick, Company K, 45th Georgia Regiment, Thomas' Brigade, Wilcox Division, Hill's Corps, CSA to His Wife Amanda Olive Elizabeth White Fitzpatrick 1862–1865*, ed. Henry M. Hammock (Nashville, Tenn.: Champion Resources, 1982), 127. Captain Charles Minor Blackford of Longstreet's First Corps, who did not share fully Ramseur's bright outlook, commented on the optimism in the army in a letter of May 3, 1864: "Grant is certainly concentrating a large army against ours. If we defeat him the military strength of the enemy will be broken, and we must have peace. . . . Officers and men are confident of success. I am so also,

Confederates—two of which were familiar leitmotifs in the saga of the Army of Northern Virginia. The chronic problem of supply continued to plague Lee. Indeed, the winter had been such a logistical nightmare that Lee confessed to Jefferson Davis on April 12, "I cannot see how we can operate with our present supplies. . . . There is nothing to be had in this section for man or animals." Shortages of food, fodder, clothing, medicine, and other necessary goods almost certainly would continue once active campaigning resumed.[2] Northern numbers constituted a second problem. Despite rumors of roughly equal strengths in the contending armies, Lee knew that his soldiers would be at a greater disadvantage than ever before. The enemy across the river mustered at least one hundred thousand men, nearly twice Lee's number.[3]

Leadership represented the third and potentially most decisive factor. The impact of Ulysses S. Grant remained to be seen, but only the most optimistic Confederate soldiers believed Grant would prove inferior to the Federal officers who had blunted Lee's offensive into Pennsylvania the previous summer and held their own during the maneuvering and fighting of late 1863. On

---

but sometimes find my fears giving away to the force of numbers!" Susan Leigh Blackford, comp., *Letters from Lee's Army: Memoirs of Life in and out of the Army in Virginia during the War between the States* (New York: Charles Scribner's Sons, 1947), 242. For a full discussion of morale in Lee's army in the spring of 1864, see Gary W. Gallagher, "Our Hearts Are Full of Hope: The Army of Northern Virginia in the Spring of 1864," in Gallagher, ed., *The Wilderness Campaign* (Chapel Hill: University of North Carolina Press, 1997).

2. R. E. Lee, *The Wartime Papers of R. E. Lee*, ed. Clifford Dowdey and Louis H. Manarin (Boston: Little, Brown, 1961), 698. For a discussion of Lee's logistical problems in the winter of 1863–64, see Douglas Southall Freeman, *R. E. Lee: A Biography*, 4 vols. (New York: Charles Scribner's Sons, 1934–35), 3:245–53; Charles W. Ramsdell, "General Robert E. Lee's Horse Supply, 1862–1865," *American Historical Review* 35 (July 1930):758–77; and Richard D. Goff, *Confederate Supply* (Durham, N.C.: Duke University Press, 1969), 212–16. Goff suggests that while morale might have been high in the infantry and artillery, "the cavalry and field transportation displayed definite signs of deterioration" (212).

3. Lee to Braxton Bragg, April 13, 1864, Lee to Jefferson Davis, April 15, 29, 1864, in Lee, *Wartime Papers*, 698–700, 706–707. F. Stanley Russell of the 13th Virginia Infantry expressed a common belief among many of Lee's troops in a letter to his sister on April 19, 1864: "It is yet hard to tell what will be the numerical strength of the two armies, for both Gen'ls. are at this time drawing troops from all quarters, but we have every reason to believe that the Yankees cannot greatly outnumber us, and where during the war have we ever been defeated? (when there was anything like an equality in number)." F. Stanley Russell, *The Letters of F. Stanley Russell: The Movements of Company H Thirteenth Virginia Regiment, Confederate States Army 1861–1864*, ed. Douglas Carroll (Baltimore: Paul M. Harrod, 1963), 67.

the southern side, leadership posed very serious problems for Lee. At the corps and division levels lurked questions of competency, attitude, and physical stamina that would be answered only on the battlefield. Should officers in these positions prove unequal to the challenge, their deficiencies, together with the shortage of qualified replacements, might compel Lee to adopt drastic measures to maintain the efficiency of his army.

Lee himself was the most important component of the army's leadership. In his twenty-three months in command of the army, he had won victories that drew the attention and admiration of the world. His penchant for the strategic and tactical offensive dominated his campaigns from the Seven Days through Gettysburg and the inconclusive maneuvering in late fall 1863. When his plans to strike George G. Meade's Army of the Potomac at Mine Run had failed in November 1863, Lee complained that he was "too old to command this army. We should never have permitted those people to get away." Unable to act comfortably on the defensive (the perceptive Edward Porter Alexander spoke of this aspect of Lee's character as his "sublime audacity"), Lee dreaded any scenario that allowed the enemy to make the offensive moves. Yet the paucity of men and supplies, not to mention the aggressive temperament of his new opponent, virtually guaranteed that he would be compelled to fight the approaching campaign on the defensive. He complained to Longstreet in late March 1864 that Grant held the initiative, and that unless the Confederates could devise some offensive scheme to disrupt Federal strategy they would have "to conform to his plans and concentrate wherever they are going to attack us."[4] Would Lee be willing to react rather than initiate the action over the course of a long campaign? Would he prove

---

4. Charles S. Venable, "General Lee in the Wilderness Campaign," in Robert Underwood Johnson and Clarence Clough Buel, eds., *Battles and Leaders of the Civil War*, 4 vols. (New York: Century, 1887), 4:240; Edward Porter Alexander, *Fighting for the Confederacy: The Personal Recollections of General Edward Porter Alexander*, ed. Gary W. Gallagher (Chapel Hill: University of North Carolina Press, 1989), 91–93; Lee to James Longstreet, March 28, 1864, in Lee, *Wartime Papers*, 684–85. Alexander remarked that not even Napoleon exceeded Lee in audacity, and he further commented that on several occasions Lee's love of the offensive threatened or inflicted serious damage to the Army of Northern Virginia. In *Lee Considered: General Robert E. Lee and Civil War History* (Chapel Hill: University of North Carolina Press, 1991), 106, Alan T. Nolan criticizes Lee's offensive tendencies: "If one covets the haunting romance of the Lost Cause, then the inflicting of casualties on the enemy, tactical victory in great battles, and audacity are enough." But if realizing Confederate independence through careful mustering and use of resources is the test, states Nolan, "a very different assessment of Lee's martial qualities is required."

adept at protracted defensive combat? These were questions that could not be answered in April 1864.

Lee wondered about his own ability to hold up physically. He had experienced problems with his health the previous spring and fall and suffered considerable discomfort during the campaign in Pennsylvania. In late summer 1863 he had offered to step down from command, citing unhappiness with the Gettysburg campaign and "the growing failure of my bodily strength." "I am becoming more and more incapable of exertion," Lee admitted, "and am thus prevented from making the personal examinations and giving the personal supervision to the operations in the field which I feel to be necessary." After fifty-seven years of often rugged living, Lee's once-strong physique betrayed inevitable decline. "I feel a marked change in my strength since my attack last spring at Fredericksburg," he confided to his son Custis on April 9, 1864, "and am less competent for duty than ever." Lee's health thus provided another question mark in any assessment of Confederate leadership.[5]

The three corps commanders in the Army of Northern Virginia presented a complex picture of ability and weakness. Senior was First Corps chief James Longstreet, whom Lee had called "the staff of my right hand" on the Peninsula and "my old war horse" at Sharpsburg. Longstreet's distinguished record boasted some of the finest accomplishments of the Army of Northern Virginia. He enjoyed an unusually warm relationship with Lee, and his facility at handling a corps in tactical situations exceeded that of any other Confederate officer. Yet Longstreet's superior reputation and obvious skills could not mask troubling episodes of the previous ten months. At Gettysburg, where he had disagreed with Lee's tactical plans, he had brooded and failed to execute orders with alacrity. Sent west in the late summer of 1863, he had hoped to find refuge from Lee's persistent reliance on assaults under the command of Joseph E. Johnston, the Confederate officer he most admired. He received instead a large dose of Braxton Bragg, whose conduct in the aftermath of Chickamauga alienated Longstreet. Eventually detached to East Tennessee to liberate Knoxville, Longstreet conducted a remarkably ineffective campaign, quarreled with subordinates Lafayette McLaws, Jerome B. Robertson, and Evander M. Law, and grew so disenchanted that he seriously considered resigning from the army.[6]

5. Lee, *Wartime Papers*, 589–90, 695–96. On Lee's "attack" in the spring of 1863 and his physical problems in late 1863 and early 1864, see Freeman, *R. E. Lee* 2:502–503, 3:156–58, 170–71, 185, 189, 204, 214.

6. Thomas J. Goree to My Dearest Mother, July 21, 1862, in Thomas J. Goree, *Longstreet's Aide: The Civil War Letters of Major Thomas J. Goree*, ed. Thomas W. Cutrer (Charlottesville:

Recalled to the Army of Northern Virginia in the spring of 1864, Long-street radiated a measure of his old spirit. In a note that likely mirrored his commander's feelings, Walter Taylor of Lee's staff welcomed Longstreet's return: "I am really beside myself, General, with joy at having you back. It is like the reunion of a family." The fact that Lee probably would take the tactical defensive against Grant—the posture Longstreet favored in almost any circumstance—boded well for Old Pete's frame of mind. Still, there had to be doubt about whether vestiges of the unhappy, contentious Longstreet of Gettysburg and East Tennessee lingered, ready to blossom anew.[7]

The Second Corps belonged to Richard Stoddert Ewell, one of the memorable characters in Lee's army. Doomed to everlasting residence in a literary aviary by Richard Taylor's classic description of him as a chirping woodcock, Ewell rarely appears in books on the war as more than a somewhat comical bundle of eccentricities. He had compiled a good record under Jackson as a division leader and had shown flashes of superior ability as a corps commander during the march to Pennsylvania in June 1863, but his subsequent record left much to be desired. His actions at Gettysburg late on July 1, and again on the second and third, left abundant room for second-guessing.[8] Problems with the stump of his amputated leg had compelled Ewell to take leave more than once

---

University Press of Virginia, 1995), 98, and William Miller Owen, *In Camp and Battle with the Washington Artillery of New Orleans* (1885; reprint, Gaithersburg, Md.: Butternut, [1982]), 157. On Longstreet's problems with McLaws, Robertson, and Law, see William Garrett Piston, *Lee's Tarnished Lieutenant: James Longstreet and His Place in Southern History* (Athens: University of Georgia Press, 1987), 76–81, and Alexander, *Fighting for the Confederacy*, 316–17, 338–39, 594 n. 13.

7. Taylor's letter to Longstreet is reproduced in full in J. William Jones et al., eds., *Southern Historical Society Papers*, 52 vols. (1876–1959; reprint, with 3-vol. index, Wilmington, N.C.: Broadfoot, 1990–92), 5:268 [hereinafter cited as *SHSP*]. Two very favorable estimates of Longstreet's career are Jeffry D. Wert, *General James Longstreet, the Confederacy's Most Controversial Soldier: A Biography* (New York: Simon and Schuster, 1993), and Piston, *Lee's Tarnished Lieutenant*. For far more critical analyses, see Robert K. Krick, "'If Longstreet . . . Says So, It Is Most Likely Not True': James Longstreet and the Second Day at Gettysburg," in Gary W. Gallagher, ed., *The Second Day at Gettysburg: Essays on Confederate and Union Leadership* (Kent, Ohio: Kent State University Press, 1993), and H. J. Eckenrode and Bryan Conrad, *James Longstreet: Lee's War Horse* (Chapel Hill: University of North Carolina Press, 1986).

8. Ewell's failure to assault Cemetery Hill and Culp's Hill on the afternoon of July 1 has been the subject of a large literature that is beyond the purview of this article; however, the fact that many officers in the Army of Northern Virginia (including, most probably, Lee) considered Ewell's conduct at Gettysburg less than adequate is pertinent to a discussion of the army's command in May 1864.

during the winter of 1863–1864, which caused Lee considerable worry. "I last spring asked for your appointment [to corps command] provided you were able to take the field," Lee wrote to his lieutenant in mid-January 1864. "You now know from experience what you have to undergo, and can best judge of your ability to endure it. I fear we cannot anticipate less labor than formerly."[9]

Ewell's uncertain health, a desire to spend time with his new wife, and a lack of decisiveness during much of his tenure at Second Corps headquarters prompted Sandie Pendleton, his chief of staff, to grouse in late November 1863 about "our superannuated chieftain, worn out as he is by the prostration incident, in a man of his age, upon the amputation and doting so foolishly upon his unattractive wife."[10] As April gave way to May 1864, questions about both Ewell's military competence and his physical stamina shadowed the forty-seven-year-old Virginian.

Ambrose Powell Hill was the last and most flamboyant of Lee's corps commanders. His achievements as a major general had stood out in an army of able division heads; at Second Manassas and Sharpsburg, especially, he had won Lee's esteem as an officer second only to Jackson and Longstreet. Hill's record as a corps commander had been considerably less impressive. At Gettysburg he rashly precipitated the first day's fighting, then essentially missed the rest of the battle. On July 3, 1863, Lee's assignment of thousands of Hill's troops to Longstreet for the climactic assault strongly suggested a lack of confidence in "Little Powell." The balance of 1863 brought nothing to raise the commanding general's opinion; in fact, Hill's ill-considered and costly attacks at Bristoe Station in October no doubt increased Lee's misgivings. As the two rode across that battleground the day after the battle, Lee grimly instructed Hill to "bury these poor dead men and let us say no more about it." High-strung, impetuous, and frequently sick, Hill, like Ewell, might demand close supervision from Lee in the upcoming campaign.[11]

9. Lee to Richard S. Ewell, January 18, 1864, in U.S. War Department, *The War of the Rebellion: A Compilation of the Official Records of the Union and Confederate Armies*, 128 vols. (Washington, D.C.: GPO, 1880–1901), ser. 1, vol. 33:1095–96 [hereinafter cited as OR; all references are to series 1]. For Taylor's memorable description of Ewell, see his *Destruction and Reconstruction: Personal Experiences of the Late War* (1879; reprint, New York: Longmans, Green, 1955), 36–37. On Ewell, see Donald C. Pfanz's *Richard S. Ewell: A Soldier's Life* (Chapel Hill: University of North Carolina Press, 1998) and Richard S. Ewell, *The Making of a Soldier: Letters of General R. S. Ewell*, ed. Percy G. Hamlin (Richmond, Va.: Whittet and Shepperson, 1935).

10. W. G. Bean, *Stonewall's Man: Sandie Pendleton* (Chapel Hill: University of North Carolina Press, 1959), 151.

11. A. L. Long, *Memoirs of Robert E. Lee: His Military and Personal History, Embracing a*

In postwar conversations with Second Corps chief of ordnance William Allan, Lee expressed displeasure with the manner in which the three corps commanders—especially Ewell—had carried out their duties at Gettysburg.[12] In regard to Longstreet, Lee almost certainly considered the poor performance in Pennsylvania an aberration in an otherwise praiseworthy career; with Ewell and Hill, however, little, if any, success as lieutenant generals counterbalanced the failures and weak performances. Doubts about at least two of the three men immediately under him must have troubled the Confederate commander as he prepared to counter the next Federal offensive.

Lee could count on ability and vigilance in the Cavalry Corps, where "Jeb" Stuart functioned as a premier practitioner of the arts of reconnaissance and screening. Like his counterparts in the infantry, Stuart had failed Lee during the Gettysburg campaign (Lee, of course, had failed at least as much as any of his subordinates), but there was no reason to suspect a reprise of that behavior in the spring of 1864. Stuart had reverted to his usual expert ways and could be relied upon to carry out whatever orders he might receive.

The picture at the division level was far from reassuring in Longstreet's First Corps, which contained only two divisions because George E. Pickett's command remained separated from the army. Gone were John Bell Hood, long the best of Longstreet's combat generals but now commanding a corps in the Army of Tennessee, and Lafayette McLaws, a usually reliable officer whose bitter quarrel with Longstreet in East Tennessee had resulted in his transfer to a post in Georgia. Longstreet favored Micah Jenkins to succeed Hood, but Evander M. Law, who had led the division after Hood suffered a disabling

Large Amount of Information Hitherto Unpublished (Philadelphia: J. M. Stoddart, 1886), 311. Henry Heth, whose division participated in the attacks at Bristoe Station, subsequently wrote: "General Lee's only remark was, addressing Hill, 'General, bury your dead.'" Henry Heth, *The Memoirs of Henry Heth*, ed. James L. Morrison (Westport, Conn.: Greenwood Press, 1974), 180. Jedediah Hotchkiss, the Confederacy's brilliant cartographer, offered a version of the incident that suggested far greater unhappiness on Lee's part: "Lee met Hill with stern rebuke for his imprudence, then sadly directed him to gather his wounded and bury his dead." Jedediah Hotchkiss, *Virginia*, vol. 4 of Clement A. Evans, ed., *Confederate Military History*, 12 vols. (1899; reprint, Wilmington, N.C.: Broadfoot, 1987), 426. On Hill's career, see William Woods Hassler, *A. P. Hill: Lee's Forgotten General* (Richmond, Va.: Garrett and Massie, 1962), and James I. Robertson Jr., *General A. P. Hill: The Story of a Confederate Warrior* (New York: Random House, 1987).

12. William Allan, "Memoranda of Conversations with General Robert E. Lee," in Gary W. Gallagher, ed., *Lee the Soldier* (Lincoln: University of Nebraska Press, 1996), 14. Lee discussed the actions of his corps commanders at Gettysburg with Allan at Washington College on April 15, 1868.

wound at Chickamauga, considered his own claim to the position stronger. After bitter wrangling among Longstreet, Jenkins, and Law, Charles W. Field had received the appointment. But Field had been out of action for twenty months because of a serious wound incurred at Second Manassas, had never led more than a brigade into action, and had received scant support from Longstreet. McLaws's replacement was South Carolinian Joseph B. Kershaw, the distinguished senior brigadier in the division but a man new to such a level of responsibility.[13]

In contrast to the First Corps, the six divisions of the Second and Third corps enjoyed veteran leadership. Edward "Allegheny" Johnson, Robert E. Rodes, and Jubal A. Early continued in the positions they had held under Ewell during the Gettysburg campaign. Johnson had a solid if unspectacular record, while Rodes had yet to fulfill the promise of his debut as head of a division at Chancellorsville. Easily the best of Ewell's major generals, Early had capably led the corps when Ewell fell ill during the winter of 1863–1864. He also nourished a thriving ambition to ascend higher on the ladder of responsibility. Gifted, outspoken, manipulative, and profane, Early exercised a good deal of influence over Ewell. Hill's divisions belonged to Richard H. Anderson, Cadmus M. Wilcox, and Henry Heth, none of whom had evidenced the spark that separated distinguished commanders from their pedestrian fellows. Overall, the divisions of the Army of Northern Virginia were in the hands of men likely to require careful direction. Should circumstances demand imagination and intellectual boldness, only Early among the six seemed a strong candidate for success.[14]

13. Documents relating to the court martial of McLaws are in *OR* 3 (1):480–508. On the question of selecting replacements for Hood and McLaws, see Douglas Southall Freeman, *Lee's Lieutenants: A Study in Command*, 3 vols. (New York: Charles Scribner's Sons, 1942–44), 3:299–312.

14. Sketches of each of the six division commanders in the Second and Third Corps are in Freeman's *Lee's Lieutenants*. Anderson and Early have been the subjects of modern biographies: Joseph Cantey Elliott's brief and admiring *Lieutenant General Richard Heron Anderson: Lee's Noble Soldier* (Dayton, Ohio: Morningside, 1985), and Charles C. Osborne's *Jubal: The Life and Times of General Jubal A. Early, C.S.A.* (Chapel Hill, N.C.: Algonquin Books, 1992). For other views of Early, see Frank E. Vandiver's introduction in Jubal A. Early, *War Memoirs: Autobiographical Sketch and Narrative of the War between the States* (Bloomington: Indiana University Press, 1960), ix–xxix, and Gary W. Gallagher's introduction in Jubal A. Early, *Lieutenant General Jubal Anderson Early C.S.A., Autobiographical Sketch and Narrative of the War between the States* (Wilmington, N.C.: Broadfoot, 1989), i–xxxvii. The last two titles are reprints of the 1912 edition of Early's autobiography and narrative.

The combat that began shortly after Grant crossed the Rapidan and continued throughout May 1864 defied all previous experience. No longer did the armies grapple, withdraw to lick their wounds, then move against one another again. From the Wilderness through the North Anna and far beyond, daily skirmishing punctuated by massive bloodlettings placed tremendous burdens on Lee and his principal subordinates. In slightly more than three weeks of campaigning, the structure of command weakened and then fractured. Casualties, failures of health, and incompetence forced Lee to adjust constantly, often in the midst of crises on the battlefield. By the end of the month, the Confederate commander had been forced to shoulder many of the duties previously discharged by his corps commanders, and he could only hope that replacements at the division level would perform adequately.

Lee's own conduct during the month of May answered any questions about his ability to accept the limitations of waging defensive warfare with only the most restricted openings to launch counterblows—although several of his decisions at both the Wilderness and Spotsylvania have been criticized. Initially, he entertained questionable hopes of taking the offensive against Grant's huge force, of dictating the action rather than responding to his new opponent's moves. (This approach had worked against Hooker's equally imposing army in May 1863.) In the Wilderness, the commitment of Ewell and Hill on widely separated fronts along the Turnpike and Plank Road on May 5 invited trouble; however, the thick vegetation between those two avenues of approach to Grant's army, together with the lack of sufficient troops to cover the entire front, largely explains Lee's actions. More problematical was Lee's decision not to rearrange the irregular and vulnerable line of Hill's Third Corps after the first day of battle. Even Douglas Southall Freeman, typically loath to acknowledge any failing on Lee's part, asserted that he "undoubtedly made a mistake in not withdrawing or fortifying the line of the Third Corps during the night of May 5."[15]

At Spotsylvania, Lee's handling of the Mule Shoe salient in Ewell's line suggests two questions. First, why did he consent to drawing the line in that

15. Freeman, R. E. Lee 4:428. For other criticisms of Lee's decision not to realign Hill's troops on the night of May 5, see Peter S. Carmichael, "Escaping the Shadow of Gettysburg: A. P. Hill and Richard S. Ewell in the Wilderness," in Gallagher, ed., The Wilderness Campaign, and Cadmus M. Wilcox, "Lee and Grant in the Wilderness," in [A. K. McClure], ed., The Annals of the War, Written by Leading Participants North and South (Philadelphia: Times Publishing, 1878), 494–95. Wilcox, who commanded one of Hill's divisions, described his unsuccessful effort to persuade Lee to adjust the lines.

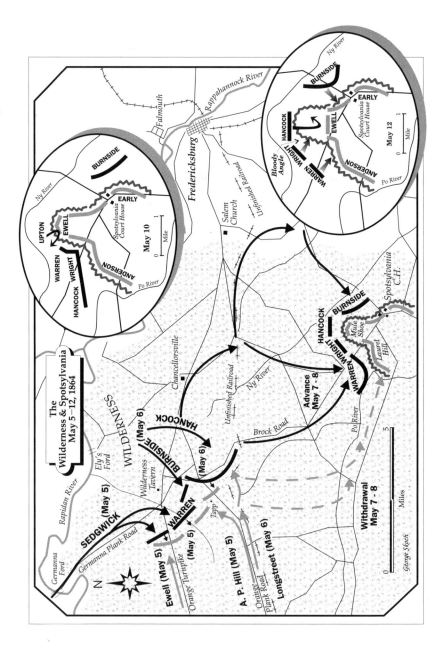

The
Wilderness & Spotsylvania
May 5–12, 1864

WILDERNESS

SEDGWICK (May 5)

WARREN

Ewell (May 5)

Orange Turnpike (May 5)

A. P. Hill (May 5)

Longstreet (May 6)

Orange Plank Road

Germanna Ford

Rapidan River

Ely's Ford

Wilderness Tavern

Germanna Plank Road

BURNSIDE (May 6)

HANCOCK (May 6)

Tapp.

Chancellorsville

Unfinished Railroad

Ny River

Brock Road

Po River

Advance May 7 - 8

HANCOCK

WARREN

BURNSIDE

WRIGHT

Mule Shoe

Laurel Hill

Spotsylvania C.H.

Withdrawal May 7 - 8

Miles

George Skoch

Falmouth

Rappahannock River

Fredericksburg

Salem Church

Unfinished Railroad

Ny River

BURNSIDE

EARLY

UPTON

EWELL

WARREN

WRIGHT

HANCOCK

ANDERSON

Spotsylvania Court House

Po River

May 10

Mile

Ny River

BURNSIDE

EARLY

EWELL

HANCOCK

WRIGHT

WARREN

ANDERSON

Spotsylvania Court House

Po River

May 12

Mile

Bloody Angle

exposed fashion? And second, knowing the importance of artillery in defending the position, why did he order its withdrawal during the night of May 11? Porter Alexander, in his usual blunt fashion, insisted that "by all the rules of military science we must pronounce these lines a great mistake." Lee apparently accepted the opinion of his chief engineer Martin Luther Smith that with proper artillery placement the line was safe. But after the war, Jedediah Hotchkiss wrote that Lee rode along the line on the morning of May 9 and "was not favorably impressed with it." According to Hotchkiss, Lee ordered construction of a second line across the base of the salient. These misgivings made all the more crucial Lee's orders to remove artillery from the Mule Shoe on May 11. He issued them in response to intelligence that Grant was shifting away from Spotsylvania; the guns could be moved more quickly in response to the Federal maneuvering if gathered somewhere outside the wooded salient. Lee later accepted full responsibility for his error. William W. Old, a member of Allegheny Johnson's staff, subsequently stated that, "After the disaster of the 12th, General Lee said to General Ewell, in my presence, that he had been misled in regard to the enemy in our front, by his scouts, and that the fatal mistake was in removing the artillery on our line."[16]

Lee committed perhaps his gravest error at the very outset of the campaign when he placed Longstreet's two divisions between Gordonsville and the hamlet of Mechanicsville some five miles south. He hoped to strike the Federal army as it marched through the Wilderness. In that scrub wasteland, northern numbers and artillery would be partially offset, a vulnerable flank might be discovered, and the enemy host would be driven back across the fords (as Joseph Hooker had been driven back almost exactly one year before). But Longstreet's ten thousand veterans were more than a day's march from the Rapidan and could not easily support Hill and Ewell. Douglas Southall Freeman excused this disposition with the comment that Lee sought to use Longstreet "as a reserve, to be employed either with the Army of Northern Virginia or against an enemy that might attack Richmond from the east or south. . . . There was as much probability that Grant would march straight for Gordonsville as there was that he would move by his left flank and cross the Rapidan and lower fords." Freeman's argument rests on a letter Lee wrote to Jefferson Davis on April 29, 1864, wherein Lee stated that he would keep

---

16. Alexander, *Fighting for the Confederacy*, 372; Hotchkiss, *Virginia*, 447; William W. Old, "Trees Whittled Down at Horseshoe," in *SHSP* 33:24.

Longstreet "in reserve" to meet a Federal thrust toward Richmond by troops other than those in the Army of the Potomac.[17]

Porter Alexander's assessment is more convincing. "At a conference with his division commanders on May 2nd held on Clark's Mountain, overlooking the Rapidan," wrote the Georgian artillerist, "Lee stated his belief that Grant would attempt to turn our right flank exactly as he did. But Mechanicsville was far behind our *left flank*, fully 33 miles in an air line & 43 by the roads we had to use from the first battlefield. Consequently, the first day's battle was necessarily fought without our presence." Alexander added that "in view of the great probabilities that Grant would move upon our right flank very early in May, it does not seem that there would have been any serious difficulty in having both Hill & Ewell out of their winter camps and extended a few miles in that direction & Longstreet's corps even as far down as Todd's Tavern." This oversight on Lee's part, concluded Alexander, was an "illustration of one of the inherent weaknesses of our army in its lack of an abundance of trained & professional soldiers in the staff corps to make constant studies of all matters of detail." Lee exercised unsound judgment in leaving Longstreet so far from the other two corps, and in doing so virtually guaranteed that he might begin a fight without his whole army on the scene.[18]

Apart from these decisions, Lee directed the campaign beautifully. His initial eagerness to bring Grant to bay in the Wilderness seemingly confirmed his habitual desire to control the action even at the risk of sustaining heavy casualties; in this case, however, he had excellent reasons for pressing his foe. Because Grant might overwhelm the Army of Northern Virginia in open country, it made sense to seek a resolution within the sheltering confines of the forest. Once the two armies began to fight, Lee made the best use of the terrain in the Wilderness, placed his army in position to thwart Grant's movements toward Spotsylvania and points south, selected strong ground, and delivered well-timed counterblows at the Wilderness and Spotsylvania. He might have accomplished much more when Grant's troops lay astride the North Anna River on May 23–26, but illness kept him confined to his cot, whence he railed helplessly at this grim turn of fortune: "We must strike them

17. Freeman, *R. E. Lee* 3:427. Lee's letter is in OR 33:1326.
18. Alexander, *Fighting for the Confederacy*, 348–49. See also his *Military Memoirs of a Confederate: A Critical Narrative* (New York: Charles Scribner's Sons, 1907), 497–98.

a blow," he muttered; "we must never let them pass us again—we must strike them a blow."[19]

Lee's conduct on the battlefields of the Wilderness and Spotsylvania showed that he considered himself responsible for a heavier share of the burden of command than ever before. At the Widow Tapp farm on the morning of May 6, he rode into the swirling chaos of Hill's retreating divisions in an attempt to restore order. For a time, only the guns of W. T. Poague's battalion of artillery shielded Lee from the advance of Winfield Scott Hancock's triumphant Federals. Similarly, during the crisis in the Mule Shoe on May 12 he recklessly placed himself at risk in an attempt to stem the massive northern assaults that had engulfed Ewell's center. In these episodes Lee revealed an uncharacteristic spectrum of emotions—extreme anxiety, exultant shouts welcoming the Texas Brigade when it appeared at the Tapp farm, and barely controlled anger.[20] Never before had he lost his composure so publicly; only once before had he showed such lack of regard for his proper place on a battlefield—on the afternoon of September 17, 1862, when he rode among the disorganized soldiers of D. R. Jones's division in an attempt to rally them to deny the enemy control of the vital Harpers Ferry Road.

What was different in May 1864? Lee's changed behavior on the battlefield probably stemmed from doubts about Ewell's and Hill's effectiveness in moments of crisis. At Second Manassas, Sharpsburg, and elsewhere, Lee left to Jackson and Longstreet full management of their sectors of the field. He conferred with them but made no effort to direct them. Hill had the responsibility of rallying his corps on the morning of May 6; Ewell had similar responsibility on May 12. Yet Lee hurried to the place of danger on each occasion. In fact, Lee seemed intent on functioning as both army and corps commander at many points during May 1864. The reason was that between the first day of the Wilderness and the retreat from the North Anna three weeks later, the corps command of the Army of Northern Virginia broke down almost com-

19. Charles S. Venable, "The Campaign from the Wilderness to Petersburg," in *SHSP* 14:535.

20. On Lee's actions at the Widow Tapp farm, see Robert K. Krick, "Lee to the Rear, the Texans Cried," in Gallagher, ed., *The Wilderness Campaign*; Dayton Kelley, *General Lee and Hood's Texas Brigade in the Battle of the Wilderness* (Hillsboro, Tex.: Hill Junior College Press, 1969), and Freeman, *R. E. Lee* 3:285–88. Freeman concluded that "For once the dignity of the commanding general was shattered; for once his poise was shaken" (287).

Lee placed himself in positions of danger several times at the Wilderness and Spotsylvania. A. R. Waud's postwar sketch depicts the first "Lee to the rear" episode, on May
6, 1864, in Widow Tapp's field.
Cooke, *Life of Gen. Robert E. Lee*

pletely. A brief review of the records of each of the men who led the corps will
illustrate this phenomenon.

Longstreet lived up to his highest reputation during the campaign. The
one negative mark usually registered against him is an alleged slowness in
reaching the field on the morning of May 6. A variety of Longstreet's enemies,
beginning with Jubal Early and extending to various twentieth-century historians, labeled this yet another example of Old Pete's inability to march
quickly. In fact, as Porter Alexander pointed out, had Lee positioned Longstreet closer to the likely field of action, the First Corps "might just as easily
have been . . . the first troops on the field, instead of the last." By Alexander's
careful reckoning, the First Corps marched thirty-six miles between 4:00 P.M.
on May 4 and 4:00 P.M. on May 5, rested until 1:00 A.M. on May 6, then
marched the remaining distance to come in behind Hill's disintegrating
lines.[21] Once on the field, Longstreet quickly examined the situation, rapidly

21. Alexander, *Fighting for the Confederacy*, 349–50. Historian Clifford Dowdey typified
those who held Longstreet rather than Lee responsible for the failure of the First Corps to arrive
at the battlefield before the morning of May 6: "As habitual with Longstreet, his troops had been

made dispositions, and in a matter of minutes sent his leading brigades crashing into Hancock's vanguard. Next he persuaded Lee to retire to a safer place; then, turning again toward the enemy, he prepared his men to launch a counterattack. An admiring gunner recalled that Longstreet, "always grand in battle, never shone as he did here."[22]

The First Corps stopped the Federals, after which Longstreet put together a flank attack that drove Hancock's troops back toward the Brock Road. Once again, Longstreet had demonstrated his tactical mastery at a crucial moment. In the midst of planning a larger flanking movement, Longstreet rode eastward on the Plank Road, where he was severely wounded in the throat by oblique fire from Confederates in the first flanking column. Lee learned that his trusted subordinate lay grievously disabled when he met Longstreet's ambulance making its way toward the rear. Francis Dawson of Longstreet's staff noted "the sadness in [Lee's] face, and the almost despairing movement of his hands, when he was told that Longstreet had fallen." Well might Lee despair, for he knew that his best corps commander had been taken from him for the foreseeable future.[23]

Lee's uncertainty about Ewell and Hill magnified the impact of Longstreet's wounding. May 1864 proved to be an especially bitter period for Ewell. He managed well enough on May 5, but on the sixth he experienced indecision reminiscent of July 1 at Gettysburg. About 9:00 A.M., Brigadier General John B. Gordon of Early's division informed Ewell that the Federal right was in the air and requested permission to attack. Early had received contradictory intelligence from scouts and insisted that such an attack would be too dangerous. Gordon had seen the exposed flank; Early had not been to the ground in person. Ewell vacillated. Campbell Brown, Ewell's assistant adjutant general,

slow to move out when they broke their temporary camp at Gordonsville on May 4th. . . . the men were put on the road methodically, and walked steadily without pressing." Dowdey, *Lee's Last Campaign: The Story of Lee and His Men against Grant—1864* (Boston: Little, Brown, 1960), 137. Dowdey wrote in the tradition of Jubal Early, who more than eighty years before had labeled it "a fact well known to the whole army, that General Longstreet was very slow in his movements on all occasions." Jubal A. Early, "Reply to General Longstreet's Second Paper," in *SHSP* 5:275.

22. John Haskell, *The Haskell Memoirs: The Personal Narrative of a Confederate Officer*, ed. Gilbert E. Govan and James W. Livingood (New York: G. P. Putnam's Sons, 1960), 63.

23. Francis W. Dawson, *Reminiscences of Confederate Service, 1861–1865*, ed. Bell I. Wiley (1882; reprint, Baton Rouge: Louisiana State University Press, 1980), 116. The loss of Longstreet, who knew Grant better than any of Lee's other principal subordinates, also denied Lee the advantage of Old Pete's insights into the Federal commander's military personality.

The Wounding of General Longstreet at the Wilderness, May 6, 1864, an engraving that appeared in Longstreet's memoirs. The loss of Longstreet left Lee without a trustworthy corps commander for the remainder of May 1864.

James Longstreet, *From Manassas to Appomattox: A Memoir of the Civil War in America* (Philadelphia: J. B. Lippincott, 1896

later asserted that "Genl Ewell was in favor of this [flanking attack] but [was] begged out of it by Early's strong personal appeals until he could go to examine the ground himself." Hours passed as fighting raged along the Plank Road on the Confederate right. About 6:30 P.M., Gordon finally advanced in an assault that bagged several hundred prisoners, including two Federal generals, before being halted by darkness. Lee properly blamed Ewell rather than Early for the failure to attack sooner. Early perhaps had acted somewhat arrogantly, but Ewell was the corps commander and held the final authority. After the war Lee remarked that he had wanted Gordon's movement to be "a full attack in flank, & intended to support it with all Ewell's corps and others if necessary, and to rout the enemy." But Ewell had deferred to Early, and "when Gordon did go," said Lee, "it was too late in the day, and he was not supported with sufficient force to accomplish anything decisive."[24]

24. Ewell Letter Book, box 2, folder 2, Campbell Brown–Richard S. Ewell Papers, Tennessee State Library, Nashville; Allan, "Memoranda of Conversations with Lee," in Gallagher, ed., *Lee the Soldier,* 11. For a careful examination of these events, see Gordon C. Rhea, *The Battle of the Wilderness: May 5–6, 1864* (Baton Rouge: Louisiana State University Press, 1994), chap. 8. Gordon's self-serving account is in John B. Gordon, *Reminiscences of the Civil War* (1903; reprint, Dayton, Ohio: Morningside, 1985), 242–61.

Ewell's actions at Spotsylvania added to doubts raised at Gettysburg and the Wilderness. On May 12, Ewell hastened forward to repair the break when Federals overran the Mule Shoe. Lee also hurried to the area of the break, where he encountered Ewell. Lieutenant Walter A. Montgomery of the 12th North Carolina vividly recalled the meeting: "General Ewell, who was on the spot, personally engaged in trying to rally the men, lost his head, and with loud curses was using his sword on the backs of some of the flying soldiers. Just then General Lee rode up and said: 'General Ewell, you must restrain yourself; how can you expect to control these men if you have lost control of yourself? If you cannot repress your excitement, you had better retire.'"[25] Lee's own iron control also was tested that day, as evidenced by his attempt to lead reinforcements into the firestorm in the Mule Shoe. But he never forgave Ewell's failure to keep his composure on May 12, nor was he pleased when Ewell bungled a probing movement on May 19 that resulted in a costly clash at the Harris Farm.

Lee commented on Ewell's failures at Spotsylvania in his postwar conversations with Colonel Allan. Allan reported that on May 12, Lee "found Ewell perfectly prostrated by the misfortune of the morning, and too much overwhelmed to be efficient." On the nineteenth, Ewell "lost all presence of mind, and Lee found him prostrate on the ground, and declaring he could not get Rodes' div[ision] out (Rodes being heavily engaged with the enemy)." Lee angrily ordered Ewell to extricate Rodes, and said that if Ewell "could not get him out he (Lee) could."[26]

Late in the month Ewell fell ill, which gave Lee a welcome pretext to remove him from command of the Second Corps. Although many contemporaries and later writers accepted Lee's public explanation, in truth he had lost faith in his subordinate. Ewell announced in early June that he had recovered sufficiently to take up command of the corps, which was about to depart for Lynchburg. Lee soon heard from a senior Second Corps officer who agreed that Ewell had to go. Robert E. Rodes had been very unhappy with his corps chief's handling of the action at the Harris farm on May 19. Learning of Ewell's application to resume his post, Rodes stepped forward and "protested against E.'s being again placed in command." Rodes's feelings against Ewell seem to have extended beyond events at Spotsylvania. According to the Reverend

25. Walter A. Montgomery, *The Days of Old and the Years That Are Past* (Raleigh, N.C.: n.p., n.d.), 28.
26. Allan, "Memoranda of Conversations with Lee," 11.

B. Tucker Lacy, Rodes had inquired of him during the winter of 1863–1864 "who commanded the Second Corps, Mrs. Ewell, General Ewell, or Sandy Pendleton, hoping it was the last" (Alexander Swift Pendleton was Ewell's chief of staff). Whatever factors prompted Rodes to complain, his action must have buttressed Lee's own feelings.

Lee's official reason for refusing Ewell's request remained one of concern about his subordinate's physical well being. "Although now restored to his usual health," Lee told Adjutant and Inspector General Samuel Cooper, "I think the labor and exposure to which he would be inevitably exposed would at this time again incapacitate him for field service. The general, who has all the feelings of a good soldier, differs from me in this opinion, and is not only willing but anxious to resume his command." In private conversation with Ewell, Lee "tried to put him off by sickness." When Ewell insisted that he should be allowed to rejoin the army, Lee told him "Plainly he could not send him in command." It was painful to do so, recalled Lee, but necessary for the good of the cause.[27]

Bitter and despondent, Ewell believed that Early and perhaps others had conspired to force him out of the army. His stepson and staff officer Campbell Brown, who remained at Second Corps headquarters after Early assumed command, shared the general's anger. "Old Early did not ask me how you were," Brown wrote Ewell on June 13, "but I made my speech so that he will hear it. . . . I intend seeing little of Early-& will get along finely. He looks at me like

27. Lacy recollections, Jedediah Hotchkiss Papers, microfilm edition, roll 39, containers 38–39, folder titled "Jackson's Staff," Library of Congress, Washington, D.C.; Lee to Samuel Cooper, June 12, 1864, in Lee, *Wartime Papers*, 776; Allan, "Memoranda of Conversations with Lee," 11. Contemporaries and later historians generally accepted Lee's official explanation of Ewell's removal. See, for example, Walter H. Taylor, *General Lee: His Campaigns in Virginia, 1861–1865, with Personal Reminiscences* (1906; reprint, Dayton, Ohio: Morningside, 1975), 249; Alexander, *Military Memoirs*, 534; Gilbert Moxley Sorrel, *Recollections of a Confederate Staff Officer* (1905; reprint, Jackson, Tenn.: McCowat-Mercer Press, 1958), 255–56; Freeman, *Lee's Lieutenants* 3: 499; and Shelby Foote, *The Civil War: A Narrative, Red River to Appomattox* (New York: Random House, 1974), 277. In *Medical-Military Portraits of Union and Confederate Generals* (Philadelphia: Whitmore, 1968), 291, Paul E. Steiner recognizes Lee's true motives (though he mistakenly states that Ewell accepted Lee's official explanation): "Lee removed him from command letting him think it was for physical reasons. . . . In actuality, there is reason to believe that he was being relieved because his military performance had been unsatisfactory—this, in turn, from both physical and mental impairment. In this case, Lee seems to have been less than candid in 1864."

a sheep-stealing dog, out of the corner of his eye." Aware of Ewell's anger, Early pleaded innocence in a letter that sought to mask his intense ambition: "I wish to say to you General that in the arrangement which has been made by which I am given the temporary command of the Corps I have had no agency directly or indirectly either by procurement or suggestion. . . . I assure you, General, I should regret excessively if any misunderstanding between ourselves should result."[28]

Hill's failures were less dramatic than Ewell's but nonetheless caused Lee major concern. His refusal to permit Harry Heth and Cadmus M. Wilcox to strengthen their positions on the evening of May 5 sprang from an admirable desire to give the men a good night's rest, but the potential consequences should have outweighed humanitarian concern. Heth and Wilcox unavailingly implored Hill to change his mind, eliciting repeated assurances that Longstreet would relieve their men before daylight. Soldierly prudence dictated that Hill give full weight to what would transpire if Longstreet were delayed for some reason, yet he decided to leave his lines in disarray. Obviously ill, Hill at length snapped, "D[amn] it Heth, I don't want to hear any more about it; the men shall not be disturbed." Near disaster followed on the morning of May 6, as Hancock routed Heth and Wilcox with ease.[29]

By May 8, Hill was so ill that he scarcely could leave his bed, and Lee replaced him temporarily with Early, who led the Third Corps at Spotsylvania. Back in command by the afternoon of May 21, Hill held the Confederate left at the North Anna. On May 23, he rashly ordered Wilcox's division to attack the Federal V Corps at Jericho Mills. Wilcox suffered about 650 casualties and gained no advantage, which prompted Lee the next day to chastise Hill in what Douglas Southall Freeman called "perhaps the stiffest rebuke ever administered to any of his generals during the war." Why, demanded Lee, did the

---

28. George Campell Brown to Richard S. Ewell, June 13, 1864, Jubal A. Early to Richard S. Ewell, June 5, 1864, box 1, folder 11, Polk, Brown, Ewell Papers, No. 605, SHC. The previous November, when Lee had placed Early in temporary command of the Second Corps because of Ewell's illness, Peter W. Hairston of Early's staff noted that Ewell "thought there had been a conspiracy to get rid of him." This same officer also recorded evidence that Ewell might have suffered from a troubled mental state in late 1863: "Genl. Ewell asked me if I ever wished myself dead. He said he sometimes thought it would save him a great deal of trouble." Peter W. Hairston Diary, November 15, December 3, 1863, Peter W. Hairston Papers, SHC.

29. Heth, *Memoirs*, 184. Wilcox, "Lee and Grant in the Wilderness," mentioned his going to see Lee but not Hill; Heth stated specifically that both he and Wilcox talked to Hill.

commander of the Third Corps "not do as Jackson would have done—thrown your whole force upon those people and driven them back?"[30] A mute Hill wisely offered no answer to this rhetorical question, and Lee let the matter drop. His profound disappointment with the chief of his Third Corps was obvious.

Three short weeks of campaigning had ravaged the army's corps command. A Confederate minié ball cost Lee the invaluable services of Longstreet, whose return to Virginia had begun on such a high note. The closest supervision from army headquarters would not overcome Ewell's weaknesses, and thus he also left the stage. Hill alone remained, fragile in health and unpredictable in action.[31] Lee would have to take up the slack, a fact underscored as he lay in agony on his cot along the North Anna. The Federal army was vulnerable on May 24–26, separated into three pieces by the looping river. Under Jackson or Longstreet, the Confederates might have struck a stunning blow. But Jackson and Longstreet were not with Lee, and he had no one else to whom he could entrust his army.

Anderson and Early stepped up in the army hierarchy with temporary promotions to lieutenant general. Anderson, whose early service had been in the First Corps, succeeded Longstreet. He secured the crossroads at Spotsylvania on May 8 following a stalwart march from the Wilderness, and afterward guided the corps with a steady hand. In short, he exceeded expectations. But Lee kept a close rein on Anderson with a constant stream of orders, behavior that would have been unthinkable and unnecessary with an officer of Longstreet's stature. Early handled the Third Corps very well at Spotsylvania and took control of the Second Corps on May 27. Whether he would blossom in his new position remained to be seen.

30. Freeman, *Lee's Lieutenants* 3:497; Hotchkiss, *Virginia*, 460. A recent treatment of the fighting at the North Anna is J. Michael Miller, *The North Anna Campaign: "Even to Hell Itself,"* *May 21–26, 1864* (Lynchburg, Va.: H. E. Howard, 1989).

31. The nature of Hill's frequent illnesses has long intrigued students of Lee's army. In *Lee's Lieutenants* 3: 442, Freeman postulates that "a psychosomatic malady" was the root of Hill's physical weakness in the Wilderness. Hill's biographers point to other possibilities. William W. Hassler concludes that "extant evidence strongly suggests that Hill suffered from chronic malaria" (Hassler, *A. P. Hill*, 237–38). James I. Robertson Jr. traces the general's troubles to chronic prostatitis arising from a case of gonorrhea contracted while he was a cadet at West Point in the 1840s (Robertson, *General A. P. Hill*, 11–12, 250). Russell P. Green, M.D., suggests that "Hill's problem was a matter of mood. He suffered from depression" (Green, "A. P. Hill's Manic Depression: 'Bury These Poor Men, and Let's Say No More about It,'" in *Virginia Country's Civil War* 4 [1986]:65–69).

Jeb Stuart's role in the campaign ended on a particularly tragic note. His troopers screened and probed the enemy with their customary skill in the Wilderness, and in the "race" for Spotsylvania on May 7–8 the Confederate mounted arm literally made the difference between disaster and successful resistance. When Philip H. Sheridan launched a raid against Richmond with more than ten thousand Federal cavalrymen during the second week in May, Stuart spurred southward to interpose part of his Cavalry Corps between the raiders and the capital. On May 11 the horsemen clashed at Yellow Tavern, where a Federal trooper fatally wounded Stuart. He was mourned in the army and across the South. Lee paid him the ultimate compliment for a cavalryman when, in a shaken voice, he affirmed that Stuart "never brought me a piece of false information."[32]

At the division level from the Wilderness to the North Anna there was much competence but scant brilliance. Kershaw and Field fought well enough to justify their selection as replacements for McLaws and Hood, yet neither displayed Hood's savage effectiveness on a battlefield (nor, it must be said, did they pile up the profusion of Confederate bodies that marked the path of every unit that Hood had commanded). Wilcox and Heth held their positions adequately on May 5, and the flight of their weary soldiers on the sixth should not count against them. Neither should Wilcox bear primary responsibility for the fiasco on May 23 at the North Anna; that dubious claim belongs to Hill. Of the major generals in the Second Corps, Rodes alone distinguished himself with memorable direction of his brigades in the Mule Shoe on May 12.

Three talented younger officers also advanced as Lee juggled commanders. John B. Gordon proposed and led the flanking attack on May 6 at the Wilderness and helped repair the break in the Mule Shoe at Spotsylvania on May 12, thereby earning command of Allegheny Johnson's battered division (Johnson himself had been captured in the breakthrough at the Mule Shoe on May 12). Stephen Dodson Ramseur, a brigadier in Rodes's division, took charge of Early's division when Early replaced Ewell. A memorable assault

---

32. On Stuart's part in the operations of May 1864, see Gordon C. Rhea's *Battle of the Wilderness* and *The Battles for Spotsylvania Court House and the Road to Yellow Tavern, May 7–12, 1864* (Baton Rouge: Louisiana State University Press, 1997), and Robert E. L. Krick, "Stuart's Last Ride: A Confederate View of Sheridan's Raid," in Gary W. Gallagher, ed., *The Spotsylvania Campaign* (Chapel Hill: University of North Carolina Press, 1998). Lee's quotation is from Robert E. Lee Jr., *Recollections and Letters of General Robert E. Lee* (1904; reprint, Wilmington, N.C.: Broadfoot, 1988), 124–25 (quoting an undated letter from W. Gordon McCabe to the junior Lee).

against long odds along the west face of the Mule Shoe salient on May 12 propelled this twenty-six-year-old North Carolinian into division command. The third new major general was William Mahone, who, as senior brigadier in Anderson's division, replaced his former chief when the latter moved to First Corps headquarters.[33]

Lee added new laurels to his record in the first month of the Overland campaign, but his principal lieutenants performed unevenly and suffered grievously. As Confederate soldiers took the roads that led to Cold Harbor and eventually to the trenches of Petersburg and Richmond, new men headed two of the three corps and three of the nine divisions, and losses among brigadiers had been catastrophic. Overall, roughly a third of the general officers in the army were dead, wounded, or absent because of illness or incompetence.[34] Lee's own health remained fragile. Ironically, the siege operations Lee feared so intensely represented his best hope for managing an army with dwindling resources of command. The works at Petersburg would ameliorate errors in judgment that might prove fatal in the open field. The lack of adequate food and fodder, and thinning ranks, circumscribed Lee's options as the summer of 1864 drew near, but the breakdown of command during May 1864 was an equally ominous factor that would affect the subsequent history of the Army of Northern Virginia.

33. On the performances of these division and brigade commanders, see Freeman, *Lee Lieutenants* 3, chap. 22; Venable, "Wilderness to Petersburg," 532–33; and Alexander, *Fighting for the Confederacy*, chaps. 15 and 16.

34. Porter Alexander included a tally of Confederate generals killed or wounded in the Wilderness and at Spotsylvania in *Fighting for the Confederacy*, 385. The roster lists Hill, who was ill rather than wounded, but omits Ewell.

II

Lee's Generals

★ 5 ★

The Making of a Hero
and the Persistence of a Legend

Stonewall Jackson during the Civil War
and in Popular History

Thomas Jonathan Jackson has inspired writers and artists for more than 130 years. In the war's literature, he generally appears as a redoubtable commander who helped fashion notable military triumphs. Many authors have pronounced his death in May 1863 a fatal blow to Confederate hopes for independence. Typical was John B. Gordon, who fought under Jackson in the Second Corps and eventually commanded that famous component of the Army of Northern Virginia. Reflecting on Confederate efforts at the battles of Gettysburg and the Wilderness, Gordon observed, in his usual hyperbolic style, that "considering them from a purely military and worldly standpoint, I should utter my profoundest convictions were I to say: 'Had Jackson been there, the Confederacy had not died.'" Robert K. Krick, whose scholarship ranks among the best on Jackson's Confederate service, reached a similar conclusion in an essay titled "The Smoothbore Volley That Doomed the Confederacy." Writing about the shots that felled Jackson at Chancellorsville, Krick concluded that "Nothing could have done more harm to the Army of Northern Virginia and to the nascent nation for which that army was the sturdiest underpinning."[1]

How did Jackson come to occupy his lofty place in the pantheon of Civil War military leaders? And why does he retain that place in the minds of so many modern students of the Civil War? His sheer brilliance as a soldier provides much of the answer, but other factors also contributed to Jackson's towering reputation in his own time and in the years since his death.

Some attention to evidence of Jackson's popularity will set the stage for discussing why he has remained such a compelling figure. The pace of publication on Jackson has been remarkable over the past few years. Commercial publishers have offered John Bowers's *Stonewall Jackson: Portrait of a Soldier*, Bevin Alexander's *Lost Victories: The Military Genius of Stonewall Jackson*, Paul D. Casdorph's *Lee and Jackson: Confederate Chieftains*, and Byron Farwell's *Stonewall: A Biography of General Thomas J. Jackson*. The contribution of these four books to the literature is debatable. For example, a photograph of someone other than Jackson stares at readers from the dust jacket of Bowers's book— surely one of the most unfortunate errors in recent Civil War studies, and unlikely to inspire confidence in the author's narrative. But each of the four books has sold well and gone into paperback printings.[2] More impressive scholarly titles also have appeared. Robert K. Krick's *Stonewall Jackson at Cedar Mountain* and *Conquering the Valley: Stonewall Jackson at Port Republic* are stunningly researched and well written. James I. Robertson Jr.'s massive *Stonewall Jackson: The Man, the Soldier, the Legend*, which like Krick's work combines wide research and literary grace, should stand for many years as the best biography.[3] Moreover, every important older book on Jackson has been re-

1. John B. Gordon, *Reminiscences of the Civil War* (1903; reprint, Dayton, Ohio: Morningside, 1985), 260–61; Robert K. Krick, "The Smoothbore Volley That Doomed the Confederacy," in Gary W. Gallagher, ed., *Chancellorsville: The Battle and Its Aftermath* (Chapel Hill: University of North Carolina Press, 1996), 134. A recent fictional treatment of Krick's subject, which posits a northern plot to assassinate Jackson, is Benjamin King, *A Bullet for Stonewall: A Novel* (Gretna, La.: Pelican, 1990). The jacket blurb for King's novel suggests that Jackson's death "altered the course of American history."

2. Bowers's book was published in 1989 (New York: William Morrow); Alexander's in 1992 (New York: Henry Holt); Casdorph's in 1992 (New York: Paragon House); and Farwell's in 1992 (New York: W. W. Norton). Apart from their success in trade hardcover and paperback editions, these books reached wider readerships through book-club adoptions.

3. Krick's two volumes were published in 1990 (Chapel Hill: University of North Carolina

printed at least once, including biographies by Frank E. Vandiver, Lenoir Chambers, G. F. R. Henderson, and Robert Lewis Dabney. The array of new books and reprints devoted to Jackson that crowd shelves at bookstores speak eloquently of a public fascination with his life and career.[4]

Jackson also has fared well outside the publishing world. For example, the Arts & Entertainment Network launched its highly successful *Civil War Journal* series in 1993 with a laudatory biographical treatment featuring Krick, Robertson, William C. Davis, and other prominent historians. The executives at A&E surely thought carefully about how best to launch their series, and their selection of Jackson attests to his position among Civil War figures. The program resoundingly promoted Jackson's greatness as a soldier, a tone set in the opening voice-over for a sequence depicting the battle of Chancellorsville. May 2 at Chancellorsville was more than just a big battle, intones the narrator, it "was there that the South's foremost general fell. . . . The man who protected the Confederate cause, the legendary war hero, the Mighty Stonewall was shot." More than just a blow to Lee's army, Jackson's death struck at his nation's morale because "along with him went the hopes and hearts" of the Confederate people.[5]

A plethora of modern artworks devoted to Jackson further attests to his popularity. Don Troiani, Dale Gallon, Mort Künstler, Don Stivers, and other prominent artists have painted or sculpted him repeatedly (only Lee has been a more frequent Confederate subject). The range of artwork featuring Jackson can be seen in advertisements in popular publications devoted to the Civil War. In the December 1995 issue of *Civil War: The Magazine of the Civil War Society*, for example, are ads for four prints, a beer stein, and two sculptures, as well as a book of Mort Künstler's paintings titled *Jackson & Lee: Legends in Gray.* Künstler's book boasts a narrative by James I. Robertson Jr., as well as more than three dozen images of Jackson. Similarly, the October 1995 issue of

---

Press) and 1996 (New York: William Morrow); Robertson's in 1997 (New York: Macmillan). Another recent title, James A. Kegel's *North with Lee and Jackson: The Lost Story of Gettysburg* (Mechanicsburg, Pa.: Stackpole, 1996), devotes considerable attention to Jackson's strategic thinking during 1861–63.

4. A complete list of reprints relating to Jackson would be too lengthy. It is worth mentioning, however, that many of the titles have been reprinted in both softcover and hardcover editions.

5. The episode is titled "Stonewall Jackson."

Civil War Times Illustrated includes ads for five prints, a commemorative plate, a pewter sculpture, and Künstler's book.[6]

Modern admiration of Jackson continues a trend begun during the Civil War and maintained among white southerners and other Americans through the late nineteenth century and into the twentieth century. The *Southern Illustrated News*, which commenced publication in Richmond, Virginia, in the fall of 1862, featured a profile of Jackson in its inaugural issue. According to this sketch, Jackson "now engrosses as much of public attention as any other man engaged in the present struggle for Southern independence." By the time he died a few months later, Jackson's fame had grown beyond the Confederacy and spread to the North and abroad. North Carolina diarist Catherine Anne Devereux Edmondston recorded a common sentiment upon learning of his death: "He died . . . in the fulness [sic] of his reputation, the brightness of his glory, a Christian patriot, unselfish, untiring, with no thought but for his country, no aim but for her advancement. I have no heart to write more, tho the paper is full of news. I care for nothing but him. . . . He was the nation's idol, not a breath even from a foe has ever been breathed against his fame. His very enemies reverenced him."[7]

The future Lord Acton noted sentiment outside the Confederacy when he observed during the fall of 1862 that "In the Northern cities Stonewall Jackson is the national hero." Just after Jackson's death, the pro-Republican Washington *Daily Morning Chronicle* paid him a strong tribute: "While we are only too glad to be rid, in any way, of so terrible a foe, our sense of relief is not unmingled with emotions of sorrow and sympathy at the death of so brave a man. Every man who possesses the slightest particle of magnanimity must admire the qualities for which Stonewall Jackson was celebrated—his heroism, his bravery, his sublime devotion, his purity of character. He is not the first instance of a good man devoting himself to a bad cause." Upon reading this piece, Lincoln wrote to the *Daily Morning Chronicle*'s editor, "I wish to lose no

6. Künstler's book was published in 1995 (Nashville, Tenn.: Rutledge Hill Press).

7. *Southern Illustrated News*, September 13, 1862; Catherine Ann Devereux Edmondston, *"Journal of a Secesh Lady": The Diary of Catherine Ann Devereux Edmondston*, ed. Beth Gilbert Crabtree and James W. Patton (Raleigh: North Carolina Division of Archives and History, 1979), 392 (entry for May 11, 1863). On Jackson's image in the Confederacy during the first eighteen months of the war, see J. Tracy Power, "'There Stands Jackson Like a Stone Wall': The Image of General Thomas J. 'Stonewall' Jackson in the Confederate Mind, July 1861–November 1862" (M.A. thesis, University of South Carolina, 1984).

time in thanking you for the excellent and manly article in the Chronicle on 'Stonewall Jackson.'"[8]

Jackson's importance in Confederate iconography stands out in Mark Neely, Harold Holzer, and Gabor Boritt's *The Confederate Image: Prints of the Lost Cause*. Numerous images of Jackson served the late-nineteenth-century market for prints associated with the Confederacy. Many were of a domestic variety, with Mrs. Jackson and their daughter; others showed the general in military settings. Still others placed a contemplative Robert E. Lee beside the grave of Jackson in Lexington, Virginia. As a group, these prints testified to Jackson's position as a leading Lost Cause hero whose visage adorned the homes of thousands of southern families.[9]

The foregoing examples from the written and artistic record demonstrate that Jackson was renowned during his lifetime and has remained so ever since. He became a hero and an enduring legend primarily because of his success in helping to translate Lee's strategic visions into battlefield victories. A brief discussion of those victories and their impact will provide context for an examination of factors beyond Jackson's performances in battle that helped shape his powerful image.

Unlike Robert E. Lee, Ulysses S. Grant, and William Tecumseh Sherman, Jackson never commanded a real army. But he did operate effectively in semi-independent command both before and after he joined Lee's Army of Northern Virginia in June 1862. He is best known for the 1862 Valley campaign, a remarkable operation that demonstrated just how much a resourceful commander of an inferior force can accomplish through speed, deception, and audacity.

The origins of this campaign lay in Richmond, where Lee was serving as chief military adviser to Jefferson Davis. George B. McClellan was approaching Richmond up the Peninsula in April 1862 with a Union force that soon would grow to 100,000. Irvin McDowell led another 30,000 northern soldiers at Fredericksburg; Nathaniel P. Banks commanded a third Yankee

8. Mark E. Neely Jr., Harold Holzer, and Gabor S. Boritt, *The Confederate Image: Prints of the Lost Cause* (Chapel Hill: University of North Carolina Press, 1987), 107 (quoting Lord Acton's published writings); Washington *Daily Morning Chronicle*, May 13, 1863; Abraham Lincoln to John W. Forney, May 13, 1863, in Abraham Lincoln, *The Collected Works of Abraham Lincoln*, ed. Roy P. Basler *et al.*, 9 vols. (New Brunswick, N.J.: Rutgers University Press, 1953), 6:214.

9. The authors emphasize that Jackson's importance as a postwar icon in the South did not equal Lee's. For their interesting discussion of why, see *Confederate Image*, 133–35.

Stonewall Jackson enjoyed considerable wartime fame beyond the borders of the Confederacy. This drawing of him by the British artist Frank Vizetelly appeared in *Harper's Weekly* on March 14, 1863.

army of 20,000 men in the lower Shenandoah Valley; and John C. Frémont a small force of about 8,000 Federals in the Alleghenies of western Virginia. Lee proposed to reinforce Jackson with Richard S. Ewell's division, bringing Jackson's force to about 17,500 men, after which he wished for Jackson to pin down all the troops belonging to Banks and Frémont so they could not join in the advance against Richmond. Jackson had gained attention with an offensive movement in late March that resulted in a sharp action at First Kernstown. Although a tactical defeat, First Kernstown had prompted the Federals to hold Banks and Frémont in the Valley, which in turn set up Jackson's subsequent campaign.

The outline of Jackson's campaign can be sketched quickly.[10] He took part of his force westward from Staunton to strike the advance element of Frémont's force under Robert H. Milroy at McDowell on May 8. With these Federals retreating into the wilds of the western Virginia Alleghenies after a largely inconclusive engagement, Jackson hastened back to the Valley, then moved northward toward New Market while Ewell's division paralleled his march to the east in the Luray Valley (the Massanutten Range divides the Shenandoah Valley into western and eastern sections for fifty miles between Harrisonburg on the south and Strasburg on the north; the Luray or Page Valley constitutes the eastern portion of the Valley). Crossing to the Luray Valley at New Market Gap, Jackson joined Ewell and captured a Federal garrison at Front Royal on May 23, defeated Banks in the battle of First Winchester on May 25, and pursued retreating Federals all the way to the Potomac River.

Jackson had placed himself in an exposed position in the extreme northern reaches of the Valley, and Federals planned a three-pronged offensive designed to cut him off north of Strasburg and destroy or capture him. Frémont would march east out of the Alleghenies, a division under James Shields would move west from Front Royal, and Banks would pursue southward from near Harpers Ferry. Jackson responded to impending disaster by driving his men to the limit. Aided by incredibly lethargic movement on the part of all the Federal commanders, he escaped the trap and marched southward to the southern end of the Massanutten Range near Harrisonburg. There he turned on his pur-

---

10. For a series of excellent maps that depict Jackson's movements in the 1862 Valley campaign, see Vincent J. Esposito, chief ed., *The West Point Atlas of American Wars*, 2 vols. (rev. ed., New York: Henry Holt, 1995), 1:Maps 48–53.

suers, defeating Frémont at Cross Keys on June 8 and Shields at Port Republic on June 9. After these twin victories, the Federals retreated northward down the Valley, and Jackson joined Lee's army outside Richmond.[11]

Jackson had accomplished his goals beautifully. He not only pinned down Frémont and Banks but also persuaded the Federals to hold McDowell at Fredericksburg. He had used rapid movement, deception, a willingness to take enormous risks, and, perhaps most important, an intimate knowledge of the geography of the Valley, supplied by his able cartographer Jedediah Hotchkiss, to achieve success. In a whirlwind of action spread over the month between McDowell and Port Republic, Jackson presented a series of victories to a Confederacy thirsting for good news from the battlefield and rapidly became his nation's greatest military hero.[12]

Jackson failed to follow up his success in the Valley with a strong effort during fighting outside Richmond. Under Lee's direct supervision for the first time, he stumbled badly at the Seven Days battles but rebounded with a memorable flanking march during the campaign of Second Manassas. During the Maryland campaign in September 1862, he sometimes commanded more than half of the army, captured Harpers Ferry, and participated in the battle of Antietam. He again led half the army at Fredericksburg and oversaw the famous Confederate flank attack against Joseph Hooker at Chancellorsville, during which he was accidentally shot by some of his own men. His death a few days later was a grim landmark in Confederate military fortunes.

Apart from his fabled Valley campaign, Jackson thus contributed to several Confederate victories as Lee's most famous lieutenant. His exploits helped convey an aura of success to the Army of Northern Virginia that lasted until very near the end of the war. That aura bolstered Confederate civilian morale when only bad news emanated from every other theater of the conflict. In this sense, Jackson's influence on Confederate fortunes reverberated well beyond

11. See Robert G. Tanner's *Stonewall in the Valley: Thomas J. 'Stonewall' Jackson's Shenandoah Valley Campaign, Spring 1862* (rev. ed., Mechanicsburg, Pa.: Stackpole, 1996) for an overview of the campaign.

12. Hotchkiss's Civil War diary is as valuable to modern historians as Hotchkiss himself was to Jackson in the Valley. See Hotchkiss, *Make Me a Map of the Valley: The Civil War Journal of Stonewall Jackson's Cartographer*, ed. Archie P. McDonald (Dallas: Southern Methodist University Press, 1973). Jackson would remain the most admired Confederate general until later in 1862, when Lee supplanted him in that position.

the specific battlefields on which he fought and continued past his death. No one but Lee could claim a greater military contribution to the Confederacy.[13]

Against these many positive elements of Jackson's record must be placed a number of less impressive performances. He rendered dismal service during the Seven Days campaign, repeatedly wasting opportunities to inflict serious harm on George B. McClellan's retreating army.[14] Jackson also botched the battle of Cedar Mountain, where on August 9, 1862, he barely wrested victory from a badly outnumbered Federal force commanded by second-line officers. Even in the Valley campaign he never delivered a crisp tactical performance, allowing smaller Union forces to escape serious harm at McDowell, First Winchester, and Port Republic. At Fredericksburg, faulty dispositions along his front permitted the enemy to achieve a breakthrough that, with better Federal coordination, might have threatened Lee's entire right flank. Even the apparently gaudy success of his celebrated flank attack at Chancellorsville on May 2, 1863, inflicted only minimal damage on the Federal army. Jackson's two and one-half divisions routed temporarily most of Oliver O. Howard's Eleventh Corps, but Joseph Hooker's larger Federal position was never in danger. Jackson's hope that he could continue the attacks after nightfall and cut off Hooker's troops from the Rappahannock River was completely unrealistic.

In short, Jackson compiled a mixed record as a general officer—though one certainly heavily weighted toward success. With this brief summary of Jackson's Confederate career as prelude, it is time to return to the question posed at the opening of this essay; namely, what factors, beyond Jackson's undeniable good days on the battlefield and on the march, contributed to his towering reputation?

The timing of Jackson's victories and failures was important. He excelled at First Manassas, providing stalwart leadership amid chaos on Henry Hill. Civilians and military figures North and South focused on Manassas during July 1861, magnifying events associated with the first big clash of the war. Because it would be many months before another major battle occurred in Virginia,

13. For a discussion of the Army of Northern Virginia as a major factor in inspiriting Confederate civilians, see chap. 3 of Gary W. Gallagher, *The Confederate War* (Cambridge, Mass.: Harvard University Press, 1997).

14. For an able defense of Jackson's role in the Seven Days, see A. Wilson Greene, "Failure or Scapegoat: Jackson at the Seven Days," in Greene, *Whatever You Resolve to Be: Essays on Stonewall Jackson* (Baltimore: Butternut and Blue, 1992).

Manassas lingered in the popular mind. Jackson came away from the battle not only as one of the primary Confederate heroes but also blessed with the nickname Stonewall. The power of a good nickname never should be underestimated; conversely, a bad one can doom a military officer to ridicule by his contemporaries and by subsequent generations of writers. Theophilus "Granny" Holmes and William Nelson Pendleton, also called "Granny" by many of the young artillerists who served under his nominal control in Lee's army, provide a pair of apt illustrations of the debilitating effect of a dismissive nickname. Jackson's new appellation added to the aura of martial power that soon surrounded him. Although he frequently insisted that Stonewall belonged to the brigade he had led rather to himself, he undoubtedly knew that the vast majority of his Confederate compatriots applied it to him as a compliment for his services at Manassas.[15]

Timing loomed even larger during the 1862 Valley campaign. The Confederacy had suffered repeated reverses during the first months of 1862. Forts Henry and Donelson had been lost, Nashville abandoned, a major counteroffensive at Shiloh smashed, and the mighty port of New Orleans surrendered. By mid-May, a Federal army of 100,000 was approaching the Confederate capital at Richmond. No good news broke this depressing spell until Jackson's first victories in the Shenandoah Valley. McDowell, Front Royal, and First Winchester came in quick succession, followed shortly by Cross Keys and Port Republic. The effect was electric. These small engagements—skirmishes, really, compared with a battle such as Shiloh—assumed enormous proportions because they inspired Confederates desperate for good news from the battlefield. Judith McGuire, a refugee living in Richmond, expressed feelings typical of many southerners upon learning of events at Cross Keys and Port Republic. "General Jackson is performing prodigies of valor in the Valley," she observed on the evening of June 9, 1862. "He has met the forces of Fremont and Shields, and *whipped them in detail.*" "We are more successful in Virginia than elsewhere," commented McGuire three days later, adding that the "whole

15. Some witnesses argued at the time that the nickname was meant derisively. Barnard Bee, they argue, wished for Jackson to advance to his support at Manassas and applied Stonewall to indicate his displeasure at the brigade's seeming immobility. However Bee meant it, almost everyone else soon used it in a positive way. For a discussion of Bee's intent, see John J. Hennessy, *The First Battle of Manassas: An End to Innocence, July 18–21, 1861* (Lynchburg, Va.: H. E. Howard, 1989), 82–83, 152 n. 52, and John J. Hennessy, "Stonewall Jackson's Nickname: Was It Fact or Was It Fiction?" *Civil War: The Magazine of the Civil War Society* 8 (March–April 1990):10–17.

Mississippi River, except Vicksburg and its environs, is now in the hands of the enemy, and .... Memphis has fallen!"[16] In the eyes of observers such as McGuire, the Valley campaign converted Jackson from a respected officer with solid service at First Manassas into the most celebrated Confederate warrior.

Timing also worked to Jackson's advantage when he failed Lee during the fighting that brought strategic Confederate victory during the Seven Days. Lost in the glow of seeing the North's largest army, commanded by its most celebrated general, turned away from Richmond, Jackson's shaky performances at Mechanicsville, Gaines's Mill, and White Oak Swamp scarcely harmed his reputation. As Walter H. Taylor of Lee's staff told Edward Porter Alexander after the war, there was "quiet talk" at army headquarters about Jackson's failures but "Nothing was said of it in a general way ... because we were so elated at raising the siege & there was no disposition to find fault."[17] Similarly, Jackson's inept tactical execution at Cedar Mountain in early August 1862 quickly receded into the shadow of his memorable flanking march around John Pope's Army of Virginia and another stunning Confederate success at Second Manassas.

The timing of Jackson's death, which came on the heels of his supreme battlefield triumph, also enhanced his reputation. Chancellorsville marked the apogee of the Lee-Jackson partnership. Because Jackson was struck down just after delivering the most storied flank attack of the war, the last military image of him conveys unqualified success. Fate took Jackson from his fellow Confederates while victory still seemed possible. He thus remained untouched by negative associations that would come with Gettysburg, the bloody Overland campaign, and the frustrating siege of Petersburg. Robert L. Dabney, a cleric who had served on Jackson's staff, spoke to this point in a biography of the general published in 1866. "His fall in the midst of the great struggle for the existence of his country," wrote Dabney, "and in the morning of his usefulness and fame, has appeared to his people a fearful mystery." But if Confederates thought only of what was best for Jackson, "it will appear a time well chosen for God to call him to rest; when his powers were in their undimmed

16. [Judith W. McGuire], *Diary of a Southern Refugee during the War* (1867; reprint, Lincoln: University of Nebraska Press, 1995), 120–21.

17. Edward Porter Alexander, *Fighting for the Confederacy: The Personal Recollections of General Edward Porter Alexander*, ed. Gary W. Gallagher (Chapel Hill: University of North Carolina Press, 1989), 569 n. 9.

prime, and his glory at its zenith; when his greatest victory had just been won; and the last sounds which reached him from the outer world were the thanksgivings and blessings of a nation in raptures with his achievements, in tears for his fall."[18] For untold thousands of Confederates, Jackson remained frozen in time as a winner who might have provided the edge that would have ensured their young republic's independence.

Because of this widely held conception of Jackson as a general who invariably triumphed, Civil War literature contains a cluster of tantalizing "what ifs" concerning him. Perhaps the most pervasive asks "What if Jackson had commanded the Second Corps on the First Day at Gettysburg?" Drawing on the postwar testimony of such witnesses as John B. Gordon and Henry Kyd Douglas, writers have frequently answered that Stonewall would have brought order out of the confusion that enveloped the divisions of Robert Rodes and Jubal Early, ignored reported threats to the Confederate left, and seized Cemetery Hill and Culp's Hill. Gettysburg then would have been a Confederate victory, and southern independence might have followed. And what if Jackson had been in the Shenandoah Valley in 1864? Many Confederates argued that he would have defeated Philip H. Sheridan, mounted a new threat to Washington, and inflicted other indignities on his Union opponents.[19]

No one has indulged in more elaborate speculation than Bevin Alexander, whose *Lost Victories: The Military Genius of Stonewall Jackson* portrayed its subject as a strategist much superior to Lee. Alexander improbably insisted that Jackson might have contrived to isolate Hooker's immense army south of the Rappahannock–Rapidan River line and force it to launch futile assaults against Confederates defending the fords across those streams. And what of Jackson at Gettysburg? Alexander conceded many obstacles to southern success but argued that his hero would have overcome them. "Would he have found another grand opportunity for victory?" asked Alexander. "Judged by the manner in which he conceived of triumph in the midst of almost certain defeat at Chancellorsville, the answer can only be guessed at, but it cannot be ruled out. Jackson could have succeeded."[20]

18. Robert L. Dabney, *Life and Campaigns of Lieut.-Gen. Thomas J. Jackson (Stonewall Jackson)* (1866; reprint, Harrisonburg, Va.: Sprinkle, 1983), 740–41.

19. See Gordon, *Reminiscences*, 154, 260–61, and Henry Kyd Douglas, *I Rode With Stonewall: Being Chiefly the War Experiences of the Youngest Member of Jackson's Staff from the John Brown Raid to the Hanging of Mrs. Surratt* (Chapel Hill: University of North Carolina Press, 1940), 246–47.

20. Alexander, *Lost Victories*, 328–29, 334–35.

Jackson and Lee on the battlefield during the Seven Days campaign, as depicted in a postwar sketch by A. R. Waud. Although Lee is the central figure in the drawing, Jackson was in fact better known at this stage of the war.
Cooke, *Life of Gen. Robert E. Lee*

Such scenarios are highly suspect. Modern readers should have empathy for Richard Ewell on July 1, 1863, and for Jubal Early during September and October 1864. Each of those men commanded Jackson's old Second Corps and labored in the immense shadow of the martyred Stonewall. Neither Ewell nor Early (nor anyone else) could have lived up to expectations based on a public memory of Jackson that had filtered out weak performances at the Seven Days and elsewhere and emphasized only heroic successes. It is highly improbable that Jackson's presence at Gettysburg would have brought a result that altered appreciably the strategic balance of power. Nor would his generalship opposite the talented and confident Sheridan in 1864 likely have yielded a different strategic result. But the golden memory of Jackson's success at Chancellorsville and on other fields led Confederates at the time and many later writers to believe that his presence would have made a difference.

Death in battle (in Jackson's case, shortly after being wounded in battle) often enhances a postwar reputation by obscuring questionable aspects of a general's record. Union generals John F. Reynolds and John Sedgwick represent two examples of this phenomenon. Neither man displayed more than ordinary competence in corps command. Yet it has become a cliché that Reynolds was the best corps commander in the Army of the Potomac, an officer whose death on July 1 at Gettysburg inflicted a grievous blow to Federal military fortunes in the eastern theater. As for Sedgwick, his dramatic death at Spotsylvania on May 9, 1864, caused innumerable writers to emphasize his lovable qualities and to overlook his subpar performances at Second Fredericksburg and elsewhere.[21]

James Longstreet, in contrast, clearly demonstrates how a high wartime reputation can sink in the mire of postwar controversy. Had Longstreet died from his dreadful wound on the Orange Plank Road on May 6, 1864, his fame today almost certainly would rival Jackson's. It is easy to imagine the likely treatment of Longstreet's last battle. Arriving on the battlefield just as A. P. Hill's corps gave way, Old Pete led his veteran soldiers into the chaotic action on the Widow Tapp farm, sent Lee to the rear, blunted the Yankee assault, and delivered a daring counterattack that might have secured victory had he not been shot down in circumstances reminiscent of Jackson's wounding the previous May. Following Longstreet's death there would be a hero's funeral with a grieving widow, anecdotes from his staff about their chief's last hours, and burial in a place that would become a Confederate shrine. Statues would be erected (including one on Monument Avenue in Richmond, where Lee, Jackson, and Jeb Stuart stand silent guard in stone and bronze), schools and roads named after him, and artworks produced to satisfy a ready market. But Longstreet lived long enough to criticize Lee, become a Republican, and run afoul of Jubal Early and others far more adept at literary combat. The world still waits for the first statue to Lee's senior lieutenant.[22]

A colorful and eccentric personality also helped to establish and then nourish Jackson's fame. Soldiers and civilians alike often prefer that their heroes be somehow different from ordinary people. Lee was different because he seemed almost too good to be true, a splendid general and Christian gentle-

21. For an example of the breathless praise often bestowed on Reynolds, see Edwin B. Coddington, *The Gettysburg Campaign: A Study in Command* (New York: Charles Scribner's Sons, 1968), 37. "He was a first-class fighting man, universally respected and admired," wrote Coddington. "If the fates had decreed other than they did, he might have gone down in history as one of the greatest generals of the Civil War."

22. A campaign to raise funds for an equestrian statue of Longstreet at Gettysburg achieved success, after years of effort, in 1998. One of the slogans employed by the group sponsoring this effort was "It's About Time." Flyer distributed by the Longstreet Memorial Fund in 1995, offering for sale T-shirts and tote bags bearing slogans paying tribute to Longstreet; flyer advertising two symposia on Longstreet, held at Gettysburg and Richmond in 1995 and 1996, respectively, mounted to raise money for the Longstreet statue. Both flyers in the possession of the author.

Artist Allen C. Redwood's *Stonewall Jackson Going Forward on the Plank Road in Advance of His Line of Battle* depicts the moment before the general was struck by musket fire from his own soldiers on May 2, 1863. Jackson's fall in the wake of his greatest triumph enhanced his already substantial reputation.
Johnson and Buel, eds., *Battles and Leaders of the Civil War*

man free of small vices and guided by an unyielding sense of duty. Jackson was different because of his sternness and his willingness to arrest subordinates, kill all the brave Yankees, and, supposedly, hang deserters.[23] He also had eccentric personal habits about which much has been written. He was the "lemon sucker," a fanatic about health who sat bolt upright to keep his internal organs

23. Despite his reputation as an officer quick to execute deserters, Jackson did not hang significantly more offenders than other leading Confederate generals.

aligned, held one hand aloft so his blood would run down and establish equilibrium, refused to eat pepper because it weakened his constitution, and so on.

Some of these habits undoubtedly have been wildly exaggerated, but stories about the general's odd personal characteristics gained wide circulation during the war and have remained firmly embedded in the literature ever since. As early as May 25, 1863, the British officer A. J. L. Fremantle noted stories of Jackson's peculiarities. "I heard many anecdotes of the late 'Stonewall Jackson,'" wrote Fremantle in his diary. "When he left the U.S. service he was under the impression that one of his legs was shorter than the other; and afterwards his idea was that he only perspired on one side, and that it was necessary to keep the arm and leg of the other side in constant motion in order to preserve circulation." People seemed to expect weirdness from Jackson, as evidenced by an article in the Atlanta *Southern Confederacy* in late October 1862. "I was surprised at Stonewall Jackson's appearance," admitted the newspaper's correspondent. "He has been described as a sort of clown. I never yet saw him riding with his knees drawn up like a monkey, and his head resting upon his breast."[24]

In the hands of postwar memoirists such as Richard Taylor, who had an eye for the telling anecdote, Jackson's quirks took on enormous proportion. Taylor's description of his first meeting with Jackson brilliantly conveyed a sense of strangeness and stern purpose. "Approaching, I saluted and declared my name and rank, then waited for a response," noted Taylor. "Before this came I had time to see a pair of cavalry boots covering feet of gigantic size, a mangy cap with visor drawn low, a heavy, dark beard, and weary eyes—eyes I afterward saw filled with intense but never brilliant light." After a short exchange, Jackson took "a contemplative suck on a lemon." Taylor claimed that "no fellow could find out" where Jackson procured his lemons (an odd statement in light of the fact that innumerable Civil War witnesses described drinking lemonade during the conflict), and closed his initial description of his new chief with a summary estimate: "He sucked lemons, ate hard-tack, and drank water, and praying and fighting appeared to be his idea of the 'whole duty of the man.'"[25]

24. Arthur James Lyon Fremantle, *Three Months in the Southern States: April–June, 1863* (1863; reprint, Lincoln: University of Nebraska Press, 1991), 132; Atlanta *Southern Confederacy*, October 31, 1862.

25. Richard Taylor, *Destruction and Reconstruction: Personal Experiences of the Late War* (1879; reprint, New York: Longmans, Green, 1955), 52.

Jackson's almost consuming religious belief also fed his legend. The Army of Northern Virginia boasted many devout officers and soldiers, including most obviously Robert E. Lee. But Old Blue Light's faith marked him as different. A Georgia cleric remarking on Jackson's triumphs in the Shenandoah Valley emulated countless other Confederates in lauding Jackson's piety. "We have cause of gratitude to God for the manifest indications of His returning favor," observed Charles Colcock Jones: "Great has been His blessing upon His servant General Stonewall Jackson. That pious man and able commander has executed one of the most brilliant passages at arms during the war." When news that Jackson had died reached Georgia in May 1863, Jones's wife Mary expressed anguish at the loss of a Christian warrior: "The death of our pious, brave, and noble General Stonewall Jackson is a great blow to our cause! May God raise up friends and helpers to our bleeding country!" Lee's official announcement of his lieutenant's death spoke of the "daring, skill, and energy of this great and good soldier." "But while we mourn his death," stated Lee in reference to Jackson's religiosity, "we feel that his spirit still lives, and will inspire the whole army with his indomitable courage and unshaken confidence in God as our hope and our strength."[26] What better object for veneration than a brilliant, eccentric man whose deep faith also inspired wonder?

Stonewall Jackson was a gifted commander who helped win some of the most famous battles in American history. His reputation rests largely on that record, but timing, a hero's death, and a personality that set him apart from his contemporaries also contributed to his fame while he lived and to his later legend. All these factors helped create the Mighty Stonewall revered by so many students of the Civil War.

26. Charles Colcock Jones to Charles C. Jones Jr., June 2, 1862, Mary Jones to Charles C. Jones Jr., May 19, 1863, in Robert Manson Myers, ed., *The Children of Pride: A True Story of Georgia and the Civil War* (New Haven, Conn.: Yale University Press, 1972), 901, 1063; General Orders No. 61, May 11, 1863, in U.S. War Department, *The War of the Rebellion: A Compilation of the Official Records of the Union and Confederate Armies*, 128 vols. (Washington, D.C.: GPO, 1880–1901), ser. 1, vol. 25 (2):793.

★ 6 ★

The Undoing of an
Early Confederate Hero

John Bankhead Magruder at the Seven Days

George B. McClellan's campaign against Richmond in 1862 marked a watershed in the development of the Confederate high command in Virginia. The cast of officers who held key positions in the Army of Northern Virginia when it marched against John Pope following the Seven Days battles differed greatly from that which two months earlier had prepared to meet the Army of the Potomac on the Peninsula. The changes began at the top, where Robert E. Lee succeeded Joseph E. Johnston after the latter's wounding at Seven Pines on May 31. A number of senior subordinates also had passed from the scene, including Benjamin Huger, Theophilus H. Holmes, W. H. C. Whiting, and Gustavus W. Smith. A fifth such officer was John Bankhead Magruder, whose performance in the Seven Days in general and at Malvern Hill in particular severely damaged his large reputation. Accusations of recklessness, drunkenness, and even cowardice bedeviled Magruder after Malvern Hill, and Lee showed no disposition to prevent his transfer away from the Army of Northern Virginia. Despite later competent service in the Trans-Mississippi theater, Magruder never fully regained his former stature in the Confederate army.

Magruder has been a somewhat shadowy figure in the literature on the

Confederacy. As careful a student as Douglas Southall Freeman got both the place and year of his birth wrong. The *Dictionary of American Biography* duplicated these errors and also mistakenly observed that Magruder had never married; a 1982 profile of the general in a leading popular magazine perpetuated other such inaccuracies.[1] These lapses in the printed record are curious, because material on Magruder's life is both plentiful and readily available. Born in 1807 in Port Royal, Caroline County, Virginia, he was a member of the first class at the University of Virginia before winning appointment to West Point in 1826.[2] A free-spirited young man who displayed a fondness for drink and a willingness to fight, Magruder came within four demerits of expulsion in his first-class (or senior) year at the academy. Despite this flirtation with disaster, he finished his career at West Point a captain of the Battalion of Cadets and graduated fifteenth in the class of 1830. Assigned to the infantry, he engineered a swap with Albert Miller Lea of the 1st Artillery and spent his antebellum military career in the long arm of the service, winning two brevets for bravery during the war with Mexico and commanding for a time the Artillery School of Instruction at Fort Leavenworth.[3]

Magruder's personality and lifestyle made him a well-known figure in the antebellum army. A dark-haired, handsome, six-footer of erect bearing and flawless manners, he had a profound attachment to elegant uniforms and a flair for the dramatic that won him the sobriquet Prince John. He loved the pomp of military reviews, conducting them with great panache even while on dis-

1. Douglas Southall Freeman, *Lee's Lieutenants: A Study in Command*, 3 vols. (New York: Charles Scribner's Sons, 1942–44), 1:15 n. 3 (stating that Magruder was born in Winchester, Virginia, on August 15, 1810); Robert Douthat Meade, "Magruder, John Bankhead," in Allen Johnson and Dumas Malone, eds., *Dictionary of American Biography*, 20 vols. (New York: Charles Scribner's Sons, 1928–36), 12:204–205; Mark Grimsley, "Inside a Beleaguered City: A Commander and Actor, Prince John Magruder," *Civil War Times Illustrated* 21 (September 1982):14–17, 33–35.

2. For a discussion of Magruder's place and date of birth, see Thomas Michael Settles, "The Military Career of John Bankhead Magruder" (Ph.D. dissertation, Texas Christian University, 1972), 5–6 n. 10.

3. *Ibid.*, 12–13, 19, 22; Francis B. Heitman, *Historical Register and Dictionary of the United States Army, From Its Organization, September 29, 1789, to March 2, 1903*, 2 vols. (Washington, D.C.: GPO, 1903), 2:684. On Magruder's tenure at the Artillery School, see A. L. Long, "Memoir of General John Bankhead Magruder," in J. William Jones *et al.*, eds., *Southern Historical Society Papers*, 52 vols. (1876–1959; reprint with 3-vol. index, Wilmington, N.C.: Broadfoot, 1990–92), 12:107–108 [hereinafter cited as *SHSP*].

tant western duty where only a handful of people might be watching. While stationed in Texas with Zachary Taylor's army in 1845–1846, he set up a theater and mounted a number of plays (he miscast James Longstreet, who was six feet, two inches tall, as Desdemona in *Othello,* replaced him with the smaller Ulysses S. Grant, and finally hired an actress to play the role). Magruder's dinner parties were lavish, expensive, and perfectly orchestrated—in one observer's words, "princely." After enjoying one of Magruder's memorable meals, an astonished English guest inquired about his host's monthly pay. "Damned if I know," answered Magruder with an affected air of detachment. Although he had a speech impediment, Magruder loved to talk and was a great raconteur. If wit and polish were needed for an evening, the urbane and well-read Magruder was a perfect guest.[4]

A junior officer's pay could not support Magruder's penchant for entertainment and personal luxury. As a second lieutenant fresh out of West Point, he courted Esther Henrietta Von Kapff, daughter of a Baltimore merchant of substantial fortune. The two were married in 1831 and eventually had two daughters and a son. But the marriage was a distant one. Mrs. Magruder lived in Baltimore while her husband received assignments to various posts, and when one of their daughters became ill in 1850 she moved to Europe with the children. Except for a year in Baltimore in the mid-1850s and a brief stay with her husband in Mexico in 1866, Mrs. Magruder spent the rest of her life in Europe. Even before she left the United States in 1850 the Magruders rarely saw one another. He relied on her to pay his debts and asked that she serve as hostess at gatherings when he returned to Baltimore on infrequent furloughs, but he seldom spoke about his wife and children to fellow officers. Indeed, many colleagues believed Magruder to be a bachelor. His private life conformed to the patterns of an unmarried man, replete with a round of parties and other activities that enabled him to display his considerable social skills.[5]

Magruder's spendthrift habits and drinking probably prompted his wife to stay in Europe. There is ample evidence of a weakness for liquor from his West Point days forward. On one occasion he stumbled to his hotel in Baltimore af-

4. Lloyd Lewis, *Captain Sam Grant* (Boston: Little, Brown, 1950), 129; James Longstreet, *From Manassas to Appomattox: Memoirs of the Civil War in America* (Philadelphia: J. B. Lippincott, 1896), 20; Long, "Magruder," 106; Daniel Harvey Hill, "Lee's Attacks North of the Chickahominy," in Robert Underwood Johnson and Clarence Clough Buel, eds., *Battles and Leaders of the Civil War,* 4 vols. (New York: Century, 1887), 2:362n.

5. Settles, "Magruder," 21–22.

ter a night of imbibing, found himself locked out, and went next door to a stage office where he passed out on a pile of mail sacks. Early the next morning a stagecoach arrived to pick up the mail and one passenger. Thinking Magruder to be his passenger, and unable to wake him, the driver put him aboard and proceeded to Washington, where he deposited his unconscious rider on a bench outside a hotel. When Magruder finally awoke, he had no idea where he was and was too embarrassed to ask anyone. After an early-morning pick-me-up, he wandered the streets until he glimpsed the Capitol. Was he in Washington? How could that be? Chancing upon a West Point classmate named Thomas Lee, Magruder hurried over to him, and blurted out, "My God, Tom, how glad I am to see you! Will you, for God's sake, tell me where I am?" Drinking of this type could not be concealed in so small an organization as the pre–Civil War army. Thus there was sufficient knowledge of Magruder's past to give credence to rumors during and after the Seven Days that he abused the bottle.[6]

When Virginia seceded from the Union on April 17, 1861, Magruder lost no time in choosing sides. He resigned his United States commission on April 20 and immediately offered his sword to the Confederacy. After an initial assignment near Richmond, he received orders on May 21 to assume command of 3,500 troops on the Peninsula between the James and York Rivers.[7]

On June 10, 1861, a portion of Magruder's troops under John Bell Hood and Daniel Harvey Hill won a skirmish at Big Bethel that was hailed, at that early time in the conflict, as "one of the most extraordinary victories in the annals of war." Magruder scarcely played a role in the modest triumph, but he took every opportunity to portray it as a decisive battle ranking with Winfield Scott's victories in Mexico. Newspapers lavished praise on him as the picture "of the Virginia gentleman, the frank and manly representative of the chivalry of the dear Old Dominion." Just as timing magnified Stonewall Jackson's accomplishments in the Shenandoah Valley in May and June 1862, so also did it enhance the impact of Big Bethel on Magruder's reputation. Writing within a year of the event, Edward A. Pollard aptly noted that the "victory was achieved at a time when the public mind was distressed and anxious on account of the constant backward movements of our forces in Virginia. . . . The

6. *Ibid.*, 24–26. On Magruder's drinking, see also Paul D. Casdorph, *Prince John Magruder: His Life and Campaigns* (New York: John Wiley and Sons, 1996), 2–3.

7. Settles, "Magruder," 171, 180.

Major General John Bankhead Magruder
Johnson and Buel, eds., *Battles and Leaders of the Civil War*

surrender of Alexandria, the surprise and dispersion of a camp at Philippi by a body of Federal troops, and the apparently uncertain movements of our forces on the Upper Potomac." Big Bethel bolstered the "confidence and ardor" of the Confederate people, wrote Pollard: "Thus regarded, it was an important event, and its effects of the happiest kind."[8]

A brigadier general's commission for Magruder followed shortly after the engagement. Within a few weeks of his arrival on the Peninsula, and on the basis of a fight directed by others, he had achieved considerable renown. Promotion to major general came on August 7, but an undercurrent of feeling against Magruder had developed in the Peninsula army. "They talk a great

8. Richmond *Dispatch*, June 13, 26, 1861; Edward A. Pollard, *Southern History of the War: The First Year of the War* (1862; reprint, New York: Charles B. Richardson, 1864), 80.

deal around here about General Magruder," wrote a Louisiana priest that fall, "and what they say is not always complimentary." Was there a feeling that luck and self-promotion rather than ability had aided Magruder? Unfortunately, the priest, who personally found the general to be "a very unpretentious and likeable gentleman," gave no specifics. Another observer commented at the time that Magruder "looks like a man too much given to dissipation, and is incapable of planning a battle, although very vigorous in fighting one."[9]

Whatever the reasons for the grumbling in the fall of 1861, few could quarrel with Magruder's masterful defense of the lower Peninsula against George B. McClellan in April 1862. Heavily outnumbered, he constructed earthworks and dammed streams to flood lowlands. Indulging his flair for drama, he shifted troops back and forth to give the appearance of greater strength, placed "Quaker guns" along his line, and conducted a bluff so successful that McClellan wasted an entire month at Yorktown. This bought time for Joseph E. Johnston to shift his army from northern Virginia to the Peninsula and to take overall command there in mid-April. Although Magruder had rendered exceptional service, his new superior was unimpressed. The Confederate works, thought the hypercritical Johnston, "had been constructed under the direction of engineers without experience in war or engineering." He asserted in Richmond that Magruder's line was poorly drawn and complained that the flooded ground around Yorktown had made offensive operations impossible. (Johnston neglected to add that he likely would not have undertaken an offensive under any circumstances.) Davis took Johnston's criticisms as evidence of negligence and offered Magruder no expression of thanks.[10]

Robert E. Lee, who functioned as the president's chief military adviser, and Secretary of War George Wythe Randolph subsequently persuaded Davis that Magruder had selected the best position to stop McClellan, but Johnston

9. Pere Louis-Hippolyte Gache to Rev. P. Phil. de Carriere, September 11, 1861, in Gache, *A Frenchman, a Chaplain, a Rebel: The War Letters of Pere Louis-Hippolyte Gache, S.J.*, ed., Cornelius M. Buckley, S.J. (Chicago: Loyola University Press, 1981), 50; [An English Combatant], *Battle-Fields of the South, From Bull Run to Fredericksburg; with Sketches of Confederate Commanders, and Gossip of the Camps* (1864; reprint, Alexandria, Va.: Time-Life Books, 1984), 117.

10. Stephen W. Sears, *To the Gates of Richmond: The Peninsula Campaign* (New York: Ticknor & Fields, 1992), chaps. 2–3, offers a good treatment of Magruder's efforts on the Peninsula prior to Johnston's arrival. Johnston's *Narrative of Military Operations, Directed during the Late War between the States* (1874; reprint, Bloomington: Indiana University Press, 1959), 111–13, details his complaints about Magruder's lines.

disagreed, and over Magruder's strenuous objections began a slow withdrawal toward Richmond in early May. During the retreat, Magruder commanded the right wing of Johnston's army, some 17,500 men. Prince John's titular superior was Gustavus W. Smith, whose commission as major general bore an earlier date and who commanded the army's reserve of 10,500 men. James Longstreet directed another 14,000 in the Confederate center and D. H. Hill 12,500 on the right.[11]

After nearly a year of independence, Magruder bridled at being subject to Smith's orders. The two quarreled immediately, then settled into a pattern of petty squabbling that ended with Magruder's refusing to obey Smith's orders and requesting, on May 23, that his "command be no longer attached to that of Major-General Smith." On that same day, orders directed Magruder to report to Richmond preparatory to taking charge of the Trans-Mississippi Department. Pleased with the reassignment, he nevertheless asked the secretary of war to postpone the transfer until the end of the current campaign. Randolph granted the request and informed Johnston that Magruder would be staying. Johnston considered Magruder a difficult subordinate and had reassigned his troops to Lafayette McLaws on May 26. Randolph insisted that Magruder stay with the army on the Peninsula, however, and Johnston grudgingly took him back.[12]

At the battle of Seven Pines on May 31, 1862, Johnston relegated Magruder to a secondary role. While the bulk of the Confederates attacked an isolated part of McClellan's force south of the Chickahominy River, Magruder and A. P. Hill remained north of the river to contain the balance of the Army of the Potomac. Johnston was severely wounded on May 31, Lee took command of the Confederate army shortly thereafter, and for the next three weeks an uneasy quiet prevailed outside Richmond. McClellan gradually shifted his strength to the south side of the Chickahominy; Lee collected troops and contemplated an offensive.

Lee had decided on a plan by the beginning of the last week in June. McClellan's army again was divided. About one-third, some 30,000 men commanded by Fitz John Porter, lay north of the Chickahominy; the other two-thirds held positions south of the river within a few miles of Richmond. Lee

11. Settles, "Magruder," 195–97.

12. *Ibid.*, 199–200; U.S. War Department, *The War of the Rebellion: A Compilation of the Official Records of the Union and Confederate Armies*, 128 vols. (Washington, D.C.: GPO, 1880–1901), ser. 1, vol. 11, pt. 3:537, 540, 551 [hereinafter cited as *OR*; all citations are to series 1].

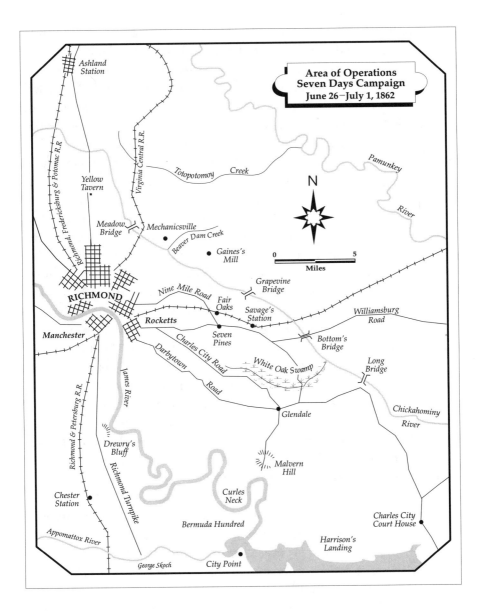

**Area of Operations
Seven Days Campaign
June 26–July 1, 1862**

N

0   5
Miles

Ashland
Station

Pamunkey
River

Totopotomoy   Creek

Yellow
Tavern

Virginia Central R.R.

Richmond, Fredericksburg & Potomac R.R

Meadow
Bridge

Mechanicsville

Beaver Dam Creek

Gaines's
Mill

Grapevine
Bridge

RICHMOND

Nine Mile Road

Fair
Oaks

Savage's
Station

Williamsburg
Road

Rocketts

Seven
Pines

Bottom's
Bridge

Long
Bridge

Manchester

James River

Charles City Road

Darbytown

Road

White Oak Swamp

Chickahominy
River

Richmond & Petersburg R.R.

Drewry's
Bluff

Richmond Turnpike

Glendale

Malvern
Hill

Chester
Station

Curles
Neck

Bermuda Hundred

Charles City
Court House

Harrison's
Landing

Appomattox River

George Skoch   City Point

hoped to mass 65,000 troops on the Confederate left—the divisions of Longstreet, D. H. Hill, and A. P. Hill, together with Stonewall Jackson's Army of
the Valley, which was en route to Richmond after its success in the Shenandoah—and crush Porter's wing with assaults. To the 25,000 men of Magruder
and Benjamin Huger would go the task of holding at bay more than 65,000
Federals south of the Chickahominy. Should the enemy on their front begin
to withdraw, Magruder and Huger were to pursue. Jefferson Davis believed
that more strength was needed south of the Chickahominy to ensure that a
swift thrust by McClellan could not take Richmond; Lee persuaded him that
Magruder, with Huger in support, would be capable of protecting the capital.[13]

Despite his assurances to Davis, Lee also doubted the security of his right.
On June 24, the day he signed the orders for the attack against Porter, he spent
time inspecting Magruder's line. The next day, first of the Seven Days, came
and went with nothing more ominous than light Federal probing in front of
Magruder. On June 26, Jackson was to open the assault on Porter at dawn. Magruder listened carefully for sounds of battle from across the Chickahominy.
He and his men were primed for a fight. "There was naturally great excitement
at our headquarters amongst our officers," recalled Joseph L. Brent of Magruder's staff. "When we considered and discussed the plan, we all thought that
the position of holding our front lines against McClellan and thereby protecting Richmond, was the post of honor as well as danger."[14] Morning passed
and mid-afternoon drew near before gunfire was audible. In the first of his
many failures during the Seven Days, Jackson never had reached his position.
A. P. Hill grew restless with the waiting and opened the battle of Mechanicsville by attacking on his own about 3:30 P.M.

Magruder immediately put up a show of force south of the river. Duplicat-
ing his tactics on the lower Peninsula, he ordered his "pickets and skirmishers
to observe the utmost vigilance; attacked the enemy's pickets from time to
time, and opened a frequent fire of artillery on his works to insure a full knowledge of his position, strength, and movements." About two o'clock, he sent a
courier to Lee with news that the Federals in his front "seemed inactive, but
alert." McClellan was so impressed with reports of Confederate activity on his
left that he sent few reinforcements to his beleaguered right. As Magruder and

13. OR 11 (2):498–99; Freeman, *Lee's Lieutenants* 1:495.
14. Joseph Lancaster Brent, *Memoirs of the War between the States* (New Orleans: Fontana,
1940), 158–59.

Huger faced down the bulk of the Federal army, Fitz John Porter's Federals fought off a series of uncoordinated assaults and before dawn on June 27 fell back to a strong position behind Powhite Creek at Gaines's Mill.[15]

Lee called for another strike against Porter on the twenty-seventh and instructed Magruder to continue his mission of the twenty-sixth for another day. Once again Prince John successfully bluffed the Federals. "So threatening were the movements of the enemy on both banks of the Chickahominy," wrote McClellan in his official report, "that it was impossible to decide until the afternoon where the real attack would be made." The Union commander added that "threatening demonstrations were frequently made along the entire line" south of the Chickahominy, which obliged him "to hold a considerable force in position to meet them." D. H. Hill thought Magruder's love of show and drama explained his ability to fool McClellan. In an often-quoted postwar passage, Hill, who personally disliked Magruder, wrote, "No one ever lived who could play off the Grand Seignior with a more lordly air than could 'Prince John,' as Magruder was called. . . . He put on naturally all those grand and imposing devices which deceive the military opponent."[16]

As on the twenty-sixth, the Confederate effort north of the Chickahominy suffered from poor coordination. A. P. Hill committed his brigades by 2:00 P.M.; D. H. Hill and Longstreet followed sometime thereafter; but Jackson, on the wrong road and engaged in leisurely countermarching, failed in his task of hitting Porter's right flank. Enormous pressure applied along a huge front finally broke Porter's line after a day of savage fighting. That night the Federals crossed the Chickahominy and rejoined the rest of the Army of the Potomac, ending Lee's best opportunity to destroy in detail a portion of McClellan's command.

Although the Army of the Potomac had suffered relatively few casualties to this point (only Porter's corps had been heavily engaged), McClellan decided to shift his base from the Pamunkey River to the James River. Late on June 28, Lee believed his opponent was retreating southward. Hoping to catch him in motion the next day, he ordered Longstreet and A. P. Hill to march southeast and strike the Federals below White Oak Swamp. Jackson, with D. H. Hill's soldiers added to his command, was to press directly against

---

15. OR 11 (2):661; Brent, *Memoirs*, 160.

16. OR 11 (1):57; Hill, "Lee's Attacks North of the Chickahominy," 362; Clifford Dowdey, *The Seven Days: The Emergence of Lee* (Boston: Little, Brown, 1964), 209.

McClellan's rear, while Magruder and Huger were to move eastward and hit the Federal right flank.

June 28 proved to be a watershed for Magruder in the Seven Days and in his larger career. To that point, while in semi-independent command south of the Chickahominy, he had been the confident, industrious commander of the early Peninsula. After the twenty-eighth, operating once again as a subordinate under close supervision, he became much less effective, repeating his experience when he had been placed under Johnston in April. Armistead Lindsey Long of Lee's staff observed Magruder closely throughout the campaign and concluded that he "belonged partly to that class of men whose genius, being unshackled, was capable of achieving the most brilliant results; but when overshadowed by authority became paralyzed." Although Long drew no parallel, the same might have been said of Jackson in comparing his activities in the Valley and outside Richmond. What Long did not know was that by the twenty-eighth Magruder had slept very little for several days and was suffering from acute indigestion made worse by the tension of holding Lee's right flank against great odds. The medication he took for his ailment probably contained some form of morphine, to which he was allergic. This combination of fatigue, nerves, and pain, together with Magruder's inherent difficulty in functioning as a subordinate, contributed to a subpar performance during the next three days.[17]

Lee wanted Magruder to advance along the Williamsburg Road on June 29. To Magruder's left, Jackson would be marching south via Grapevine Bridge; to his right, Huger would proceed along Charles City Road. Despite a meeting with Lee that morning, Magruder was confused about the plan. He thought he was to act in concert with Jackson and Huger, when in fact Lee wished for him to assault the Federal rear guard as soon as he made contact. Reluctant by himself to bring on a major engagement, Magruder cautiously inched toward an enemy who had retreated from the area of Fair Oaks to a position near Savage Station on the Richmond & York River Railroad. At Savage Station his brigadiers reported Federals in manifest strength, and Magruder, who had been awaiting word that Jackson and Huger were within supporting range, requested reinforcements. Lee detached two brigades from Huger for the purpose but recalled them when the Federals opposing Magruder exhibited no aggressive tendencies. Lee then ordered Magruder to at-

17. Long, "Magruder," 110; Brent, *Memoirs*, 192.

tack. About 5:00 P.M., Prince John finally ordered a "general" assault; however, fewer than half his men became actively engaged and the attacks sputtered. Darkness and a drenching thunderstorm brought an end to the battle of Savage Station.[18]

Lee laid principal blame on Magruder for his bitter disappointment with the action on June 29. "I regret much that you have made so little progress today in the pursuit of the enemy," Lee wrote his lieutenant. "In order to reap the fruits of our victory the pursuit should be most vigorous. I must urge you, then, again to press on his rear rapidly and steadily. We must lose no more time or he will escape us entirely." Armistead Long reflected this unhappiness with Magruder at army headquarters, asserting later that Magruder's failure to attack on June 28 cost Lee his best chance to harm the retreating McClellan. "[O]n the 28th the audacity which was so conspicuous on the Peninsula seemed to abandon him," observed Long of Magruder, "for he closely hugged his breastworks with thirty thousand men, while McClellan was in active preparations for retreat. The advantage thus gained [by the enemy] could never be overcome."[19]

Long's criticism was patently unfair. Lee had not even determined his strategy in time for Magruder to launch attacks on the twenty-eighth. As for Lee, it is difficult to explain why he failed to make similarly pointed comments to Jackson, who had spent the entire day rebuilding Grapevine Bridge (a suitable ford was nearby) and had refused a direct plea for cooperation from Magruder because he "had been ordered on other important duty." Walter Taylor of Lee's staff had apprised his chief on the twenty-ninth that Magruder believed Jackson must be operating under orders not to support the attack at Savage Station. "On the contrary," Lee informed Magruder in a postscript to the message urging a vigorous pursuit, Jackson had been directed to assist Magruder "and to push the pursuit vigorously." Without help from Huger and especially Jackson, Magruder, who faced a superior enemy force, could not have attacked successfully. Lee nevertheless had lost confidence in Prince John and ordered him to march to the Darbytown Road and follow Longstreet. Henceforth, Magruder would not be trusted with a leading role.[20]

18. OR 11 (2):494, 662–64; Freeman, *Lee's Lieutenants* 1:552–53.

19. OR 11 (2): 687; Long, "Magruder," 110.

20. OR 11 (2):664, 495, 687; Freeman, *Lee's Lieutenants* 1:555–56. Freeman argued that Magruder's operations on June 27 "were more censurable than those of the 29th" because he failed to discern the movements of a Federal division opposite his lines.

By the morning of June 30, Magruder's physical condition had so deteriorated that his staff grew concerned. He displayed great nervous energy, galloping back and forth to no apparent purpose, reversing orders, and bogging down in details better handled by junior officers. (Douglas Southall Freeman dismissively referred to him as the "galloping Magruder" on June 30 and July 1.) Major Brent found a quiet moment to ask if the general was unwell. "Why do you think so?" snapped Magruder. "I hope you will pardon me," said Brent gently, "but I have never seen your usual calmness so much lost by an extreme irritability, sometimes exhibited without any apparent cause, and hence I inferred that you must be feeling badly." "Well, Major, you are right," Magruder admitted. "I am feeling horribly." He went on to mention two days of indigestion, medicine he believed had triggered an allergic reaction, and loss of "so much sleep that it affects me strangely." Magruder thanked his staff officer for his concern and vowed to try to regain his "self control." Brent felt "greatly relieved when I saw that the General did not resent my interference, but actually strove to assume his usual deportment."[21]

Unfortunately, the events of June 30 offered nothing but continued aggravation. Instructed initially to support Longstreet, Magruder reached the Darbytown Road by 2:00 P.M., shortly after which Lee instructed him "to halt and rest my men, but to be ready to move at any time." About 4:30 came orders from Longstreet to proceed to the aid of Theophilus Holmes, whose command was on the New Market Road near Malvern Hill. A confusion of routes delayed Magruder's reaching Holmes, and in gathering twilight he received word to return to Longstreet's position. Not until 3:00 A.M. on July 1, after replacing Longstreet's soldiers in line, could Magruder's men go into bivouac. They had been on their feet for eighteen hours, had marched twenty miles, and had not fired a shot.[22] During Magruder's travail on the roads, Longstreet and A. P. Hill fought the bitter battle of Glendale (or Frayser's Farm). Again they did so without assistance from Stonewall Jackson, who had made an unhurried crossing at Grapevine Bridge that afternoon, dawdled north of White Oak Swamp Creek, and only feebly tested the Federal right flank late in the day. Huger also failed to add his weight to the Confederate effort. Glendale,

21. Brent, *Memoirs*, 192; Freeman, *Lee's Lieutenants* 1:586, 598 (Freeman titled chap. 36 "Holmes Advances and Magruder Gallops in Vain").

22. OR 11 (2):495, 666–67.

Confederate assault at Glendale (Frayser's Farm), June 30, 1862. While the soldiers of A. P. Hill and James Longstreet engaged the Federals, Magruder's troops marched and countermarched but saw no action.
Johnson and Buel, eds., *Battles and Leaders of the Civil War*

the sixth of the Seven Days, provided further evidence of Lee's inability to coax a coordinated effort from his lieutenants.[23]

Magruder retired after 3:00 A.M. on Sunday morning, July 1, for his second hour's sleep in three days. Up before daylight, he sorted out his lines, which had become tangled in the darkness earlier that morning. Both he and his men looked exhausted. A staff officer brought some welcome food, Magruder's first in nearly twenty-four hours. Not far to the south, thousands of Federals with abundant artillery stood crowded atop Malvern Hill. Frustrated at the failures of the past week, and still seeking to deliver a knockout blow, Lee decided to attack into the teeth of the Army of the Potomac. Jackson, Huger, and Ma-

23. See Freeman's *Lee's Lieutenants* 1:563–64 for an appraisal of Lee's division commanders on the thirtieth.

gruder would lead the offensive, with Longstreet and A. P. Hill, whose losses on the thirtieth had been heavy, in reserve. Magruder was to take the Quaker Road and form on Jackson's right flank in front of Malvern Hill. Huger would be on Magruder's right.[24]

Once again ignorance of roads hampered the Confederates. It turned out that there were two Quaker Roads. Three soldiers who were natives of the area led Magruder to a path that ran west. Longstreet presently inquired whether Magruder was moving in the wrong direction. No, the trio of guides insisted, they had taken the proper line of march. With misgivings, Longstreet deferred to their local knowledge. But they proved to be mistaken. Magruder should have taken the Willis Church Road, sometimes also called the Quaker Road. Many hours slipped by as Magruder's troops retraced their steps, finally to arrive about 4:00 P.M. behind Huger's command on the Confederate right.[25]

Much had happened by then. Lee's battle plan, issued at 1:30 P.M., called for Lewis A. Armistead's brigade of Huger's division to charge with a shout after Confederate artillery had punched a hole in McClellan's line. Other units would then take up the assault. Unbelievably, Lee issued no orders to William Nelson Pendleton's reserve artillery, which contained the heavy guns needed to implement the plan. Division field batteries went into action, achieved no concentration of fire, and quickly were disabled by superior Union artillery. In a famous criticism, D. H. Hill described the southern artillery effort as "of the most farcical character." Sometime after three o'clock, Hiram Berdan's Federal sharpshooters advanced against Armistead's brigade, which repelled the attack and pursued the retreating enemy for a quarter mile.[26]

24. OR 11 (2):667, 496; Brent, *Memoirs*, 196.

25. OR 11 (2):668; "Justice to General Magruder—Letter from Rev. P. G. Robert," in *SHSP* 5:249–50; Freeman, *Lee's Lieutenants* 1:590–91. Freeman blamed Magruder for the confusion about roads: "Apparently the galloping Magruder did not ask to examine Lee's map—the only one available—nor does he seem to have inquired of the commanding General where the road ran. . . . He had three guides from the neighborhood and, still without explanation, bade them conduct him to the Quaker road." Brent, *Memoirs*, 203, stated that during a conference with Jackson, Huger, and Magruder on the morning of July 1, "General Lee produced a map which he unrolled and held open, while the Generals bent down and examined it as they rode along." In *R. E. Lee: A Biography*, 4 vols. (New York: Charles Scribner's Sons, 1934–35), 2:205, Freeman had been more gentle with Magruder, attributing the error "to poor guides and poorer maps."

26. Freeman, *R. E. Lee* 2:207–209; OR 11 (2):628, 819; Dowdey, *Seven Days*, 334; Freeman, *Lee's Lieutenants* 1:599–600.

About this time, Magruder arrived on the scene in a state of agitation similar to that which had alarmed Brent the previous morning. Want of sleep and the reaction to his medicine continued to take a toll. "The wild expression of his eyes and his excited manner," remembered one Confederate officer, "impressed me at once with the belief that he was under the influence of some powerful stimulant, spirits or perhaps opium." Lee's 1:30 P.M. attack order was shown Magruder. After a quick reconnaissance on Armistead's front, he summoned thirty rifled pieces under Colonel Stephen D. Lee and sent instructions for his infantry to hasten forward. He also dispatched a courier to find General Lee, perhaps to convey news of Armistead's activity against Berdan. Back from Lee came plain orders: "General Lee expects you to advance rapidly. He says it is reported the enemy is getting off. Press forward your whole line and follow up Armistead's successes."[27]

Many authors have claimed that through his courier Magruder must have given Lee a false impression of Armistead's movement. Otherwise, they argue, Lee never would have ordered a general assault without adequate artillery support.[28] There is not a shred of direct evidence to support this view, however, and Magruder certainly was not the source of Lee's fear that the enemy might "get off" unharmed. Lee himself had been agitated all day, frustrated with the week's string of failures and eager to punish the enemy.[29] With the same audacious aggressiveness that would prompt him to order the Pickett-Pettigrew assault at Gettysburg almost exactly a year later, he opted for a massed infantry attack to drive McClellan's army back against the James River.

Magruder hoped to muster 15,000 men against the Federals in his sector but managed to send forward only about one-third that number in disjointed attacks by brigades and regiments.[30] Some of Huger's, Jackson's, and D. H. Hill's brigades followed suit, and soon 5,000 Confederate bodies littered the slopes of Malvern Hill. The crushing repulse brought to an end a bloody week of Confederate offensives. At a cost of 20,000 casualties, Lee had saved the capital and thoroughly overawed his cautious opponent without inflicting ma-

---

27. Greenlee Davidson to A. P. Hill, April 23, 1863, in Greenlee Davidson, *Captain Greenlee Davidson, C.S.A.: Diary and Letters, 1851–1863*, ed. Charles W. Turner (Verona, Va.: McClure Press, 1975), 71; OR 11 (2):668–69, 677–78.

28. See for example Dowdey, *Seven Days*, 338, and Editors of Time-Life Books, *Lee Takes Command* (Alexandria, Va.: Time-Life Books, 1984), 68.

29. Freeman, *R. E. Lee* 2:200, 209–10.

30. OR 11 (2):669–71.

jor physical damage on the Army of the Potomac. It was a stumbling tactical victory made possible by the timidity of McClellan, who on the night of July 2 began a retreat to Harrison's Landing.

Across the Confederacy tactical details mattered less than the broader result. Lee's offensive campaign had reversed a tide of woeful military news that had undermined southern civilian morale during the first half of 1862. The Seven Days ushered to the Confederacy's center stage the general who soon would personify the national strivings of his people.

Despite happiness at McClellan's retreat, the Confederate press and people wondered whom to blame for failing to destroy the Union army. Lee largely escaped these criticisms; Jackson, the hero of the Valley and idol of the Confederacy, also emerged relatively unscathed. More often than not, Magruder stood out as the prime villain.[31] On the evening of July 1, John B. Jones, the famous rebel diarist, noted that "To-day Gen. Magruder led his division into action at Malvern Hill, it is said, contrary to the judgment of other commanders. The enemy's batteries commanded all the approaches in most advantageous position, and fearful was the slaughter." Later that night, as Magruder prepared to lie down on blankets that had been spread for him, Lee rode into his camp. According to John Lamb, an officer who acted as Magruder's aide at Malvern Hill, the army commander asked: "General Magruder why did you attack?" Aware of the implications of Lee's question, Magruder answered without hesitation, "In obedience to your orders, twice repeated." Others in the army echoed Jones and Lee in criticizing Magruder's actions on July 1. Thomas J. Goree of Longstreet's staff, for example, informed his mother that "Genl. Magruder, contrary to orders had attacked them [the Federals on Malvern Hill]. The result was that Magruder having engaged his Division, others had to come to his support and very soon the Divisions of Huger, D. H. Hill & Jackson were also engaged."[32]

The next day Magruder told the secretary of war that with McClellan's threat to Richmond removed, he was ready to proceed to the Trans-

31. Magruder's two biographers devote little attention to Magruder's difficulties in the wake of the Seven Days. See Settles, "Magruder," 217–18, and Casdorph, *Magruder*, 187–88.

32. John B. Jones, *A Rebel War Clerk's Diary at the Confederate States Capital*, 2 vols. (1866; reprint, Alexandria, Va.: Time-Life Books, 1982), 1:140; John Lamb, "Malvern Hill—July 1, 1862," in *SHSP* 25:217; Freeman, *R. E. Lee* 2:218–19; Thomas Jewett Goree to Sarah Williams Kittrell Goree, July 21, 1862, in Goree, *Longstreet's Aide: The Civil War Letters of Major Thomas J. Goree*, ed. Thomas W. Cutrer (Charlottesville: University Press of Virginia, 1995), 96.

Mississippi. Without comment, Lee instantly relieved him of all duties with the Army of Northern Virginia.[33]

Meanwhile, ugly rumors spread about Magruder's conduct at Malvern Hill. Colonel Thomas R. R. Cobb informed his wife four days after that engagement that "Old Magruder made no reputation in this battle. He lost rather than gained. He was depressed, and I fear was drinking." The charge that Magruder had been intoxicated on July 1 quickly gained wide currency, a phenomenon encouraged, no doubt, by his long-standing reputation as a bon vivant. One participant spewed vitriol in an account published during the war. Magruder ordered the rash attacks at Malvern Hill, insisted this man. "*He was the only one responsible. . . . Was he tipsy?* I know not, though common report avows he was; and passing, I wondered whether he had returned to his old habits at such an important moment, to frustrate all our designs by passion and intoxication!" Richmonder Sallie Brock Putnam wrote soon after the war that following Malvern Hill "General Magruder was accused of great rashness, and many declared that he was under the intoxicating influence of ardent spirits." Another Richmonder also suggested widespread unhappiness with Prince John, although she did not mention his drinking. "Our people think that their whole army might have been captured but for the dilatoriness of some of our generals," wrote diarist Judith McGuire on July 15, 1862. "General Magruder is relieved, and sent to command in the West."[34]

An even more damaging accusation spread that Magruder had screened "himself from the enemy's fire" as his gallant soldiers bled and died on Malvern Hill. Magruder defended himself against what he called "strictures which had been made by an officer of inferior rank on my military operations near Richmond." Among the documents he submitted to army headquarters was a statement signed by Surgeon E. J. Eldridge of the 16th Georgia Infantry. Eldridge stated that he had seen Magruder twice during the battle and again immediately afterward and detected "no excitement or want of self-possession beyond the ordinary excitement of the battle-field." There had been no evidence of cowardice. As for Magruder's being intoxicated, Eldridge testified "most posi-

33. *OR* 11 (3):630; Freeman, *Lee's Lieutenants* 1:606–607.

34. Thomas R. R. Cobb, "Extracts from Letters to His Wife, February 3, 1861–December 10, 1862," in *SHSP* 28:293; [An English Combatant], *Battle-Fields of the South*, 373; Sallie Brock Putnam, *Richmond during the War: Four Years of Personal Observation* (1867; reprint, Lincoln: University of Nebraska Press, 1996), 148; [Judith W. McGuire], *Diary of a Southern Refugee during the War* (1867; reprint, Lincoln: University of Nebraska Press, 1995), 127.

tively that if he was under the influence of liquor I failed entirely to see it. . . . [I] am positive, as far as my judgment goes, that he had not even taken a drink—most certainly was not the least excited from any cause." Staff officer Lamb later seconded Eldridge's statements, writing that "General Magruder was perfectly sober the whole day"—a day on which Lamb "did not leave his side, except to carry some order."[35]

On July 11, Colonel Robert H. Chilton of Lee's staff urged Confederate adjutant and inspector general Samuel Cooper to revoke Magruder's assignment to the Trans-Mississippi Department on grounds of unfitness for command. Chilton pronounced Magruder "utterly incompetent and deficient" and claimed that "General Lee concurs in my belief of his incompetency, but will not act unless directly asked by the President for his opinion." Chilton added darkly that David R. Jones, who commanded a division under Magruder during the Seven Days, "charges him [Magruder] with something worse than incompetency." Nine days later Chilton admitted to the president that Lee knew nothing of the letter to Cooper; moreover, Chilton's statement about Lee's attitude toward Magruder was "not based upon what I had heard Genl. Lee state, but my observation of facts which I knew must be within the knowledge of Genl Lee."[36]

Communications from Chilton and Cooper persuaded Davis to delay Magruder's transfer until all questions about his conduct during the Seven Days had been considered. Magruder already had left for the Trans-Mississippi, but he returned to Richmond to speak with Davis and to prepare an official response. By mid-August he had completed a detailed account of his activities during the Seven Days and passed it on to Lee with a request that it "be forwarded to the President at the very earliest moment." After giving the document a "cursory examination," Lee sent it to Secretary Randolph with a set of comments that took issue with a number of Magruder's statements. "General Magruder appears to have greatly exerted himself to accomplish the duty devolved to him," read Lee's tactful cover letter, "and I can bear testimony to the uniform alacrity he displayed in its execution. He had many difficulties to contend with, I know. I regretted at the time, and still regret, that they could not have been more readily overcome. I feel assured, however, that General

35. OR 11 (2):682–83; Lamb, "Malvern Hill," 217. In *Lee's Lieutenants* 1:607 n. 24, Freeman speculated that D. H. Hill was the officer who made the "strictures" against Magruder.

36. Jefferson Davis, *The Papers of Jefferson Davis: 1862*, ed. Lynda Lasswell Crist *et al.* (Baton Rouge: Louisiana State University Press, 1995), 296–97, 297 n. 1.

Magruder intentionally omitted nothing that he could do to insure success." Three months dragged by until finally, on October 10, Magruder received orders to report to a new post. By then Theophilus Holmes had been given command of the Trans-Mississippi Department. Magruder protested that he should have his original posting but in the end accepted assignment to command the District of Texas, New Mexico, and Arizona.[37]

Why was Magruder singled out for special blame after the Seven Days? By no reasonable measure was his performance open to greater censure than Jackson's. His execution of Lee's orders on June 26–27 had been sound. His tentative advance on the twenty-ninth stemmed from a misunderstanding of the roles to be played by Jackson and Huger. At least he went into action at Savage Station; Jackson dallied the entire day at Grapevine Bridge, lost in his own murky activities. Ignorance of roads and repeated changes of destination kept Magruder's soldiers marching rather than fighting on June 30, while Jackson crept toward White Oak Swamp and eventually mounted a feeble attack. Much has been made of Jackson's exhaustion during the Seven Days. By June 30, Magruder had gone without significant sleep for several days. That condition, together with stomach problems and his physician's ill-advised prescription, made him edgy and easily flustered. With only a single hour's sleep on the night of June 30, he continued in this state on July 1. Dashing around after he arrived behind Huger's lines, issuing rapid-fire orders and restless at delay, he appeared to be out of control and possibly inebriated.

Magruder attacked at Lee's order on July 1 but failed to deliver a single, powerful blow. That was unfortunate but typical of the overall Confederate effort throughout the Seven Days. The Confederate people may have settled on Magruder, and to a lesser degree Benjamin Huger, as culprits because they could not believe Jackson, who had provided such magnificent news from the Valley in May and early June, capable of a less-than-sterling effort.[38]

Factors beyond the specifics of the Seven Days may have influenced Lee's judgments about Magruder. Deeply religious and guided by duty and moderation in private affairs, Lee may have viewed the pattern of Magruder's life as

37. Davis, *Papers of Davis,* 297 n. 1; *OR* 11 (2):679–80; (3):641; 15:826. Magruder's final report of his part in the Seven Days' campaign, dated August 12, 1862, and other documents he submitted as attachments are in *OR* 11 (2):660–88.

38. For a lengthy but ultimately unpersuasive defense of Huger's role in the Peninsula campaign, see Jeffrey L. Rhoades, *Scapegoat General: The Story of Major General Benjamin Huger, C.S.A.* (Hamden, Conn.: Archon Books, 1985).

significant. Lee's father, the flamboyant and financially reckless Light Horse Harry Lee, had come to grief and shame in a debtor's prison because he lacked self-control. Magruder resembled Harry Lee in a number of ways. Prince John had long lived beyond his means and piled up debt. His reputation as an officer who sometimes drank to excess was well known in the Old Army. A poor father and husband, he impressed friends as a man of little religious conviction.[39] In short, he seemingly lacked self-control and devotion to duty. Perhaps Lee chose not to tolerate a mediocre performance from a man he could not respect. With Jackson, the stern Presbyterian who gave all credit to God, much more could be forgiven. Whatever Lee's thinking, he expressed no regret at Magruder's departure.

Ahead of the Army of Northern Virginia lay campaigns that would become legendary. From those operations, the Confederate people would draw confidence and resolve to maintain their struggle for independence. Few of John Bankhead Magruder's fellow citizens, whether inside or outside the army, would wonder what his role might have been in those stirring events.

39. Elizabeth Lindsay Lomax's diary entry for March 29, 1858, sheds light on perceptions about Magruder's religious convictions: "We attended early service at St. John's, where we found many friends. . . . I must confess that I was surprised to find John Bankhead Magruder at early service. I think of him as a very clever man, a fine soldier, but not religious—but 'Who knows?'" Elizabeth Lindsay Lomax, *Leaves from an Old Washington Diary, 1854–1863*, ed. Lindsay Lomax Wood (Mount Vernon, N.Y.: Books, Inc., 1943), 83.

★ 7 ★

Scapegoat in Victory

James Longstreet and the Battle of Second Manassas

James Longstreet watched as long lines of his infantry poured eastward toward the shaken Federal units deployed on both sides of the Warrenton Turnpike. It was about four-thirty on the afternoon of August 30, 1862, and the battle of Second Manassas was entering its final phase. Gathering his horse, which pranced and reared in response to the tumult of the massive Confederate counterattack, Longstreet turned to see Robert E. Lee riding toward him. Longstreet had anticipated his commander's order to press an enemy unnerved by southern cannon that shredded their exposed left flank, and now the fighting had turned decisively in favor of the Army of Northern Virginia. For a few minutes the commanders observed the action together. Off to their left, Stonewall Jackson's troops, who had carried the brunt of the combat for two days, prepared to add their weight to the assault. Lee presently rode off, but Longstreet remained to watch. Terrain and events conspired to provide him and his staff with a memorable panorama of triumph, as Confederate infantry and artillery moved up and then down and then up again across undulating ridges in furious pursuit of the Union forces. By nightfall southern arms had secured a second great victory on the ground where thirteen months earlier the war had begun in earnest.[1]

Following closely the successful defense of Richmond during the Seven Days, Second Manassas ignited the imagination of the people of the Confederacy. Optimism replaced the awful memories of the spring of 1862, when a seemingly endless series of disasters had befallen their western armies. Tributes from the southern press lauded the performances of Lee, Longstreet, and Jackson. From the welter of senior generals who had fought in the Seven Days, Longstreet and Jackson emerged as Lee's principal lieutenants. Lee himself gave equal praise to his two wing commanders, who had confirmed his faith in their abilities to handle large numbers of men.[2] Under the guidance of this triumvirate, the Army of Northern Virginia had made a critical passage toward maturity.

Fifteen years after the victory at Second Manassas, James Longstreet's conduct at the battle would come under severe criticism. With Lee and Jackson in their graves and thus unable to testify, a coterie of former officers in the Army of Northern Virginia claimed that Longstreet had failed his chief and placed at peril his fellow wing commander. Their charges were serious: Longstreet had been slow to reach the battlefield; he thrice had refused Lee's call for an attack on August 29 while Jackson's hard-pressed brigades fought alone; he had failed to commit his troops as quickly as possible on August 30; and he

1. James Longstreet, *From Manassas to Appomattox: Memoirs of the Civil War in America* (Philadelphia: J. B. Lippincott, 1896), 188–89; Gilbert Moxley Sorrel, *Recollections of a Confederate Staff Officer* (1905; reprint, Jackson, Tenn.: McCowat-Mercer Press, 1959), 91–92; Douglas Southall Freeman, *R. E. Lee: A Biography*, 4 vols. (New York: Charles Scribner's Sons, 1934–36), 2:334–35.

2. On the Virginia press, see Douglas Southall Freeman, *Lee's Lieutenants: A Study in Command*, 3 vols. (New York: Charles Scribner's Sons, 1942–44), 2:136, and J. Tracy Power, "'There Stands Jackson Like a Stone Wall': The Image of General Thomas J. 'Stonewall' Jackson in the Confederate Mind, July 1861–November 1862" (M.A. thesis, University of South Carolina, 1984), 134. Power emphasizes that southern editors did not single Jackson out "as the particular hero of the battle." Lee's comments are in U.S. War Department, *The War of the Rebellion: A Compilation of the Official Records of the Union and Confederate Armies*, 128 vols. (Washington, D.C.: GPO, 1880–1901), ser. 1, vol. 12, pt. 2:551–59 [hereinafter cited as OR; all citations are to series 1]; R. E. Lee, *Lee's Dispatches: Unpublished Letters of General Robert E. Lee, C.S.A. to Jefferson Davis and the War Department of the Confederate States of America, 1862–1865*, ed. Douglas Southall Freeman and Grady McWhiney (1915; reprint, New York: G. P. Putnam's Sons, 1957), 60.

subsequently had claimed far more than his share of credit for the success on that day. In sum, they argued, Longstreet at Second Manassas gave ample evidence of the plodding, stubborn, self-centered behavior that would be repeated at Gettysburg. These criticisms deserve close review because they have colored subsequent treatment of Longstreet's part in the campaign. Without an appreciation of their origins and the extent to which they were accurate, a full understanding of the Confederate side of the battle is impossible.

Disputes about Longstreet's performance at Second Manassas grew out of the larger Gettysburg controversy that raged from the early 1870s into the twentieth century. At the January 1873 dedication of the Lee Chapel in Lexington, Virginia, William Nelson Pendleton, Lee's former chief of artillery, blamed Longstreet for the defeat at Gettysburg. Jubal A. Early, J. William Jones, Fitzhugh Lee, Richard Taylor, and others seconded Pendleton, who alleged that Longstreet's slowness to attack on the morning of July 2 and again on July 3 was decisive.[3] These men were leaders in a movement to canonize Lee as the transcendent hero of the Lost Cause; they demanded that Lee's war record be utterly without blemish. They needed scapegoats, and Longstreet was an ideal candidate.[4] As early as 1865, Longstreet had told northern journalist William Swinton that Lee had erred at Gettysburg, a judgment Swinton cited in his *Campaigns of the Army of the Potomac*. In 1867, Longstreet had called for the South to accept defeat, reconcile with the North, and get on

3. Pendleton's speech, which he delivered many times throughout the South, was published in *Southern Magazine* 15 (December 1874); Jubal Early had made essentially identical charges against Longstreet a year earlier at Lexington in an address on Lee. Susan P. Lee, *Memoirs of William Nelson Pendleton* (Philadelphia: J. B. Lippincott, 1893), 285–86. Representative comments by Fitzhugh Lee and Taylor are in J. William Jones *et al.*, eds., *Southern Historical Society Papers*, 52 vols. (1876–1959; reprint, with 3-vol. index, Wilmington, N.C.: Broadfoot, 1990–92), 5:138–39, 162–94 [hereinafter cited as *SHSP*].

4. William Garrett Piston's *Lee's Tarnished Lieutenant: James Longstreet and His Place in Southern History* (Athens: University of Georgia Press, 1987) is easily the best treatment of Longstreet's postwar years; Piston's dissertation, "Lee's Tarnished Lieutenant: James Longstreet and His Image in American Society" (University of South Carolina, 1982), contains significantly more detail than the book. See also Thomas L. Connelly, *The Marble Man: Robert E. Lee and His Image in American Society* (New York: Alfred A. Knopf, 1977), esp. chaps. 2 and 3; Connelly and Barbara Bellows, *God and General Longstreet: The Lost Cause and the Southern Mind* (Baton Rouge: Louisiana State University Press, 1982), esp. chap. 1; and Gaines M. Foster, *Ghosts of the Confederacy: Defeat, the Lost Cause, and the Emergence of the New South* (New York: Oxford University Press, 1987), esp. chaps. 3–7.

Lieutenant General Longstreet in a photograph probably taken in 1863.

Miller, ed., *Photographic History of the Civil War*

with rebuilding its shattered economy—suggestions that prompted many southerners to label him a traitor. Finally, he became a Republican and received appointive offices from U. S. Grant.[5] Any of these actions would have caused trouble; together they isolated Longstreet as a convenient target.

Champions of Lee portrayed Longstreet as willful, unreliable, slow, clumsy in movement and thought, and given to magnifying his own importance. They emphasized that, in Lee's mind, Jackson was his preeminent subordinate and could be trusted to function with relative freedom, while Longstreet required close supervision. In 1878, Fitzhugh Lee quoted an anonymous source who claimed that Robert E. Lee had told him that "General Longstreet,

5. Longstreet, *Manassas to Appomattox*, 635–38; William Swinton, *Campaigns of the Army of the Potomac* (New York: Charles Scribner's Sons, 1866), 340–41. Swinton quoted Longstreet as the authority for his conclusion that Lee deserved most of the blame for the debacle at Gettysburg.

when once in a fight, was a most brilliant soldier; but he was the hardest man to move I had in my army." Jubal Early asserted, also in 1878, that during the war Lee had said to him, "Longstreet is a very good fighter when he gets in position and gets everything ready, but he is so slow."[6] Such statements countered one piece of evidence that bedeviled the anti-Longstreet camp: Lee habitually pitched his tent near Longstreet, a fact that seemingly supported the latter's assertion that he and Lee always enjoyed the warmest relations and cared deeply for one another.[7] Early and others implied that the commanding general bivouacked near Longstreet rather than Jackson in order to expedite his marches.

In a book published well before the controversies of the 1870s, Edward A. Pollard affirmed that Longstreet's "relations with Gen. Lee . . . were not only pleasant and cordial, but affectionate to an almost brotherly degree; an example of beautiful friendship in the war that was frequently remarked by the public."[8] This bond—so strong and open that the Confederate people recognized it—explains why Lee camped near Longstreet. With his sense of humor and fondness for social intercourse, Lee doubtless also found Longstreet's convivial headquarters more pleasant than those of the dour Jackson. It takes nothing away from Lee's great respect and admiration for Jackson to admit that their private relationship was not especially close.

Later writers who drew on the work of Lee's partisans, however, gave continuing force to their opinions. In his widely popular *Lee the American*, Gamaliel Bradford stated that "Lee's deep affection for his great lieutenant [Jackson]

6. Many of those who attacked Longstreet aired their views in the pages of the *SHSP*, whose editor, J. William Jones, had been a chaplain in the Army of Northern Virginia and was a staunch supporter of the effort orchestrated by Jubal Early to present Lee as a warrior without blemish (see esp. vols. 4–6 of the *SHSP*). The quotations from Fitzhugh Lee and Early are in *SHSP* 5:193, 274.

7. Raphael J. Moses, Longstreet's commissary officer, noted in his autobiography, "I saw General Lee almost daily, while in Virginia, for his headquarters were very near General Longstreet's always." Raphael J. Moses, "Autobiography," No. 529, p. 54, Moses Papers, Southern Historical Collection, Wilson Library, University of North Carolina, Chapel Hill. Examples of Longstreet's many statements about his close relations with Lee are in *SHSP* 5:71, and Helen D. Longstreet, *Lee and Longstreet at High Tide: Gettysburg in Light of the Official Records* (1904; reprint, Millwood, N.Y.: Kraus Reprint, 1981), 79–84.

8. Edward A. Pollard, *Lee and His Lieutenants: Comprising the Early Life, Public Services, and Campaigns of General Robert E. Lee and His Companions in Arms, with a Record of Their Campaigns and Heroic Deeds* (New York: E. B. Treat, 1867), 420.

and perfect confidence in him are beyond question. It has been well pointed out that this was proved practically by the fact that the commander-in-chief always himself remained with Longstreet and left Jackson to operate independently, as if the former were more in need of personal supervision." Most influential was Douglas Southall Freeman, who observed that Lee "camped near Longstreet in order to hasten the movements of that leisurely general."[9]

Usually overlooked or relegated to a footnote is contradictory testimony such as that quoted in George Cary Eggleston's 1875 reminiscence. "General Lee himself said in the presence of a distinguished officer from whose lips I heard it," wrote Eggleston, "that Jackson was by no means so rapid a marcher as Longstreet, and that he had an unfortunate habit of *never being on time.*" Eggleston, who ranked Jackson second only to Lee as "the greatest military genius we had," did not mention whether Lee spoke in the wake of Jackson's chronic tardiness during the Seven Days. William P. Snow's early postwar work on Confederate generals seconded Eggleston's assessment of Longstreet, describing Old Pete as "bold, daring, dashing" and a rapid marcher.[10]

Freeman and other authors shaped by the late-nineteenth-century writings of those who insisted on Lee's perfection even refused to grant Longstreet his full physical stature. At six feet, two inches tall, Longstreet was an imposing figure. Major J. W. Ratchford of D. H. Hill's staff called him a "handsome man of fine physique." Moxley Sorrel, a member of Longstreet's staff who knew his chief as well as anyone during the war, described him as "a soldier every inch, and very handsome, tall and well proportioned, strong and active, a superb horseman and with an unsurpassed soldierly bearing." Yet the prevailing image of him is of a shorter, rather ponderous man. For example, Freeman shrank Longstreet to five feet, ten and a half inches, and Frank E. Vandiver, in his able biography of Jackson, called him "rather heavy-set, not tall" with an "air of languor" about him.[11]

9. Gamaliel Bradford, *Lee the American* (Boston: Houghton Mifflin, 1912), 139; Freeman, *R. E. Lee* 2:484 (citing Henry Alexander White's undocumented *Robert E. Lee and the Southern Confederacy, 1807–1870* [New York: G. P. Putnam's Sons, 1904]). Freeman unabashedly revealed his bias when he wrote of Jackson in vol. 2 of *Lee's Lieutenants* (p. xv): "The history of the Army from Cedar Mountain to Sharpsburg and back again to the Rappahannock is, in its finest lines, his military biography." See Piston, *Lee's Tarnished Lieutenant,* 174–78, on Freeman's impact on later historians.

10. George Cary Eggleston, *A Rebel's Recollections* (1875; reprint, Bloomington: Indiana University Press, 1959), 133; William P. Snow, *Lee and His Generals* (1867; reprint, New York: Fairfax Press, 1982), 321, 323, 330, 336, 338.

11. J. W. Ratchford, *Some Reminiscences of Persons and Incidents of the Civil War* (1909; re-

Longstreet's own postwar writings gave ammunition to his enemies and provided an opening for Jubal Early, who by the mid-1870s was his principal antagonist, to spread the controversy beyond Gettysburg to Second Manassas. Fierce attacks on Longstreet in the 1870s prompted him to mount an intemperate defense. In an important article first published in the *Philadelphia Weekly Times*, Longstreet insisted that after negotiations on strategy Lee had promised to fight on the tactical defensive in Pennsylvania, implied that in other ways he and Lee were peers rather than commander and subordinate, and offered a precise listing of all of Lee's errors during the campaign. As proof of Lee's respect for his judgment, Longstreet mentioned the events of the afternoon of August 29, 1862, at Manassas. Between noon and evening that day, wrote Longstreet, Lee three times expressed a desire that he attack and each time deferred to his belief that an attack was not advisable. This series of exchanges, asserted Longstreet, illustrated the character of "the relations that existed between us."[12]

Longstreet added that at the critical moment on August 30 when Lee ordered him to move to Jackson's support, he decided to break up the Federal assault with artillery: "Instead of moving to reinforce Jackson, therefore, I sent dispatches for batteries to hurry to where I was." A battery quickly appeared, fired into the flank of the advancing Union troops, and stopped them. Other batteries then arrived, and their enfilading fire scattered a second Union assault. After his artillery blunted a third Federal attempt, Longstreet "sprung every man that I had to the charge, and swept down upon them like an avalanche. The effect was simply magical. The enemy broke all to pieces."[13]

Jubal Early immediately responded to Longstreet's discussion of Second Manassas. "Though professing to be on 'The Mistakes of Gettysburg,'" wrote Early of Longstreet's piece, "one of the prime objects of the last article . . .

print, Austin, Tex.: Shoal Creek, 1971), 65; Sorrel, *Recollections*, 17; Freeman, *Lee's Lieutenants* 1:xliv; Frank E. Vandiver, *Mighty Stonewall* (New York: McGraw-Hill, 1957), 295. For a full-length photograph that conveys a sense of Longstreet's stature, see Editors of Time-Life Books, *Lee Takes Command: From Seven Days to Second Bull Run* (Alexandria, Va.: Time-Life Books, 1984), 153. For a review of Longstreet's image in the literature on the war, see chap. 11 of Piston, *Lee's Tarnished Lieutenant*.

12. James Longstreet, "The Mistakes of Gettysburg," *Philadelphia Weekly Times*, February 23, 1878 (reprinted in [A. K. McClure], ed., *The Annals of the War, Written by Leading Participants North and South, Originally Published in the Philadelphia Weekly Times* [Philadelphia: Times Publishing, 1879], 619–33, and in *SHSP* 5:257–70).

13. *SHSP* 5:267–68. Longstreet gave a slightly different version of these events in *Manassas to Appomattox*, 186–90.

seems to have been to claim for General Longstreet the principal credit for the victory gained at the second battle of Manassas, at the expense of both General Lee and General Jackson." "If there was any doubt before of a fact well known to the whole army, that General Longstreet was very slow in his movements on all occasions," continued Early, "he has now furnished very conclusive evidence of its truth, in his narrative of incidents connected with the second battle of Manassas." Arriving on the field about noon on the twenty-ninth, he did not commit any of his troops until near nightfall and then only in a feeling movement. "In the meantime General Jackson's command had sustained and repulsed seven different attacks in heavy force during the afternoon." The next day, "though there was skirmishing and fighting in Jackson's front all day, General Longstreet was not ready to go into action until after 3 P.M. . . . It was twenty-seven hours after his arrival on the field before he was ready to begin." Early suggested that Lee, who had wanted Longstreet to attack on the twenty-ninth, must have asked Longstreet to advance before three o'clock on the thirtieth. Throughout that day and a half, asserted Early, Jackson's command (Early was in that command) thought it an "almost interminable period before [Longstreet's troops] were brought into action." Exhausted by four days of "confronting and fighting Pope's accumulating columns," they anxiously asked one another, "Will Longstreet never begin?"[14]

Longstreet's implication that his troops had won the battle almost single-handed on the afternoon of August 30 galled Early most of all. "General Jackson merely withstood the enemy's attacks, while Longstreet was getting ready," noted Early with a touch of his famous sarcasm, "and the question comes in here very naturally: What would have been the result, if Jackson and his men had not been of the stuff to withstand the shock of more than three times their numbers, for the long hours it took Longstreet to get ready?"[15]

Stephen D. Lee, whose battalion of artillery occupied the ground between Jackson's and Longstreet's troops, subsequently pointed out that it was his eighteen guns, not the batteries Longstreet ordered forward after receiving Lee's message to help Jackson, that broke up the Union attacks. Lee showed

14. *SHSP* 5:274–78.

15. *Ibid.*, 276. Early was much less critical of Longstreet in his memoir titled *Lieutenant General Jubal Anderson Early C.S.A.: Autobiographical Sketch and Narrative of the War between the States* (Philadelphia: J. B. Lippincott, 1912), 122–28. Although it was not published until after his death, Early completed this narrative before the contentious debates about Gettysburg and Second Manassas broke out in the 1870s.

Defeat of the Federal Troops by Longstreet's Corps, Second Manassas, a late-nineteenth-century engraving depicting the massive Confederate assault on the afternoon of August 30, 1862. Longstreet, *Manassas to Appomattox*

that the batteries Longstreet summoned were too far away and not positioned to enfilade the Federal formations: "They no doubt did good service—as good service as any batteries could have done at their distance, but all the honor of crushing that terrible onslaught on Jackson by the surging masses, so vividly described by Longstreet, does not belong to them. Jackson and eighteen other pieces of artillery, much nearer, are entitled to that honor, which, as indicated by General Longstreet, was the turning point of the battle."[16] In an addendum to S. D. Lee's article, Early admitted that Longstreet probably was too far away from Lee's guns to be aware of their part in the battle and might have assumed that the batteries he called into action had greater effect. Adopting a conciliatory pose at the end of the article, Early stated that "Longstreet won sufficient glory at Second Manassas for him to permit others to share with him their well-earned laurels."[17]

Early really wanted the greatest possible censure of Longstreet, and the exchange relating to Second Manassas in the *Southern Historical Society Papers* helped to accomplish that goal. The writings of Walter H. Taylor, Lee's adjutant general, illustrate the success of Early and his supporters. Taylor's wartime correspondence with Longstreet was of the warmest type,[18] and his 1874 memoir *Four Years with General Lee*, published before the Second Manassas controversy, contained no hint that Longstreet's part in the battle had been less than satisfactory. When he published *General Lee: His Campaigns in Virginia, 1861–1865* in 1906, however, Taylor included what was by then the standard criticism of Longstreet. On the afternoon of August 29, wondered Taylor, "Why did not Longstreet attack, and so relieve the heavy pressure on Jackson?" Taylor then quoted G. F. R. Henderson, the British officer who wrote a classic—and near idolatrous—life of Jackson: "Longstreet, with a complacency it is hard to understand, has related how he opposed the wishes of his commander-in-chief [that he attack]." "As matters turned out, it was all right," said Taylor in conclusion. "General Jackson had succeeded in holding his lines, so fiercely and continuously assailed. General Longstreet, perhaps, found his justification

---

16. *SHSP* 6:59–62. For Longstreet's response to S. D. Lee and the latter's rejoinder, see *ibid.*, 215–17, 250–54. Lee had much the better of the exchange.

17. *Ibid.*, 64–70.

18. When Longstreet and the First Corps returned from Tennessee to Virginia in the spring of 1864, for example, Taylor wrote, "I really am beside myself, General, with joy at having you back. It is like the reunion of a family." Taylor's entire letter is reproduced in *SHSP* 5:268, and in Helen Longstreet's *Lee and Longstreet at High Tide*, 79.

in the success that crowned the efforts of the Confederates the next day; and yet I know of no good reason to doubt that the same success would have been attained the first day had the same energy been displayed."[19]

Later writers accepted this view. Clifford Dowdey remarked that Longstreet was "dangerously slow at Second Manassas, but criticisms were forgotten in the glow of final victory." Douglas Southall Freeman insisted that Longstreet managed to exert his dominance over Lee on the afternoon of August 29. "The seeds of much of the disaster at Gettysburg," wrote Freeman in a sentence that damned Longstreet's conduct in two battles, "were sown in that instant—when Lee yielded to Longstreet and Longstreet discovered that he would." Freeman asked darkly whether Longstreet had come to believe that "no matter what the public might say of Jackson, he and not 'Stonewall' had the large influence on Lee." Hamilton J. Eckenrode and Bryan Conrad, Longstreet's first biographers, concurred that Lee "let Longstreet persuade him to wait and wait again." Longstreet had done well when he finally attacked on the thirtieth, "but his long delay had imperiled Jackson and caused the latter heavy losses." Edward J. Stackpole's popular *From Cedar Mountain to Antietam*, among many other accounts, took a similar view.[20]

Longstreet wrote a letter to former Union general Fitz John Porter in April 1878 that Jubal Early and his cohorts would have used to great advantage. "I failed to obey the orders of the twenty-ninth," stated Longstreet, "and on the 30th, in direct opposition to my orders, made the battle from my position and won it." Here was an admission from Longstreet's own pen that he had violated orders and a bald assertion that his troops alone had won the battle. Placed in context, however, it is not quite so damning. Porter had been court-martialed and cashiered for failing to carry out an impossible order from John Pope to launch an assault against Jackson's right flank on August 30 (Porter knew Longstreet's 30,000 men were in the way, but Pope refused to believe it). During and after the war, Republicans had hounded Porter unmerci-

19. Walter H. Taylor, *Four Years with General Lee* (1875; reprint, Bloomington: Indiana University Press, 1962), and *General Lee: His Campaigns in Virginia, 1861–1865, with Personal Reminiscences* (1906; reprint, Dayton, Ohio: Morningside, 1975), 107–10.

20. Clifford Dowdey, *Lee's Last Campaign: The Story of Lee and His Men against Grant—1864* (Boston: Little, Brown, 1960), 11; Freeman, *R. E. Lee* 2:325; Freeman, *Lee's Lieutenants* 2:137–38; Hamilton J. Eckenrode and Bryan Conrad, *James Longstreet: Lee's War Horse* (Chapel Hill: University of North Carolina Press, 1936), 110–11; Edward J. Stackpole, *From Cedar Mountain to Antietam* (Harrisburg, Pa.: Stackpole, 1959), 203–206.

fully for his Democratic political views. In 1878 he was in the midst of a protracted effort to clear his name; he would not be exonerated until 1886.[21]
Longstreet clearly empathized with Porter and was telling him that he, too,
had received an unwise order, had acted on his own better judgment, and had
won a great victory. But Longstreet knew he had not disobeyed orders on August 29—Lee had accepted his reasons for not attacking. As for the thirtieth,
Longstreet's employment of artillery rather than infantry to relieve the pressure on Jackson was in only the very narrowest sense "direct opposition" to
Lee's order. Thus the letter to Porter probably was a case of Longstreet's indulging in hyperbole to buoy the spirits of a man he saw as a fellow victim of slan-
derous attacks.

What is a fair assessment of Longstreet's role in the campaign of Second
Manassas? Did Early, Pendleton, and the rest have even a partially valid case?
It is very important to keep in mind that the charges were not leveled against
Longstreet until Lee was dead. Surely this was no coincidence. Many men who
assailed Longstreet attributed to Lee comments and attitudes that have absolutely no support in surviving direct evidence from Lee.[22] Many of the statements so attributed were blatant lies, such as Pendleton's claim that he had
heard Lee order Longstreet to attack at dawn on July 2 at Gettysburg. In rela-
tion to Lee, it must be added that anyone who accepts the case against Longstreet in its full form must also accept an interpretation of Lee as a weak leader
whom Longstreet could dominate at will. Eckenrode and Conrad believed
that Lee "permitted Longstreet to shape events somewhat, because Longstreet
was so masterful, so certain of himself, so self-expressive, while he, Lee, was
uncertain of himself and always repressed."[23] Although he surely would have

21. James Longstreet to Fitz John Porter, April 15, 1878, Porter Papers, Library of Congress. On Porter's difficulties, see *OR* 12 (2), supplement (the entire volume is devoted to Porter's
court-martial), and Otto Eisenschiml, *The Celebrated Case of Fitz John Porter: An American Drey-
fus Affair* (Indianapolis: Bobbs-Merrill, 1950).

22. An undated, typewritten transcript of a May 7, 1868, conversation between Lee and
William Preston Johnston (son of Albert Sidney Johnston and a member of the faculty at Wash-
ington College while Lee was president) includes the statement, "He [Lee] said Longstreet was
often slow." Because it is impossible to tell when Johnston reconstructed the conversation, it
must be used with caution. The typescript is in the McCormick Library at Washington and Lee
University, Lexington, Virginia. For the text of Johnston's notes of conversations with Lee, see
William Preston Johnston, "Memoranda of Conversations with General R. E. Lee," in Gary W.
Gallagher, ed., *Lee the Soldier* (Lincoln: University of Nebraska Press, 1996), 25–28. Johnston
also published "Reminiscences of Robert E. Lee" in *Belford Monthly* 5 (June 1890).

23. Eckenrode and Conrad, *James Longstreet*, 364–65.

denied it, even Freeman sometimes left a similar impression. His sketch of Longstreet in *Dictionary of American Biography,* for example, argued that Longstreet successfully resisted Lee's instructions at Second Manassas, during the Suffolk campaign in the spring of 1863, and at Gettysburg.

Specific distortions relating to Longstreet at Second Manassas may be dealt with briefly in turn. The implication that Lee viewed Jackson rather than Longstreet as his principal lieutenant during the campaign is inaccurate. Unfortunately, it mars the work of even such respected authors as Jennings C. Wise, who relegated Longstreet to a decidedly inferior position in the army when he labeled the victory at Manassas "Lee's and Jackson's success."[24] In the wake of the Seven Days, Lee secured the transfer of a number of senior major generals serving with the Army of Northern Virginia, leaving Longstreet his ranking subordinate. Lee gave generous credit to Longstreet for his part in the Seven Days, prompting a staff officer to remark that "Genl. Longstreet has undoubtedly acquired as much or more reputation than any other officer in this army. He is now next in command in Virginia to Genl. Lee."[25] Similarly, when Lee reorganized the Army of Northern Virginia into two corps after Second Manassas, he chose Longstreet as his second in command. Moreover, Lee sent Longstreet's name to Jefferson Davis for promotion to lieutenant general without qualification, but in recommending Jackson, Lee told the president: "My opinion of the merits of General Jackson has been greatly enhanced during this expedition [the 1862 Maryland campaign]. He is true, honest, and brave; has a single eye to the good of the service, and spares no exertion to accomplish his object." Why would Lee take pains to qualify his endorsement of Jackson unless he harbored some doubts about him? Did he believe that Jackson had given less than full exertion at times?[26] Whatever the answer, the evidence makes amply clear that Lee did not consider Jackson the superior and Longstreet the inferior subordinate.

24. Jennings C. Wise, *The Long Arm of Lee; or, The History of the Artillery of the Army of Northern Virginia, with a Brief Account of the Confederate Bureau of Ordnance,* 2 vols. (Lynchburg, Va.: J. P. Bell, 1915), 1:276. Among the officers assigned elsewhere were Gustavus Woodson Smith, Benjamin F. Huger, Theophilus H. Holmes, and John Bankhead Magruder; all but Magruder ranked Longstreet.

25. Thomas J. Goree to My Dearest Mother, July 21, 1862, in Thomas J. Goree, *Longstreet's Aide: The Civil War Letters of Major Thomas J. Goree,* ed. Thomas W. Cutrer (Charlottesville: University Press of Virginia, 1995), 98.

26. OR 19 (2): 643. Freeman speculated about Lee's choice of language in *Lee's Lieutenants* 2:247, concluding that the "evidence does not permit an answer."

The charge that Longstreet was slow in reaching the battlefield at Second Manassas also lacks foundation. Lee ordered him to leave his position along the Rappahannock on the afternoon of August 26; after an eleven-mile march, Longstreet's divisions (except R. H. Anderson's, which was left to watch the Rappahannock line and would follow when it could) bivouacked that night in Orleans. Moving without adequate cavalry (virtually all of the cavalry had been sent with Jackson), the column suffered a number of delays on August 27 but made it past Salem to spend the night near White Plains. The first phase of Longstreet's march almost exactly matched the performance of Jackson's "foot-cavalry" over the same route a day and a half before. On the road again before dawn, the first of Longstreet's troops reached Thoroughfare Gap by mid-afternoon of the twenty-eighth.[27] Lee was pleased with Longstreet's progress. A courier from Jackson had informed Lee of Jackson's position; other messengers brought news that the gap was clear of Federals. Confident that the situation was well in hand, Lee ordered Longstreet's column to bivouac for the night so the men would be fresh on the twenty-ninth.[28] Those instructions manifestly did not come from a commander unhappy with the pace of his subordinate's march.

As it turned out, the Confederates did have to fight for Thoroughfare Gap on the evening of August 28. After clearing away Union defenders commanded by Brigadier General James B. Ricketts, the divisions of D. R. Jones and John Bell Hood camped for the night on the eastern slope of the gap. James Kemper's division did not participate in the fighting that evening and remained just west of the gap. Cadmus M. Wilcox's command, which had passed through Hopewell Gap some three miles north of Thoroughfare Gap, spent the night at Antioch Church. The soldiers of Longstreet's wing were in motion again at daylight on August 29, with Hood in the lead followed by the divisions of Kemper, Jones, and Wilcox. Through Haymarket and Gainesville they moved purposefully, striking the Warrenton Turnpike about 9:00 A.M.

27. Longstreet, *Manassas to Appomattox*, 170–73; OR 12 (2): 555, 564; Freeman, *R. E. Lee* 2:304–13 (the best account of the march).

28. John J. Hennessy, *Historical Report on the Troop Movements for the Second Battle of Manassas, August 28 through August 30, 1862* (Denver: National Park Service, 1985), 22. This deeply researched work, with its sixteen detailed maps, is indispensable to any serious study of the battle. It was published for wider distribution under the title *Second Manassas Battlefield Map Study* (Lynchburg, Va.: H. E. Howard, n.d.), as a volume in the Virginia Civil War Battles and Leaders series.

Within another hour the head of Hood's column reached Jackson's right. Lee and Longstreet both arrived on the field about ten o'clock, and by noon Longstreet had deployed almost all of his men.[29]

To summarize, in less than three days Longstreet's veterans shifted from their position on the Rappahannock to the battlefield. They did so without the help of an adequate cavalry screen, and in the course of their journey fought for possession of Thoroughfare Gap. By any reasonable standard, it was an excellent march that compared favorably with what Jackson's troops accomplished in covering the same ground.

Longstreet was now on the field, and it is at this point that critics have painted the most unflattering picture of his performance. They argue that he stubbornly refused to attack despite three requests by Lee, while to his left Jackson's exhausted soldiers fought off wave after wave of Union assaults. Lee first urged Longstreet to strike the Union left just after noon. Longstreet quite properly wanted to check the ground first (had John Pope taken this elementary precaution the next day he would have been spared a good deal of grief). In an hour's reconnaissance he found that the Federals extended well south of the Warrenton Turnpike and occupied strong ground. There was also an unconfirmed report of Union troops at Manassas Junction. If that were true, it was possible a Federal flanking movement could strike the right of any assaulting column Longstreet might form. Lee was somewhat skeptical but, as he and Longstreet discussed the problem, Confederate cavalry chief Jeb Stuart sent news that a Union force was indeed approaching from the southeast along the Manassas-Gainesville road. A disappointed Lee agreed that nothing should be done until he knew more about the Union threat.[30]

Longstreet reinforced his right with Wilcox's brigades and rode out for another look. He returned to tell Lee, who had been joined by Stonewall Jackson, that the threat in his immediate front was not too serious but that a significant volume of dust rising from the direction of Manassas indicated that more Federals might be on their way. Lee listened, then suggested for a second time that Longstreet attack. Longstreet preferred to wait for concrete word

29. Hennessy, *Report on Manassas Troop Movements*, 56–57, 85, 123; OR 12 (2):555–56, 564; Longstreet, *Manassas to Appomattox*, 180–81.

30. Longstreet, *Manassas to Appomattox*, 181–83; Longstreet, "Our March against Pope," in Robert Underwood Johnson and Clarence Clough Buel, eds., *Battles and Leaders of the Civil War*, 4 vols. (New York: Century, 1887), 2:519 [hereinafter cited as *B&L*]; OR 12 (2):556, 736; Hennessy, *Report on Manassas Troop Movements*, 151.

about the Federals at Manassas, and Lee reluctantly agreed to postpone the assault a while longer. Before many minutes had passed, Stuart joined Lee and Longstreet (Jackson had left) with the intelligence that the troops coming from Manassas were almost surely Fitz John Porter's Union Fifth Corps. Lee decided that it would be unsound to move with a potentially serious threat to Longstreet's right; however, he determined to look at the situation himself.[31]

In an hour Lee was back. He and Longstreet, who also had taken another look at the situation, concurred that the Union menace, as Longstreet put it, "was hardly strong enough to mean aggressive work from that quarter." For a third time Lee called for an assault. It was well past four o'clock. Longstreet cited the lateness of the hour as a deterrent to launching a decisive attack and called instead for a reconnaissance-in-force later that evening. If an opening were found, preparations could be made during the night for a massive counterstroke along the Warrenton Turnpike at dawn on the thirtieth. Lee hesitated, then consented to follow Longstreet's proposed course.[32]

Just after 6:00 P.M., Hood advanced and engaged in a confusing, bitter fight with Federals along the turnpike. Hood was a bold, even reckless fighter, but he quickly decided to oppose an attack in the morning over that ground. "My line was in the midst of the enemy," Hood later wrote, "the obscurity of the night, which was deepened by a thick wood, made it almost impossible to distinguish friend from foe, and for the same reason I was unable to select a position and form upon it for action the next morning." Federals and Confederates became tangled in the darkness, making effective control impossible. "In view of this condition of affairs," Hood continued, "I determined to . . . inform Generals Lee and Longstreet of the facts, and to recommend that I retire and resume the line from which I had advanced just before sunset."[33] Sup-

31. Longstreet, *Manassas to Appomattox*, 183; Freeman, *R. E. Lee* 2:323–24.

32. Longstreet, *Manassas to Appomattox*, 183–84; Hennessy, *Report on Manassas Troop Movements*, 184, 218. Douglas Southall Freeman wrote that "Longstreet was obdurate" in opposing Lee's third suggestion that he attack (*R. E. Lee* 2:324).

33. John Bell Hood, *Advance and Retreat: Personal Experiences in the United States and Confederate States Armies* (1880; reprint, Bloomington: Indiana University Press, 1959), 34–35. See also Hood's report in *OR* 12(2): 604–606. Lee's memory failed him when he discussed Hood's probing attack with William Allan (Jackson's ordnance officer and subsequently a member of the faculty at Washington College) on February 19, 1870. Allan quoted Lee as stating that Hood "drove the Yankees handsomely, and after night returned to Lee delighted & excited." William Allan, "Memoranda of Conversations with General Robert E. Lee," in Gallagher, ed., *Lee the Soldier*, 17.

port for Hood's recommendation came from Cadmus M. Wilcox, who spent more than two hours examining the Union lines after the fighting died down. Faced with such advice, Lee canceled plans to assault the next morning. He hoped that Pope would attack him and leave an opening for a counterattack.[34]

It had been a difficult day for Lee. Naturally aggressive, he inclined toward attacking almost from the moment Longstreet was in position. In line with the style of command he exhibited both before and after Second Manassas, Lee sought the opinion of a trusted subordinate—in this instance Longstreet, who three times counseled against launching an assault. In every instance subsequent intelligence proved Longstreet's caution well grounded. Longstreet was not a headstrong or sullen lieutenant on August 29; he was alert and careful and served his chief well. And it is pertinent to note that his conduct on the twenty-ninth was dramatically different from that of Jackson several weeks earlier, when Stonewall and thousands of troops lay idle at White Oak Swamp as their comrades waged a furious battle a short distance away.[35]

The allegation that Longstreet was slow to attack and relieve pressure on Jackson on the afternoon of August 30 can be dismissed quickly. Lee wanted to see Pope resume the offensive that day. Colonel Charles Marshall of Lee's staff recalled that "We hoped we would be attacked. I think the hope that we might be attacked caused General Lee to defer any action that he might have taken [that morning]." As the morning slipped by with no renewal of the Union assaults, Lee met with Jackson and Longstreet to plan a movement that night to get around Pope's right and cut him off from Washington. Jackson would make that effort, while Longstreet created a diversion on the Union left. In the meantime, Longstreet and Jackson were to prepare to receive new attacks.[36] When the Union assaults did come and Jackson asked Lee and

34. Hennessy, *Report on Manassas Troop Movements*, 246–47, quoting the testimony of Colonel Charles Marshall of Lee's staff.

35. Apologists for Jackson's failures during the Seven Days have pointed to his exhaustion after weeks of hard campaigning. See for example R. L. Dabney, *Life and Campaigns of Lieut.-Gen. Thomas J. Jackson (Stonewall Jackson)* (1866; reprint, Harrisonburg, Va.: Sprinkle, 1983), 466–67, and Clifford Dowdey, *The Seven Days: The Emergence of Lee* (Boston: Little, Brown, 1964), 314–15. For less charitable explanations, see Edward Porter Alexander, *Military Memoirs of a Confederate: A Critical Narrative* (1907; reprint, Bloomington: Indiana University Press, 1962), 133–55, and Daniel Harvey Hill, "McClellan's Charge of Base and Malvern Hill," *B&L* 2:389–90.

36. Hennessy, *Report on Manassas Troop Movements*, 283. Longstreet left the only accounts of this meeting among the top Confederate leaders in *Manassas to Appomattox*, 186–87, and "Our

James Longstreet in 1894, just before publishing a memoir giving Jackson's troops little credit for their service at Second Manassas.
Collection of the author

Longstreet for help, Longstreet responded quickly by summoning batteries to help break up the Federal formations. Then, anticipating Lee's order, he sent his entire wing forward in a well-executed counterattack (his troops were in good position because he had prepared them to launch the diversion later that night). This commitment of 30,000 men in half an hour was a remarkable per-

March against Pope," 520. Lee's report stated only that "on the morning of the 30th the enemy again advanced, and skirmishing began along the line. The troops of Jackson and Longstreet maintained their positions of the previous day." OR 12 (2):557.

formance, unmatched on any other battlefield of the war. Lee could not have asked for a better response from a subordinate than he got from Longstreet on the afternoon of August 30.

The final criticism of Longstreet at Second Manassas centers on his failure to give adequate credit to the splendid fighting of Jackson's wing. In terms of his postwar writings this certainly is true. Longstreet's articles written after Early and the others had begun their campaign against him, as well as his memoir *From Manassas to Appomattox*, accorded Jackson and his men less than their share of glory for the victory.[37] The reason was that he believed most writers in the years after the war had magnified Jackson's role in the Army of Northern Virginia. In short, Longstreet was distinctly jealous of Jackson's reputation. "That Jackson was clever there is no doubt," he wrote a northern friend in 1885, "but that he was superhuman as Virginians who have written about him would have the world believe there is room for grave doubts."[38] Longstreet's desire to strike back at Early, Jones, Pendleton, and their allies does not excuse his ungenerous treatment of Jackson at Second Manassas—but it makes it understandable.

Overall, James Longstreet performed very capably during the entire campaign of Second Manassas. The evidence strongly suggests that Lee took a similar view. He continued to rely on Longstreet, made him the ranking corps commander when the Army of Northern Virginia officially reorganized later that fall, and without exception demonstrated trust and affection for Old Pete.[39] The story of James Longstreet and Second Manassas is a primer on how politics, prejudice, and self-interest often influence the way in which subsequent generations perceive historical events.

37. Longstreet's principal discussions of Second Manassas are in *Manassas to Appomattox*, 163–98; "Campaign against Pope"; "The Artillery at Second Manassas—General Longstreet's Reply to General S. D. Lee," in *SHSP* 6:215–17; and the article cited in n. 16 above. Chaps. 7–9 of Piston, *Lee's Tarnished Lieutenant*, contain a full discussion of Longstreet's writings.

38. James Longstreet to John P. Nicholson, July 12, 1885, quoted in Piston, *Lee's Tarnished Lieutenant*, 146.

39. In the summer of 1864, Thomas J. Goree reported that "after one of the battles Genl. Lee said that Longstreet's Corps attacked the enemy with greater dash, repulsed them with more steadiness, had fewer stragglers, and kept better in hand than any corps in his army." Thomas J. Goree to Sarah Williams Kittrell Goree, July 14, 1864[?], Goree, *Longstreet's Aide*, 124. For a sampling of Lee's warm correspondence with Longstreet, see Helen D. Longstreet, *Lee and Longstreet at High Tide*, 78–82.

★ 8 ★

Confederate Corps Leadership on the First Day at Gettysburg

A. P. Hill and Richard S. Ewell in a Difficult Debut

Former Confederates pursued the question of responsibility for the defeat at Gettysburg with almost religious zeal in the years following Appomattox. Accusations about the culpability of Lee's principal lieutenants had surfaced well before the end of the war, but not until the mid-1870s did the debate take on the character of an internecine brawl. At the heart of the controversy lay an attempt on the part of Jubal A. Early, Fitzhugh Lee, J. William Jones, and others to refute James Longstreet's suggestion, first given wide circulation in William Swinton's history of the Army of the Potomac, that Lee had erred badly at Gettysburg. Early and the others sought to absolve Lee of responsibility for any military failures during the war and singled out Longstreet as their primary villain. Longstreet had ignored orders to launch an assault against the Federal left at dawn on July 2, they argued, thereby denying the South a victory at Gettysburg and probably its independence. Although Longstreet stood at the vortex of this war of words, other ranking Confederates also received substantial criticism during and after the war—Jeb Stuart for a ride around the Union army that prevented his keeping Lee informed of Federal movements, A. P. Hill for precipitating the battle against Lee's orders and then mounting a weak pursuit of routed Federals, and Richard Stoddert Ewell for failing to seize Cemetery Hill and Culp's Hill late in the first day's fighting.[1]

Lost opportunities on July 1 loomed large because the troops of Hill and Ewell had gained a decided advantage over their opponents west and north of Gettysburg by midafternoon. To many Confederate observers it seemed that one more round of assaults would have carried Cemetery Hill and Culp's Hill and sealed a major victory. Loath to engage the enemy in the first place, Lee had reached the field in time to recognize the opening presented by Hill's earlier decision to commit two divisions and had sought to press the Confederate advantage. But first Hill and then Ewell declined to renew the offensive, observed their critics, affording desperate Federals time to patch together a strong line on high ground south of the town. Their failure set the stage for two more days of bloody battle during which the commanders of the Second and Third corps became little more than bystanders in a drama dominated on the Confederate side by Lee and Longstreet.

Hill and Ewell entered Pennsylvania in June 1863 burdened with the legacy of Stonewall Jackson. Between them they commanded the four divisions of the old Second Corps. Lee's reorganization of the army after Jackson's death had assigned three of Jackson's divisions to Ewell as chief of a smaller Second Corps, while Hill's Light Division, long a bulwark of Jackson's corps, supplied six of the thirteen brigades in "Little Powell's" new Third Corps.[2] Perhaps inevitably, estimates of the performances of Hill and Ewell on July 1 frequently included invidious comparisons to the heroic Jackson of the 1862 Valley campaign and Chancellorsville rather than to the eminently fallible "Old Jack" of the Seven Days or Cedar Mountain.

Less than a month after Gettysburg, Surgeon Spencer Glasgow Welch of

1. Much of the controversial writing about Gettysburg appeared in the pages of J. William Jones *et al.*, eds., *Southern Historical Society Papers*, 52 vols. (1876–1959; reprint, with 3-vol. index, Wilmington, N.C.: Broadfoot, 1990–92 [hereinafter cited as SHSP]; see esp. vols. 4–6 for the opening arguments by Jubal A. Early, James Longstreet, and other principals in the debate. Important modern works include Thomas L. Connelly, *The Marble Man: Robert E. Lee and His Image in American Society* (New York: Alfred A. Knopf, 1977), esp. chaps. 2 and 3; Glenn Tucker, *Lee and Longstreet at Gettysburg* (Indianapolis: Bobbs-Merrill, 1968), which devotes considerable attention to Richard S. Ewell; and William Garrett Piston, *Lee's Tarnished Lieutenant: James Longstreet and His Place in Southern History* (Athens: University of Georgia Press, 1987).

2. On the reorganization of the army and the importance of Jackson's legacy, see Douglas Southall Freeman, *Lee's Lieutenants: A Study in Command*, 3 vols. (New York: Charles Scribner's Sons, 1942–44), 2:683–714.

Ambrose Powell Hill in a photograph taken in 1862 while he was a brigadier general.

Miller, ed., *Photographic History of the Civil War*

the 13th South Carolina complained to his wife that Hill had mishandled his troops on July 1. Had he not done so, the Third Corps could have captured "the strong position last occupied by the enemy . . . and the next day when Ewell and Longstreet came up the victory completely won." "If 'Old Stonewall' had been alive and there," suggested Welch (whose regiment served in Hill's Third Corps), "it no doubt would have been done. Hill was a good division commander, but he is not a superior corps commander. He lacks the mind and sagacity of Jackson." Henry Heth's division led the Third Corps toward

Gettysburg and suffered severe casualties during the fighting on July 1. Writing about the battle in 1877, Heth refrained from making direct comments about Hill's actions but did mention the public's questioning "whether if Stonewall Jackson had been in command of Hill's corps on the first day—July 1st—a different result would have been obtained."[3]

Other critics focused on Hill's decision to send Heth's division into Gettysburg despite Lee's orders to avoid a general engagement. In his history of Virginia during the war, Jedediah Hotchkiss observed that "A. P. Hill, always ready and anxious for a fight, but so far as known without orders from General Lee, sent the divisions of Heth and Pender toward Gettysburg. . . . [He thus] brought on an engagement with two corps of Meade's army." The careful Edward Porter Alexander averred that "Hill's movement to Gettysburg was made of his own motion, and with knowledge that he would find the enemy's cavalry in possession." "Lee's orders were to avoid bringing on an action," continued Alexander, who added that Hill's "venture is another illustration of an important event allowed to happen without supervision." No postwar critic savaged Hill more completely than John S. Mosby. In an extended apology for Jeb Stuart's absence from the army, the famous partisan officer insisted that Hill had miscalculated in sending Heth's division toward Gettysburg on the morning of July 1. "Hill and Heth in their reports, to save themselves from censure, call the first day's action a reconnaissance; this is all an afterthought," wrote Mosby. "They wanted to conceal their responsibility for the final defeat. Hill said he felt the need of cavalry—then he ought to have stayed in camp and waited for the cavalry." No one ordered Hill to advance, concluded Mosby, and Lee "never would have sanctioned it."[4]

Modern historians have joined this chorus. For example, in his massive chronicle of the artillery in Lee's army, Jennings C. Wise observed that Hill's "orders were specific not to bring on an action, but his thirst for battle was unquenchable, and . . . he rushed on, and . . . took the control of the situation

3. Spencer Glasgow Welch, *A Confederate Surgeon's Letters to His Wife* (1911; reprint, Marietta, Ga.: Continental, 1954), 66–67; Henry Heth, "Letter from Major-General Henry Heth, of A. P. Hill's Corps, A.N.V.," in *SHSP* 4:155.

4. Jedediah Hotchkiss, *Virginia*, vol. 4 of Clement A. Evans, ed., *Confederate Military History*, 12 vols. (1899; reprint, Wilmington, N.C.: Broadfoot, 1987), 403; Edward Porter Alexander, *Military Memoirs of a Confederate: A Critical Narrative* (1907; reprint, Dayton, Ohio: Morningside, 1977), 381; John S. Mosby, *Stuart's Cavalry in the Gettysburg Campaign* (1908; reprint, Gaithersburg, Md.: Olde Soldier Books, 1987), 141, 155.

out of the hands of the commander-in-chief." Warren W. Hassler's *Crisis at the Crossroads*, a monograph devoted to the action on July 1, stated unequivocally that "Hill certainly erred, as evidenced by Lee's later painful surprise, in permitting Heth to march on Gettysburg for forage and shoes." Hassler believed that Hill should have exercised greater caution "in developing the situation in the event that Federal troops were present there in numbers." Even Edwin B. Coddington, whose admirable study of the campaign set a standard for meticulous scholarship, speculated that Hill expected to find a fight as well as some shoes and provisions on the morning of July 1. Mosby may have been correct, stated Coddington, "when he charged Hill with planning a 'foray' and calling it a 'reconnaissance.'" Douglas Southall Freeman labeled the manner in which the Army of Northern Virginia stumbled into a confrontation on the first day "incautious," apportioning most of the responsibility to Jeb Stuart. "Obvious blame, also, would be charged against Powell Hill," remarked Freeman, "if he had not been sick on the 1st." That illness prevented his monitoring Heth's advance more closely and, in Freeman's view, absolved him of criticism.[5]

Richard S. Ewell's decision not to attack Cemetery Hill and Culp's Hill on the afternoon of July 1 inspired more heated discussion—and more direct comparisons with Jackson—than did Hill's conduct. Major General Isaac Ridgeway Trimble held no command on July 1 but found himself in Gettysburg with Ewell about midafternoon. "The fighting ceased about 3 P.M.," Trimble noted in his diary, "Genl. Ewell saying he did not wish to bring on a hurried engagement without orders from Lee. This was *a radical error,* for had we continued the fight, we should have got in their rear & taken the Cemetery Hill & Culps Hill." Trimble expanded on his diary entry in a speech prepared after the war and published in the 1870s. He described a tense confrontation between himself and Ewell, during which he told Ewell that Culp's Hill held the key to the Federal position and advised that a brigade be sent to occupy it. Ewell asked if Trimble were certain the hill commanded the town, prompting Trimble to reply that the general could see for himself that it did and ought to

5. Jennings C. Wise, *The Long Arm of Lee; or, The History of the Artillery of the Army of Northern Virginia, With a Brief Account of the Confederate Bureau of Ordnance,* 2 vols. (1915; reprint, Richmond, Va.: Owens, 1988), 2:615; Warren W. Hassler, *Crisis at the Crossroads: The First Day at Gettysburg* (University: University of Alabama Press, 1970), 153; Edwin B. Coddington, *The Gettysburg Campaign: A Study in Command* (New York: Charles Scribner's Sons, 1968), 273–74; Freeman, *Lee's Lieutenants* 3:170–71.

be seized at once. "General Ewell made some impatient reply," remembered Trimble, "and the conversation dropped."[6]

Junior officers also sensed a passing opportunity. J. A. Stikeleather of the 4th North Carolina, a regiment in Stephen Dodson Ramseur's brigade of Robert E. Rodes's division, entered Gettysburg on the heels of the retreating Federals and estimated that five hundred troops could have captured Cemetery Hill at that point. "The simplest soldier in the ranks felt it," he wrote his mother soon after the battle. "But, timidity in the commander that stepped into the shoes of the fearless Jackson, prompted delay, and all night long the busy axes from tens of thousands of busy hands on that crest, rang out clearly on the night air, and bespoke the preparation the enemy were making for the morrow." Another Confederate witness, writing twenty-two years after the battle, professed to have heard Brigadier General Harry Hays urge Jubal Early to strike Culp's Hill with his entire division. Early agreed that the eminence "should be occupied on the spot" but felt constrained by Ewell's orders not to advance beyond the town. Turning away from Hays and the writer, Early then muttered, "more to himself than Hays, 'If Jackson were on the field I would act on the spot.'"[7]

Influential postwar accounts by Henry Kyd Douglas and John B. Gordon were equally damning. Douglas recalled in his memoirs (written late in the nineteenth century but not published until 1940) that Ewell's staff lost heart when the general failed to follow his initial success with an assault against Cemetery Hill. According to Douglas, chief of staff Sandie Pendleton, when just out of Ewell's hearing, said "quietly and with much feeling, 'Oh, for the presence and inspiration of Old Jack for just one hour!'" Gordon characteristically placed himself at center stage in a dramatic account. His brigade, which belonged to Early's division, had pursued the broken Federals into Gettysburg;

6. William Starr Myers, ed., "The Civil War Diary of General Isaac Ridgeway Trimble," *Maryland Historical Magazine* 17 (March 1922):11 (Trimble's use of "Cemetery Hill" and "Culp's Hill," local place names that he almost certainly did not know at the time of the battle, suggests that he revised his diary after the fact); Isaac R. Trimble, "The Battle and Campaign of Gettysburg, from the Original MS. Furnished by Major Graham Daves of North Carolina," in *SHSP* 26:123–24. A more dramatic version of the meeting between Ewell and Trimble is in Randolph H. McKim, "The Gettysburg Campaign," in *SHSP* 40:273.

7. Glenn Tucker, *High Tide at Gettysburg: The Campaign in Pennsylvania* (Indianapolis: Bobbs-Merrill, 1958), 186 (quoting Stikeleather's letter, which was published in the *Raleigh* [N.C.] *Semi-Weekly Standard* on August 4, 1863); W. H. Swallow (a pseudonym), "The First Day at Gettysburg," *Southern Bivouac,* New Series, 1 (December 1885):441–42.

Lieutenant General Richard Stoddert Ewell
Library of Congress

looking southward toward the high ground, Gordon saw an opening and believed that in "less than half an hour my troops would have swept up and over those hills, the possession of which was of such momentous consequence." Two times, claimed Gordon, he ignored instructions to halt: "Not until the third or fourth order of the most peremptory character reached me did I obey." "No soldier in a great crisis ever wished more ardently for a deliverer's hand," stated Gordon, "than I wished for one hour of Jackson when I was ordered to halt. Had he been there, his quick eye would have caught at a glance the entire situation, and instead of halting me he would have urged me forward and have pressed the advantage to the utmost."[8]

8. Henry Kyd Douglas, *I Rode with Stonewall, Being Chiefly the War Experiences of the Youngest Member of Jackson's Staff from the John Brown Raid to the Hanging of Mrs. Surratt* (Chapel Hill: University of North Carolina Press, 1940), 247; John B. Gordon, *Reminiscences of the Civil War* (New York: Charles Scribner's Sons, 1903), 154–55.

Although he gave no hint of it in his official report or in his correspondence with President Davis, Robert E. Lee apparently also felt keen disappointment in Ewell. He told former Second Corps chief of ordnance William Allan in April 1868 that he could not get Ewell "to act with decision." "Stuart's failure to carry out his instructions *forced the battle of Gettysburg*," Allan paraphrased Lee in notes written immediately after their conversation, "& *the imperfect, halting way in which his corps commanders* (especially Ewell) *fought the battle, gave victory . . . finally to the foe.*" Nearly two years later, Lee confided to Allan that he often thought that "if Jackson had been there [at Gettysburg] he would have succeeded."[9] Three months before he died, Lee discussed Gettysburg with his cousin Cassius Lee, again saying that Jackson's presence would have brought victory. "Ewell was a fine officer," Lee commented, "but would never take the responsibility of exceeding his orders, and having been ordered to Gettysburg, he would not go farther and hold the heights beyond the town."[10]

In the face of such an array of evidence (and these examples only hint at its extent), it is scarcely surprising that most historians have taken Ewell to task for his decision not to assault Cemetery Hill. Douglas Southall Freeman handled this phase of Gettysburg in *Lee's Lieutenants* in a chapter titled "Ewell Cannot Reach a Decision." Granting Ewell every extenuating circumstance, concluded Freeman, the "impression persists that he did not display the initiative, resolution and boldness to be expected of a good soldier." Clifford Dowdey, whose gracefully written books on Lee and his army gained wide popularity, portrayed Ewell as a man frozen by irresolution, dependent upon Jubal Early's counsel, and fearful of Lee's adverse opinion. By the evening of July 1, argued Dowdey, Lee realized that "paralysis of will marked Ewell like a fatal disease. . . . [He] saw that Jackson's great subordinate had failed in his hour of decision." Hill had drawn Lee into a battle he did not want, believed Dowdey; then "the commander of the mobile Second Corps had robbed the army of its chance to win the field." Warren Hassler hedged on the issue of Cemetery Hill and Culp's Hill: "Ewell—a new corps commander—proved that he was by no means up to stepping into Jackson's shoes and filling them, though he was perhaps correct in not launching an attack on these eminences, as the Unionists,

9. William Allan, "Memoranda of Conversations with General Robert E. Lee," in Gary W. Gallagher, ed., *Lee the Soldier* (Lincoln: University of Nebraska Press, 1996), 14, 18.

10. Robert E. Lee Jr., *Recollections and Letters of General Robert E. Lee* (1904; reprint, Wilmington, N.C.: Broadfoot, 1988), 415–16. These quotations are as remembered by Cassius Lee's son Cazenove Lee, who passed them along to Robert E. Lee Jr.

by 5 o'clock, were well on their way toward rendering the elevations impregnable." Coddington defended Ewell's decision not to order an assault more directly, though he, too, could not resist adding that if "Ewell had been a Jackson he might have been able to regroup his forces quickly enough to attack within an hour after the Yankees had started to retreat through the town."[11]

Any judgments about the conduct of Hill and Ewell on July 1 necessarily rest on an imperfect body of evidence. It is important to evaluate the individuals who kept diaries, wrote letters or memoirs, or reported on conversations they overheard. Did they have motivations that colored their accounts? For example, is it possible that Trimble, a major general without portfolio, resented Ewell's offhand dismissal of his counsel and consequently exaggerated the lieutenant general's confusion? It is also pertinent to inquire whether soldiers who had fought under Jackson in the glory days of the Second Corps too quickly assumed that their old chief might have acted differently and accomplished more. Finally, did writers unintentionally (or intentionally) allow postwar interpretations to shape their testimony as eyewitnesses?

Among the leading examples of participants whose postwar writings must be used with great care is John B. Gordon. Few witnesses matched Gordon in his egocentrism or his willingness to play loose with the truth, and his recollections leave unwary readers with a distinct impression that the Confederacy would have triumphed if only misguided superiors such as Ewell and Early had acted on his advice. Henry Kyd Douglas displayed similar tendencies to magnify his own role and choose the embellished anecdote over mundane facts—leading some to suggest that his book should be titled *Stonewall Rode with Me* rather than *I Rode with Stonewall*. Yet these men saw so much and wrote so well that their books are cited with great frequency in the literature. Modern judgments based on such testimony necessarily reflect the flaws of the originals.[12]

---

11. Freeman, *Lee's Lieutenants* 3:172–73; Clifford Dowdey, *Death of a Nation: The Story of Lee and His Men at Gettysburg* (New York: Alfred A. Knopf, 1958), 152–53; Hassler, *Crisis at the Crossroads*, 155; Coddington, *Gettysburg Campaign*, 320–21. For a treatment of Ewell on July 1 that generally accepted the traditional interpretation (and differs markedly from the present essay), see Gary W. Gallagher, "In the Shadow of Stonewall Jackson: Richard S. Ewell in the Gettysburg Campaign," *Virginia Country's Civil War* 5 (1986):54–59.

12. A glaring example of Gordon's confident dissembling may be found in his *Reminiscences of the Civil War*, 160, where he stated that "impartial military critics, after thorough investigation, will consider . . . [it] as established . . . [that] General Lee distinctly ordered Longstreet to attack early the morning of the second day" at Gettysburg. By the time Gordon wrote this in the early twentieth century, a mass of evidence, much of it from men who had served on Lee's own staff, left little doubt that Lee had given Longstreet no such order.

Discrimination is especially important evaluating literature that embraces the myth of the Lost Cause, much of which sought to canonize Lee. As a rough yardstick, students may assume that the later the account by a soldier, the less likely it is to offer dispassionate analysis of Lee. (There are exceptions to this rule, E. Porter Alexander's writings being the most obvious.) Jubal Early anticipated this trend in postwar literature with the publication of his address on Lee delivered at Washington and Lee University on the general's birthday in 1872. Early reviewed at length "those grand achievements which have placed the name of Robert E. Lee among the foremost of the renowned historic names of the world." Because he combined the most spotless of characters with unmatched military ability, insisted Early, Lee stood alone as the greatest man yet produced by the American people. More than that, as a brilliant representative of the antebellum South's civilization, Lee offered reassuring proof that the Confederate people had waged an honorable war for independence. This vision of Lee precluded serious criticism lest an author raise doubts about his own southern loyalty, a fact not lost on those who wrote about the campaigns of the Army of Northern Virginia. This is not to say that the scores of articles published in the *Southern Historical Society Papers*, in which Early and others orchestrated a massive examination of Gettysburg, and the vast body of other postwar testimony cannot be examined with profit. Indeed, some of the most valuable information on the Confederate side of the campaign can be found in such sources. But readers should be aware that they contain much special pleading, selective recall, and even outright falsehood.[13]

Just as the evidence relating to Hill and Ewell on July 1 must not be accepted uncritically, so also must modern students resist the temptation to judge the generals outside of their historical context. Both men made decisions based on available intelligence about the Union army and an imperfect understanding of the terrain. What they did not know should not be held

13. Jubal A. Early, *The Campaigns of Gen. Robert E. Lee. An Address by Lieut. General Jubal A. Early, before Washington and Lee University, January 19th, 1872* (Baltimore: John Murphy, 1872), 3, 45. For some of the richest collections of postwar testimony by Confederate participants, see Robert Underwood Johnson and Clarence Clough Buel, eds., *Battles and Leaders of the Civil War*, 4 vols. (New York: Century, 1887) [hereinafter cited as *B&L*]; [A. K. McClure], ed., *The Annals of the War, Written by Leading Participants North and South, Originally Published in the Philadelphia Weekly Times* (Philadelphia: Times Publishing, 1879); and the periodicals *The Land We Love* (published 1866–69), *Our Living and Our Dead* (published 1874–76), *Southern Bivouac* (published 1882–85), and *Confederate Veteran* (published 1893–1932).

against them. For example, many writers have buttressed their case against Ewell by quoting a letter Winfield Scott Hancock wrote to Fitzhugh Lee in January 1878. "In my opinion," stated Hancock in response to a query from Lee, "if the Confederates had continued the pursuit of General Howard on the afternoon of the 1st July at Gettysburg, they would have driven him over and beyond Cemetery Hill." Such a statement from the man who commanded the Federal defense late on July 1 seemingly carried great weight. But should it? Hancock knew how weak the Federal defenders were at that point in the battle; Ewell did not and should not be criticized for failing to understand the situation on high ground he could not see.[14]

Factors such as the nature of Lee's orders, the condition of Hill's and Ewell's troops following their midafternoon success, problems of communication, and the normal chaos of a large battlefield also should be weighed. Finally, the fair question is whether Hill and Ewell discharged their duties reasonably well on July 1—not whether they matched the standard of excellence set by Stonewall Jackson in the campaigning from Second Manassas through Chancellorsville.

Hill almost certainly went into the Gettysburg campaign with his commanding general's full confidence. As early as October 1862, Lee had told Jefferson Davis that next to Jackson and Longstreet, "I consider A. P. Hill the best commander with me. He fights his troops well, and takes good care of them." "At present," added Lee, "I do not think that more than two commanders of corps are necessary for this army." Eight months later, in the wake of Jackson's death, Lee opted to add a third corps. "I have for the past year felt that the corps of this army were too large for one commander," Lee explained to the president, contradicting his statement of October 1862. "Nothing prevented my proposing to you to reduce their size and increase their number but my inability to recommend commanders." Lee reaffirmed his belief that Hill was "the best soldier of his grade" with the army and asked Davis to agree to

14. "Letter from General Winfield Scott Hancock," in *SHSP* 5:168–72 (quotation on page 168). Among the many Confederates who quoted Hancock to prove that Ewell should have mounted assaults against Cemetery Hill were John B. Gordon, *Reminiscences of the Civil War*, 156, and Fitzhugh Lee, *General Lee* (New York: D. Appleton, 1894), 272–73. As careful a student as Coddington, *Gettysburg Campaign*, 318, 320–21, stated that Hancock's letter indicated that to "achieve complete success after smashing the Union positions north and west of the town the Confederates would have had to continue their drive through the streets and up Cemetery Hill without a letup." Jackson might have accomplished this, observed Coddington, but Ewell could not.

his heading the new Third Corps.[15] Hill took his famous Light Division, less two brigades and led by William Dorsey Pender, with him from the Second to the Third Corps; there it joined Richard H. Anderson's division, shifted over from Longstreet's First Corps, and a new division under Henry Heth composed of two brigades from the Light Division and two others transferred to the army from Mississippi and North Carolina.

As the bulk of the Army of Northern Virginia prepared to march toward the Potomac during the first week in June, Lee instructed Hill to watch and react to the Army of the Potomac along the Rappahannock River. "You are desired to open any official communications sent to me," the commanding general told his lieutenant, "and, if necessary, act upon them, according to the dictates of your good judgment." Reminiscent of the freedom previously accorded Jackson, this grant of wide discretion suggests that Lee harbored few doubts about Hill's ability to restrain the headlong impulse to fight that had been so obvious in his conduct at Mechanicsville and elsewhere.[16]

Hill's first substantial test in his new position came on July 1 and raised questions about his impetuosity as well as his broader capacity to command a corps. Did he needlessly trigger a battle Lee hoped to avoid? And once on the verge of sweeping success late in the afternoon, did he fail to use his men to best advantage? Affirmative answers to these questions not only constitute an indictment of Hill's generalship, but they also affect any assessment of Lee's role in shaping the ultimate Confederate defeat.

Lee learned from Longstreet's scout Harrison on the night of June 28 that the Federal army had crossed the Potomac. In the absence of more substantial intelligence from his own cavalry—and fearing a Union movement against his supply line in the Cumberland Valley—Lee aborted a planned movement toward Harrisburg and issued orders on June 29 for the reconcentration of the Army of Northern Virginia on the east side of the South Mountain range. Hill and Longstreet were "to proceed from Chambersburg to Gettysburg," toward which point Ewell's divisions would march from their positions to the north and east.[17]

A surgeon on James Longstreet's staff remembered a relaxed Lee talking

15. Lee to Jefferson Davis, October 2, 1862, in U.S. War Department, *The War of the Rebellion: A Compilation of the Official Records of the Union and Confederate Armies*, 128 vols. (Washington, D.C.: GPO, 1880–1901), ser. 1, vol. 19, pt. 2:643 [hereinafter cited as *OR*; all references are to series 1]; Lee to Jefferson Davis, May 20, 1863, *ibid.*, 25 (2):810–11.

16. Lee to A. P. Hill, June 5, 1863, *OR* 27 (3):859–60.

17. *OR* 27 (2):307.

to a group of officers at his headquarters shortly after dispatching these orders: "To-morrow, gentlemen, we will not move to Harrisburg as we expected, but will go over to Gettysburg and see what General Meade is after." Heth's division of Hill's corps led the way eastward from Chambersburg to Cashtown, a hamlet eight miles west of Gettysburg, on the twenty-ninth; Pender and the Light Division followed the next day, and Anderson's orders called for his division to take the same route on July 1.[18]

On the morning of June 30, Heth sent his largest brigade, four North Carolina regiments under Brigadier General James Johnston Pettigrew, to Gettysburg in search of shoes and other supplies. A nonprofessional soldier who had compiled a dazzling record as a student at the University of North Carolina, Pettigrew spotted northern cavalry as he neared the western edge of Gettysburg and elected to withdraw rather than risk battle against a foe of unknown size and composition. He subsequently told Heth about the Federal cavalry, adding that some of his officers also had heard drums on the far side of Gettysburg, indicating the presence of Union infantry. Hill soon joined Heth and Pettigrew, and the brigadier repeated his story. Hill doubted that Pettigrew had seen more than a small detachment (he had in fact seen part of John Buford's two full brigades): "I am just from General Lee, and the information he has from his scouts corroborates that I have received from mine—that is, the enemy are still at Middleburg [some sixteen miles from Gettysburg], and have not yet struck their tents."[19]

Some of the West Pointer's disdain for civilian soldiers may have been manifest in this discussion—a professional questioning a talented amateur's observations. Perhaps sensing this, Pettigrew asked Captain Louis G. Young of his staff, who knew Hill from their service together during the Seven Days, to speak to the corps commander. Young insisted that the troops he saw were veterans rather than Home Guards; however, Hill "still could not believe that any portion of the Army of the Potomac was up; and in emphatic words, expressed the hope that it was, as this was the place he wanted it to be." Heth reiterated that he wanted the shoes. "If there is no objection," he said to Hill,

18. J. S. D. Cullen to James Longstreet, May 18, 1875, quoted in James Longstreet, *From Manassas to Appomattox: Memoirs of the Civil War in America* (Philadelphia: J. B. Lippincott, 1896), 383; OR 27 (3):943–44 (the letter from Lee to Ewell dated June 28 should be dated June 29; see Coddington, *Gettysburg Campaign,* 189).

19. OR 27 (2):607, 637; Henry Heth, "Letter from Major-General Henry Heth, of A. P. Hill's Corps, A.N.V.," in *SHSP* 4:157.

"I will take my division to-morrow and go to Gettysburg and get those shoes!" "None in the world," came the nonchalant reply. "A courier was then dispatched with this information to the general commanding," noted Hill in his official report, "and with orders to start Anderson early; also to General Ewell, informing him, and that I intended to advance the next morning and discover what was in my front."[20]

Hill's message to Ewell and Young's postwar recollection indicate that Hill considered Heth's movement on July 1 a reconnaissance-in-force. Young's account might also be construed to mean that Hill hoped to find the Federals at a disadvantage so that he could strike a blow; however, Heth stated categorically after the war that his chief stressed the importance of not precipitating an engagement. Whatever Hill's full intention, he ordered Pender to support Heth while he awaited Anderson in Cashtown.[21]

When Heth's division took the pike eastward from Cashtown just after daylight on July 1, Hill lay at his headquarters contending with an unknown malady.[22] Heth collided with Buford's cavalry about 8:00 A.M. and soon committed two brigades. The fighting swelled rapidly as Confederate artillery went into action. Back at Cashtown, Hill listened to the distant rumble and discussed its import with Lee, who had arrived shortly after the battle began. Hill

20. Louis G. Young, "Pettigrew's Brigade at Gettysburg, 1–3 July, 1863," in Walter Clark, ed., *Histories of the Several Regiments and Battalions from North Carolina in the Great War, 1861–'65*, 5 vols. (1901; reprint, Wendell, N.C.: Avera Press for Broadfoot's Bookmark, 1982), 5:116–17; Heth, "Letter from Major-General Heth," 157; *OR* 27 (2):607. A somewhat different version of the episode involving Hill, Heth, and Pettigrew appears in Henry Heth, *The Memoirs of Henry Heth*, ed. James L. Morrison (Westport, Conn.: Greenwood Press, 1974), 173. The memoirs were written in 1897, some twenty years after the letter published in *SHSP*.

21. Walter Kempster, "The Cavalry at Gettysburg," in Ken Bandy and Florence Freeland, comps., *The Gettysburg Papers*, 2 vols. (Dayton, Ohio: Morningside, 1978), 1:402; *OR* 27 (2):607. In his paper, originally presented in 1913, Kempster quoted a postwar conversation between himself and Heth.

22. Arthur James Lyon Fremantle, an English officer accompanying Longstreet at Gettysburg, recorded his impressions of Hill about 4:30 that afternoon: "General Hill now came up and told me he had been very unwell all day, and in fact he looks very delicate" (Fremantle, *Three Months in the Southern States: April–June, 1863* [1863; reprint, Lincoln: University of Nebraska Press, 1991], 254). Both of Hill's biographers make the point that Hill would have accompanied Heth's advance on July 1 if he had thought there was any chance of a major engagement. See William Woods Hassler, *A. P. Hill: Lee's Forgotten General* (Richmond: Garrett and Massie, 1962), 158–59; James I. Robertson Jr., *General A. P. Hill: The Story of a Confederate Warrior* (New York: Random House, 1987), 215.

informed Lee that Heth's instructions called for him to report the presence of any Union infantry immediately "without forcing an engagement."[23] After a short conversation with his chief, Hill rode to the front, where he arrived about noon to find that Heth had stirred a hornet's nest of Union cavalry and infantry and withdrawn to a position on Herr Ridge west of Willoughby Run. Lee joined Hill before long, and shortly after two o'clock the pair watched an artillery duel between Hill's guns and those of the Federal First Corps east of Willoughby Run.[24]

Once Lee was on the field, responsibility for the battle passed to him. In his postwar memoirs, Walter H. Taylor of Lee's staff wrote that when Lee reached the battlefield he "ascertained that the enemy's infantry and artillery were present in considerable force. Heth's division was already hotly engaged, and it was soon evident that a serious engagement could not be avoided." In fact, at that juncture only the infantry brigades of James J. Archer and Joseph Davis in Heth's division had seen serious action. The Army of Northern Virginia had not been drawn into a general battle, and it was Lee rather than Hill who subsequently decided when the other brigades of Heth's division and Pender's division would be sent forward.[25]

In sum, the charge that Hill brought on a major battle against Lee's orders simply does not hold up under careful scrutiny. He did approve a heavy reconnaissance-in-force for the morning of July 1—a movement that would have been unthinkable had Jeb Stuart been performing his duties. The need for such an action certainly is open to debate; however, Hill informed Lee and Ewell of his intentions, cautioned Heth to be careful, and arranged for Pender to be within supporting distance of Heth. Had Lee wished for Hill to exercise more restraint, he could have communicated with him on the night of June

23. *OR* 27 (2):607, 637; Walter H. Taylor, *Four Years with General Lee* (New York: D. Appleton, 1877), 92–93. Lee had told Ewell on the morning of July 1 that "he did not want a general engagement brought on till the rest of the army came up." (*OR* 27 [2]:444.) He likely communicated the same sentiment to Hill.

24. Taylor, *Four Years with Lee*, 93; Heth, *Memoirs*, 175; *OR* 27 (2):348.

25. Taylor, *Four Years with Lee*, 93. Heth went to Lee rather than Hill for permission to continue the assaults when Robert E. Rodes's division of Ewell's corps appeared on the Federal right (Heth, *Memoirs*, 175). Coddington discussed Heth's failure to go through channels (i.e., through Hill) in *Gettysburg Campaign*, 309. Hill's uncertain health and Heth's friendship with Lee might help to explain the division commander's actions. Robertson, *General A. P. Hill*, 215, argued that Hill should not be held responsible for initiating the action between Heth and Buford, but he "did become culpable once Heth became locked in combat."

30. He chose not to do so; neither did he shrink from battle when the tactical situation seemed propitious on July 1. Stuart's absence set in motion the sequence of events that erupted in fighting on July 1, and Lee gave the orders that turned a meeting engagement into a full-scale battle.

What of Hill's responsibility for failing to press the Confederate assault late in the afternoon? Between 3:00 and 4:30 P.M., Heth's division and three brigades of Pender's division, together with Rodes's division on their left, forced the Federal First Corps toward Gettysburg and finally to Cemetery Hill. To the northeast, Jubal Early's division of the Second Corps enjoyed similar success against the Union Eleventh Corps. Fortune had guided Lee's infantry to the battlefield in precisely the right places to achieve tactical success; as he watched the Union retreat from atop Seminary Ridge, Lee sensed a great opportunity if the Army of Northern Virginia took the high ground below Gettysburg. Still hamstrung by a lack of intelligence concerning the enemy's location and strength, however, he worried about "exposing the four divisions present, already weakened and exhausted by a long and bloody struggle, to overwhelming numbers of fresh troops."[26]

Hill and Lee were together on Seminary Ridge about 4:30 P.M. Nearly four hours of daylight remained. Despite his vaunted reputation as an offensive fighter, Hill evinced little enthusiasm for renewed assaults on his front. He told Lieutenant Colonel A. J. L. Fremantle, a British observer, that the Federals had fought with unusual determination all day. Heth had been wounded, many field officers were down, and casualties in some units approached critical levels. "Under the impression that the enemy were entirely routed," noted Hill in his official report, "[and with] my own two divisions exhausted by some six hours' hard fighting, prudence led me to be content with what had been gained, and not push forward troops exhausted and necessarily disordered, probably to encounter fresh troops of the enemy."[27] Hill undoubtedly shared these views with Lee, who had seen with his own eyes the condition of Hill's men. Apparently persuaded that no more could be expected of Heth's and Pender's divisions, Lee turned his attention to Ewell's corps.

Neither Lee's allusion to "four divisions present" nor Hill's description of his "exhausted" divisions acknowledged the presence near the battlefield of Richard H. Anderson's five brigades. Third Corps surgeon Welch wrote about

26. OR 27 (2):317–18.
27. Fremantle, *Three Months*, 254; OR 27 (2):607.

a month after the battle that Heth and Pender "should have been immediately reinforced by Anderson with his fresh troops." Colonel Abner Perrin, who led a brigade in Pender's division, complained bitterly to Governor Luke Bonham of South Carolina on July 29, 1863, that Anderson's division (the largest in the Third Corps) took no part in the action on the afternoon of July 1. Whether Anderson or Hill was to blame, conceded Perrin, he could not say, but he considered this to be *"the cause of the failure of the campaign."* Captain Young of Pettigrew's brigade related a conversation with Anderson after the war in which the latter stated that Lee had ordered his division to halt some two miles west of Gettysburg. Puzzled by these instructions when sounds of heavy fighting were audible nearby, Anderson sought out Lee for clarification. "General Lee replied that there was no mistake made," Anderson told Young, "and explained that his army was not all up, that he was in ignorance as to the force of the enemy in front, that . . . [Anderson's] alone of the troops present, had not been engaged, and that a reserve in case of disaster, was necessary."[28]

Hill and Lee both knew of Anderson's presence. Hill also must have known that James H. Lane's and Edward L. Thomas's brigades of Pender's division had suffered relatively light casualties. Together these troops likely could have mounted a strong assault in the available daylight. Why did Hill choose not to advocate their deployment for another attack? Perhaps Lee had told him he considered Anderson's division a reserve. Or, as William Woods Hassler has suggested, Hill may have thought that "since [he] and Lee were together . . . it was up to Lee to decide whether Anderson's division should be employed."[29] Whatever the explanation, Lee's presence on Seminary Ridge and knowledge of the pertinent facts rendered him rather than Hill primarily responsible for the decision not to press the Federals along Hill's front after 4:30 P.M.

Hill's withdrawal from the fighting shifted the spotlight to Richard S. Ewell. Before the death of Jackson, Ewell had served only briefly under Lee. The commanding general knew that soldiers in the Second Corps liked and respected "Old Bald Head" and may have heard rumors that on his deathbed

<hr/>

28. Welch, *Surgeon's Letters*, 66; Perrin's letter is reproduced in Milledge L. Bonham Jr., ed., "A Little More Light on Gettysburg," *Mississippi Valley Historical Review* 24 (March 1938):523; Young, "Pettigrew's Brigade at Gettysburg," 121.

29. William Woods Hassler, "A. P. Hill at Gettysburg: How Did He Measure Up As Stonewall Jackson's Successor?" *Virginia Country's Civil War* 5 (1986):51.

Jackson expressed a preference for Ewell as his successor.[30] Convinced that Ewell had recovered from the loss of a leg at Groveton the previous August, Lee settled on him to receive a revamped Second Corps containing Ewell's old division, under Jubal A. Early, the division once commanded by Jackson himself, now under Edward "Allegheny" Johnson, and Robert E. Rodes's division, formerly directed by D. H. Hill. In sending Ewell's name to Jefferson Davis for promotion to lieutenant general, Lee termed him "an honest, brave soldier, who has always done his duty well"—far fainter praise than that accorded Hill in the same letter. He sent Ewell's name forward, said Lee to Colonel Allan after the war, with full knowledge of "his faults as a military leader—his quick alternations from elation to despondency[,] his want of decision &c." Lee talked frankly with Ewell when he made him a lieutenant general, stressing that as a corps commander Ewell would have to exercise independent judgment. As the army embarked on the Gettysburg campaign, Lee remarked to Allan, he had hoped Ewell no longer needed minute supervision.[31]

As with Hill, Ewell's first moment of truth as a corps chief came on July 1. Recalled from his advance against Harrisburg on June 29, he placed his divisions on roads whence they might march toward Chambersburg. The next day another directive named Gettysburg as the point of concentration. By that time, Johnson's division was well on the road to Chambersburg. On the morning of July 1, Rodes's division was a few miles north of Gettysburg at Heidlersburg, and Early's brigades were some three miles east of Rodes. Allegheny Johnson's division was far to the west, just outside Chambersburg near Scotland. Ewell's orders for July 1 permitted him to march to Cashtown or Gettysburg. When Hill informed Ewell on the morning of July 1 that Heth was moving toward Gettysburg, Ewell instructed Rodes and Early to march there as well. "I notified the general commanding of my movements," wrote Ewell in his official report, "and was informed by him that, in case we found the enemy's force very large, he did not want a general engagement brought on till the

---

30. For rumors about Jackson's deathbed preference for Ewell, see Douglas Southall Freeman, *R. E. Lee: A Biography*, 4 vols. (New York: Charles Scribner's Sons, 1934–36), 3:8; Freeman, *Lee's Lieutenants* 2:690; William Dorsey Pender, *The General to His Lady: The Civil War Letters of William Dorsey Pender to Fanny Pender*, ed. William Woods Hassler (Chapel Hill: University of North Carolina Press, 1965), 237.

31. *OR* 25 (2):810; Allan, "Memoranda of Conversations with Lee," in Gallagher, ed., *Lee the Soldier*, 11.

rest of the army came up." By the time Lee's message reached him sometime after noon, Ewell knew that Hill's corps was in a fight. Indeed, some of Rodes's artillery had reached Oak Ridge and opened on the Federals in Hill's front. "It was too late to avoid an engagement without abandoning the position already taken up," Ewell later explained, "and I determined to push the attack vigorously."[32]

Rodes's infantry went into action against the Union First Corps north and northwest of Gettysburg shortly after 2:30 P.M., followed by Early's division, which approached from the north and northeast and struck the Union Eleventh Corps about an hour later. Outnumbered Federals offered stiff resistance for a time, then fell back to Cemetery Hill in the face of relentless Confederate pressure. Several thousand prisoners and some artillery fell into southern hands as Ewell's triumphant infantry surged into Gettysburg. Ewell's decision to press the attack after receiving Lee's cautionary orders had been vindicated. To the west, Hill's brigades also had advanced and taken position on Seminary Ridge. It was between 4:30 and 5:00 P.M. Ewell's critics would insist that he lost a fabulous opportunity during the next hour—the time when Hancock later told Fitzhugh Lee that the Federals were vulnerable on Cemetery Hill.[33]

Perhaps the most meticulous account of Ewell's movements after he entered Gettysburg came from the pen of George Campbell Brown. As Ewell's stepson and staff officer, Brown had direct knowledge of the events. It is true that he wrote in December 1869, a time when he believed that his stepfather had been wronged by those who said he vacillated at the decisive moment. Nonetheless, his version of what transpired accords with most of the known facts. "I shall set down facts as well & truly as I can," he wrote, "remembering them more distinctly because [they were] discussed & seem[ed] to be important at the time & soon after."[34]

Brown met Ewell as the latter entered Gettysburg amid the soldiers of

32. OR 27 (2):443–44.

33. OR 27 (2):444–45, 468–69, 552–55. For examples of postwar claims that Ewell frittered away this crucial opportunity, all of which compare Ewell to Jackson in the most unfavorable terms, see Douglas, *I Rode with Stonewall*, 247; Gordon, *Reminiscences*, 154–56; and James Power Smith, "General Lee at Gettysburg. A Paper Read before the Military Historical Society of Massachusetts, on the Fourth of April, 1905," in *SHSP* 33:143–44. Douglas and Smith had served on Jackson's staff.

34. George Campbell Brown Memoir, p. 57, Brown-Ewell Papers, Tennessee State Library and Archives, Nashville.

Rodes and Early, who "were mingling in their advance." Early soon appeared and joined Ewell. Riding forward, they "surveyed the ground & examined the position & force on Cemetery Hill. Having concluded to attack, if Hill concurred, Gen'l Ewell ordered Early & Rodes to get ready." Just then a messenger arrived from William "Extra Billy" Smith, one of Early's brigadiers, with news of Federals in the Confederate left rear. Early doubted the accuracy of this intelligence but suggested that he suspend his movements long enough to make certain the flank was secure. Ewell told him to do so: "Meantime I shall get Rodes into position & communicate with Hill."[35]

A staff officer galloped in search of Hill, eventually returning with word that he had not advanced against Cemetery Hill and that Lee, who was with Hill on Seminary Ridge, "left it to Gen'l Ewell's discretion, whether to advance alone or not." The enemy on the high ground looked formidable, continued Brown; any assault would entail moving Rodes's and Early's divisions around either end of town and reuniting them in the open ground in front of Cemetery Hill. There the troops would be "within easy cannon shot & in open view of an enemy superior in numbers & advantageously posted." Hill clearly intended to offer no support, and Johnson's division had not yet reached the battlefield. Moreover, Rodes reported that just three of his brigades were in good condition; Early also had just three within easy distance.

"It was, as I have always understood, with the express concurrence of both Rodes & Early," concluded Brown, "& largely in consequence of the inactivity of the troops under Gen'l Lee's own eye . . . that Gen'l Ewell finally decided to make no direct attack, but to wait for Johnson's coming up & with his fresh troops seize & hold the high peak [Culp's Hill] to our left of Cemetery Hill." The notion that Ewell's decision lost the battle was, in Brown's opinion, "one of those frequently recurring but tardy strokes of military genius, of which one hears long after the minute circumstances that rendered them at the time impracticable, are forgotten."

Brown's narrative includes no mention of dramatic confrontations with Trimble or Gordon. Early and Ewell are the principals, and it is thus instructive that Early's official report agrees in essentials with Brown. As he rode into town in the wake of retreating Federals, Early took in a chaotic scene. Ahead, to the south, loomed Cemetery Hill, presenting a "very rugged ascent" and defended by enemy artillery that disputed the Confederate advance. Union pris-

35. This and the following two paragraphs are based on *ibid.*, 59–61.

oners were so numerous as "really to embarrass" the southern infantry. Far from a dramatic rout (as many postwar writers would describe it), the Federal withdrawal, especially to the west, was carried out in "comparatively good order." Still, Early believed an immediate advance would expand on the success already won, and he set out to find Ewell or Hill.

Before he could locate either lieutenant general, a message arrived from Extra Billy Smith telling of a Federal threat approaching on the York Road. Early doubted the veracity of this report but thought it "proper to send General Gordon with his brigade to take charge of Smith's also, and to keep a lookout on the York road, and stop any further alarm." He also sent word to Hill, by a member of Pender's staff he had met in the town, that "if he [Hill] would send up a division, we could take the hill to which the enemy had retreated." Shortly thereafter, Early found Ewell, conveyed his views, and was "informed that Johnson's division was coming up, and it was determined with this division to get possession of a wooded hill to the left of Cemetery Hill, which it commanded."[36]

Both Brown's and Early's accounts suggest that Ewell and Early discussed the situation and concluded that a successful assault against Cemetery Hill would require help from A. P. Hill. Failing in that, Culp's Hill should be the target once Allegheny Johnson's division arrived.

Robert Rodes's report provides additional information relating to the situation at about 4:30 P.M. Even before the Federals had been cleared from Gettysburg, asserted Rodes, "the enemy had begun to establish a line of battle on the heights back of the town, and by the time my line was in a condition to renew the attack, he displayed quite a formidable line of infantry and artillery immediately in my front, extending smartly to my right, and as far as I could see to my left, in front of Early." To have assaulted that line with his division, which had suffered more than two thousand five hundred casualties, "would have been absurd." With no Confederates in evidence on Rodes's right— where Hill's corps held the southern line—and no specific orders to continue the advance, Rodes assumed that Lee's previous instructions to avoid a general engagement still held and began to place his troops in a defensive posture.[37] Brown's observation that Ewell instructed Rodes to "get ready" to advance

36. OR 27 (2):469–70. See also Early's account in Jubal A. Early, *Lieutenant General Jubal Anderson Early, C.S.A.: Autobiographical Sketch and Narrative of the War between the States* (1912; reprint, Wilmington, N.C.: Broadfoot, 1989), 269–71, which conforms closely to his official report.

37. OR 27 (2):555.

does not necessarily contradict Rodes's statement that he received no "specific orders" to do so. The division leader might well have received an initial directive to prepare his men, concluding later, when no follow-up order came, that there would be no renewal of the assault.

Three last pieces of evidence suggest that the Federals presented a daunting front along Cemetery Hill as soon as the Confederates took possession of Gettysburg. Ewell's report mentioned that the "enemy had fallen back to a commanding position known as Cemetery Hill, south of Gettysburg, and quickly showed a formidable front there." An absence of favorable positions for artillery prevented Ewell's bringing guns to bear on the Federals. Second Corps topographer Jedediah Hotchkiss's entry in his journal for July 1 noted "complete success on our part. . . . The pursuit was checked by the lateness of the hour and the position the enemy had secured in a cemetery." Even John Gordon offered testimony radically at odds with his postwar posturing. In a letter to his wife written six days after the fighting, Gordon observed that his brigade "drove [the Federals] before us in perfect confusion; but night came on [and] they fell back to a strong position & fortified themselves."[38]

While Ewell and his subordinates continued to gather the scattered Second Corps units, James Power Smith of Ewell's staff rode in search of Lee. The commanding general, meanwhile, had sent Walter Taylor to find Ewell. The two messengers undoubtedly passed each other somewhere on the field. Taylor soon reached Ewell with word that Lee had "witnessed the flight of the Federals through Gettysburg and up the hills beyond. . . . It was only necessary to press 'those people' in order to secure possession of the heights, and that, if possible, he wished him to do this." Ewell expressed no objection, remembered Taylor after the war, thereby conveying the impression that he would seek to implement Lee's order. "In the exercise of that discretion, however, which General Lee was accustomed to accord to his lieutenants," added Taylor, "and probably because of an undue regard for his admonition, given early in the day, not to precipitate a general engagement, General Ewell deemed it unwise to make the pursuit. The troops were not moved forward, and the enemy proceeded to occupy and fortify the position which it was designed that General Ewell should seize."[39]

38. OR 27 (2):445; Jedediah Hotchkiss, *Make Me a Map of the Valley: The Civil War Journal of Stonewall Jackson's Topographer*, ed. Archie P. McDonald (Dallas: Southern Methodist University Press, 1973), 157; John B. Gordon to My own *precious wife*, July 7, 1863, Gordon Family Papers (MS 1637), University of Georgia Special Collections, Athens.

39. Taylor, *Four Years with Lee*, 95–96.

Taylor's account is notable for its distortion of the conditions on Ewell's end of the field. It describes a Federal "flight" when most of the Union troops maintained some order to their lines; it claims that Ewell failed to execute Lee's order to take the heights when Lee had only suggested an attack against the high ground if the situation seemed favorable; and it speaks of Federals, as a result of Ewell's dereliction, "occupying and fortifying ground" that they already held and were fortifying. Overall, Taylor's narrative illustrates nicely the degree to which officers not present on the Confederate left, including Lee in his postwar statements, minimized the obstacles faced by Ewell and exaggerated the Second Corps chief's indecision.

Ewell confronted a very difficult choice on the late afternoon of July 1. Lee manifestly wished for him to capture Cemetery Hill. Accomplishment of this object would have entailed not a continuation of the previous assaults, as so many of Ewell's critics blithely claimed, but the preparation and mounting of an entirely new assault using portions of Rodes's and Early's divisions. With enough time to gather the troops and stage them south of town, Ewell might have brought to bear six brigades—at most six to seven thousand men. Numerous factors militated against a rapid deployment of such a striking force. The streets of Gettysburg were clogged with men, and units were intermixed; the soldiers were tired after a long day of marching and fighting; thousands of Union prisoners demanded attention; Extra Billy Smith's warning of Federals on the York Pike and later cavalry reports of menacing Union troops were potentially ominous. Most important, Union strength on the heights was unknown, though clearly growing, and Allegheny Johnson's division had yet to reach a position from which it might support an assault.

Douglas Southall Freeman wrote that Ewell could not reach a decision. But Ewell did reach a decision—not to attack Cemetery Hill. Although it was not the decision that Lee wished him to make, it certainly was reasonable given the situation. None of which answers the question of whether Ewell lost his nerve that eventful afternoon. Perhaps he did. Perhaps, as Lee and other critics of Ewell later suggested, the general's old inability to function without specific orders paralyzed him.

If that was the case, Lee must shoulder at least some of the responsibility for Ewell's failure. At Gettysburg, Lee applied the same loose rein with Ewell and Hill that had worked so well with Longstreet and Jackson during the previous year. He as yet had no concrete evidence that his new lieutenants would prove unequal to the task of directing a corps (that evidence would accumulate rapidly from July 1863 onward), and it made sense to give them latitude. But if, as he told Colonel Allan after the war, Lee knew that Ewell lacked decisiveness, perhaps he should have modified his method of command on the afternoon of July 1. If he issued a discretionary order when he really wanted Ewell to take those heights (as Taylor's testimony implied), Lee should have known that an indecisive Ewell might react as he did. Direct instructions would have avoided any confusion.

A. P. Hill and Richard S. Ewell have suffered more than a century's carping about their conduct on July 1, 1863. Neither of them performed brilliantly; each worked in the immense shadow of Stonewall Jackson, whose greatest triumph remained vividly present in the minds of soldiers in the Army of Northern Virginia. Hill did not cause the battle to be fought, nor did he or Ewell cost the Confederacy a more impressive victory. At every crucial moment, Lee was on the field and able to manage events. In the end, he more than any of his lieutenants controlled the first day's action. Anyone seeking to apportion responsibility for what transpired on the Confederate side on the opening day at Gettysburg should look first to the commanding general.

★ 9 ★

Revisiting the 1862 and 1864 Valley Campaigns

Stonewall Jackson and Jubal Early in the Shenandoah

The campaigns waged in the Shenandoah Valley by Stonewall Jackson and Jubal A. Early have inspired dramatically different sets of images. Jackson's campaign in April–June 1862 usually has been analyzed with almost breathless admiration for the audacity and resolve that yielded Confederate triumph against long odds. With fewer than 20,000 soldiers, Jackson confounded Federal opponents who collectively led more than 60,000 men, won battles that lifted morale across the Confederacy, and gained renown on both sides of the Potomac and among European observers. Early's campaign during June–October 1864 has garnered far fewer accolades. Commanding a smaller force than Jackson had led, Early crafted several victories and tied down thousands of Federal troops but ultimately suffered shattering defeat. Reviled by fellow Confederates as the man who "lost" the Valley, Early ended the war in disgrace.[1]

1. Lee alluded to public unhappiness with Early when he informed his lieutenant in late March 1865 that he was removing him from command in the Shenandoah Valley. See Lee to

Popular perceptions of the two Valley campaigns remain highly favorable to Jackson and far more critical of Early. The ultimate results of the operations are beyond debate—Jackson emerged victorious and Early did not. But if available resources, quality of Federal opponents, tactical efficiency, and the degree to which each man accomplished his strategic goals are taken into account, Early's effort stands up well against Jackson's in many respects.

A few words about the commanders and their campaigns will set the stage for a comparative assessment. Jackson's fame is such that he requires little introduction.[2] He ranks among the best-known figures of the war, a towering presence on the military landscape of Virginia defined in a handful of famous vignettes. In the July heat at First Manassas in 1861, he prodded his brigade into an effort on Henry Hill that secured its everlasting fame and his wonderful nickname Stonewall. He pushed his soldiers unsparingly during the campaign of Second Manassas, confirming their reputation as "foot cavalry" in a prodigious march around John Pope's Army of Virginia, and once on the battlefield he staged a stalwart defense against heavy Federal assaults. Along the Orange Turnpike west of Chancellorsville on May 2, 1863, he reached the apogee of his storied collaboration with Robert E. Lee when he quietly ordered young Robert E. Rodes to launch the most storied flank attack of the war.

Several characteristics marked Jackson as a Confederate commander. Secretive and hard-hitting, he demanded a great deal of himself and of his officers and men. He embraced a hard vision of war and always sought to inflict the greatest possible damage on the enemy. His personality and attitudes stood in stark contrast to the romantic traits often associated with Confederate officers. Clear evidence of Jackson's harsh notions about war may be found in the wartime notebooks of a member of Confederate general Richard H. Anderson's staff, who recorded that Jackson "once said the only objection he had to Genl Lee was that he did not hate Yankees enough." A woman in North Carolina spoke to the unrelenting quality of Jackson's leadership in June 1862, remarking that "he is the only one of our generals who gives the enemy no rest,

Early, March 30, 1865, reproduced in Jubal A. Early, *Lieutenant General Jubal Anderson Early, C.S.A.: Autobiographical Sketch and Narrative of the War between the States* (1912; reprint, Wilmington, N.C.: Broadfoot, 1989), 468–69.

2. The best biography of Jackson is James I. Robertson Jr., *Stonewall Jackson: The Man, the Soldier, the Legend* (New York: Macmillan, 1997). Of the older biographies, Frank E. Vandiver's *Mighty Stonewall* (New York: McGraw-Hill, 1957) stands out as both well researched and gracefully written.

no time to entrench themselves." A northern diarist, writing from New York City in September 1862, agreed, terming Jackson "our national bugaboo."[3]

Jackson's personal beliefs and habits added to his fame. Contemporaries and generations of later readers noted his deep Christian faith and compared him to other great religious warriors, labeling him the Confederate Cromwell or the southern Joshua. They also savored—and undoubtedly exaggerated— his notions about health, his alleged love of lemons, and other elements of his odd personality.

For the purposes of this comparison, it is crucial to note that Jackson began the Valley campaign in March 1862 with a reputation as a good soldier and emerged three months later as the military idol of the South. Few campaigns in any American war have propelled a commander to such fame in so short a time.

Jubal A. Early went to the Valley in 1864 as commander of Jackson's old Second Corps.[4] A Virginian and an 1837 graduate of West Point, Early had resigned from the army after about a year to become a lawyer in Rocky Mount, Virginia. He returned to military service as major of the 1st Virginia Volunteers during the war with Mexico, resuming his law practice after that conflict ended. A member of the Virginia state convention in 1861, he opposed secession but joined the Confederate army after his state left the Union. He fought well from First Manassas through the beginning stage of the Overland campaign, rising to the rank of lieutenant general.

A capable soldier, Early displayed energy and initiative on many battlefields and earned Jackson's and Lee's high opinion. Lee understood Early's strengths—especially his self-reliance and daring—as well as his weaknesses, which included extreme ambition and a dismissive attitude toward the Confederate cavalry. It was a measure of Lee's confidence in Early, whom he called

3. William McWillie Notebooks, Mississippi Department of Archives and History, Jackson; Catherine Ann Devereux Edmondston, *"Journal of a Secesh Lady": The Diary of Catherine Ann Devereux Edmondston, 1860–1866,* ed. Beth Gilbert Crabtree and James W. Patton (Raleigh: North Carolina Division of Archives and History, 1979), 191–92 (entry for June 11); George Templeton Strong, *Diary of the Civil War, 1860–1865,* ed. Allan Nevins (New York: Macmillan, 1962), 252 (entry for September 3). On Jackson's hard view of war, see Charles Royster, *The Destructive War: William Tecumseh Sherman, Stonewall Jackson, and the Americans* (New York: Alfred A. Knopf, 1991).

4. Early's *Autobiographical Sketch and Narrative,* which has an undeserved reputation as being untrustworthy, is indispensable to any consideration of his Confederate career. The best biography is Charles C. Osborne, *Jubal: The Life and Times of General Jubal A. Early, CSA, Defender of the Lost Cause* (Chapel Hill, N.C.: Algonquin Press, 1992).

Thomas Jonathan "Stonewall" Jackson in a photograph taken in February 1862, on the eve of his Valley campaign.
Miller, ed., *Photographic History of the Civil War*

affectionately "my bad old man," that he often gave him difficult assignments. Confederate artillerist Robert Stiles remarked about this phenomenon in his often-quoted postwar memoir: "The commanding general reposed the utmost confidence in him. This he indicated by selecting him so frequently for independent command, and to fill the most critical, difficult, and I had almost said hopeless, positions, in the execution of his own great plans; as for example, when he left him at Fredericksburg [during the Chancellorsville campaign] with nine thousand men to neutralize Sedgwick with thirty thousand."[5]

5. Robert Stiles, *Four Years under Marse Robert* (1903; reprint, Dayton, Ohio: Morningside, 1977), 188–89. For a wartime mention of Lee's nickname for Early, see the letter signed "Phax" in the Mobile *Advertiser*, September 15, 1864.

Lieutenant General Jubal Anderson Early
Johnson and Buel, eds., *Battles and Leaders of the Civil War*

Early was in many ways as much of a character as the weirdly brilliant Jackson. An exceedingly sarcastic man, he found frequent targets for his jibes. G. Moxley Sorrel of James Longstreet's staff praised Early's soldierly abilities while noting his "snarling, rasping disposition" and "biting tongue [that] made him anything but popular."[6] A lifelong bachelor who nonetheless fathered several children, Early often singled out happily married men as targets for special scorn. He also stood among the most accomplished cursers in the Army of Northern Virginia, who, according to many witnesses, strung together imagi-

6. Gilbert Moxley Sorrel, *Recollections of a Confederate Staff Officer* (1905; reprint, Jackson, Tenn.: McCowat-Mercer, 1957), 43, 50.

native combinations of profanity that provoked both outrage and laughter. Although no contemporary recorded any of Early's more enthusiastic outbursts of profanity, an incident at Lynchburg in June 1864 conveys some sense of this element of his personality. Arriving at the outskirts of the city with his veteran Second Corps just as Federal troops approached, Early drew rein among some artillerists, raised himself in his saddle, and, shaking his fist at the enemy, shouted in a piercing treble: "No buttermilk rangers after you now, you God-damned Blue-butts!"[7]

Few men professed great affection for Early, who once wrote a very revealing estimate of himself. "I was never blessed with popular or captivating manners," he observed, "and the consequence was that I was often misjudged and thought to be haughty and disdainful in my temperament. . . . I was never what is called a popular man." Many of his soldiers, who called him Old Jube or Old Jubilee, did admire his personal bravery under fire. "Troops that can win the approbation of General Early for coolness and courage on the field of battle, are entitled to it," observed an Augusta, Georgia, newspaper in 1863, "for no officer we have possesses more of these qualities or despises more heartily the lack of them in others."[8]

Early departed for the Shenandoah Valley in June 1864 with a substantial military reputation if few friends. The death of Jackson thirteen months earlier and the wounding of James Longstreet at the Wilderness had left Early the best corps commander in the Army of Northern Virginia, and Lee's decision to entrust this major operation to him bespoke a high opinion of his prickly lieutenant. Four months later, Early's reputation had been savaged because of his defeats at the hands of Philip H. Sheridan. Civilians and soldiers alike blamed him for Confederate disasters in the Valley, and almost always there was a statement that went something like, "If we had only had Jackson in the Valley again, none of this would have happened."

Operations in the Valley thus wrought opposite transformations on the reputations of Jackson and Early. Did their contemporaries, as well as generations of later critics, judge fairly in evaluating the two campaigns?

Robert E. Lee served as principal architect of both Valley campaigns, envisioning them in large measure as strategic diversions to weaken pressure on

7. Rebecca Yancey Williams, *The Vanishing Virginian* (New York: E. P. Dutton, 1940), 85–86 (quoting John Warwick Daniel, Early's assistant adjutant general).

8. Early, *Autobiographical Sketch and Narrative*, xxiv–xxv; Augusta *Daily Constitutionalist*, January 6, 1863.

Richmond. In late April 1862, George B. McClellan's massive Army of the Potomac advanced toward Richmond up the Peninsula between the York and James rivers. Irvin McDowell menaced the Confederate capital from the vicinity of Fredericksburg with another major Federal force. Smaller armies under Nathaniel P. Banks in the Shenandoah Valley and John C. Frémont in the Alleghenies farther west completed the roster of northern threats in the Old Dominion. Lee wanted Jackson, who commanded a modest force in the Valley, to occupy all the Federals west of the Blue Ridge; otherwise, they might join McDowell at Fredericksburg for an advance against Richmond in conjunction with McClellan's movements on the Peninsula. Jackson had attacked a piece of Banks's army at Kernstown on March 23, thereby preventing its transfer to McClellan. In late April, Lee gave Jackson authority over Richard S. Ewell's division, which brought his strength to about 17,500 men, and encouraged Stonewall to strike a blow against Banks.

Jackson quickly demonstrated how a resourceful commander of an inferior force could use speed and audacity to achieve great results. On May 8, 1862, he concentrated part of his troops at the village of McDowell, in the Alleghenies west of Staunton, stopping the advance guard of Frémont's army and knocking it deeper into western Virginia. Returning to the Valley, he marched northward, crossed the Massanutten Range to the Luray Valley, and captured several hundred Federals in a skirmish at Front Royal on May 23. Two days later he won the battle of First Winchester against Banks, driving the enemy toward the Potomac River. By May 29, Jackson's troops skirmished with Federals near Harpers Ferry, having cleared most of the lower Valley of Union forces.

Positioned near Harpers Ferry, Jackson lay vulnerable to a three-pronged Federal pincers movement designed to isolate him in the lower Valley. Frémont would march from the west, a division under James Shields would move east from Front Royal, and Banks would apply pressure from the north. But Jackson pushed his men unmercifully and, assisted by indifferent performances by all three Federal commanders, escaped the trap and marched south to near Harrisonburg. There he defeated Frémont at Cross Keys on June 8 and Shields at Port Republic on June 9, after which he moved to reinforce Lee's army outside Richmond while the Federals retreated down the Shenandoah and Luray valleys.[9]

9. Two good general studies of Jackson's Valley campaign are William Allan's *History of the Campaign of Gen. T. J. (Stonewall) Jackson in the Shenandoah Valley of Virginia. From November 4, 1861, to June 17, 1862* (1880; reprint, Dayton, Ohio: Morningside, 1987) and Robert G. Tan-

Jackson had accomplished his strategic goals beautifully. He pinned down Banks and Frémont and convinced the Federals to hold McDowell at Fredericksburg as well, thereby denying McClellan thousands of reinforcements. He had used speed, intimate knowledge of the Valley's geography (supplied by cartographer Jedediah Hotchkiss), and a willingness to assume risks to earn success. None of his battles had been a tactical masterpiece; indeed, he had struggled to win despite having superior numbers at McDowell and again at Port Republic, and Banks's soldiers had escaped from the battlefield at First Winchester with minimal damage. Still, these small victories reached a Confederate populace starved for good news from the military front. A string of defeats had befallen Confederate arms in the western theater between February and mid-May 1862, and McClellan had reached Richmond's suburbs virtually without a fight. The timing of Jackson's successes in the Valley could not have been more opportune, and the Confederate people responded by making Stonewall a transcendent hero.

Two years later, Lee selected Jubal Early to lead Jackson's old Second Corps into the Valley for another crucial operation. With Grant's army pressing against the defenses of Richmond, a Federal force under David Hunter marched southward up the Valley, burning as it went and heading for Lynchburg. A key city in terms of supply and communications, Lynchburg could not be sacrificed. Lee gave Early orders on June 12, 1864, that included a range of goals. Old Jube was to prevent Hunter from capturing Lynchburg, then march down the Valley clearing it of Federals, and finally, cross the Potomac River and threaten Washington. If all went well, Early's campaign would oblige Grant to weaken the Army of the Potomac by dispatching units to protect Washington, perhaps opening the way for Lee to launch a blow against Federals investing the southern capital. In this last element, Early faced a task similar to Jackson's when he had undertaken his campaign in the Valley.

Early moved toward Lynchburg in mid-June. He defeated Hunter there on June 18–19, pursuing him into western Virginia before turning north for a swift march down the Valley. His soldiers crossed the Potomac into Maryland, swung north and east over South Mountain and the Catoctin Range, and de-

---

ner's *Stonewall in the Valley: Thomas J. "Stonewall" Jackson's Shenandoah Valley Campaign, Spring 1862* (revised ed., Mechanicsburg, Pa.: Stackpole, 1996). See also Douglas Southall Freeman's excellent analytical narrative in vol. 2 of *Lee's Lieutenants: A Study in Command*, 3 vols. (New York: Charles Scribner's Sons, 1942–44). The best work on any of the episodes that made up Jackson's campaign is Robert K. Krick's exhaustive *Conquering the Valley: Stonewall Jackson at Port Republic* (New York: William Morrow, 1996).

scended on Washington. On July 9, Early's men defeated a motley array of northern troops under Lew Wallace in the battle of the Monocacy, just south of Frederick, Maryland, after which they proceeded through stifling heat and dust toward the United States capital. Hard marching brought Early's tired soldiers to the outer defenses of Washington on July 11. A day of skirmishing ensued, during which Abraham Lincoln briefly came under fire. Early learned that elements of the Federal Sixth Corps had reinforced the Washington garrison, and, outnumbered and unable to force his way into the city, he decided to withdraw to Berryville in the lower Shenandoah Valley.

Thus ended the first phase of Early's Valley campaign. In a month's marching and fighting, he had accomplished everything Lee asked. He had saved Lynchburg, cleared the Valley of Federals, threatened Washington, and compelled Grant to dispatch reinforcements from the Army of the Potomac.[10] Lincoln's somewhat panicked request to Grant on the afternoon of July 10 betrayed northern concern about Early's activities. The president urged Grant to leave enough men at Petersburg "to retain your hold" and to bring the rest of the army to Washington and "make a vigorous effort to destroy the enemie's force in this vicinity." Early provided his summary of the campaign in a typically salty remark to an officer as the Confederates began their withdrawal to Virginia: "Major, we haven't taken Washington, but we've scared Abe Lincoln like hell!"[11]

The concluding phase of the 1864 Valley campaign began in late July and soon developed into a fluid second front in Virginia. With Lee and Grant mired in siege operations around Richmond and Petersburg, Early remained in the Valley, threatening to move back into Maryland, protecting the Confederate harvest, and forcing the Federals to deploy thousands of men to oppose him. After a Confederate victory at Second Kernstown on July 24 and the burning of Chambersburg, Pennsylvania, on July 30, Grant assigned Philip H.

---

10. On Early's campaign between mid-June and mid-July 1864, see Frank E. Vandiver's *Jubal's Raid: General Early's Famous Attack on Washington in 1864* (New York: McGraw-Hill, 1960), Benjamin Franklin Cooling's *Jubal Early's Raid on Washington, 1864* (Baltimore: Nautical and Aviation Publishing, 1989), and vol. 3 of Freeman's *Lee's Lieutenants*.

11. Abraham Lincoln to Ulysses S. Grant, July 10, 1864, in Abraham Lincoln, *The Collected Works of Abraham Lincoln*, ed. Roy P. Basler, 9 vols. (New Brunswick, N.J.: Rutgers University Press, 1953), 7:437; Henry Kyd Douglas, *I Rode with Stonewall: The War Experiences of the Youngest Member of Jackson's Staff* (Chapel Hill: University of North Carolina Press, 1940), 295–96.

Sheridan the task of defeating Early and destroying the Valley as a Confederate granary. A period of maneuvering with little combat followed during August and the first two weeks of September, during which Sheridan built the Army of the Shenandoah into a force of more than 40,000 men to oppose Early's 14,000.

Early's Valley campaign climaxed in three battles between mid- September and mid-October 1864. On September 19, Sheridan attacked in the battle of Third Winchester or the Opequon. Stubborn Confederate resistance collapsed late that afternoon, as Sheridan's overwhelming advantage in numbers (especially cavalry) carried the field. Three days later at Fisher's Hill, just south of Strasburg, Sheridan trounced Early's Army of the Valley again. This time the Confederates retreated southward to Rockfish Gap, and Sheridan systematically burned a swath through the lower Valley.

Lee sent reinforcements to Early in October, and the Confederates pursued Sheridan to the vicinity of Middletown, just north of Strasburg. In the battle of Cedar Creek on October 19, Early launched the most impressive surprise attack of the war. This assault involved a night march, two crossings of the North Fork of the Shenandoah River, and the coordination of four Confederate columns at dawn on the nineteenth. Jubilant Confederates routed two-thirds of Sheridan's much larger army during a remarkable five-hour morning offensive. A combination of hesitation on Early's part; exhaustion and hunger among Confederate soldiers, who fell away from the ranks to plunder Union camps; and Sheridan's rallying his men to mount a powerful counterattack turned the tide, and northern numbers again brought utter defeat to the Army of the Valley. Cedar Creek ended major operations in the Shenandoah. The Confederacy would never again use the area as a route of invasion or as a vital source of foodstuffs and livestock.[12]

Early lingered in the Valley until the spring of 1865. On March 2, he and a pathetic remnant of his Valley command were crushed at the battle of Waynesboro. Public outcry in the South compelled Lee to remove Early from

12. On the concluding phase of Early's Valley campaign, see Jeffry D. Wert, *From Winchester to Cedar Creek: The Shenandoah Campaign of 1864* (Carlisle, Pa.: South Mountain Press, 1987); Gary W. Gallagher, ed., *Struggle for the Shenandoah: Essays on the 1864 Valley Campaign* (Kent, Ohio: Kent State University Press, 1991); and vol. 3 of Freeman's *Lee's Lieutenants*. The best tactical study of any of Early's engagements in the Valley is Theodore C. Mahr, *The Battle of Cedar Creek: Showdown in the Shenandoah, October 1–30, 1864* (Lynchburg, Va.: H. E. Howard, 1992).

command, and Early left active service a thoroughly discredited figure. Few Confederates realized that he had compelled Grant to detach for lengthy service away from the Army of the Potomac one of the best Union commanders in Sheridan, and to concentrate more than 40,000 men to deal with Early's 12,000 to 14,000. It had been a good trade-off for Lee, but one almost completely obscured by the ultimate Confederate defeat in the Valley. Even Lee had not realized the odds Early faced against Sheridan. "Lee consistently and most seriously underestimated the force Sheridan employed in the Valley," noted Douglas Southall Freeman: "No other mathematical calculation made by Lee during the war was so much in error."[13]

Stonewall Jackson's Valley campaign always will be studied as a classic example of brilliant military maneuvering and fighting. Early's campaign probably never will be seen in a similarly glowing light. Jackson certainly performed in exemplary fashion, but Early's activities in the Valley measure up very well against the Mighty Stonewall's. Several comparative dimensions of the two operations suggest why this is so.

The quality of northern leadership heavily favored Jackson. Nathaniel P. Banks, a politician turned general, compiled a record of unbroken futility against a range of Confederate commanders in theaters from the Red River in Louisiana to the Shenandoah Valley. He fully earned the derisive nickname "Commissary" bestowed upon him by contemptuous Confederates. John C. Frémont manifested similar ineptitude as a general. His many failures during the Civil War suggest that he probably had reached the peak of his abilities when he led a handful of hungry explorers across rugged western mountains during the antebellum years. Between them, Banks and Frémont demonstrated nothing but incompetence in the Valley, a record matched or only modestly improved upon by other Federal generals such as Robert H. Milroy and James Shields. Perhaps most important, no Union commander exercised overall control in the Valley in 1862, which virtually guaranteed problems of coordination.

Early's initial opponents proved equally inept, and he easily defeated David Hunter at Lynchburg and Lew Wallace at the Monocacy. But Philip Sheridan brought considerable military gifts to the later phase of the 1864 campaign. Although Sheridan suffered tactical lapses at both Third Winchester and Fisher's Hill, he had an ability to inspirit troops on a battlefield rivaled by few commanders on either side during the war. "God *damn* you, don't cheer

13. Freeman, *Lee's Lieutenants* 3:611.

me! There's lots of fight in you men yet! God damn you! Come up!" he had shouted to Union soldiers upon reaching the battlefield at Cedar Creek after his army had been pushed back several miles.[14] Sheridan's fiery example more than once brought impressive results during fighting in the Valley. The Federal commander also understood how to use his superior numbers, pressing Early relentlessly and ruthlessly carrying out Grant's orders to destroy the Valley as a breadbasket for Lee's army (Grant hoped Sheridan would accomplish even more). Beyond Sheridan, the Army of the Shenandoah counted such able men as George Crook, Horatio Wright, and George A. Custer among its generals. Moreover, Sheridan exercised overall control in the Valley, answering only to Grant, who gave him a free hand, and to the secretary of war. During his entire Confederate career, Jackson never faced an opponent of Sheridan's ability. Nor did Jackson face the task of influencing a Union general-in-chief as resolute as Grant. Early's operations in June and July, which placed Washington at much greater risk than anything Jackson did in May and June 1862, had relatively little impact on the northern high command because Grant was in charge. Unlike McClellan and other Union officers in 1862, Grant simply could not be stampeded.

Jackson also enjoyed an edge over Early in the troops he led and faced. In terms of Confederate soldiers, Jackson possessed a slight advantage in numbers and quality. He commanded just more than 17,000 men for most of his campaign, almost all of whom were original volunteers who willingly had gone to war. The Stonewall Brigade, for example, was in its fighting prime. Early commanded 14,000 men or fewer for most of his campaign. They also served well but were neither as fresh nor as well supplied as Jackson's men had been. Early did have superior subordinates. Robert E. Rodes, John B. Gordon, Stephen Dodson Ramseur, and Joseph B. Kershaw performed ably as division chiefs (Rodes and Ramseur lost their lives at Third Winchester and Cedar Creek respectively), exceeding the records of Richard S. Ewell, Richard Taylor, and Jackson's other principal lieutenants. Neither Jackson nor Early could count on competent cavalry support.

As for Federal troops, Jackson fought against much weaker foes. Writers

14. Sheridan is quoted in A. Wilson Greene, "Union Generalship in the 1864 Valley Campaign," in Gallagher, ed., *Struggle for the Shenandoah,* 72. For a comparison of Early and Sheridan in the Valley, see Gary W. Gallagher, "Jubal A. Early and Philip H. Sheridan in the 1864 Valley Campaign: A Comparative Assessment," in Barbara Hughett, ed., *Civil War Leadership: Essays Presented at the 50th Anniversary Symposium of the Civil War Round Table of Chicago* (Dayton, Ohio: Morningside, 1992), 61–70.

frequently state that he defeated more than 60,000 of the enemy with his 17,000 men, but there never were nearly that many Union troops *together* in the Valley. The number 60,000 includes troops stationed far from the Valley with McDowell or other commanders. Union strength in a single force seldom reached even 20,000 against Jackson, and the men represented some of the poorest northern troops. They suffered from low morale, exhibited little confidence in their leaders, and contended with problems of supply.

Early labored under far more difficult circumstances. He fought an army of 35,000 to 45,000 directed by the aggressive Sheridan, including the veteran Sixth Corps and the competent Nineteenth Corps. At no time could Early have gained a tactical advantage in numbers against Sheridan. Even after the brilliant flanking movement at Cedar Creek, his troops assaulted more numerous Federals. Jackson receives well-earned plaudits for placing the bulk of his small army in a position to strike fragments of the Union forces. But no Confederate commander, including Jackson, could have duplicated that achievement against Sheridan in September and October 1864.

The scale of marching and fighting offers a final useful point of comparison. By Jedediah Hotchkiss's careful reckoning, Early's soldiers marched more than 1,500 miles between mid-June and mid-October 1864, a figure about two and one-half times larger than the distance Jackson's men traversed between late March and the second week of June 1862.[15] Casualties tell a similar story. Jackson's six largest engagements—First Kernstown, McDowell, Front Royal, First Winchester, Cross Keys, and Port Republic—resulted in approximately 5,500 northern and 2,750 Confederate casualties (prisoners accounted for half of the northern total), modest losses when compared to even a mid-sized Civil War battle. Of the six, only First Winchester and Port Republic properly should be called battles. The rest amounted to large-scale skirmishes in which each side lost fewer than 1,000 men. In contrast, Early's six largest engagements—Lynchburg, the Monocacy, Second Kernstown, Third Winchester, Fisher's Hill, and Cedar Creek—produced more than 15,000 Union and about 10,000 Confederate casualties. At both Third Winchester and Cedar Creek, Sheridan lost approximately as many men in one day as all of Jackson's opponents combined during the entire 1862 Valley campaign.[16]

15. Jedediah Hotchkiss, *Make Me a Map of the Valley: The Civil War Journal of Stonewall Jackson's Topographer*, ed. Archie P. McDonald (Dallas, Tex.: Southern Methodist University Press, 1973), 244.

16. Casualties for battles in the 1862 Valley campaign break down as follows: Kernstown

Jackson manifestly possessed several advantages that rendered his task in 1862 much easier than Early's in 1864. Against weak opponents leading second-line troops, he won a series of small victories that enabled him to accomplish the strategic goals laid out by Lee. Against equally weak Union officers in June and July 1864, Early also won victories and achieved his strategic goals. He managed far less success against the talented Sheridan, though he still occupied more than 40,000 Federals and denied Grant Sheridan's services on the Richmond front for nearly three months.

For those who like to indulge in comparisons, two questions naturally arise concerning the Valley campaigns. First, could Early have duplicated Jackson's dazzling performance in the spring of 1862? The answer must be probably not—although he almost certainly would have bested the undistinguished cast of Union commanders. Second, would Jackson have defeated Sheridan in the battles of September and October 1864? Again, the answer must be no. The campaign would have been different, but not its outcome. Sheridan had the ability and the numbers to vanquish any opponent laboring under the handicaps imposed on Jubal Early. Both Jackson and Early deserve high marks for their work in the Valley. But if forced to choose one or the other operation to command, most reasonable people would ask to be placed in Jackson's rather than Early's position.

(March 23), 590 U.S. and 720 C.S.; McDowell (May 8), 250 U.S. and 500 C.S.; Front Royal (May 23), 900 U.S. and 50 C.S.; First Winchester (May 25), 2,019 U.S. and 400 C.S.; Cross Keys (June 8), 685 U.S. and 690 C.S.; Port Republic (June 9), 1,000 U.S. and 800 C.S.—total, just fewer than 5,500 U.S. (more than half of whom were captured) and just more than 2,750 C.S. Casualties for the 1864 Valley campaign were: Lynchburg (June 16–18), 950 U.S. and 500 C.S.; Monocacy (July 9), 2,000 U.S. and 700 C.S.; Second Kernstown (July 24), 1,200 U.S. and 500 C.S.; Third Winchester or Opequon (September 19), 5,000 U.S. and 4,000 C.S.; Fisher's Hill (September 22), 525 U.S. and 1,200 C.S.; Cedar Creek (October 19), 5,600 U.S. and 2,900 C.S.—total, just more than 15,000 U.S. and just fewer than 10,000 C.S. (about half of whom were prisoners at the last three battles). These figures are approximate, especially on the Confederate side.

III

Fighting for Historical Memory

★ IO ★

Jubal A. Early, the Lost Cause, and Civil War History

A Persistent Legacy

Jubal Anderson Early understood the power of the printed word to influence perceptions of historical events. One of Robert E. Lee's principal lieutenants during the Civil War, he sought to create a written record celebrating the Confederacy's military resistance. Early hoped that future generations would rely on this record, the essence of which can be distilled into a few sentences. Lee was a heroic soldier who led an outnumbered army of Confederate patriots against a powerful enemy. With Stonewall Jackson initially at his side, he faced northern generals of minimal talent who later lied in print to explain their failures. Against these men and later against Ulysses S. Grant, a clumsy butcher who understood only that vast northern resources of men and maté- riel must be expended freely, the Confederate commander worked his magic across a Virginia landscape that functioned as the cockpit of the war. Lee and his Army of Northern Virginia set a standard of valor and accomplish- ment equal to anything in the military history of the Western world until finally, worn out but never defeated, they laid down their weapons at Appo- mattox. If the youth of the white South and succeeding generations of Amer- icans and foreign readers accepted his version of the war, believed Early, ex-

Confederates would have salvaged their honor from the wreck of seemingly all-encompassing defeat.

These ideas constitute part of what has come to be called the Myth of the Lost Cause, an explanation for secession and Confederate defeat propagated in the years following the Civil War. Early's role as a leading Lost Cause warrior has been explored by several talented historians, all of whom portray him as so violently antinorthern that he eventually isolated himself from the southern white mainstream. Resolutely unreconstructed, goes the common argument, Early watched disapprovingly as proponents of the New South gained increasing power and ultimately rendered him a crabby anachronism long before his death in 1894.[1] This interpretation neglects Early's long-term impact on the ways in which Americans have understood the Civil War. Clear-eyed in his determination to sway future generations, Early used his own writings and his influence with other ex-Confederates to foster a heroic image of Robert E. Lee and the southern war effort. Many of the ideas these men articulated became orthodoxy in the postwar South, eventually made their way into the broader national perception of the war, and remain vigorous today. To put this phenomenon within the context of current historical work, Early understood almost immediately after Appomattox that there would be a struggle to control the public memory of the war. He worked hard to help shape that memory and ultimately enjoyed more success than he probably imagined possible.[2]

Before examining Early's largely persuasive efforts in this regard, it is worth noting that many of his other ideas found little favor in the postwar

1. The most influential interpretations of Early as a Lost Cause figure have been Thomas L. Connelly, *The Marble Man: Robert E. Lee and His Image in American Society* (New York: Alfred A. Knopf, 1977), and Gaines M. Foster, *Ghosts of the Confederacy: Defeat, the Lost Cause, and the Emergence of the New South* (New York: Oxford University Press, 1987). Also useful is William Garrett Piston, *Lee's Tarnished Lieutenant: James Longstreet and His Place in Southern History* (Athens: University of Georgia Press, 1987), and Thomas L. Connelly and Barbara L. Bellows, *God and General Longstreet: The Lost Cause and the Southern Mind* (Baton Rouge: Louisiana State University Press, 1982). Each of these books depicts Early as a soldier of limited talent who worked out his personal and professional frustrations after the war by championing Robert E. Lee—an interpretation open to revision but beyond the scope of this essay to examine.

2. A useful introduction to the subject of historical memory is David Thelen, ed., *Memory and American History* (Bloomington: Indiana University Press, 1990). See also Michael Kammen's *Mystic Chords of Memory: The Transformation of Tradition in American Culture* (New York: Alfred A. Knopf, 1991), esp. part 2.

South. A conservative Whig who venerated property and rule by the slave-holding class during the antebellum period, he had resisted changes to the existing order.[3] After Appomattox, Early remained a self-styled conservative Whig who never relinquished his elitist conception of how society should be organized. While other southern whites trimmed their ideological sails to suit changed times, he clung tenaciously to every element of his antebellum world view.[4] Gaines M. Foster has shown that most southerners were disinclined to embrace Early's elitist and nostalgic views. They preferred the vision of John Brown Gordon and others, which acknowledged that the war had altered their world while still honoring Confederate leaders and the motives for secession. Foster likens Early and those who agreed with him to the Native American ghost dancers of the late nineteenth century: "They appeared captivated by a dream of . . . a return to an undefeated Confederacy. This aspect of their historical vision does not appear very different from another revitalization movement of the late nineteenth century, the Ghost Dance among the Plains Indians. . . . They clung to the past, defended old values, and dreamed of a world untouched by defeat." In the end, adds Foster, very few white southerners "joined the ghost dance."[5]

Because of Early's passionate interest in how the future would judge the Confederacy, however, it is a mistake to see him as looking only to the past. His opinions about Confederate military history, which he hoped would influence subsequent generations, earned a receptive hearing across the postwar South. Before any other principal Civil War commander, he began to write his

3. Jubal A. Early, "To the Voters of Franklin, Henry & Patrick Counties," July 20, 1850, Scrapbook, Jubal A. Early Papers, Library of Congress, Washington, D.C. [repository hereinafter cited as LC]. See George H. Reese, ed., *Proceedings of the Virginia Secession Convention of 1861*, 4 vols. (Richmond: Virginia State Library, 1965), 1:428, for Early's description of himself as a Whig in 1861.

4. For an example of Early's describing himself as a Whig after the war, see Jubal A. Early to J. Randolph Tucker, August 8, 1884, Tucker Family Papers, Southern Historical Collection, Wilson Library, University of North Carolina, Chapel Hill [repository hereinafter cited as SHC]. Early's obituary in the March 3, 1894, edition of the Lynchburg *News* described him as "a lifelong Whig, of the most conservative type." See Jack P. Maddex Jr., *The Virginia Conservatives, 1867–1879: A Study in Reconstruction Politics* (Chapel Hill: University of North Carolina Press, 1970), and James Tice Moore, *Two Paths to the New South: The Virginia Debt Controversy, 1870–1883* (Lexington: University Press of Kentucky, 1974), for some of the postwar debates that revealed Early's conservatism. Foster's analysis is in chap. 4 of *Ghosts of the Confederacy*.

5. Foster, *Ghosts of the Confederacy*, 60–61.

memoirs of the war. But first he left the United States. A much-maligned figure in the Confederacy after his army was defeated by Philip H. Sheridan's
forces in the Shenandoah Valley, Early was relieved of command in March
1865 and missed the surrender of the Army of Northern Virginia at Appomattox. Upon hearing of Lee's capitulation, the forty-eight-year-old Early traveled
westward with the hope of joining Confederates in the Trans-Mississippi theater. He learned en route that they also had surrendered and decided, as he put
it, to leave the United States "to get out from the rule of the infernal Yankees. . . . I cannot live under the same government with our enemies. I go
therefore a voluntary exile from the home and graves of my ancestors to seek
my fortunes anew in the world." Traveling first to Havana, then to Mexico,
and eventually settling in Canada, Early spent four years abroad before returning to Virginia in 1869. From Canada he followed events in the United
States with mounting bitterness, declaring at one point, "I have got to that
condition, that I think I could scalp a Yankee woman and child without wink-
ing my eyes."[6]

While in Mexico during the winter of 1865–1866, Early crossed pens with
his old foe Sheridan in a newspaper exchange that anticipated in tone and focus his later writings about the war. At dispute were the strengths and casualties of the forces in the Shenandoah campaign. Sheridan asserted that Early
had lost nearly 27,000 men killed, wounded, and captured; Early countered
that his force had consisted of fewer than 14,000 men and could not have suffered the losses claimed by Sheridan. Early's numbers were more accurate, but
winning this argument constituted only a means to the larger end of compiling
a written record aimed at both contemporary and future readers. By insisting
that he had commanded far fewer men than Sheridan, Early cast his own performance in a better light and sustained the honor of hopelessly outnumbered
Confederates. "Sheridan's letter has furnished another evidence of the propri-
ety of my caution to all fair minded men of other nations," insisted Early, "to
withhold their judgments upon the reports of our enemies until the truth can
be placed before them."[7]

Robert E. Lee figured prominently in Early's crusade to establish the Con-

---

6. Jubal A. Early to John Goode, June 8, 1866, Early Papers, LC; Jubal A. Early to Lee, October 30, 1865, Mss3 L515a, Virginia Historical Society, Richmond [repository hereinafter cited
as VHS]; Jubal A. Early to John C. Breckinridge, March 27, 1867, collection of William C. Davis.

7. Philip H. Sheridan to editors of the New Orleans *Daily Crescent*, January 8, 1866, and
Jubal A. Early to editor of the New York *News*, February 5, 1866, newspaper clippings in Scrapbook, Early Papers, LC.

Jubal Early at age forty-eight, shortly after he left the United
States in 1865.
Library of Congress.

federate side of the war's military history. Early had expressed unbounded admiration for Lee even before the Civil War, agreeing with other Virginians
that Lee's record during the conflict with Mexico marked him as a brilliant soldier. In the spring of 1862, a witness noted that Early, who habitually criticized
Confederate civilian and military leaders, never spoke negatively about Lee.
"For Lee he seemed to have a regard and esteem and high opinion felt by him
for no one else," remarked this man.[8] During the war, Lee appreciated Early's
talents as a soldier and displayed a personal fondness for his cantankerous and

8. John S. Wise, *The End of an Era* (Boston: Houghton Mifflin, 1899), 228.

profane lieutenant. Only Stonewall Jackson among Lee's corps commanders received more difficult assignments from Lee, a certain indication of the commanding general's high regard.

Lee ensured his subordinate's utter devotion by his gentle handling of Early's removal from command in the spring of 1865. He expressed regret at having to replace Early but noted that defeats in the Shenandoah Valley had alienated that vital region's citizens and raised doubts among Early's soldiers. "While my own confidence in your ability, zeal, and devotion to the cause is unimpaired," stated Lee, "I have nevertheless felt that I could not oppose what seems to be the current of opinion, without injustice to your reputation and injury to the service." Lee closed with thanks for "the fidelity and energy with which you have always supported my efforts, and for the courage and devotion you have ever manifested in the service of the country."[9]

In late November 1865, a letter arrived from Lee that likely inspired Early to begin work on his memoirs. Lee intended to write a history of the Army of Northern Virginia, but the loss of official papers during the chaotic retreat from Richmond to Appomattox had left him without sufficient information about the period from 1864 to 1865. Would Early send whatever materials he had relating to that last phase of the conflict? Seven and a half months earlier Lee had spoken of the Union's "overwhelming resources and numbers" in his farewell order to the Army of Northern Virginia. Now he specifically asked Early for information about Confederate strengths at the principal battles from May 1864 through April 1865. "My only object," concluded Lee in language Early would echo many times in his own writings, "is to transmit, if possible, the truth to posterity, and do justice to our brave Soldiers."[10]

Lee sent Early another request in March 1866 for "reports of the operations of your Commands, in the Campaign from the Wilderness to Richmond, at Lynchburg, in the Valley, Maryland, &c." Lee wanted all "statistics as regards numbers, destruction of private property by the Federal troops, &c." because he intended to demonstrate the discrepancy in strength between the

9. Lee to Early, March 30, 1865, reproduced in Jubal A. Early, *Lieutenant General Jubal Anderson Early, C.S.A.: Autobiographical Sketch and Narrative of the War between the States* (Philadelphia: J. B. Lippincott, 1912), 468–69.

10. Lee to Early, November 22, 1865, George H. and Katherine Davis Collection, Howard-Tilton Memorial Library, Tulane University, New Orleans [repository hereinafter cited as TU]; Lee, General Order No. 9, April 10, 1865, in R. E. Lee, *The Wartime Papers of R. E. Lee*, ed. Clifford Dowdey and Louis H. Manarin (Boston: Little, Brown, 1961), 934.

two armies and believed it would "be difficult to get the world to understand the odds against which we fought." "The accusations against myself," Lee wrote in reference to various newspaper accounts, "I have not thought proper to notice, or even to correct misrepresentations of my words & acts. We shall have to be patient, & suffer for awhile at least. . . . At present the public mind is not prepared to receive the truth."[11]

Three months after he received Lee's letter, Early had completed a draft of his wartime memoirs. He published the last section of this manuscript—the first book-length reminiscence by any major Civil War commander—in late 1866 as *A Memoir of the Last Year of the War for Independence, in the Confederate States of America*. Lee's letter of March 1866 can be read as an outline for Early's book, which covered precisely the period the letter defined, strongly emphasized the North's advantage in numbers, and detailed Federal depredations in the Shenandoah Valley. A desire to satisfy Lee's request for information about the conflict's final year may have prompted Early to hurry this portion of his larger narrative into print. The fact that he never published the whole memoir suggests that he contemplated revisions and printed only the chapters that would serve Lee's most immediate needs (as well as place his own controversial activities in the Shenandoah Valley in the best possible light).[12]

Early also may have read Lee's letter of March 1866 as an unintentional summons to champion Lee against all detractors. Distressed by the mention of attacks on Lee, Early may have decided to persuade the public to "receive the truth" about his old commander—to spell out in vigorous detail, and with an attention to evidence befitting Early's years of experience as a lawyer, a case for the greatness of both Lee and his army.

Early discussed the need to tell the Confederate side of the war in a letter to Lee in late November 1868. Decrying the proliferation of errors in every-

11. Lee to Early, March 15, 1866, George H. and Katherine M. Davis Collection, TU.

12. Early to John Goode, June 8, 1866, Early Papers, LC. The first edition of *A Memoir of the Last Year of the War* was printed in Toronto by Lovell and Gibson. Subsequent editions, each slightly revised, were published in 1867 in New Orleans, Lynchburg, Virginia, and Augusta, Georgia. Early's full memoir, edited by his niece Ruth H. Early, was published eighteen years after his death under the title *Lieutenant General Jubal Anderson Early, C.S.A.: Autobiographical Sketch and Narrative of the War between the States*. For Early's sending Lee portions of his manuscript devoted to campaigns prior to May 1864, see Lee to Early, October 15, 1866, George H. and Katherine M. Davis Collection, TU, and Early to Lee, November 20, 1868, box 25, folder titled "Introductory Chapter (Notes & Pages of a Rough Draft) I," John Warwick Daniel Papers, Alderman Library, University of Virginia, Charlottesville [repository hereinafter cited as UVa].

thing he had read about the conflict, Early urged Lee not to "abandon your purpose of writing a history of the operations of the Army of Northern Virginia." In one passage Early got to the heart of his concern about the published record: "The most that is left to us is the history of our struggle, and I think that ought to be accurately written. We lost nearly everything but honor, and that should be religiously guarded."[13]

Apart from his concern about future perceptions of Lee and his army, Early also sought to guard his own long-term reputation. "According to my view," he wrote to another former Confederate officer, "the most important books of all are those put into the hands of the rising generation." One new school book implied that Early should have captured Washington during his raid across the Potomac in the summer of 1864. "It is by no means a pleasant reflection that I am to be held up in that light before not only the rising generation of this day," groused Early, "but all those to come hereafter." He warned that former Confederates must try to get the correct version of the war into print immediately because "we all know how hard it is to eradicate early impressions."[14]

In lectures, writings, and personal correspondence over the last twenty-five years of his life, Early put his impressions of the war on record. He took an active role in publishing the *Southern Historical Society Papers*, wherein former Confederates reexamined old battles and assessed both comrades and enemies. Thomas L. Connelly, Gaines M. Foster, William Garrett Piston, and other historians have explored this aspect of Early's postwar career in detail. Although some of their conclusions are open to debate, the focus of this essay must remain elsewhere. It is enough to note that Early achieved a position in the South as a leading arbiter of questions relating to Confederate military history. He orchestrated the effort to isolate James Longstreet—Lee's senior subordinate throughout the war—as a pariah because he had dared to criticize Lee in print. Other former Confederates took notice. If Early could savage a soldier of Longstreet's wartime accomplishments and reputation, scarcely anyone could be safe criticizing Lee. Robert Stiles, a former Confederate artillerist who wrote a much-quoted volume of recollections, commented about Early's influence among ex-Confederates who wrote about the war: "[A]s long as 'the

13. Early to Lee, November 20, 1868, Daniel Papers, UVa.
14. Early to Charles Venable, June 9, 1871, Charles Scott Venable Papers, SHC.

old hero' lived," stated Stiles, "no man ever took up his pen to write a line about the great conflict without the fear of Jubal Early before his eyes."[15]

Early interpreted key military events and personalities in a series of publications between 1866 and 1872. His major points can be summarized quickly: (1) Robert E. Lee was the best and most admirable general of the war; (2) Confederate armies faced overwhelming odds and mounted a gallant resistance; (3) Ulysses S. Grant paled in comparison to Lee as a soldier; (4) Stonewall Jackson deserved a place immediately behind Lee in the Confederate pantheon; and (5) Virginia was the most important arena of combat.

Lee towers above all other Civil War figures in Early's writings. The preface to *A Memoir of the Last Year of the War* unabashedly announced Early's "profound love and veneration" for Lee. In an address at Washington and Lee University in 1872, which was widely distributed as a pamphlet and stands as a classic Lost Cause tract, Early hoped to help the audience form "a really correct estimate of [Lee's] marvellous ability and boldness as a military commander." Defending his subject at every turn, Early explained Gettysburg as an instance where Lee's subordinates (especially James Longstreet) failed to execute a sound plan of battle. The public misunderstood the campaign only because Lee's magnanimity had prevented his revealing the true causes of that defeat. Early explained the fall of Richmond in April 1865 and the surrender of Lee's army as "consequences of events in the West and Southwest, and not directly of the operations in Virginia." In rendering this judgment that failures elsewhere had undone Lee, Early professed to shun invidious comparisons between his hero and Confederate leaders in other theaters. He closed with an affirmation of Lee's personal and professional greatness, insisting that his hero had no equal during the Civil War or among earlier military figures.[16]

Northern numerical superiority rendered Lee's successes all the more remarkable to Early. He repeatedly stressed the unequal pools of Confederate and Federal manpower, heaping scorn on northern officers who overestimated Lee's strength. Northern attempts to play down Grant's advantage in man-

15. Robert Stiles, *Four Years under Marse Robert* (1903; reprint, Dayton, Ohio: Morningside, 1977), 190–91. On Early's stature as a Confederate historian, see Virginia General Assembly joint resolution quoted in the Lynchburg *News*, March 4, 1894.

16. Early, *A Memoir of the Last Year of the War*, vii; Jubal A. Early, *The Campaigns of Gen. Robert E. Lee. An Address by Lieut. General Jubal A. Early, before Washington and Lee University, January 19th, 1872* (Baltimore: John Murphy, 1872), 3–4, 29–33, 40–41, 45.

power over Lee elicited an especially strident reaction. When Adam Badeau, Grant's military secretary during 1864–1865, placed Union and Confederate numbers in early May 1864 at 98,000 and 72,000 respectively, Early characterized the article as part of "a persistent and systematic effort to falsify the truth." Addressing his reply to the editor of the London *Standard*, he gave the numbers as 141,000 and 50,000 (Grant actually outnumbered Lee by about two to one). Again with an eye on history's verdict, Early pointed out that a people "overpowered and crushed in a struggle for their rights" had but one resource upon which to rely for vindication—an appeal to "foreign nations and to the next age."[17]

Early found only honor in the Confederate performance against daunting odds. In his scenario, a band of noble Confederates led by the peerless Lee held off a mechanistic North blessed with inexhaustible reserves of men and matériel for nearly three years. Exploiting an array of scientific breakthroughs applicable to military use and relentlessly piling in men, the Federals "finally produced that exhaustion of our army and resources, and that accumulation of numbers on the other side, which wrought the final disaster." The Army of Northern Virginia "had been gradually worn down by the combined agencies of numbers, steam-power, railroads, mechanism, and all the resources of physical science." Early repeatedly juxtaposed steadfast Confederates against craven northern soldiers who manipulated numbers to rationalize their defeats at the hands of Lee's smaller army. A passage from an address to the South Carolina Survivors' Association in late 1871 typifies Early's tendency to question the virility of Federal officers and their men: "I might multiply the instances of the attempts of our enemies to falsify the truth of history," he said after discussing George B. McClellan's habit of grossly inflating Lee's strength, "in order to excuse their manifold failures, and to conceal the inferiority of their troops in all the elements of manhood, but I would become too tedious."[18]

17. Jubal A. Early, "Address of General Jubal A. Early," in *Proceedings of the Third Annual Meeting of the Survivors' Association, of the State of South Carolina; and the Annual Address by Jubal A. Early, Delivered before the Association, November 10, 1871* (Charleston: Walker, Evans & Cogswell, Printers, 1872), 20–21 [hereinafter cited as "Address to S.C. Survivors"]; Jubal A. Early, *The Relative Strength of the Armies of Genl's Lee and Grant. Reply of Gen. Early to the Letter of Gen. Badeau to the London Standard* (n.p.: n.p., 1870), 1–2, 5.

18. Early, *Campaigns of Lee*, 40; Early, "Address to S.C. Survivors," 31–32. Walter H. Taylor of Lee's staff spent more time than any other ex-Confederate attempting to show that the Federals vastly outnumbered Lee. See his *Four Years with General Lee* (1877; reprint, Bloomington: Indiana University Press, 1962).

Jefferson Davis and His Generals, a popular Lost Cause engraving from 1890. Despite the title, Lee dominates the grouping. Each of the generals served all or part of his career in the eastern theater. Jackson is to Lee's right. Early stands at the far right.
Collection of the author

Early cast Ulysses S. Grant as the principal agent of northern power, a butcher who threw unending ranks of his hapless soldiers against Lee's veterans. His analysis contained no hint of Grant as a master of maneuver whose willingness to take breathtaking risks and ability to rebound from reverses brought victory at Vicksburg, Chattanooga, and elsewhere.[19] Unwilling to concede anything to Grant, Early insisted that he "had none of the requisites of a great captain, but merely possessed the most ordinary brute courage, and had the control of unlimited numbers and means." Were Grant to publish a work on strategy, the appropriate title would be "The Lincoln-Grant or Pegging-Hammer Art of War."[20]

Stonewall Jackson, rather than Grant, received Early's nod as the second superior military leader of the war. Lee was the unsurpassed chief, Jackson the peerless subordinate who "always appreciated, and sympathized with the bold conceptions of the commanding General, and entered upon their execution with the most cheerful alacrity and zeal." Early often linked Lee with Jackson, urging fellow white southerners to "be thankful that our cause had two such champions, and that, in their characters, we can furnish the world at large with the best assurance of the rightfulness of the principles for which they and we fought." Always conscious of the need to influence future generations, Early counted on this team to garner sympathy for the Confederacy: "When asked for our vindication, we can triumphantly point to the graves of Lee and Jackson and look the world square in the face." The pious Lee and sternly Calvinist Jackson easily lent themselves to religious imagery, which Early employed in calling on Virginians "to remain true to the memory of your venerated leaders. . . . Let the holy memories connected with our glorious struggle, afford stronger incentives to renewed efforts to do our duty."[21]

With Lee and Jackson so important to his vision of the Confederate experience, Early inevitably defined the war as predominantly a Virginia phenomenon. He only occasionally mentioned events west of the Appalachians and usually avoided overt criticism of the Confederacy's western leaders and their armies. Yet his writings consistently identified Richmond as the ultimate target of northern military planning and credited Lee and his soldiers with extending the war through their dogged defense of the Confederate capital.[22]

19. Early, "Address to S.C. Survivors," 33; Early, *Campaigns of Lee*, 39.
20. Early, *A Memoir of the Last Year of the War*, 34–35; Early, *Campaigns of Lee*, 44.
21. Early, *Campaigns of Lee*, 27, 31, 44, 47.
22. Ibid., 39.

The *Southern Historical Society Papers*, whose contents Early influenced to a greater degree than anyone else, were published in Richmond and leaned very heavily toward topics associated with Lee and the eastern theater. This bias prompted some ex-Confederates who had fought elsewhere to find other forums for their writings about the war. The *Southern Bivouac* and the *Confederate Veteran*, begun respectively in Louisville and Nashville in 1882 and 1893, paid a great deal of attention to campaigns and leaders outside Virginia but never approached the *Southern Historical Society Papers* in terms of influencing historians.[23]

At a convention of the Southern Historical Society held in August 1873, Early explained the organization's goals. "The history of our war has not been written," he said in the keynote address, "and it devolves upon the survivors of those who participated in that war, to furnish the authentic materials for that history." A flyer subsequently circulated by the society announced that "generations of the disinterested must succeed the generations of the prejudiced before history, properly termed such, can be written. This, precisely, is the work we now attempt, to construct the archives in which shall be collected . . . memoirs to serve for future history." Ever since the society first described its purpose, legions of historians and other writers have mined the fifty-two volumes of its papers for material on the Confederate war effort.[24]

Disseminated by Early and other former Confederates through publications including the society's *Papers*, Lost Cause interpretations of the war gained wide currency in the nineteenth century and remain remarkably persistent today. These ideas have lasted so long partly because they are grounded in fact. Robert E. Lee *was* a gifted soldier who inspired his army to accomplish prodigious feats on the battlefield. The Army of Northern Virginia and other Confederate forces consistently fought at a disadvantage in numbers and often

23. Gaines M. Foster correctly noted that the *Veteran* enjoyed a far wider circulation than the *Papers* but did not address the question of which publication wielded greater influence on the writing of Confederate military history. (Foster, *Ghosts of the Confederacy*, 106.)

24. *The Proceedings of the Southern Historical Convention, Which Assembled at the Montgomery White Sulphur Springs, Va., on the 14th of August, 1873; and of the Southern Historical Society, As Reorganised, with the Address by Gen. Jubal A. Early, Delivered before the Convention on the First Day of Its Session* (Baltimore: Turnbull Brothers, [1873]), 37–38; Southern Historical Society, *Official Circular* ([Richmond]: [Southern Historical Society, 1876]), 3. A measure of the enduring influence of the fifty-two-volume *Southern Historical Society Papers* (J. William Jones et al., eds. [Richmond: Southern Historical Society, 1876–1959]) is that they have been reprinted twice in the past two decades.

of matériel. A number of northern newspapers as well as some soldiers in the Army of the Potomac joined Confederates in complaining about Grant's "hammering" tactics in 1864. Stonewall Jackson won his reputation honestly and served Lee as a superb lieutenant. Many people at the time—northern, southern, and European—looked to Virginia as the crucial arena of the war, as have a number of historians since. The distortion came when Early and other proponents of the Lost Cause denied that Lee had faults or lost any battles, focused on northern numbers and material superiority while ignoring Confederate advantages, denied Grant any virtues or greatness, and noticed the Confederacy outside the eastern theater only when convenient to explain southern failures in Virginia. With these thoughts in mind, I will turn to a brief review of recent scholarly and popular literature, fiction, documentaries and films, and the thriving market in Civil War art that reveals trends that almost certainly would bring a smile to Jubal Early's lips.

A striking irony of the Civil War is that the rebel Lee rather than the Union's protector Grant has joined Lincoln as one of the conflict's two great popular figures.[25] Frederick Douglass complained of friendly treatments of Lee in the North soon after the general's death in October 1870. "Is it not about time that this bombastic laudation of the rebel chief should cease?" asked the nation's most famous black leader. "We can scarcely take up a newspaper . . . that is not filled with *nauseating* flatteries of the late Robert E. Lee." Douglass would surely lament the fact that the United States government, whose sovereignty Lee nearly compromised, has honored the Confederate leader with five postage stamps and made his antebellum home at Arlington a national memorial. Douglas Southall Freeman's Pulitzer Prize–winning *R. E. Lee: A Biography* was issued to a chorus of praise in the mid-1930s and cemented in American letters an interpretation of Lee very close to Early's utterly heroic figure. In the annotated bibliography, Freeman acknowledged his debt to the *Southern Historical Society Papers* by stating that they contain "more valuable, unused data than any other unofficial repository of source material on the War Between the States."[26]

25. The best examination of the process by which Lee became a national hero is Connelly's *Marble Man*, chaps. 4, 6. Readers should approach this work, which combines insights and distortions in about equal measure, with an understanding that Connelly grossly underestimated Lee's stature as the preeminent hero in the Confederacy from early 1863 through the close of the war.

26. David W. Blight, *Frederick Douglass' Civil War: Keeping Faith in Jubilee* (Baton Rouge:

Anyone writing about Lee since the mid-1930s has contended with Douglas Southall Freeman's immense shadow. Historians such as Thomas L. Connelly and Alan T. Nolan have discovered that challenging the heroic Lee triggers a response reminiscent of Early's attacks on James Longstreet. Nolan's *Lee Considered: General Robert E. Lee and Civil War History*, which appeared in 1991, followed a trail blazed in 1977 by Connelly's starkly revisionist *The Marble Man: Robert E. Lee and His Image in American Society*. Questioning several elements of what he labeled "the Lee tradition," Nolan argued that Lee's famous victories came at so high a cost in manpower that they probably shortened the life of the Confederacy. Many academic reviewers welcomed Nolan's study, but the book took a severe beating from Lee's admirers. One historian called it an "anti-Lee" book that used "always-perfect hindsight" to reach flawed conclusions. A prominent student of the Army of Northern Virginia termed Nolan "a bootless revisionist" with "a total lack of perspective of historical time and sense." Even more to Jubal Early's taste would have been the plea mailed to Civil War scholars from a retired military officer: "I call upon every true student of the Civil War, every son and daughter of the veterans of that war both North and South, and every organization formed to study, research, reenact, perserve [sic] and remember our Civil War heritage not to purchase Nolan's book.... If you have it already, burn it as it is not worth recycling."[27]

Those who prefer Lee as Early's icon have found much to applaud in re-

---

Louisiana State University Press, 1989), 229; Douglas Southall Freeman, *R. E. Lee: A Biography*, 4 vols. (New York: Charles Scribner's Sons, 1934–35), 4:558. Freeman summed up his interpretation of Lee as a man and a soldier in chaps. 11 and 28 of vol. 4. The five stamps appeared in 1937 (Lee and Stonewall Jackson with Stratford Hall in the background), 1949 (Lee and George Washington with Washington and Lee University in the background), 1955 (a bust of Lee), 1970 (Lee with Jackson and Jefferson Davis on the Confederate memorial at Stone Mountain, Georgia), and 1995 (a three-quarter-length portrait of Lee). Pictures of the five stamps can be found in U.S. Postal Service, *The Postal Service Guide to Stamps*, 23rd edition (Crawfordsville, Ind.: R. R. Donnelley & Sons, 1996).

27. Reviews of *Lee Considered* by James I. Robertson Jr., in the Richmond *News Leader* (May 29, 1991), Robert K. Krick in the Fredericksburg (Va.) *Free Lance-Star* (July 20, 1991), and Dennis E. Frye in *Blue and Gray Magazine* 9 (February 1992), 26; Brig. Gen. (Ret.) M. H. Morris to "Dear Civil War Scholar," April 28, 1992 (copy in author's files). For a positive reaction by an academic historian, see Drew Gilpin Faust's review on the front page of the *New York Times Book Review*, July 7, 1991.

cent literature. A pair of works published within the past six years that have reached wide audiences through book clubs and paperback editions typify this phenomenon. Paul D. Casdorph's *Lee and Jackson: Confederate Chieftains* bluntly claimed that Lee forged "the foremost military career in the American saga." Describing Grant as "the Yankee Goliath" who outnumbered Lee by two to one in the spring of 1864, Casdorph judged Lee "nothing short of brilliant in the campaign of attrition that followed." At Lee's side through most of Casdorph's book is Stonewall Jackson, whose "eagerness to undertake independent orders had insured Lee's great successes throughout the battles of 1862." In his study of the Chancellorsville campaign, Ernest B. Furgurson invoked superlatives in describing Lee and Jackson, claiming that "American history offers no other pair of generals with such perfect rapport, such sublime confidence in each other" (this view overlooked the obvious tandem of Grant and William Tecumseh Sherman).[28]

Winston Groom's *Shrouds of Glory: From Atlanta to Nashville, The Last Campaign of the Civil War* also illustrated that Lost Cause arguments remain current. Although Groom treated a campaign far removed from the eastern theater, his narrative included numerous references to Lee and Jackson and to Grant's inability, despite superior manpower, to subdue his wily opponent. Grant had introduced "a new kind of war, a grinding nightmare of armed embrace in which the victorious dog never turns loose of his victim, but pursues him relentlessly, attacking whenever he can." Earlier in Virginia, Confederates had learned that their "esprit tended to offset federal superiority in numbers and manufacturing. . . . Northern armies, on the other hand, had come to rely on their overwhelming numbers to wreck the Confederates' logistics system, then simply grind their armies down by attrition." Grant's strategy against Lee in 1864 earned him "a reputation in certain quarters on both sides as a 'butcher' or 'murderer' rather than a general. . . . Deserved or undeserved as such sobriquets might have been, the fact was that the North was becoming war wearier by the day." Greeted by generally favorable reviews, selected by book clubs, awarded a prize within weeks of its publication, and beneficiary of its author's wide name recognition because of his success with the novel *For-*

---

28. Paul D. Casdorph, *Lee and Jackson: Confederate Chieftains* (New York: Paragon House, 1992), 403, 401, 400, 194; Ernest B. Furgurson, *Chancellorsville 1863: The Souls of the Brave* (New York: Alfred A. Knopf, 1992), 146.

rest Gump, Shrouds of Glory seemed destined to reinforce Lost Cause images among thousands of readers.[29]

The wide availability of hundreds of reprinted older titles also keeps Early's Lost Cause arguments current. New paperback editions of books by Clifford Dowdey illustrate this point. A gifted writer who inherited Douglas Southall Freeman's mantle as the principal chronicler of the Army of Northern Virginia, Dowdey published between 1958 and 1964 a biography of Lee and studies of the Seven Days, Gettysburg, and the Overland campaign. "Out of the crucible of the Seven Days," Dowdey wrote of Lee, "he molded an army that would be man for man the greatest fighting force ever on the continent." By the time Lee perfected his organization of the Army of Northern Virginia, however, he faced an impossible task: "He would no longer be fighting off only another army, or even other armies. Lee's Army of Northern Virginia," concluded Dowdey in language reminiscent of Early's address at Washington and Lee University, "was a personally designed, hand-wrought sword fending off machine-tooled weapons that kept coming in immeasurable, illimitable numbers." The most important fact about Lee's image, argued Dowdey elsewhere, "is that the legendary aspects were always present. There was no later building of the legend, no collections of sayings or anecdotes; the Lee of the legend emerged full-scale, larger than life, during his command of the army."[30] Here Dowdey reinforced Early's interpretation of Lee—while at the same time ignoring the postwar efforts by Early and many other Lost Cause writers to burnish Lee's image and defend it against any assailants.

During the 1860s and 1870s, Jubal Early exhibited special interest in how successive generations of young people and foreign readers would view the Confederate struggle. Lost Cause writings have carried great weight with both audiences in the twentieth century. Books on the Civil War for young readers in the 1950s and 1960s emphasized Lee and his campaigns within an

29. Winston Groom, *Shrouds of Glory: From Atlanta to Nashville, The Last Great Campaign of the Civil War* (New York: Atlantic Monthly Press, 1995), 8–9, 11. On the reception of Groom's book, see " '95 Kirkland Book Award Goes to Winston Groom," *Civil War News*, August 1995, 24. For a dissenting view, see my review in the *New York Times Book Review*, April 16, 1995, 23.

30. Clifford Dowdey, *The Seven Days: The Emergence of Lee* (1964; reprint, Lincoln: University of Nebraska Press, 1993), 358; Dowdey, *Lee's Last Campaign: The Story of Lee and His Men against Grant—1864* (1960; reprint, Lincoln: University of Nebraska Press, 1993), 5–6.

interpretive framework substantially attuned to the writings of Early and Freeman.

The roster of ninety titles in Random House's Landmark Books on American history included four relating to the military side of the Civil War—all of which featured Lee as a major actor. Hodding Carter's *Robert E. Lee and the Road of Honor* affirmed that Lee should be admired "so long as men respect and remember courage and high purpose and a sense of duty and honor." Visitors entered Lee's burial crypt at Lexington, Virginia, "as if it were a hallowed place," wrote Carter. "That is as it should be." Jonathan Daniels's *Stonewall Jackson* lauded the virtues of Lee and his lieutenant as soldiers and men, and MacKinlay Kantor's *Gettysburg* praised Lee and described units of the Army of Northern Virginia "as the most capable troops ever to go into action." The Landmark series offered neither a biography of Grant (or Sherman or any other Union general) nor a narrative of any of his victories in the western theater. Only MacKinlay Kantor's *Lee and Grant at Appomattox* devoted appreciable attention to Grant, and it followed conventions far more favorable to Lee than to Grant. Kantor's Grant was a "silent, shabby, stubborn" man who liked animals more than people: "Maybe it is necessary to be like that, if one is to squander a thousand lives through some mistake of judgment during a battle." For Lee, who had a "grave magnificence," Kantor chose knightly and religious allusions: "You could imagine him in the wars of long ago, in polished armor. You could imagine him in the wars of Biblical times, proud in his chariot, facing the Philistines."[31]

Houghton Mifflin's North Star Books for children also ignored Grant but offered Jonathan Daniels's appreciative *Robert E. Lee*. Daniels's penultimate sentence could have been written by Jubal Early. "He went almost as though he rode into eternity," wrote Daniels of Lee's death, "again at the head of a column—a long gray line, ragged and barefoot, lean and hungry, but on its certain way to glory of which no power on earth could deprive it."[32]

No foreign nation has manifested more interest in the Civil War than

31. Hodding Carter, *Robert E. Lee and the Road of Honor* (New York: Random House, 1955), 174, 176; Jonathan Daniels, *Stonewall Jackson* (New York: Random House, 1959); MacKinlay Kantor, *Gettysburg* (New York: Random House, 1952), 19; MacKinlay Kantor, *Lee and Grant at Appomattox* (New York: Random House, 1950), 26–27, 32–33. Each of these titles went through many printings in the 1950s and 1960s. The Landmark Books also included two titles on Abraham Lincoln.

32. Jonathan Daniels, *Robert E. Lee* (Boston: Houghton Mifflin, 1960), 180.

Great Britain, whose authors generally have followed Lost Cause interpretive contours. Field Marshal Viscount Garnet Wolseley, Arthur James Lyon Fremantle, and Francis C. Lawley, all of whom spent time with Lee as observers or reporters, between 1863 and 1890 wrote very favorably about the Confederate leader and his soldiers.[33] George Francis Robert Henderson's *Stonewall Jackson and the American Civil War,* first published in England in 1898 and reprinted there and in the United States numerous times in the twentieth century, marked a milestone of laudatory British writing about the Confederacy. Douglas Southall Freeman remarked in 1939 that no author before or after Henderson "succeeded so well in capturing in print the spirit of the Army of Northern Virginia. . . . The reception of *Stonewall Jackson* by old Confederates was, needless to say, enraptured." In 1933, Maj. Gen. J. F. C. Fuller departed from these earlier British historians in *Grant & Lee: A Study in Personality and Generalship,* wherein he dismissed Henderson's biography of Jackson as "almost as romantic as Xenophon's *Cyropaedia.*" Fuller also questioned Lee's strategic grasp and accused him of too often taking the tactical offensive. "In several respects," stated Fuller, Lee "was one of the most incapable Generals-in-Chief in history."[34]

The most renowned British author to write seriously about the Civil War was Winston Churchill, whose assessments echoed Henderson rather than Fuller. In the late 1950s, Churchill told readers that Lee's "noble presence and gentle, kindly manner were sustained by religious faith and exalted character." Lee and Jackson formed a brilliant partnership that faced awful odds: "Against Lee and his great lieutenant, united for a year of intense action in a comradeship which recalls that of Marlborough and Eugene, were now to be marshalled the overwhelming forces of the Union." Churchill's Grant also filled a

33. See Garnet Wolseley, *The American Civil War: An English View,* ed. James A. Rawley (Charlottesville: University Press of Virginia, 1964), which collects Wolseley's writings about the Civil War; A. J. L. Fremantle, *Three Months in the Southern States: April–June, 1863* (Edinburgh: W. Blackwood and Sons, 1863; reprinted in New York and Mobile, Ala., 1864); and Francis C. Lawley, "General Lee," *Blackwood's Edinburgh Magazine* 101 (January 1872):348–63. Lawley's piece and Wolseley's "General Lee" are reprinted in Gary W. Gallagher, ed., *Lee the Soldier* (Lincoln: University of Nebraska Press, 1996).

34. Douglas Southall Freeman, *The South to Posterity: An Introduction to the Writing of Confederate History* (New York: Charles Scribner's Sons, 1939), 165; J. F. C. Fuller, *Grant and Lee: A Study in Personality and Generalship* (1933; reprint, Bloomington: Indiana University Press, 1957), 8. Longmans, Green and Company of London published the first edition of Henderson's *Jackson.*

typical Lost Cause role. Mentioning "Grant's tactics of unflinching butchery" during the Overland campaign, Churchill observed that "more is expected of the high command than determination in thrusting men to their doom." The former prime minister also touched on the theme of honor so important to Early and other Lost Cause advocates. "By the end of 1863 all illusions had vanished," claimed Churchill. "The South knew they had lost the war, and would be conquered and flattened. It is one of the enduring glories of the American nation that this made no difference to the Confederate resistance."[35]

Two imperfect but highly suggestive measures of Lee's triumph over Grant as a popular figure can be found in late-twentieth-century Civil War fiction and art. Lee and his army have been central to a number of successful novels. Harry Turtledove's *The Guns of the South* presents Lee with the tantalizing prospect of overcoming northern numbers and superior military hardware by acquiring modern automatic weapons from time-traveling South Africans (who hope to gain a twentieth-century ally by helping the Confederacy win its independence). Douglas Savage's *The Court Martial of Robert E. Lee* posits a scenario wherein Lee faces charges from his own government for the defeat at Gettysburg, M. A. Harper's *For the Love of Robert E. Lee* details the process by which a woman in the 1960s becomes infatuated with Lee and imagines the details of his life, and Richard Adams's *Traveller* follows the Confederate commander from the perspective of his favorite horse. Lee's victory at Second Manassas serves as the backdrop for Tom Wicker's sprawling *Unto This Hour*, Bernard Cornwell's *Battle Flag*, and a significant portion of Thomas Keneally's *Confederates*—all of which include long sections devoted to Stonewall Jackson. Jackson predictably looms large in another novel, *A Bullet for Stonewall*, the literary merits of which could be exhausted in a sentence.[36]

35. Winston Churchill, *The American Civil War* (New York: Dodd, Mead, 1961), 39, 41, 123, 119. This book is a reprint of the chapters on the Civil War from vol. 4 of Churchill's *A History of the English Speaking Peoples: The Great Democracies*, 4 vols. (New York: Dodd, Mead, 1958). Echoes of Early's unflattering interpretation of Grant also can be found in William S. Mc-Feely's Pulitzer Prize–winning *Grant: A Biography* (New York: W. W. Norton, 1981).

36. Harry Turtledove, *The Guns of the South: A Novel of the Civil War* (New York: Ballantine Books, 1992); Douglas Savage, *The Court Martial of Robert E. Lee: A Historical Novel* (Conshohocken, Pa.: Combined Books, 1993); M. A. Harper, *For the Love of Robert E. Lee* (New York: Soho Press, 1992); Richard Adams, *Traveller* (New York: Alfred A. Knopf, 1988); Tom Wicker, *Unto This Hour* (New York: Viking Press, 1984); Bernard Cornwell, *Battle Flag* (New York: HarperCollins, 1995); Thomas Keneally, *Confederates* (New York: Harper & Row, 1979); Benjamin King, *A Bullet for Stonewall* (Gretna, La.: Pelican, 1990).

By far the most widely read of Civil War novels published in the last quarter century was *The Killer Angels*, which features Lee as one the six characters around whom author Michael Shaara built his narrative. This Pulitzer Prize–winning novel—as well as *Gettysburg*, the sprawling four-hour film based closely on its text—would by turns delight and upset Lost Cause adherents. The primacy of the eastern theater shines through both the novel and the screenplay, which understandably define Gettysburg as the decisive moment of the conflict. "I think if we lose this fight," remarks Union colonel Joshua Lawrence Chamberlain at one point, "the war will be over." Early and other Lost Cause writers also treated Gettysburg as the most important battle, repeatedly reexamining it in the *Southern Historical Society Papers* and other publications. If only Longstreet had obeyed Lee's orders more expeditiously, they insisted, Gettysburg would have been a great victory and Confederate independence a reality. So Early would have approved of a film devoted to Gettysburg, and appreciated as well Shaara's tribute to an Army of Northern Virginia that maintained a jaunty confidence despite being outnumbered and outgunned: "It is an army of remarkable unity, fighting for disunion. . . . They share common customs and a common faith and they have been consistently victorious against superior numbers. They have as solid a faith in their leader as any veteran army that ever marched." Elsewhere the novelist stated that Lee's army was "unbeatable, already immortal." Shaara's portrayal of Lee as an aging and ill lion, blindly insistent on attacking despite James Longstreet's sagacious advice to the contrary, would have riled Lee's nineteenth-century champions, however, and Early would have seethed at Shaara's description of his own conduct at Gettysburg as timid and motivated by concern for reputation and position.[37]

Jeff Shaara's *Gods and Generals: A Novel of the Civil War* represents a dis-

37. Michael Shaara, *The Killer Angels* (New York: David McKay, 1974), 33, ix, 85. *Gettysburg* debuted in theaters in 1993 and later was shown on television in an expanded version. Almost all of the film's dialogue comes directly from the novel. Like Jubal Early, Union hero Joshua Lawrence Chamberlain understood the power of the printed word. His publications rank among the most evocative by any veteran and have impressed generations of historians and other writers. Shaara's fascination with Chamberlain prompted him to make the Maine soldier a key character in *The Killer Angels*, which in turn helped convince the public that Chamberlain was perhaps the best regimental commander on the field at Gettysburg. Visitation at the site on Little Round Top where Chamberlain and his 20th Maine fought at Gettysburg increased dramatically following publication of *The Killer Angels* and again after the release of the film *Gettysburg*. (Telephone conversation with Kathy Georg Harrison, historian at Gettysburg National Military Park, August 11, 1995.)

tant aftershock of his father's novel about Gettysburg. Set in the period September 1859 to June 1863, it serves as what the film and television industries, with typical disregard for the English language, would call a prequel to *The Killer Angels*. Once again Lee is one of the main characters, and the younger Shaara's treatment of the Confederate hero virtually never departs from Lost Cause orthodoxy. Lee literally sheds tears when he decides he must go with Virginia and against the Union in April 1861, achieves strategic brilliance at Second Manassas and Chancellorsville, and enjoys a magnificent military relationship with Stonewall Jackson. In the wake of Chancellorsville, with Jackson dead, Lee knows Union numbers are lengthening the odds against the Confederacy. "If we are to end this war," he tells Longstreet in May 1863, "we must *win* this war, and I believe it [an invasion of the North] is the only way." The book closes with Lee and his army on the march northward in June 1863, thus anticipating the clash at Gettysburg that so fascinated Early and other Lost Cause writers.[38]

What of Grant? He appears along with Lee in Richard Slotkin's *The Crater*, a masterful evocation of the botched Federal attempt to breach the Confederate lines at Petersburg in July 1864. He is also the protagonist in Robert Skimin's *Ulysses: A Biographical Novel of U. S. Grant*. Offered to a largely indifferent reading public in 1994, *Ulysses* gives a mixed reading of Grant as a man and a general. In the opening two sentences, however, Skimin adopts a tone entirely absent from novels that sketch Lee: "As he looked blearily into the cracked mirror, Grant tried to recall his foray, but only glimpses returned. His hands shook, his eyes were blood red, and his filthy uniform reeked of whiskey and vomitus."[39] No successful novels have been built around Grant, his campaigns, or the armies he led. The fact that the Confederate commander's horse has gotten as much recent novelistic attention as the general-in-chief of the United States armies delineates the chasm separating Lee and Grant in fiction (the notion that someone might write a novel about Cincinnati, Grant's favorite horse, is beyond imagining). Novelists admittedly have portrayed Lee in different ways; some sketching military limitations and others falling closer to Jubal Early on the interpretive scale.[40] Interpretations

38. Jeff Shaara, *Gods and Generals: A Novel of the Civil War* (New York: Ballantine Books, 1996), 487.

39. Richard Slotkin, *The Crater* (New York: Atheneum, 1980); Robert Skimin, *Ulysses: A Biographical Novel of U. S. Grant* (New York: St. Martin's Press, 1984), xi. Like Harry Turtledove, Slotkin is a professional historian.

40. Douglas Savage, for example, credited the writings of Douglas Southall Freeman,

aside, however, Lee's presence dwarfs that of Grant in novels published during the last twenty-five years.

The same pattern holds true in Civil War art. The past decade has witnessed a proliferation of artists who cater to the Civil War market. Their advertisements adorn the pages of leading popular magazines devoted to the subject, a perusal of which leaves no doubt that Jubal Early's heroes have dominated the war on canvas and in clay to a degree they never achieved against the Union armies. Lee and Jackson far outstrip Grant as subjects for prints, sculptures, and other items. During the period 1983–1995, *Blue and Gray Magazine* ran advertisements for more than twenty-five works with Lee as the primary subject, more than fifteen featuring Jackson, and more than a dozen of the two men together. No ads for works highlighting Grant appeared during these years. During the same dozen years in *Civil War: The Magazine of the Civil War Society*, the totals were thirty ads for Lee, seventeen for Jackson, three for the pair together, and two for Grant. The magazine with the largest circulation in the field is *Civil War Times Illustrated*. Its first issue for 1995 contained advertisements for a print of Lee, a framed *carte de visite* of Lee, a bust of Lee, a Lee commemorative china plate, a "Robert E. Lee Limited Edition 1851 Navy Colt Revolver," rubbings from the gravestones of Lee and Jackson, a print of Lee and Jackson at Chancellorsville, and a print of Jackson and his wife Mary Anna. Prospective buyers could find only two opportunities to acquire something featuring Grant—a Civil War chess set that also included Lee and Jackson as Confederate king and bishop respectively, and a catalog of autographs with Lee and Lincoln sharing space with Grant as the highlighted subjects.[41]

A recent flyer announced publication of *Jackson & Lee: Legends in Gray*, a coffee-table book featuring seventy-five paintings by Mort Künstler and a narrative by Civil War historian James I. Robertson Jr. Many parts of the accompanying brochure echo Jubal Early's language. "In the pantheon of American soldiers, none stands taller than Confederate generals Thomas J. 'Stonewall' Jackson and Robert E. Lee," reads one passage. Another affirms that "these two Southern generals forged the greatest partnership in command in American history." Although they fought for a cause that would have dis-

---

Thomas L. Connelly, and Alan T. Nolan for influencing his portrait of Lee. One advertisement for the book included a blurb from William Garrett Piston calling it "a remarkable accomplishment."

41. *Civil War Times Illustrated* 33 (January–February 1995), advertisements on pp. 4, 5, 13, 14–15, 21, 64, 66, 73, 75.

membered the United States, Lee and Jackson are described as men who "epitomized the virtues of duty, valor and honor that patriotic Americans hold so dear."[42]

Grant has been the subject of no such book—for the apparent reason that despite *his* sense of duty, unquestioned valor, and unmatched contributions to Union victory, there is no comparable market among Civil War enthusiasts for works of art devoted to him. What explains this situation more than 130 years after he extended generous and honorable terms of surrender to Lee at Appomattox? Part of the answer probably lies in the often repeated stories about Grant as a drunkard and prewar failure that contrast so dramatically with descriptions of Lee as a devout Christian who made self-denial and self-control cardinal elements of his personal philosophy. Grant's scandal-ridden presidency also influenced his later reputation. Another major factor must be Grant's enduring image—carefully nurtured by Jubal Early and other Lost Cause writers—as an unimaginative officer who bludgeoned the Army of Northern Virginia into submission.

In 1987, Mark E. Neely, Harold Holzer, and Gabor S. Boritt published *The Confederate Image: Prints of the Lost Cause*, a superb analysis of nineteenth-century prints depicting Lost Cause themes. They concluded that by the end of the century, "throughout the South, and particularly in the iconography of the Lost Cause, Robert E. Lee had emerged as first in war, first in peace, and first in the hearts of his countrymen." Stonewall Jackson also inspired a number of nineteenth-century prints, and "one of the most enduring" of all Lost Cause images was an engraving of E. B. D. Julio's *The Last Meeting of Lee and Jackson*—a subject that has been painted repeatedly by modern artists.[43] Current Civil War art demonstrates that, if anything, Lee and Jackson are more dominant than in the heyday of the original Lost Cause writers.

Apart from their penchant for depicting Lee and Jackson, modern artists

42. The flyer was produced by Easton Press of Norwalk, Connecticut. Künstler also published a book titled *Gettysburg: The Paintings of Mort Künstler*, with text by James M. McPherson (Atlanta: Turner, 1993). Issued in conjunction with the release of the film *Gettysburg*, this book includes eight depictions of Lee at Gettysburg.

43. Mark E. Neely Jr., Harold Holzer, and Gabor S. Boritt, *The Confederate Image: Prints of the Lost Cause* (Chapel Hill: University of North Carolina Press, 1987), 168, color plate 11. On Lee and Jackson, see esp. chaps. 6, 10, and 11. Julio's famous interpretation of *The Last Meeting* remains available in a variety of prints as well as in one bas-relief version.

The Last Meeting of Lee and Jackson, an engraving of E. B. D. Julio's painting, a vastly popular Lost Cause representation of the two generals at Chancellorsville. Several versions of this engraving remain in print.

Collection of the author

select topics using other criteria that conform to Early's framework for under-standing the war. For example, Confederate topics outnumber Union ones by two or three to one (and according to price sheets for prints and sculpture typi-cally appreciate more rapidly). Subjects associated with the eastern theater are painted four or five times as often as those relating to all other theaters com-bined. Modern artists and the Civil War public to which they cater clearly join Early in considering the arena of Lee's activities the most important of the conflict.[44]

On October 30, 1865, Early composed his last letter to Lee before leaving the country for self-imposed exile. "I have brought away with me feelings of the highest admiration and respect for yourself," he wrote, "and I am satisfied history will accord to you the merit of retiring from the struggle with far more true glory than those who, by overwhelming numbers and resources, were en-abled to thwart all your efforts in defence of the liberties and independence of our unfortunate country." Five years later, Early struggled to come to terms with Lee's death. "The loss is a public one," he remarked, "and there are mil-lions of hearts now torn with anguish at the news that has been flashed over the wires to all quarters of the civilized world." He asked a former comrade to suggest a "suitable mode by which the officers who served under General Lee can give expression to their sentiments, and manifest to the world their appre-ciation of his talents, his virtues, and his services."[45] Deciding that Lee's mem-ory could best be served by attention to the written record of the war, Early worked tirelessly in the vineyards of Lost Cause advocacy. He proved himself a devoted lieutenant of Lee to the end of his life—and together with other Lost Cause authors helped demonstrate that the victors do not always control how historical events are remembered.

As much as anyone, then, Jubal Early constructed the image of the Civil War that many Americans North and South still find congenial. To explain why they do so would require another essay far longer than this. It would have to address the degree to which Lost Cause warriors wrote accurately about their war against the Union, what subsequent generations of Americans

---

44. These comparative figures were compiled from advertisements in *Civil War Times Illus-trated, Civil War: The Magazine of the Civil War Society,* and *Blue and Gray Magazine.* The data on prices come from sheets listing out-of-print works by Don Troiani, Dale Gallon, Mort Künstler, Don Stivers, and other leading Civil War artists.

45. Early to Lee, October 30, 1865, Mss3 L515a, VHS; Early to William Nelson Pendleton, October 13, 1870, William Nelson Pendleton Papers, SHC.

Lee and His Generals rivals Julio's *Last Meeting of Lee and Jackson* as a ubiquitous Lost Cause print. Published early in the twentieth century, it presents Lee as slightly taller than the other Confederate generals, who in turn are shown as nearly identical in height.

Collection of the author

really wanted when they called for states' rights, how conservatism and race fit into the equation, and why the ultimate goals of Union and freedom—for which more than a third of a million northern soldiers perished—often have figured only marginally in the popular understanding of the conflict.

A Widow and Her Soldier

LaSalle Corbell Pickett as the Author
of George E. Pickett's Civil War Letters

In the spring of 1913, fifty years after the climactic Confederate assault on the third day of Gettysburg, LaSalle Corbell Pickett published *The Heart of a Soldier: As Revealed in the Intimate Letters of Genl. George E. Pickett, C.S.A.*[1] The book contained forty-four letters supposedly written to Mrs. Pickett by the general between September 1861 and the mid-1870s. The publisher touted the book's personal glimpses of Robert E. Lee, Stonewall Jackson, James Longstreet, and other Confederate luminaries; its narration of interesting episodes of the war; and the touching love story of George and LaSalle Pickett. Quoting a reviewer who labeled the letters the "finest literary product of the Civil War," one advertisement predicted the Pickett letters would "make the literary fame of their soldier-author as immortal as his military glory." The *Confederate Veteran*, a magazine with a large southern audience, announced that the book would take its place "as a vital part of the courage and heroism that lives in the history of our great war."[2] Sales of the 1913 printing went well, and fifteen years later Arthur Crew Inman issued a slightly re-

1. New York: Seth Moyle, 1913.
2. *Confederate Veteran* 21 (1913):189, 360 [hereinafter cited as CV].

vised second edition under the title *Soldier of the South: General Pickett's War Letters to His Wife*.[3]

A group of letters relating to the 1863 Confederate invasion of Pennsylvania and the battle of Gettysburg formed the centerpiece of the volume. Rich with anecdotes and revealing Pickett's innermost thoughts and feelings—enthusiasm and confidence before the grand assault that became known as Pickett's Charge, anger and bewilderment following its bloody repulse—the letters display a vividness and immediacy that have attracted the attention of several generations of historians and popular writers. "Poor old Dick Garnett did not dismount, as did the others of us," read one passage describing Pickett's brigadiers during the assault, "and he was killed instantly, falling from his horse. Kemper, desperately wounded, was brought from the field and subsequently, taken prisoner. Dear old Lewis Armistead, God bless him, was mortally wounded at the head of his command after planting the flag of Virginia within the enemy's lines."[4] The letters dealing with Seven Pines, the Appomattox campaign, and other episodes of Pickett's wartime career, though less frequently cited, are similar in character. A student of General Pickett, or of Lee's army and its operations, could scarcely ask for better material from which to fashion a narrative.

Almost from the time of its publication, however, LaSalle Pickett's edition of her husband's letters was controversial—accepted by some writers, rejected by others, and questioned, at least in part, by most. A standard bibliography on the Civil War described the book's contents as "forty-eight highly edited—and probably highly abridged—letters of one of Lee's infantry commanders; Mrs. Pickett prepared the text."[5] Douglas Southall Freeman included the letters in the bibliography of his *R. E. Lee* with the curt observation that "they are rarely quoted in these volumes." Less reticent in private conver-

3. Boston: Houghton Mifflin, 1928. A native of Georgia then living in Boston, Inman (1895–1963) had published several volumes of poetry but had no formal credentials as a historian. For a revealing view of Inman, see Daniel Aaron, ed., *The Inman Diary: A Public and Private Confession*, 2 vols. (Cambridge, Mass.: Harvard University Press, 1985). The diary contains only a handful of entries pertinent to *Soldier of the South*.

4. Pickett, ed., *Heart of a Soldier*, 107.

5. Allan Nevins, James I. Robertson Jr., and Bell I. Wiley, eds., *Civil War Books: A Critical Bibliography*, 2 vols. (Baton Rouge: Louisiana State University Press, 1967–69), 1:145. The entry for Inman's *Soldier of the South* reads: "A reissue of . . . [*Heart of a Soldier*], with two letters and a new title added; in neither work does a clear picture emerge of Pickett the general" (p. 146).

sation than in print, Freeman expressed his unvarnished opinion that historians "should never believe anything that LaSalle Corbell Pickett had written about her husband."[6]

The first published discussion of the letters was a two-page appendix in George R. Stewart's *Pickett's Charge: A Microhistory of the Final Attack at Gettysburg, July 3, 1863*. After a careful review of the letters relating to Gettysburg, Stewart decided that they could not be "considered original historical sources." "I have come to this conclusion regretfully," he went on, "because I would have been glad to use some of the vivid details there presented." Stewart cited several reasons for his suspicions. First, Freeman and "another Civil War expert" doubted the authenticity of the letters; second, Stewart could find no originals for any of the letters, and Mrs. Pickett included facsimiles of none in her book; third, the writing was "lusciously sentimental"; and fourth, the letters betrayed knowledge of things Pickett could not have known at the time he supposedly wrote them. As examples of this last point, Stewart cited Pickett's use of such battlefield place names as Little Round Top, Cemetery Ridge, and Culp's Hill in a letter dated July 3, 1863. The Confederates did not know these names at the time of the battle and did not use them in their official battle reports. Acknowledging that the letters pertaining to Gettysburg might be heavily edited versions of originals, Stewart thought it more likely, "as data and occasional wordings would indicate," that Mrs. Pickett constructed them using *Pickett's Men: A Fragment of War History* by Walter H. Harrison, her husband's inspector general through most of the war.[7]

The authors of three of the most widely read books on Gettysburg did make use of the Pickett letters. Clifford Dowdey's *Death of a Nation: The Story of Lee and His Men at Gettysburg* listed the Inman edition in a note on sources with the comment that the letters had been "doctored for publication." "It can only be assumed," stated Dowdey, "that Mrs. Pickett included in her version of her husband's letters material which he had told her, as some of the questionable passages . . . equate with known facts." Proceeding on the as-

6. Douglas Southall Freeman, *R. E. Lee: A Biography*, 4 vols. (New York: Charles Scribner's Sons, 1934–35), 4:563; Glenn Tucker, *Lee and Longstreet at Gettysburg* (Indianapolis: Bobbs-Merrill, 1968), 270. The second quotation is from Tucker, who, without naming the person, explains in a note that "Douglas S. Freeman was quoted by a correspondent (to this author)."

7. George R. Stewart, *Pickett's Charge: A Microhistory of the Final Attack at Gettysburg, July 3, 1863* (Boston: Houghton Mifflin, 1959), 297–98; Walter H. Harrison, *Pickett's Men: A Fragment of War History* (1870; reprint, Gaithersburg, Md.: Butternut Press, 1984).

LaSalle Corbell Pickett
Miley Collection, Virginia Historical Society, Richmond

sumption that the material at least came from Pickett, Dowdey quoted the letters many times in his account of events on July 3 at Gettysburg.[8] In his exhaustive *The Gettysburg Campaign: A Study in Command*, Edwin B. Coddington used Inman's book to address the question of who commanded the Confederate brigades in the assault on Cemetery Ridge. "The latest edition of Pickett's letters," wrote Coddington in reference to *Soldier of the South*, "has concluded that Pickett did not consider himself in command of more than his

8. Clifford Dowdey, *Death of a Nation: The Story of Lee and His Men at Gettysburg* (New York: Alfred A. Knopf, 1958), 371. Dowdey's book has been very popular, going through five printings in its first nine years and remaining in print today.

own division." He cited excerpts from two of the general's letters written on July 3 and one on July 4 to the future Mrs. Pickett.[9]

Two recent biographers also used both LaSalle Pickett's and Arthur Crew Inman's editions of the letters. In *"Faithfully and Forever Your Soldier": Gen. George E. Pickett, CSA*, Richard F. Selcer implies that LaSalle Pickett's editing of the correspondence was primarily cosmetic. "When LaSalle published her wartime letters from George," writes Selcer, "she wielded a heavy editorial hand. Among other changes, she changed the sign-off from 'faithfully yours' to 'faithfully your soldier' or just 'your soldier.'" Edward G. Longacre, in *Pickett, Leader of the Charge: A Biography of General George E. Pickett, C.S.A.*, observes that LaSalle Pickett "fabricated many of the wartime and postwar letters," but he nonetheless quotes passages from several of them.[10]

LaSalle Pickett's strongest defender has been Glenn Tucker, whose *High Tide at Gettysburg* and *Lee and Longstreet at Gettysburg* won favorable reviews from many scholars.[11] Tucker quotes freely from the Pickett letters in both books, and his chapter in the latter titled "Pickett's Missives and Missing Report" examines the letters as historical evidence and finds them "essentially genuine." Chiding "overcautious historians who reject almost everything that cannot be verified by an additional source," Tucker argues that the letters contain "little if any information that fails to harmonize with what is known from other sources about Pickett's share in the campaign." Tucker believes Mrs. Pickett to have been a woman of high integrity who approached her editing project from a nineteenth-century perspective. "The practice today in editing letters and the like," writes Tucker, "is to leave them unaltered down to the

9. Edwin B. Coddington, *The Gettysburg Campaign: A Study in Command* (New York: Charles Scribner's Sons, 1968), 793–94 n. 68. Considered a classic treatment of the campaign, this volume has been reprinted several times.

10. Richard F. Selcer, *"Faithfully and Forever Your Soldier": Gen. George E. Pickett, CSA* (Gettysburg, Pa.: Farnsworth House Military Impressions, 1995), 65 n. 46; Edward G. Longacre, *Pickett, Leader of the Charge: A Biography of General George E. Pickett, C.S.A.* (Shippensburg, Pa.: White Mane, 1995), xi. Lesley J. Gordon's biography of Pickett, which was available only in manuscript at the time this essay was prepared, includes a careful evaluation of Mrs. Pickett's edition of her husband's letters.

11. Glenn Tucker, *High Tide at Gettysburg: The Campaign in Pennsylvania* (Indianapolis: Bobbs-Merrill, 1958). For reviews of Tucker's books, see *Civil War History* 5 (1959): 431–33 (*High Tide at Gettysburg* reviewed by Brainerd Dyer) and 14 (1968):367–68 (*Lee and Longstreet at Gettysburg* reviewed by Richard R. Duncan).

Major General George Edward Pickett
Miller, ed., *Photographic History of the Civil War*

crossing of a'T.'" Such was not always the rule, and if "Mrs. Pickett did make alterations in the interest of clarity, but did not alter the meaning of the original letters, it was quite within the proprieties." Tucker finds it significant that Mrs. Pickett published the letters at a time when many of her husband's veterans were alive and could have pointed out glaring errors. That none did, that in fact the old warriors "appear to have believed and lingered over every word" of the letters, spoke well for *The Heart of a Soldier*. "What better test of authenticity could be devised than this?" asks Tucker.[12]

12. Tucker, *Lee and Longstreet at Gettysburg*, 148, 156, 271 n. 1. On pages 155–56, Tucker specifically addresses the anachronisms that bothered Stewart. A number of writers on Gettysburg have followed Tucker rather than Stewart. One recent book on the battle, Champ Clark *et al.*, *Gettysburg: The Confederate High Tide* (Alexandria, Va., 1985), opens its chapter on Pickett's Charge with a quotation from *Heart of a Soldier*.

Although more than eight decades have passed since Mrs. Pickett first offered *The Heart of a Soldier* to the public, extant evidence permits a definitive answer to the question of whether the letters have any value as historical documents. Sadly, a careful review of this evidence leads to the conclusion that the correspondence published in *The Heart of a Soldier*, which represents a significant portion of the known Pickett letters of wartime date, is worthless as a source on the general's Confederate career. LaSalle Pickett concocted the letters, relying on plagiarism and her own romantic imagination, and Arthur Crew Inman compounded the problem by reprinting them when he knew her handling of the material was questionable.[13]

The most damning proof of Mrs. Pickett's authorship is her systematic plagiarism of Harrison's *Pickett's Men*.[14] As Pickett's inspector general for much of the war, Harrison had participated in most of the division's operations. His book, published in 1870 and based on surviving records and interviews with former officers, was filled with information unavailable elsewhere. Going far beyond the "data and occasional wordings" on Gettysburg mentioned by George Stewart, Mrs. Pickett's plagiarism of Harrison permeates all eighteen letters in *The Heart of a Soldier* that deal significantly with battles from Seven Pines through Appomattox.[15] In these eighteen letters are more than forty instances of nearly verbatim plagiarism, ranging in length from one sentence to entire paragraphs, together with dozens of paraphrases.

The extent of Mrs. Pickett's borrowing can be fully appreciated only through a close reading of the two books, but a few representative illustrations will make the point. Harrison narrates Pickett's Charge: "The three brigades

---

13. Other Confederate primary accounts have come under scrutiny over the years. Perhaps the most famous is Mary Chesnut's diary, first published in 1905 in a version expanded and rewritten by Chesnut herself in the 1880s and subsequently reprinted. Not until C. Vann Woodward and Elisabeth Muhlenfeld edited *The Private Mary Chesnut: The Unpublished Civil War Diaries* (New York: Oxford University Press, 1984) was an accurate edition of the real diaries made available.

14. For a sketch of Harrison and background on his book, see Gary W. Gallagher's introduction to the Butternut Press reprint of Harrison's *Pickett's Men* (Gaithersburg, Md., 1984).

15. The letters in *Heart of a Soldier* are numbered. Those devoted to battles are numbers 4 (Seven Pines), 5 (Gaines's Mill), 8–9 (the Maryland campaign and the Stonewall Jackson–Richard B. Garnett feud), 10 (Fredericksburg), 11, 13 (the Suffolk campaign), 14, 16–19, 21–22 (the Gettysburg campaign), 24 (New Bern), 28 (Bermuda Hundred), 37 (Five Forks), and 38 (Appomattox). Other letters briefly mention battles, but they deal principally with social activities, Pickett's courtship of LaSalle Corbell, the birth of their first child, politics, and postwar events.

moved across this field of death and glory as steadily as a battalion forward in line of battle upon drill. The three brigade commanders were conspicuously in front of their commands, leading and cheering them on." Mrs. Pickett has her husband narrate Pickett's Charge: "My three brigades . . . moved across that field of death as a battalion marches forward in line of battle upon drill, each commander in front of his command leading and cheering on his men."[16]

Harrison writes that before the battle of Fredericksburg, James Longstreet "had left directions with his Division-commanders, Pickett and Hood, to hold their ground simply in defence, unless an opportunity should occur to pitch into the enemy while he was engaged with A. P. Hill on the right." Pickett's letter on Fredericksburg states that "Old Peter's orders were that Hood and myself were to hold our ground of defense unless we should see an opportunity to attack the enemy while engaged with A. P. Hill on the right." In his chapter on fighting at Bermuda Hundred, Harrison mentions a "line of breastworks, important as the main line of defence between Richmond and Petersburg, and opposing any advance of the enemy upon the peninsula of Bermuda Hundreds." A letter in *The Heart of a Soldier* reads, "the line of breastworks . . . is most important, as the main line of defense between Richmond and Petersburg and opposing any advance of the enemy upon the peninsula of Bermuda Hundred."[17]

Harrison's account of Pickett's last major battle includes a description of the crossroads where the fighting occurred: "Situated in a flat, thickly wooded country, Five Forks, as its name indicates, is simply a crossing, at nearly right angles, of two country roads, and the deflection of a third road, bisecting one of those angles." LaSalle Pickett has her husband state that "Five Forks is situated in a flat, thickly wooded country and is simply a crossing at right angles of two country roads and a deflection of a third bisecting one of these angles." A final set of quotations concerns the retreat toward Appomattox Court House after Five Forks. "I will not attempt to describe the sufferings of this march to Amelia Court-House, and thence to Sailor's Creek," writes Harrison, "when for forty-eight hours the man or officer who had a handful of parched corn in his pocket was fortunate." Pickett's letter on the subject declares that "the horrors of the march from Five Forks to Amelia Court House and thence to Sailor's Creek beggars all description. For forty-eight hours the

16. Harrison, *Pickett's Men*, 97; Pickett, ed., *Heart of a Soldier*, 106.
17. Harrison, *Pickett's Men*, 71, 131; Pickett, ed., *Heart of a Soldier*, 65, 136.

man or officer who had a handful of parched corn in his pocket was most fortunate."[18]

Although Harrison was her principal source, LaSalle Pickett undoubtedly drew on other Confederate writings. From the letters dated July 3 and July 4, 1863, especially the conversations between Lee and Longstreet and Longstreet and Pickett, one can infer that she used Longstreet's articles on Gettysburg, published in the *Southern Historical Society Papers* and *The Annals of the War*, and Edward Porter Alexander's long letter on the cannonade preceding Pickett's Charge, published in the *Southern Historical Society Papers*.[19] One example concerns a conference between Lee and Longstreet early on the morning of July 3. Lee rode to his corps commander's headquarters that morning, where, according to Longstreet, he pointed his fist at Cemetery Hill and said, "The enemy is there, and I am going to strike him." Mrs. Pickett places her husband at this conference and has him report, " 'The enemy is there, General Longstreet, and I am going to strike him,' said Marse Robert in his firm, quiet, determined voice."[20]

Two other incidents from Mrs. Pickett's writings merit attention. In *Pickett and His Men*, a history of her husband's division, and an article in *McClure's Magazine* titled "My Soldier," she quotes portions of letters supposedly written to Pickett by Abraham Lincoln. She claims that Lincoln, while a congressman from Illinois, had learned through Pickett's uncle, with whom he practiced law, that Pickett had been unable to secure an appointment to West Point from any member of his own state's congressional delegation. Lincoln arranged for the appointment and wrote to the young cadet soon after he reached West Point. "I have just told the folks here in Springfield on this 111th anniversary of the birth of him whose name, mightiest in the cause of civil liberty, still mightiest in the cause of moral reformation, we mention in

18. Harrison, *Pickett's Men*, 139, 155; Pickett, ed., *Heart of a Soldier*, 171–72, 177.

19. James Longstreet, "Lee in Pennsylvania" and "The Mistakes of Gettysburg," originally published in 1876 in the *Philadelphia Weekly Times* and reprinted in [A. K. McClure], ed., *The Annals of the War, Written by Leading Participants North and South Originally Published in the Philadelphia Weekly Times* (Philadelphia: Times Publishing, 1879), 414–46, 619–33, and in J. William Jones and others, eds., *Southern Historical Society Papers*, 52 vols. (1876–1959; reprint, with 3-vol. index, Wilmington, N.C.: Broadfoot, 1990–92), 5:54–86, 257–70 [hereinafter cited as *SHSP*]; E. P. Alexander, "Letter from General E. P. Alexander, Late Chief of Artillery First Corps, A.N.V.," *SHSP* 4:97–111. The conversations are in letters 18, 19, and 21 of Pickett, ed., *Heart of a Soldier*.

20. Longstreet, "Lee in Pennsylvania," 429; Pickett, ed., *Heart of a Soldier*, 94.

solemn awe, in naked, deathless splendor," begins one turgid excerpt, "that the one victory we can never call complete will be that one which proclaims that there is not one slave or one drunkard on the face of God's green earth. Recruit for this victory."[21] Bearing all the earmarks of LaSalle Pickett's writing style and none of Lincoln's, the letter found its way into Ida Tarbell's biography of Lincoln, with ownership of the letter credited to Mrs. Pickett. Half a century later, the editors of the comprehensive edition of Lincoln's works pronounced Mrs. Pickett's Lincoln materials a forgery.[22]

Another highly questionable letter, also in *Pickett and His Men*, figures in a typically dramatic anecdote. Having received Longstreet's unspoken order to make his famous assault, Pickett galloped off, only to remember that in his pocket was a letter to his fiancée. Scribbling on the corner of the envelope, "If Old Peter's nod means death good-by, and God bless you, little one!" Pickett hastened back to Longstreet and asked him to mail the letter. Longstreet not only agreed to do so but, according to Mrs. Pickett, took the time right then, with several thousand of his men about to launch an attack, to compose a cover letter. "General Pickett has just intrusted to me the safe conveyance of the inclosed letter," it began. "If it should turn out to be his farewell the penciled note on the outside will show you that I could not speak the words which would send so gallant a soldier into the jaws of a useless death." Struggling with his emotions, Longstreet continued: "As I watched him, gallant and fearless as a knight of old, riding to certain doom, I said a prayer for his safety and made a vow to the Holy Father that my friendship for him, poor as it is, should be your heritage."[23]

As with the Lincoln letters, the prose and the sentiments here are LaSalle Pickett's. Longstreet left three detailed accounts of the afternoon of July 3, none of which mentions this episode. His memoirs describe the interview with Pickett as follows: "Pickett said, 'General, shall I advance?' The effort to speak

21. LaSalle Corbell Pickett, *Pickett and His Men* (Atlanta: Foote and Davis, 1899), 127; LaSalle Corbell Pickett, "My Soldier," *McClure's Magazine* 30 (1908):563–71. The two versions vary slightly; that quoted here is from *Pickett and His Men*, which, as might be expected, is a panegyric.

22. Ida M. Tarbell, *The Life of Abraham Lincoln* (1900; reprint, 2 vols., New York: Doubleday, 1928), 11, 401; Abraham Lincoln, *The Collected Works of Abraham Lincoln*, ed. Roy P. Basler *et al.*, 9 vols. (New Brunswick, N.J.: Rutgers University Press, 1953–55), 8:439.

23. Pickett, *Pickett and His Men*, 301. See also letter 19 in Pickett, ed., *Heart of a Soldier*.

the order failed, and I could only indicate it by an affirmative bow. He accepted the duty with seeming confidence of success, leaped on his horse, and rode gayly to his command. I mounted and spurred for Alexander's post." Longstreet wrote a short introduction for *Pickett and His Men.* Why would he have done so if Pickett's letter of July 3 was not legitimate? The likely explanation is that he wrote his introduction (an appreciation of Pickett that makes no reference to the substance of the book) without having read Mrs. Pickett's narrative. If he later discovered what she had done, he chose not to accuse her publicly.[24]

The fifty-one Pickett letters in the papers of Arthur Crew Inman shed further light on the published correspondence. This material, sent to Inman by LaSalle Pickett, consists of typescripts of the bogus letters in *The Heart of a Soldier,* which arrived in envelopes marked "Copies of My Soldier's Letters," together with eleven authentic originals in Pickett's hand (two of the eleven are fragments).[25] For the reissue of the correspondence as *Soldier of the South,* Inman dropped two of the letters in *The Heart of a Soldier* and added three of the eleven originals.[26] He took his text directly from Mrs. Pickett's typescripts, on which his editorial changes are clearly marked, and from the three original letters. Yet he deceptively implies that he worked only with originals, written on "yellow pages, crisp with age, carrying down through unrolling years, in neatly-penciled or penned sentences, the flavor of the past." Inman thus perpetuates the false impression conveyed by Mrs. Pickett's statement in *The*

24. Longstreet's accounts are in *SHSP* 5:69–70 and *Annals of the War,* 430–31 (the same version); James Longstreet, "Lee's Right Wing at Gettysburg," in Robert Underwood Johnson and Clarence Clough Buel, eds., *Battles and Leaders of the Civil War,* 4 vols. (New York: Century, 1887), 3:345; and James Longstreet, *From Manassas to Appomattox: Memoirs of the Civil War in America* (Philadelphia: Lippincott, 1896), 392 (quotation).

25. The Arthur Crew Inman Papers are in the John Hay Library, Brown University, Providence, R.I. There are no typescripts for letters 2, 7, 19, 33, 39, and 42 in *Heart of a Soldier;* Inman made typescripts for five of the eleven originals and duplicates of LaSalle Pickett's typescripts. Item 51 on the inventory of *Soldier of the South* material in the Inman Papers is mistakenly described as a letter in Pickett's hand and signed by him. The written fragment in this case is in Inman's hand.

26. Inman omitted letters 31 and 44, both of which concern Pickett's children. In addition to the three originals (numbers 24, 29, and 35 in *Soldier of the South*), he included one letter in typescript not in *Heart of a Soldier* (number 21 in *Soldier of the South*). The net gain was thus two, for a total of forty-six letters in *Soldier of the South.*

Heart of a Soldier that "for half a century these letters have lain locked away from the world, the lines fading upon the yellowed pages."[27]

Inman had both the original and typescript of a fragment dated July 23, 1863, that Mrs. Pickett had printed in *Pickett and His Men*.[28] Although she had moved words and sentences around and added or deleted phrases, Inman chose to reproduce the mutilated letter in *Soldier of the South*. One of his plates, positioned opposite the text, is a facsimile of part of the original. "It is evident from comparison with the original fragment, and from the altered style," he concedes in a note, "that the quoted letter has been to some extent changed." Worried that the original "does differ considerably from the form in which the same matter appears in the text," editors at Houghton Mifflin considered Inman's note insufficient explanation and suggested that he correct the text. Inman declined. What was worse, he asserted that he had adhered "scrupulously to the exact historical statements" in the letters—letters his readers had every reason to believe were originals.[29]

A comparison of the eleven originals in the Inman papers with the published correspondence in *The Heart of a Soldier* strongly suggests that LaSalle Pickett composed the latter. The originals are signed "George" or "G . . ." while the published letters are signed "Your Soldier," a closing no doubt preferred by LaSalle Pickett, who always called Pickett "My Soldier."[30] The writing styles also differ significantly. Pickett was a romantic, given to tender expressions such as, "Bye Bye my love. I think of you by day, dream of you by night, and my heart is ever with you. Forever yours and *only* yours, George." Or this: "Oh my own sweet wife, keep up your heart bravely, and think of your husband who lives but for you; you *know* it, you *feel* it. I would my baby give anything in the world anything to see my wife this evening."[31] But the letters

27. Inman, ed., *Soldier of the South*, vii–ix; Pickett, ed., *Heart of a Soldier*, [v].

28. Pickett, *Pickett and His Men*, 316–17. The typescript letter that Inman added to *Soldier of the South* had also been printed in *Pickett and His Men*.

29. Inman, ed., *Soldier of the South*, 78, ix; M. Allen to Arthur Crew Inman, January 14, 1928, Inman Papers. As he observes in his introduction, Inman deleted much "personal" as opposed to "historical" material from the original letters.

30. Presumably for the sake of consistency, Inman changed the closings of the three originals in *Soldier of the South* to "Your Soldier."

31. George E. Pickett to LaSalle Corbell Pickett, Thursday evening [1863], [July 3, 1864?], Inman Papers. On Pickett's romantic nature, see Gilbert Moxley Sorrel, *Recollections of a Confederate Staff Officer* (1905; reprint, Jackson, Tenn.: McCowat-Mercer, 1958), 146–47. Sorrel, who served as Longstreet's chief of staff, wrote that "Pickett was a widower, but had recently suffered

in his own hand lack the overpowering sentimentality and gushy prose of the published letters: "Now, my Sally, how I hate to say it—adieu. Do you remember how many times we said good-by that last evening? And then as I heard the latch of the gate click and shut me out, I was obliged to go back. I could not stand the cruelty of the sound of the latch—it seemed to knife my soul. I turned back and said 'Good night!' The door was open; I came in. You thought I had gone. I can't just remember how many times I said good night. I know I did not close the gate as I went out again. Keep another gate open for the good morning, my precious bride-to-be. Oh, the bliss to be—the bliss to be then for *YOUR SOLDIER*."[32]

Several of the published letters, but none of the originals, have lengthy passages in which Pickett recounts in black dialect the humorous adventures of his body servant.[33] Speech patterns of slaves fascinated LaSalle Pickett, it must be noted, and she wrote four volumes of stories in what Joel Chandler Harris called an "absolutely faithful reproduction of the dialect of the old Southern slave."[34] In the original letters Pickett often mentions fellow officers but seldom quotes them, while in the printed ones he attributes improbable statements to them. In one such tale Lewis A. Armistead, just before leading his brigade forward at Gettysburg, pulls a ring from his finger and says, "Give this little token, George, please, to her of the sunset eyes, with my love, and tell her the 'old man' says since he could not be the lucky dog he's mighty glad that you are." Here as elsewhere LaSalle Pickett is the subject of the quotation.[35] Pickett's way of alluding to superiors is also inconsistent. Nicknames

---

himself to fall in love with all the ardor of youth. The object of these fiery, if mature, affections, dwelt not far from Suffolk." Referring to Pickett's habit of leaving his headquarters at night to visit LaSalle Corbell, Sorrel observed, "I don't think his division benefited by such carpet-knight doings in the field."

32. Pickett, ed., *Heart of a Soldier*, 80.

33. See, for example, letters 7, 25, 34, and 42 in Pickett, ed., *Heart of a Soldier*.

34. Robert K. Krick, *Neale Books: An Annotated Bibliography* (Dayton, Ohio: Morningside, 1977), 145–46. The four books, known collectively as the *In de Miz* series, are: *Kunnoo Sperits and Others, Yule-Log and Others, Ebil Eye and Others,* and *Jinny and Others* (Washington, D.C.: Neale, 1900–1901). Mrs. Pickett also used black dialect in her novel *The Bugles at Gettysburg* (Chicago, 1913) and in many of her stories. A contemporary sketch of her noted that "in dialect work she is at her best" (Lucian Lamar Knight, comp., *Biographical Dictionary of Authors*, in Edwin A. Alderman and Joel Chandler Harris, eds., *Library of Southern Literature*, 15 vols. [Atlanta: 1910], 15:343).

35. Pickett, ed., *Heart of a Soldier*, 93.

are almost universal in the printed letters—"Marse Robert" for Lee, "Old Jack" for Jackson, "Old Peter" for Longstreet, "Little Mac" for McClellan; in the originals, ranks and last names predominate.[36]

A final point of difference between the originals and the published letters concerns length. There is a six-page letter in *The Heart of a Soldier* supposedly written at Gettysburg on July 3 while Pickett awaited orders to advance. "How Pickett found time to write these lines," marvels Glenn Tucker, "is one of the astonishing things of the battle."[37] No original dated July 3, 1863, has surfaced, probably because Major General Pickett had his hands full preparing his division for the assault. Other published letters written on the march to Pennsylvania run two to four pages and give details of the army's position, expected movements, and morale. Two originals, dated June 26 and June 30 from Greencastle and Chambersburg, Pennsylvania, respectively, are only one page long and confined to personal matters. In each Pickett explains that he is afraid to write more because the letters could be intercepted.[38]

Anachronisms and other factual problems in the published letters go beyond the famous examples relating to Gettysburg.[39] Commenting on the battle of Antietam in a letter of September 25, 1862, for instance, Pickett observes that "in its wake came Lincoln's great political victory, proving the might of the pen, in his Emancipation Proclamation—winning with it the greatest victory yet for the North." He goes on to urge emancipation for all southern slaves lest Europe shun the South. Southern emancipation and foreign intervention would end the war, and, he concludes, "I pray God that the powers that reign will have the wisdom and foresight to see this in its true and all-pervading light." Here Pickett displays remarkable political insight in recognizing, just three days after the preliminary proclamation was issued, the vast potential of Lincoln's actions. And his call for freeing southern slaves puts him well in the vanguard on an issue that would not surface in the Confederacy for many months.[40]

36. For the flavor of LaSalle Pickett's use of nicknames, see *ibid.*, 42, 46, 59, 62, 65–66, 70, 92, 94, 109, 117, 130–33.

37. *Ibid.*, 91–96 (letter 18); Tucker, *High Tide at Gettysburg*, 354.

38. Letters 14–17 in Pickett, ed., *Heart of a Soldier*; George E. Pickett to LaSalle Corbell, June 26, 30, 1863, Inman Papers.

39. See above, page 229.

40. Pickett, ed., *Heart of a Soldier*, 60.

Although the evidence reveals that LaSalle Pickett composed the letters in *The Heart of a Soldier*, it does not explain her motive. Long active in the affairs of the United Daughters of the Confederacy, a favorite at reunions of the United Confederate Veterans, and revered as the "child bride of the Confederacy" and widow of a famous southern hero, she risked alienating the people whose opinions meant most to her. She was a writer by profession, who belonged to the Women's National Press Association and served as president of the League of American Pen-women. Disclosure of her fabrication almost certainly would have elicited harsh judgments from her peers.[41]

Why did she take such a chance? Money may have been one reason. George Pickett did not prosper in the postwar years, and his widow was left to support herself. Perhaps her publisher projected large sales on a book of her husband's letters. The threat of exposure probably seemed remote. The men who might have detected her plagiarism—Walter Harrison, James Longstreet, and Porter Alexander—were all dead. No one else had any of Pickett's letters to her, so comparisons of original and published texts were impossible. The phony Lincoln material had been accepted and printed by a leading expert on the president.

Another factor might have been a wish to bolster with her husband's own testimony the intensely romantic portrait of him Mrs. Pickett had drawn in *Pickett and His Men* and elsewhere. Imbued as she was with the romance of the Old South and a gallant Confederacy, she may have relished the opportunity to present herself as the quintessential southern belle, worshiped by her soldier husband and admired and flattered by his fellow generals. The Pickett letters, together with most of LaSalle Pickett's other writings, fit into the Lost Cause literature of the late nineteenth and early twentieth centuries. They dwell on such tragic aspects of the Confederate experience as the defeat at Gettysburg and celebrate a chivalric people battling to preserve their superior civilization. Doomed to defeat in the face of overwhelming numbers, the Confederacy, exemplified by her husband in LaSalle Pickett's writings, fought nobly to the end.

"These letters are sacred," stated Mrs. Pickett in her foreword to *The Heart of a Soldier*, "and they are given to the world with great reluctance." Dedicating them to the memory of "the Great Soldier and True Man" who

---

41. For sketches of Mrs. Pickett, see Tucker, *Lee and Longstreet at Gettysburg*, 148–49, 156–58, 271 n. 1; CV 39 (1931):151; and Knight, comp., *Biographical Dictionary*, 343.

wrote them, she voiced the hope that they would inspire people who honored "courage, loyalty and the love of man for woman."[42] If that was her goal, she failed miserably. For instead of honoring George Pickett, the letters cast a shadow on him that will be lifted only if a cache of genuine letters comes to light.[43]

42. Pickett, ed., *Heart of a Soldier*, [v].

43. The city of Harrisburg, Pennsylvania, purchased approximately 150 allegedly authentic Pickett letters in 1995 as part of a campaign to build a significant collection of documents and letters for a museum. Subsequent fiscal difficulties forced the city to return the letters to the owner. The final disposition of this Pickett material, to which scholars have been denied access, remains uncertain.

IV

Distant Reverberations

★ I2 ★

How Familiarity Bred Success

Military Campaigns and Leaders
in Ken Burns's The Civil War

Ken Burns's television series on the Civil War provoked lively debate about its vision of the great American trauma. Especially in the area of military operations and commanders, discussion highlighted a gulf often separating academic historians from the public. Most viewers responded positively to the series, although they disagreed about its relative treatment of North and South, the degree to which it stressed slavery as a cause of secession, and whether it glorified war by emphasizing the bravery and devotion of common soldiers or conveyed an antiwar subtext through repeated shots of bloated corpses and blasted landscapes. Academic historians centered much of their attention on whether Burns had spent inordinate time on military campaigns and thereby obscured larger and more important issues. In the procession of battles and generals, believed many academics, viewers probably missed the broader context within which the armies contended for supremacy. Any consideration of Burns's work raises two questions: Did the series properly balance military and nonmilitary topics? And did Burns develop each appropriately?

Most of the discussion to date has centered on the question of balance. In a cover story on what it termed a "stunning television documentary," *News-*

week magazine remarked that "fourteen million Americans, more than the entire population of the Confederacy, gave themselves over to 'The Civil War'
last week." Most of those viewers probably would have agreed with the editor
of Civil War Times Illustrated, a widely read popular publication about the war,
who wrote that the series "distills—but does not dilute—some of the most
complex issues in our national history into a readily understandable form" and
"helps set new standards in using the documentary medium to both interpret
history and entertain Americans." As good as it was, added this writer, The
Civil War neglected the battle of South Mountain, Winfield Scott's strategic
contribution to Union victory, and other "minor but pertinent pieces" of the
military picture. Blue and Gray Magazine, a bimonthly published in Columbus,
Ohio, similarly called the documentary "powerful, moving, and educational"
but asserted that the issue of slavery was "extremely over-treated" while military events such as South Mountain and James Harrison Wilson's destructive
raid through Alabama in 1865 were ignored. Overall, nonscholarly magazines
devoted to the Civil War typically praised the series but complained about errors of fact or omissions concerning specific battles or campaigns.[1]

Academic historians frequently expressed unhappiness with what they
perceived as uncritical popular acceptance of Burns's work. Many of their
comments betrayed an impatience toward military topics, which they saw as
inherently less interesting and important than the social and political dimensions of the war. One typical evaluation pronounced the "commercial success
of The Civil War to be symptomatic of the problem of historical representation
in the media" and worried about "the canonization of the narrative strategies
embedded in the production of such programs" (the latter statement speaks
volumes about why so few lay readers find academic history to their taste).
Agreeing with others who voiced unhappiness with Burns's "conception of
the Civil War as a history of war," this scholar quoted with thinly disguised
sarcasm the filmmaker's statement that "'only' 40 percent of the eleven hours
depicted battles." "The Civil War is luxuriant on military detail and very thin
on political context," complained another academic reviewer. "Each major
battle is separately portrayed, the character of its generals dissected, and its
battlefields, now quiet and reflective, filmed in long, beautiful shots; this is the

1. "Revisiting the Civil War," Newsweek 106 (October 8, 1990):58–59; John E. Stanchak,
"A Big War on a Small Screen," Civil War Times Illustrated 29 (October 1990):50–51; Gregg
Biggs, "Audio/Video Reviews," Blue and Gray Magazine 8 (December 1990):42.

visual version of the approach taken by generations of Civil War buffs, for whom reenacting battles is a beloved hobby. Missing are the truly decisive *political* battles, which determined what the armies of the North and South brought to each of their physical confrontations."[2]

Much of the scholarly criticism reflected changes in the historical profession that have brought attention to people and issues previously slighted. The desire to make American history more inclusive and to reveal its ambiguities and tensions is certainly laudable, but it is important to remember that the subject of Burns's documentary was a mammoth *war* that unfolded chronologically. Would avoiding chronological narrative and muting the role of armies make the experience of 1861–1865 more intelligible to nonspecialists? In their haste to deny the centrality of military events, many of Burns's critics overlook that what occurred on battlefields profoundly influenced virtually every aspect of life behind the lines. Military results often shaped the "truly decisive *political* battles." Neither the home front nor the battlefield can be understood without attention to reciprocal influences that determined actions and decisions in both spheres.

Nor does it help to label readers (or viewers) interested in military campaigns and leaders "buffs" eager to dress up and restage battles. The vast majority of "buffs" have neither donned a uniform nor attended a Civil War reenactment. Their interests usually extend well beyond questions of where regiments and brigades fought on individual battlefields. Many academic historians, content to speak to one another in language that excludes anyone outside the university community, ignore a literate lay audience that consistently has manifested interest in the Civil War. A sense of "we know best" permeates much of their commentary about Burns. Put off by the public's fondness for generals, battles, and narrative integrity, these academics insist that lay readers and viewers should be given "real history" as defined by scholars.

In fact, any documentary about the Civil War that failed to place military events at or near center stage would itself be open to charges of distortion. Moreover, the notion that any documentary on a cataclysmic conflict should play down the importance of military events almost certainly would amuse most nonacademics. Millions of people North and South eagerly followed the

2. Daniel J. Walkowitz, "Telling the Story: The Media, the Public, and American History," *Perspectives* 31 (October 1993):1, 6–7; Ellen Carol DuBois's review of *The Civil War*, in *American Historical Review* 96 (October 1991):1141.

progress of Union and Confederate armies on a daily basis, according more attention to strategic maneuvers and battles than to any of the nonmilitary topics favored by modern scholars. Perceptions about the military situation influenced how people voted, whether they bought government bonds, and many of their other activities. One university professor may have been too harsh when he ascribed "nitpicking" academic criticisms of Burns to jealousy over the commercial success of *The Civil War*; however, he was correct in stating that "Burns has made history live, giving it a human face and vivid texture rarely achieved in Academe." Indeed, Burns's greatest achievement lay in his ability to fire the imaginations of millions of Americans, sending them in large numbers to libraries and bookstores in search of more information.[3]

Many academic scholars revealed their lack of interest in soldiers and battles by questioning how much time Burns spent on the battlefield but never asking how well he covered military events. I have tipped my hand about the first question. I think Burns strikes a reasonable balance between military and nonmilitary coverage. But how sound is his treatment of matters military? Does *The Civil War* incorporate recent scholarship? Is the geographical coverage balanced? Are the major actors on each side given appropriate attention? Does Burns evaluate available sources judiciously? And does he strive to explain the connections between the home front and the battlefield? Regrettably, the answers to these questions suggest an utterly conventional approach that leaves the viewer with a skewed sense of the war's military dimension.[4]

Although Burns consulted a number of prominent historians, many parts of *The Civil War* betray a curious ignorance of modern scholarship. The first episode sets the military stage with a flawed examination of resources at the opening of the conflict. Stressing the North's industrial capacity and vastly larger pool of manpower, Burns concludes that "the odds against a southern victory were long." While true as far as it goes, this approach overlooks important Confederate advantages that evened the initial balance sheet. The Confederacy had only to defend itself and could win if the North did nothing; moreover, its armies could stand on the defensive while Union forces faced the

3. The professor who criticized Burns's detractors was Gordon Zimmerman of the University of Nevada, whose comments appeared as a letter to the editors in *Newsweek* 106 (October 29, 1990):14.

4. The book that accompanied the documentary, *The Civil War: An Illustrated History*, by Geoffrey C. Ward, Ric Burns, and Ken Burns (New York: Knopf, 1990), follows an almost identical interpretive path.

task of conquering and occupying the South. The immense size of the Confederacy (at 750,000 square miles it was double the size of the American colonies during the Revolutionary War) and its 3,500-mile coastline posed daunting obstacles to northern arms. In works such as James M. McPherson's *Ordeal by Fire* and *Battle Cry of Freedom* and Herman Hattaway and Archer Jones's *How the North Won*, Burns had readily available analyses of each side's strengths and weaknesses. Inexplicably, he chose to overlook their insights.[5]

Burns's appraisal of resources drapes a mantle of hopelessness over the Confederate resistance, imparting an especially tragic quality to the costly battles that follow. Here *The Civil War* echoes Lost Cause writers such as Jubal A. Early, who often attributed Confederate defeat to the enemy's material strength. Gallant struggle against impossible odds elevated Confederate soldiers, as Early suggested in an 1872 address on Robert E. Lee: "General Lee had not been conquered in battle. . . . He surrendered . . . the mere ghost of the Army of Northern Virginia, which had been gradually worn down by the combined agencies of numbers, steam-power, railroads, mechanism, and all the resources of physical science." This interpretive tradition extends back to Lee himself, who had assured his soldiers at Appomattox on April 10, 1865, that the enemy's "overwhelming numbers and resources" had compelled him to surrender.[6]

Other passages reinforce the initial image of badly outnumbered Confederates. In Episode III, for example, Burns describes Lee's army on June 26, 1862, as a "tiny force" facing a juggernaut in George B. McClellan's Army of the Potomac. The ensuing Seven Days battles assume the character of an

5. On this question, see chap. 12 of James M. McPherson, *Ordeal by Fire: The Civil War and Reconstruction* (New York: Alfred A. Knopf, 1982); chap. 10 of McPherson, *Battle Cry of Freedom: The Civil War Era* (New York: Oxford University Press, 1988); and chap. 1 of Herman Hattaway and Archer Jones, *How the North Won: A Military History of the Civil War* (Urbana: University of Illinois Press, 1982).

6. Jubal A. Early, *The Campaigns of Gen. Robert E. Lee. An Address by Lieut. General Jubal A. Early, before Washington and Lee University, January 19th, 1872* (Baltimore: John Murphy, 1872), 39–40; Lee's quotation is from General Orders No. 9, the text of which is reproduced in Douglas Southall Freeman, *R. E. Lee: A Biography*, 4 vols. (New York: Charles Scribner's Sons, 1934–35), 4:154–55. On Lost Cause writers who pointed to northern resources to explain defeat, see chap. 2 of Thomas L. Connelly, *The Marble Man: Robert E. Lee and His Image in American Society* (New York: Knopf, 1977), and chap. 4 of Gaines M. Foster, *Ghosts of the Confederacy: Defeat, the Lost Cause, and the Emergence of the New South* (New York: Oxford University Press, 1987).

underdog southern force vanquishing a much larger but inept opponent—a conception at odds with the facts. When Lee took charge of Confederate troops outside Richmond in early June 1862 he summoned reinforcements from many quarters. By the end of the month, he commanded approximately 90,000 soldiers in the largest army ever fielded by the Confederacy. Although McClellan's Federals outnumbered the Confederates by 10,000 to 15,000 men, Lee came nearer to parity with his opponent than in any subsequent operation. Far from a mismatch, the Seven Days witnessed two roughly equal antagonists square off on Confederate home ground.[7]

The series similarly misrepresents the impact of technology on late-antebellum American military officers. Following a segment in Episode II on the slaughter at Shiloh, which details how the battle's horrific casualties shocked civilians on both sides, Burns takes up the topic of technological advances. Viewers learn that the "most important innovation of the whole war was the rifled musket, along with a French refinement, Captain Claude Minié's new bullet, an inch-long lead slug that expanded into the barrel's rifled grooves and spun as it left the muzzle" and "was accurate at 250 yards, five times as far as any other one-man weapon." "The age of the bayonet charge had ended," announces the narrator, "though most officers did not yet know it when the war began and some had not learned it when the war was over."

This narration and the juxtaposition of graves at Shiloh with the new weaponry misled viewers by suggesting that Civil War officers first contemplated rifle-muskets and minié balls during the war. The United States army had converted from smoothbores to rifle-muskets in the mid-1850s, necessitating revision of the tactical manuals to cope with the weapon's increased distance and accuracy. "The introduction of the rifle had produced changes in tactical thinking," noted Grady McWhiney and Perry D. Jamieson in an excellent summary of late-antebellum developments, "but the changes were not extensive enough to compensate for the firepower of the new weapon." Official army doctrine thus recognized a new tactical era well before the cannons fired at Fort Sumter in April 1861. Although the war saw many costly infantry

---

7. Thomas L. Livermore's *Numbers and Losses in the Civil War in America: 1861–65* (1900; reprint, Bloomington: Indiana University Press, 1957), the standard work on the subject, places Lee's total engaged strength during the Seven Days at 95,481 (p. 86). In *To the Gates of Richmond: The Peninsula Campaign* (New York: Ticknor & Fields, 1992), 156, Stephen W. Sears, who acted as a consultant to Burns, places Lee's strength at 92,400 men.

assaults at Shiloh and elsewhere, they cannot be explained as mistakes by officers innocent of the improved weaponry.[8]

The most obvious shortcoming of Burns's military coverage is its geographical imbalance. His war is preeminently a struggle between the famous armies that operated in Virginia and the rest of the eastern theater. For the purpose of this essay, it is crucial that Burns neither justifies his emphasis on the East nor acknowledges the views of historians who complain of a Virginia bias. Apparently unconcerned with how people at the time perceived the relative importance of campaigns in the East and West (and perhaps influenced by the richer store of photographs of eastern armies and battlefields), he assumes the greater importance of military operations in Virginia, Maryland, and Pennsylvania. In doing so he again follows a Lost Cause tradition exemplified artistically by Charles Hoffbauer's famous murals depicting the *Seasons of the Confederacy*. Gracing one gallery of the Virginia Historical Society in Richmond, the murals equate Virginia with the Confederacy: *Spring* depicts Stonewall Jackson's infantry on the march in the Shenandoah Valley, *Summer* a tableau of Lee and his generals on a Virginia hillside, *Autumn* a ragged line of troopers following Jeb Stuart amid blazing fall colors, and *Winter* a Confederate artillery battery going into action at snowy Fredericksburg.

I happen to believe that during the war events in the East did overshadow those beyond the Appalachians. European political leaders, many politicians in Washington, and civilians in the Union and the Confederacy most often looked to Virginia to gauge the war's progress. The presence of the opposing capitals and each side's largest army, as well as the increasingly dominant figure of Robert E. Lee, help to explain this phenomenon. Psychologically and politically, what happened in the eastern theater heavily influenced both sides. Lee and the Army of Northern Virginia came to embody the Confederacy in the minds of many southern whites. As long as Lee's army remained in the field, hopes for Confederate independence remained alive. Similarly, victories in the West could not counter the North's frustration with repeated defeats at Lee's hands. The northern public insisted in March 1864 that Ulysses

8. Grady McWhiney and Perry D. Jamieson, *Attack and Die: Civil War Military Tactics and the Southern Heritage* (University, Ala.: University of Alabama Press, 1982), 48–58 [quotation on p. 58]. Edward Hagerman, *The American Civil War and the Origins of Modern Warfare: Ideas, Organization, and Field Command* (Bloomington: Indiana University Press, 1988), 16–20, also discusses antebellum efforts to adjust to rifled weaponry.

Detail of *Summer,* one of four murals by the French artist Charles Hoffbauer depicting the seasons of the Confederacy. Lee, mounted on Traveller, occupies the center of this group of generals who were never together except in the artist's imagination. From the left, Stonewall Jackson, Fitzhugh Lee, A. P. Hill, Lee, James Longstreet, J. E. Johnston, George E. Pickett, P. G. T. Beauregard, and Jeb Stuart. All but Johnston and Beauregard served their entire Confederate careers in the eastern theater. Four other eastern-theater officers—Richard S. Ewell, John B. Gordon, Wade Hampton, and John Bell Hood—appear in a portion of the mural omitted here.
Virginia Historical Society, Richmond

S. Grant, recently made general-in-chief of the Union armies, take the field in Virginia, hoping their best general would bring victory against the rebel chieftain.[9]

I hasten to add that many scholars dispute the primacy of the eastern theater. Thomas L. Connelly, Archer Jones, Richard M. McMurry, and others have complained of an undue preoccupation with the East in too much military literature on the war, arguing that Union achievements in the West

9. For a more detailed discussion of the relative importance of the eastern and western theaters, see Gary W. Gallagher, "'Upon Their Success Hang Momentous Issues': Generalship," in Gabor S. Boritt, ed., *Why the Confederacy Lost* (New York: Oxford University Press, 1992), 90–107.

largely decided the contest. Beginning with the capture of Confederate Forts Henry and Donelson in early 1862 and progressing through victories at Shiloh, Vicksburg, and Chattanooga to Sherman's success in Georgia and the Carolinas in 1864–1865, northern armies gutted the logistical heartland of the Confederacy, crippled civilian morale, and rendered further struggle impossible. Anyone searching for the key to northern victory, insist these authors, must look outside Virginia.[10]

How pronounced is the eastern thrust of *The Civil War?* The best evidence concerns Gettysburg and Vicksburg, for which Burns followed popular impressions rather than the scholarly literature. Historians often describe the Union triumphs at Gettysburg and Vicksburg as twin calamities for the Confederacy. The one repulsed Lee's second raid across the Potomac River and inflicted stupendous losses on the Army of Northern Virginia; the other gave the North control of the Mississippi River and removed an entire Confederate army from the field. "We have certain information that Vicksburg surrendered to General Grant on the 4th of July," a joyful Abraham Lincoln wrote on July 7, 1863: "Now, if General Meade can complete his work, so gloriously prosecuted thus far [at Gettysburg], by the literal or substantial destruction of Lee's army, the rebellion will be over." James M. McPherson echoed many other historians in observing that "the losses at Gettysburg and Vicksburg shook the Confederacy to its foundations." A concomitant Federal success in the West, William S. Rosecrans's virtually bloodless maneuvering of Braxton Bragg and the Army of Tennessee out of middle Tennessee during the Tullahoma campaign of June–July 1863, added to the laurels won by U. S. Grant at Vicksburg.[11]

Despite these major Union victories along the Mississippi River and in the Confederate heartland, Burns elected to reinforce the common misconception that Gettysburg dominated that remarkable season of combat. He lavishes nearly forty-five minutes on the campaign in Pennsylvania versus fewer than eleven on the marching and fighting between December 1862 and July

10. Studies that argue for the primacy of the western theater include Thomas L. Connelly and Archer Jones, *The Politics of Command: Factions and Ideas in Confederate Strategy* (Baton Rouge: Louisiana State University Press, 1973), Richard M. McMurry, *Two Great Rebel Armies: An Essay in Confederate Military History* (Chapel Hill: University of North Carolina Press, 1989), and Hattaway and Jones, *How the North Won.*

11. Abraham Lincoln to Henry W. Halleck, July 7, 1863, in Abraham Lincoln, *The Collected Works of Abraham Lincoln,* ed. Roy P. Basler *et al.,* 9 vols. (New Brunswick, N.J.: Rutgers University Press, 1953), 6:319; McPherson, *Ordeal by Fire,* 333.

One of the many representations of the Pickett-Pettigrew assault at Gettysburg that feature Lewis A. Armistead (with hat on sword point) of Pickett's division. Like this engraving, Ken Burns's documentary of the Civil War gives the impression that Pickett and his Virginians carried the entire burden of the attack.

Louis Shepheard Moat, ed., *Frank Leslie's Illustrated History of the Civil War* (New York: Mrs. Frank Leslie, 1895)

1863 that settled Vicksburg's fate. Rosecrans's Tullahoma campaign, which helped set the stage for the Union advance from Chattanooga to Atlanta in 1864, receives not a single mention.

Treatment of other operations reflects a similar bias. Strategic offensives in late summer and fall 1862 marked the only time Confederate armies penetrated Union territory in the eastern and western theaters almost simultaneously. Lee's march into Maryland and the battle of Antietam (the eastern element of these offensives) receive twenty-five minutes, movements into Kentucky by Confederate forces under Braxton Bragg and Edmund Kirby Smith (the western component) only fleeting attention. Similarly, Episode IV allocates a twelve-minute section to Lee's battle at Fredericksburg, Virginia, in December 1862, while the clash at Murfreesboro, Tennessee, a bloodier western counterpart fought on December 31, 1862, and January 2, 1863, flashes past viewers in less than a minute. When Ulysses S. Grant planned his five-pronged advance against the Confederacy in the spring of 1864, he considered William Tecumseh Sherman's strike against Atlanta the first priority and his own campaign against Lee a secondary element designed to tie down and bleed Confederate forces in Virginia. Burns inexplicably reverses this ranking, stating that "Grant entrusted his friend with the second most important part of his grand strategy—to seize Atlanta and smash the combined Confederate armies of Tennessee and Mississippi under Joseph E. Johnston."

The Trans-Mississippi theater fares worst of all the geographical areas. Burns disregards Pea Ridge and Wilson's Creek (except for mentioning casualties at the latter), battles that helped decide the fate of Missouri, a slaveholding state that Lincoln believed must be held if the Union were to be preserved. Similarly, viewers learn nothing about Henry Hopkins Sibley's Confederate invasion of New Mexico in 1862, Nathaniel P. Banks's Federal advance up the Red River in the spring of 1864, Confederate general Sterling Price's raid into Missouri later that year, and numerous other noteworthy military events west of the Mississippi. Episode VII does furnish a glimpse of Missouri's brutal guerrilla war in a snippet about the vicious Confederate irregular "Bloody Bill" Anderson. Shelby Foote, whose appearance in the documentary made him something of a media star, apparently failed to influence Burns regarding the Trans-Mississippi. The documentary's neglect of that sprawling region contrasts sharply with Foote's own narrative history of the Civil War, which gives it a generous number of pages.[12]

Even when engaged with the eastern theater, Burns often follows hoary interpretive conventions that obscure almost as much as they reveal. He reduces the battle of Fredericksburg to the infamous slaughter of Union attackers below the Sunken Road on Marye's Heights, offering no substantive attention to action on the southern end of the field where Union troops achieved some success against Stonewall Jackson's defenders. Gettysburg supplies a number of comparable examples. Traditionally given far less attention than either of the other two days, the first day's fighting appears in Episode V as "a skirmish" compared with what was to come. Burns thus brushes aside a compelling meeting engagement that escalated into savage combat claiming thou-

12. In *The Civil War: A Narrative*, 3 vols. (New York: Random House, 1958–74), Foote devotes ten pages to Pea Ridge and nearly seventy to the Red River campaign.

sands of Union and Confederate casualties. He offers equally predictable emphases for the rest of the battle. The Federal defense of Little Round Top dominates coverage of the second day, with action at the Peach Orchard, Wheatfield, and Devil's Den playing decidedly secondary roles and the contest for Culp's Hill altogether absent. The climactic Confederate assault on the third day is "Pickett's Charge," leaving uninformed viewers with the impression that George E. Pickett's division of Virginians made up all, rather than considerably less than half, of the assaulting column and that Pickett, rather than James Longstreet, oversaw the Confederate effort. (LaSalle Corbell Pickett would no doubt cheer Burns's decision to make her husband the central figure of the famous assault.)

Perhaps Burns's deep admiration for Michael Shaara's novel *The Killer Angels* contributed to this unbalanced treatment of Gettysburg. Of the characters whom Shaara featured on July 1, only John Buford, whose Federal cavalry gave way to supporting infantry before the battle escalated, actively participated in the fighting. Shaara built his account of the second day's fighting around Joshua Lawrence Chamberlain and the 20th Maine on Little Round Top and used Lewis A. Armistead and his brigade in Pickett's division to take readers through the final Confederate assault on July 3.[13]

Several sections on the war in the East demonstrate Burns's capacity to rise above trite conceptions—which makes the weaker passages all the more frustrating. With Stonewall Jackson's 1862 Shenandoah Valley campaign, for example, Burns avoids the ubiquitous stereotype of 17,000 rugged Confederate "foot cavalrymen" defeating more than 60,000 Federals. No extravagant claims accompany the treatment of how Jackson bested several inept Union generals and tied down some 40,000 enemy troops while strategists in Richmond worked to stop George B. McClellan's advance up the Peninsula.

Robert E. Lee, Ulysses S. Grant, and William Tecumseh Sherman rightly dominate Burns's cast of generals. Collectively, the three wielded far greater influence on military affairs than any of their peers. Could the Confederacy have mounted a four-year resistance without Lee's ability to build and sustain

---

13. The back cover of a recent paperback edition of *The Killer Angels* contains a quotation by Burns that leaves no doubt about his debt to Shaara: "A book that changed my life. . . . I had never visited Gettysburg, knew almost nothing about the battle before I read the book, but here it all came alive." Michael Shaara, *The Killer Angels* (New York: Ballantine Books, 1993 [38th printing]).

morale through battlefield victories? Was ultimate Union success possible without the strategic and operational contributions of Grant and Sherman? A positive answer to either question strains credulity.

Having selected the three key military figures, however, Burns fails to follow through with satisfying portraits of them. *Newsweek* reported that "a substantial minority of northern scholars, especially blacks," believed "sympathy for the colorful rascals and noble, long-suffering patricians of the Confederacy—the 'Lee cult' in other words"—undermined the series. Part of this critique no doubt stemmed from Burns's treatment of Lee. If the filmmaker was aware of Thomas L. Connelly's revisionist work on Lee, he chose to ignore it in crafting a comfortable portrait well attuned to Lost Cause images. Episode I tells viewers that Lee opposed slavery—a correct statement only if one applies the most expansive definition of "antislavery." Episode V repeats a common misconception that after the second day's fighting at Gettysburg, Lee believed an all-out attack on the Federal center would carry the field; he actually planned strikes against both Federal flanks and settled for the option of a frontal attack only with great reluctance on the morning of July 3. The biographical sketch in Episode VI alludes to Lee's habitually referring to Federals as "those people rather than the enemy." Even a cursory canvass of Lee's own writings, which bristle with references to Federals as "the enemy," would have spared Burns this last error.[14]

Nowhere does the series take up the questions about Lee's generalship that have inspired vigorous debate over many decades. Did his strategic grasp serve the Confederacy well, or was he blinded by a determination to protect his native Virginia? Did the benefits of his legendary victories outweigh their terrible price in casualties? How did Confederate civilians respond to his battles and campaigns? Did he and his army divert attention from more important events in the West? What was his ultimate impact on the fortunes of the Confederacy? Shelby Foote turns a nice phrase in observing that "Gettysburg was the price the South paid for having Robert E. Lee," but such statements are a poor substitute for analysis. In the end, viewers see an aristocratic, bountifully

---

14. "Revisiting the Civil War," 61–62. Connelly's *Marble Man* sparked controversy by questioning many of the traditional assumptions about Lee that Burns accepted. Alan T. Nolan's *Lee Considered: General Robert E. Lee and Civil War History* (Chapel Hill: University of North Carolina Press, 1991) continued the debate with a similarly pointed critique of what he terms the mythic Lee.

gifted officer who wins most of his battles and confronts defeat with dignity. Both Lee and Burns's audience deserve a more sophisticated treatment.[15]

The relationship between U. S. Grant and William Tecumseh Sherman forms an appealing leitmotif in the documentary. Burns understands the importance of this most productive professional collaboration of the war but fails to stress Grant's dominant role in the partnership. During a period of early independent command, Sherman had been beset by doubt and by fear of the enemy. Grant's steadiness and unshakable commitment to victory freed his mercurial lieutenant to blossom as a successful field commander. Aware of his role as the subordinate member of the team, Sherman perceptively summarized the strengths that he and his fellow Ohioan brought to command: "I am a damned sight smarter man than Grant; I know a great deal more about war, military history, strategy, and grand tactics than he does; I know more about organization, supply, and administration and about everything else than he does; but I'll tell you where he beats me and where he beats the world. He don't care a damn for what the enemy does out of his sight, but it scares me like hell!" In March 1864, as Grant prepared to assume responsibility for all Union land forces, Sherman revealed how important his friend's reassuring presence had been during previous campaigns: "I knew wherever I was that you thought of me," he wrote Grant, "and if I got in a tight place you would come—if alive."[16]

Through Shelby Foote, Burns characterizes Sherman as perhaps the first "modern" general because he realized that war on civilians would mark future conflicts. In fact, well before Sherman began his "March to the Sea" in November 1864, Grant had formulated a strategy of exhaustion that targeted the logistical underpinnings of the Confederacy. Philip H. Sheridan cheerfully carried out Grant's orders to apply this strategic concept to the Shenandoah Valley in October 1864. "Do all the damage to railroads and crops you can,"

15. For negative assessments of Lee's strategic ability, see chap. 3 of Connelly and Jones, *Politics of Command*, and chap. 4 of Nolan, *Lee Considered*; for a response to Lee's critics that summarizes the principal arguments on both sides, see Gary W. Gallagher, "Another Look at the Generalship of R. E. Lee," in Gallagher, ed., *Lee the Soldier* (Lincoln: University of Nebraska Press, 1996), 275–290.

16. James Harrison Wilson, *Under the Old Flag: Recollections of Military Operations in the War for the Union, the Spanish War, the Boxer Rebellion, Etc.*, 2 vols. (New York: D. Appleton, 1912), 2:17; William Tecumseh Sherman to Ulysses S. Grant, March 10, 1864, printed in William Tecumseh Sherman, *Memoirs of General W. T. Sherman*, ed. Charles Royster (New York: Library of America, 1990), 428.

read Grant's instructions. "Carry off stock of all descriptions, and negroes, so as to prevent further planting. If the war is to last another year, we want the Shenandoah Valley to remain a barren waste." Sheridan's soldiers subsequently destroyed huge quantities of civilian property in what embittered Confederates called "The Burning."[17]

The Union's military effort in the West belongs to Grant and Sherman in *The Civil War*, leaving other prominent Federal officers unfairly in the shadows. John Charles Frémont, Don Carlos Buell, and William S. Rosecrans all held important western commands but play only the smallest of bit parts in the documentary. The most obvious omission concerns Henry W. Halleck, whom Burns casts briefly as a jealous administrator hoping to push Grant aside after Shiloh. Under Halleck's supervision, Grant, John Pope, and other officers brought Union victories that cleared rebels from Missouri, made deep inroads into Arkansas, and captured immensely rich logistical areas in western and middle Tennessee (Halleck took credit for most of these successes). At the time, Grant called Halleck "one of the greatest men of the age," and Sherman pronounced him the "directing genius" behind Union successes in the West during the winter and spring of 1862. Halleck's achievements earned him promotion to general-in-chief of the Union armies in July 1862; however, frustration and failure in that position tarnished his earlier accomplishments and colored most subsequent estimates of his abilities. Apparently distracted by Halleck's career in Washington, Burns overlooked his more impressive earlier service.[18]

On the Confederate side, viewers might infer that cavalryman Nathan Bedford Forrest ranked as the most important officer in the West. Shelby Foote relates a number of colorful anecdotes about the roughhewn general and, incredibly, places him alongside Abraham Lincoln as one of the war's "two authentic geniuses." Although Forrest never commanded more than a few thousand men, his appearances in the series outnumber those of Braxton Bragg, Albert Sidney Johnston, Joseph E. Johnston, P. G. T. Beauregard, and

17. U.S. War Department, *The War of the Rebellion: A Compilation of the Official Records of the Union and Confederate Armies*, 128 vols. (Washington, D.C.: GPO, 1880–1901), ser. 1, vol. 43, pt. 1:917. For good discussions of Grant and Sherman, see chap. 5 of Joseph T. Glatthaar, *Partners in Command: The Relationships between Leaders in the Civil War* (New York: Free Press, 1994), and Hattaway and Jones, *How the North Won*, 686–87.

18. The quotations by Grant and Sherman are in Hattaway and Jones, *How the North Won*, 150.

others who led southern armies during major campaigns. This treatment grossly inflates Forrest's prominence. His wartime contemporaries in the Confederacy typically saw Forrest as a peer of John Hunt Morgan and Earl Van Dorn, other successful raiders whose exploits vexed the Federals, but scarcely conceived of him as a general whose impact rivaled that of senior officers.[19] Northerners loathed Forrest for his slaughter of the black and white troops who surrendered to his men at Fort Pillow in April 1864 (to his credit, Burns does not play down this episode in Forrest's career) and probably wished him dead—few, however, considered him as big a threat to the Republic as the Army of Tennessee under Braxton Bragg or Joseph E. Johnston.

Brevity and predictability characterize Burns's portrayals of other generals, encouraging viewers, perhaps inadvertently, to adopt simplistic notions about officers whose careers deserve a more layered understanding. John Pope and Joseph E. Johnston illustrate this phenomenon. Burns's Pope is the posturing braggart familiar even to casual students of the war. Pope may have blustered (though he did not habitually locate his "headquarters in the saddle," as the film claims), but he was more than a buffoon. His actions in northern Virginia during July 1862 reflected a shift in Union policy toward a harsher style of war embracing private property and civilians as well as Confederate armies. Johnston comes across as an avuncular figure who looked after his soldiers and skillfully husbanded meager southern resources. Although Johnston may have been "very nearly worshiped by his men" during his withdrawal from north Georgia to Atlanta in May and June 1864, many civilians, politicians, and others in the Confederacy deplored his constant retreating and insisted on a more active opposition to Sherman. John Bell Hood understood why Jefferson Davis substituted him for Johnston in mid-July and immediately mounted an offensive. In these and many other cases, the addition of political and social context to a military discussion—which is very different, I should emphasize, from a reduction of the amount of military coverage—would have strengthened Burns's work.[20]

19. James Ramage's *Rebel Raider: The Life of General John Hunt Morgan* (Lexington: University Press of Kentucky, 1986), as well as contemporary southern newspapers, letters, and diaries, strongly suggest that Morgan probably eclipsed Forrest during the war as a Confederate hero.

20. A succinct discussion of the political dimension of Pope's conduct in Virginia is in McPherson, *Battle Cry of Freedom*, 501–502; Mark Grimsley provides a more detailed examination in "Conciliation and Its Failure, 1861–1862," *Civil War History* 39 (December 1993):317–36. Richard M. McMurry, *John Bell Hood and the War for Southern Independence* (Lexington: Univer-

Throughout the series Burns missed opportunities to show that generals cannot operate in a vacuum during a war between democratic societies. The allocation of resources, selection of targets, appointment of officers, definition of operational goals, and timing of campaigns often represented a compromise between military and political imperatives. Lincoln waited until after the elections in November 1862 to remove the popular George B. McClellan (a staunch Democrat), kept political generals such as Nathaniel P. Banks and Benjamin F. Butler in command despite their well-documented ineptitude, postponed his preliminary proclamation of emancipation until he had a victory in the eastern theater, and otherwise adjusted his military goals to suit political realities. Similarly, Jefferson Davis deployed precious men and material to defend peripheral areas because civilians in those regions demanded protection.

Generals bowed to public opinion on numerous occasions, as when Grant took the field against Lee in May 1864 and Lee removed the unpopular Jubal A. Early from command in the Shenandoah Valley in March 1865. Political constraints also affected officers in the field. John Frémont and David Hunter, while Federal commanders in Missouri in 1861 and along the South Atlantic coast in 1862, respectively, issued sweeping orders emancipating slaves, only to have Lincoln insist that he alone possessed the authority for such actions. Sometimes these connections stand out in *The Civil War*—the relationship between Antietam and the Emancipation Proclamation is one example—but more often than not generals and their armies appear to operate in an environment devoid of nonmilitary pressures.

The correlation between events on the battlefield and morale behind the lines also remains underdeveloped. Lee's stunning triumphs in 1862–1863 convinced many white southerners (as well as a number of soldiers in the Army of the Potomac) that he could not be beaten. For the rest of the war, an expectation of success from the Army of Northern Virginia helped maintain Confederate morale as southern arms suffered setbacks almost everywhere else. The Army of the Potomac's string of losses more than once spread turmoil through northern society. Defeats at the Seven Days and Second Manassas triggered a diplomatic crisis; another pair of setbacks at Fredericksburg and

---

sity Press of Kentucky, 1982), 116–23, and Thomas L. Connelly, *Autumn of Glory: The Army of Tennessee, 1862–1865* (Baton Rouge: Louisiana State University Press, 1971), 399–425, offer perceptive analyses of Johnston's removal from command of the Army of Tennessee.

Chancellorsville fueled support for the antiwar Copperheads; and Grant's inability to deliver a knockout blow to Lee's army during May and June 1864 helped drive northern morale to its lowest point of the conflict. More specific development of these connections between the battlefield and the home front would have formed a useful theme in Burns's documentary, while also deflecting complaints that he gave too much attention to the military.

The common denominator for most of my criticisms lies in Burns's failure to sift carefully through the best literature on the war. Much of his material comes from highly quotable but problematic postwar memoirs and reminiscences such as Sam Watkins's *"Co. Aytch"* and John B. Gordon's *Reminiscences of the Civil War*. Full of comfortable old stories that undoubtedly move audiences when told well, these books are also full of inaccuracies. Some manipulate the truth to even old scores or place their authors in the best light; others simplify and sanitize issues and leaders—especially those which, like Gordon's book, appeared during the era of sectional reconciliation. A systematic use of modern scholarship would have provided a check on these older accounts and enabled Burns to avoid many errors and distortions. I am not arguing that *The Civil War* should have adopted a scholarly format. That would have driven viewers off in droves as surely as dry historiographical lectures send students reeling from college classrooms. But with the latitude afforded by an eleven-hour format, Burns could have injected more complexity into his military narrative and his sketches of leading soldiers while still including an ample number of fetching anecdotes.

Numerous small errors mar the narrative. John Singleton Mosby was not a general, the British observer with Lee's army at Gettysburg was A. J. L. (not A. S.) Fremantle, an image of Federal wagons parked on the Peninsula in 1862 does not belong in the sequence on Gettysburg, and so on. The cumulative effect of these lapses weakens the viewer's confidence and makes one wish that a scholar had given the final script a careful proofreading. But I do not believe such errors materially compromise the documentary.

My critique may strike many viewers of *The Civil War* as unduly harsh, another piece of academic carping about a popular success. But that is not the case. I applaud Burns for taking on such a monumental and potentially controversial subject when he must have anticipated intense scrutiny from both academics and the public. He brought to the project a record of superb documentary filmmaking and sufficient funding to treat the Civil War on an expansive scale. He sought the advice of historians, searched for the right nineteenth-century and modern images, and apparently read widely in the literature. He settled on a good balance between military and nonmilitary coverage. With so many crucial elements in place, the likelihood of success was great.

My disappointment stems from a sense of missed opportunity. Burns could have used his undeniable narrative gifts to present the broad context as well as the drama and pathos of military campaigns. Instead, he maneuvered comfortably along well-trod paths, employing durable anecdotes, serving up leaders in familiar interpretive garb, and never challenging his viewers with choices or enabling them to see how campaigns and battles merged with civilian affairs to create a magnificent historical tapestry.

★ 13 ★

Battlefields, the Lost Cause, and the Legacy of the Civil War

Threats of development thrust the issue of Civil War battlefield preservation into the headlines during the 1980s and 1990s. The debate over how much historic ground should be set aside raised issues relating to the ways in which Americans remember the conflict. Historians squared off against one another, some arguing for greater protection of battle sites and others insisting that such places already had been accorded too much attention. Opponents of preserving additional acreage at battlefields sometimes suggested that these sites celebrated Confederate generals and armies in a way that ratified, at least implicitly, Lost Cause arguments about the war. Preservationists often countered that the battlefields honored all Americans who struggled with profound political and social questions in the 1860s. Too often lost in the rhetoric was an understanding of the immense value of these sites as teaching tools to explore and understand the complexity of our nation's most critical era.

I will not examine in detail specific confrontations between developers and preservationists. This is not because I am neutral on the subject—far from it. I am deeply concerned about the fate of battlefields. Moreover, I believe the clashes in 1987 over a proposed mall adjacent to Manassas National Battlefield Park, in 1994 over the Disney theme park planned for nearby Haymarket, from the late 1980s to 1997 over a pair of developments at Brandy Station, and during the last decade at many other sites, to be both fascinating and instructive.[1] But here my focus will be on two questions, one directly related to the main themes in the other essays in this book and the other cast more broadly. First, do Lost Cause interpretations of Robert E. Lee, his lieutenants, and the Army of Northern Virginia still resonate at battlefields in the war's eastern theater? And second, do these battlefields, on balance, enrich or hinder modern understanding of the conflict?

As background for my consideration of the first question, I will note that symbols of the Lost Cause increasingly have come under fire. The most visible of those symbols has been the Confederate flag, around which recent controversies have swirled in Georgia (the Confederate flag constitutes two-thirds of the state flag), Maryland (the state approved and then withdrew a vanity license plate that incorporated a Confederate flag), and South Carolina (citizens debated whether the Confederate flag should continue to fly over their state capitol). A pair of letters to the editor in *Newsweek* reflected the passionate reaction to a proposal from South Carolina governor David Beasley to remove the flag from the capitol and place it elsewhere on the statehouse grounds. "I am very glad to see someone trying to get rid of a symbol of hatred in America," wrote one reader: "Hatred is all the Old South flag represents. . . . The last place a symbol of racism belongs is atop a governmental building in America." In contrast, a man with "20 ancestors who served in the armed forces of the Confederate States of America . . . [was] highly offended by Governor Beasley's suggestion," maintaining that the flag honored "the

---

1. On the often rancorous debate among historians and in the public arena regarding Disney's proposed theme park, see "A House Divided: Historians Confront Disney's America," *OAH Newsletter* 22 (August 1994):1, 8–9; Deborah Fitts, "The Disney Park Looms," *Civil War: The Magazine of the Civil War Society* (June 1994):14–22; *Los Angeles Times*, July 11, 1994, pp. B5–B6; *New York Times*, May 12, 1994, p. A16; *Wall Street Journal*, August 25, 1994, p. A13; and *Washington Post*, May 15, 1994, pp. B1, B5, June 17, 1994, pp. A1, A10. On legal issues raised by the earlier struggle between a mall developer and preservationists at Manassas, see Charles P. Lord, "Stonewalling the Malls: Just Compensation and Battlefield Protection," *Virginia Law Review* 77 (November 1991):1637–72. For typical coverage of Brandy Station, see Brooke A. Masters, "Battle Rejoined at Civil War Site in Virginia," the lead article in the Metro section of the Washington *Post*, July 12, 1991.

sacrifices, suffering and heroism of our people during their struggle for independence."[2]

Everyone in this debate agrees that the Confederate flag frequently turns up in connection with repellent acts. During the public exchanges sparked by Governor Beasley, a black lawyer from Columbia, South Carolina, observed, "We all know that at the Klan rallies, at incidents of hate crime, this flag is their symbol. The flag embraces and perpetuates the ideology of white supremacy." For this man, "That flag tells me that, because of the color of my skin, I am considered a second-class citizen. If it represents history," he concluded, "put it in a museum." The chairman of the heritage committee of the Sons of Confederate Veterans had admitted earlier in 1996 that various groups "misappropriate our Confederate symbols for their own vile use"—but also had charged that the "media portrays to the world that the Confederate Battle Flag stands for nothing but perverted honor." For members of the SCV, he emphasized, the flag stood for pride in ancestors who had fought for "States Rights, self-determination and freedom from oppression."[3]

Outside the large community of lay readers, reenactors, and others specifically interested in the Civil War, it is probably fair to say that many Americans who recognize the Confederate flag at all view it with mixed emotions. Although few likely endorse facile comparisons of the Confederacy and its flag with Nazi Germany and its swastika, most cannot be unaware that various extremist groups have appropriated the battle flag for their bigoted purposes.[4]

Confederate monuments have prompted similarly heated exchanges. Typically erected in southern towns during the late nineteenth or early twentieth centuries, they often graced courthouse lawns and honored soldiers who served in the Confederacy's armies. A controversy in Sylvania, Georgia, illus-

2. *Newsweek*, January 13, 1997, p. 16. On the controversies in Georgia and Maryland, see the Atlanta *Journal/Constitution*, May 22, 28, 1994, and Marsha Rader, "Maryland Rescinds SCV License Plate with the Battle Flag," *Civil War News* 23 (February/March 1997):1, 30–31. Under the headline "Diehard Maryland Rebels," *Time* reported on March 10, 1997, the latest twist in the Maryland story: "A Federal judge lifts the state's ban on license plates that fly the Confederate battle flag" (p. 21).

3. Rick Bragg, "Southern Leader Urges Furling Rebel Flag," New York *Times*, November 27, 1996, p. A10; "Forward the Colors: A Report from the Heritage Committee," *Confederate Veteran*, vol. 4 of 1996 [no date on title page], 6.

4. For examples of equating the Confederacy to Nazi Germany, see Gordon Hickey, "City Tourism Idea Hits Reality," Richmond *Times-Dispatch*, December 8, 1994, p. B1, and "The Flag and the Fury," *U.S. News and World Report* 122 (March 10, 1997):13.

trates how these statues sometimes have divided communities. Sylvania's Confederate monument was moved in the 1970s after demolition of the Screven County Courthouse, in front of which the memorial had stood for many decades. A 1996 economic plan called for restoring downtown Sylvania to its historic appearance and returning the monument, which bears the inscription "Never Rose A Nation So Fair and White and Fell So Pure of Crime," to a place near its original location. A group of citizens termed this feature of the plan "a slap in the face to African Americans." Sylvania's mayor answered that the statue honored men who had lost their lives during the war but did not glorify slavery. Except for the provision dealing with the monument, the plan was generally supported in Sylvania.[5]

Such controversies related to Confederate monuments echo earlier African American protests against perceived glorification of the Lost Cause. In 1925, for example, the National Urban League's *Opportunity* clipped an article from a Pittsburgh newspaper applauding the fact that a lack of funding had stopped work on the gigantic Confederate memorial at Stone Mountain, Georgia. Labeling the sculpture "a living reminder of the cause to which they [the white South] have dedicated their lives: human slavery and color selfishness," this piece pronounced it "the irony of fate that the work should stop at its present stage. Just enough work has been done to remind the traveler that 'there is the lost cause, conceived in hatred, and interrupted in its course for want of support.' Nothing could constitute a more appropriate insignia to a lost cause than an unfinished monument halted in its rise for want of sympathy."[6]

The series of commemorative Civil War stamps issued by the United

5. Hilary Miller, "Confederate Memorial in Sylvania, Ga., Under Fire," *Civil War News* 22 (November 1996):60. For a photograph of Sylvania's monument, see Ralph W. Widener Jr., *Confederate Monuments: Enduring Symbols of the South and the War between the States* (Washington, D.C.: Andromeda, 1982), 77.

6. "Let Stone Mountain Alone," *Opportunity* 3 (April 1925):125. The carvings at Stone Mountain eventually were completed, and in 1970 the United States Postal Service issued a "Stone Mountain Memorial" six-cent stamp. A theme park also opened at Stone Mountain in 1970 and now attracts five million tourists a year. The Confederate sculpture at Stone Mountain periodically returns to the headlines in controversies relating to its status as a symbol of the Lost Cause. On the history of the Confederate sculpture, see David Freeman, *Carved in Stone: The History of Stone Mountain* (Macon, Ga.: Mercer University Press, 1997). For an example of recent controversies, see Duane D. Stanford, "Must Park's Rebel Image Be Written?" *Atlanta Journal/Constitution*, April 17, 1994, p. F7.

States Postal Service in 1994 suggests that many Americans hold a far less antagonistic attitude toward the Confederacy and its symbols. The twenty-stamp set featured sixteen individuals (eight Confederate and eight Union) and four battles. Three of the stamps depicting battles—Chancellorsville, Gettysburg, and the *Monitor* versus the *Virginia*—included Confederate battle flags. Lost Cause icons Robert E. Lee, Stonewall Jackson, and Jefferson Davis—the three men whose images are carved into the side of Stone Mountain—were among the eight Confederates. A handsome companion book paid tribute to the men and women who struggled for both the Union and the Confederacy. "Even more than the American Revolution, the Civil War has defined our national character," read the introduction: "The violence and valor, and the nobility of the combatants' cause, each fighting to preserve a 'sacred' truth, are enshrined in the American consciousness." Twenty stamps could not touch on all the episodes and major personalities of the conflict, "but the people and battles that we have selected truly do epitomize the virtues that both sides adhered to—courage, duty and above all a shared conviction that right would prevail."[7]

Battlefields stand for these same virtues in the minds of most people who visit them. They have become hallowed historic ground for citizens from all parts of the United States who walk their hills and fields and often pay homage to both Union and Confederate soldiers. The one-dollar silver coin from a 1995 Civil War commemorative set issued by the United States Mint captured perfectly this notion of sacred ground. Against the background of the 44th New York Infantry's monument on Little Round Top, the coin—sales of

7. U.S. Postal Service and the Editors of Time-Life Books, *The Civil War, 1861–1865: A Collection of U.S. Commemorative Stamps* (n.p.: U.S. Postal Service, 1995), 4. In addition to Lee, Jackson, and Davis, the subjects were Clara Barton, Mary Chesnut, Frederick Douglass, David Farragut, Ulysses S. Grant, Winfield Scott Hancock, Joseph E. Johnston, Abraham Lincoln, Phoebe Pember, Raphael Semmes, William Tecumseh Sherman, Harriet Tubman, and Stand Watie. Shiloh was the fourth battle depicted. A company selling replicas of Union and Confederate flags in the late 1990s praised both sets of banners in a breathless brochure: "They were bold in design. Brilliant in color. Rousing symbols of the causes each side fought and died for. As one Confederate color sergeant so poignantly said of his regimental battle flag: *'Comrades . . . may it ever guide and guard you . . . In the smoke, glare, and din of battle . . . let its bright folds inspire you. . . .'* Now, in all their stirring magnificence, the regimental flags of the Union and Confederacy are yours to treasure always in a spectacular new commemorative series: *Battle Flags of the Civil War!*" Promotional literature for "Battle Flag Replicas of the Civil War" (Norwalk, Conn.: Willabee and Ward, 1997).

which generated money for battlefield preservation—featured a quotation from Union hero Joshua Lawrence Chamberlain: "In Great Deeds Something Abides. On Great Fields Something Stays. Forms Change And Pass: Bodies Disappear: But Spirits Linger To Consecrate Ground For The Visionplace Of Souls." Chamberlain uttered these words in October 1889 at ceremonies dedicating the Twentieth Maine Infantry's monuments at Gettysburg. In his address, Chamberlain left no doubt that northern soldiers fought for the more righteous cause of Union, but he also struck a conciliatory note in paying tribute to the "manly qualities and earnest motives" of Confederate soldiers.[8]

Chamberlain's ascribing positive attributes to his former opponents fit a pattern of reconciliation that grew increasingly powerful as the nineteenth century drew to a close. He stressed that the war had been a test of Union, alluding to emancipation only once in his speech at Gettysburg. "The Union was the body of a spiritual Unity," he said: "Of this we were part—responsible to it and for it—and our sacrifice was its service." Others in the North similarly trumpeted Union, embraced reconciliation, and neglected slavery and emancipation as central events in the war. Former Confederates, most of whom denied in retrospect that a desire to protect slavery had been at the root of secession, likewise reached out to their former enemies. In contrast to the vitriolic anti-Yankee rhetoric of Jubal Early and others among the founding group of Lost Cause warriors, these southern reconciliationists celebrated the manly virtues and honest patriotism of soldiers in both armies. This new strain of Lost Cause thinking continued to venerate Lee and Jackson, to extol Confederate gallantry in the face of severe trials, and to find only noble impulses behind the movement for Confederate independence; however, it also celebrated a United States poised on the brink of the twentieth century as worthy of the loyalty of all Americans.[9]

John Brown Gordon of Georgia personified this new Lost Cause approach. In an overblown style befitting a man who had enjoyed a successful political career at the state and national levels, Gordon wrote in his memoirs

8. Joshua Lawrence Chamberlain, *"Bayonet! Forward"*: *My Civil War Reminiscences* (Gettysburg, Pa.: Stan Clark Military Books, 1994), 193, 202.

9. *Ibid.*, 195. For a good overview of the reconciliation movement, see Pt. 2 of Michael Kammen, *Mystic Chords of Memory: The Transformation of Tradition in American Culture* (New York: Alfred A. Knopf, 1991). The best analysis of changes in Lost Cause thinking is in Gaines M. Foster's *Ghosts of the Confederacy: Defeat, the Lost Cause, and the Emergence of the New South* (New York: Oxford University Press, 1987).

that the "unseemly things which occurred in the great conflict between the States should be forgotten, or at least forgiven, and no longer permitted to disturb complete harmony between North and South." Young Americans should be instructed "to hold in perpetual remembrance all that was great and good on both sides," and to recognize that the two sections fought "to protect what they conceived to be threatened rights and imperilled liberty." The conflict's blood and tears in the long term would contribute to "the upbuilding of American manhood and . . . the future defence of American freedom." Gordon closed his narrative with a paean to the modern nation: "So the Republic, rising from its baptism of blood with a national life more robust, a national union more complete, and a national influence ever widening, shall go forward forever in its benign mission to humanity."[10]

Battlefields attracted veterans and other Americans who shared Gordon's views. The most famous gatherings occurred at Gettysburg in 1913 and 1938 on the fiftieth and seventy-fifth anniversaries of the battle. Large crowds of onlookers descended on the small town in 1913 to join thousands of former Union and Confederate soldiers. Newsreels captured the old adversaries, many of them with long white beards, shaking hands, quietly talking, or staging mock confrontations at famous sites on the battlefield. Far fewer veterans survived to gather at Gettysburg in 1938, but once again photographers caught them in a number of friendly poses, perhaps the most poignant of which showed aged Confederates clasping hands with equally venerable Federals across the famous stone wall on Cemetery Ridge.[11]

Woodrow Wilson delivered remarks on the fiftieth anniversary, and Franklin D. Roosevelt spoke at the unveiling of the Eternal Peace Light Memorial during the seventy-fifth reunion. Both presidents emphasized reconciliation, the bravery of Union and Confederate soldiers, and the mighty nation that came out of the conflict; neither mentioned emancipation. "These gallant men in blue and gray sit all about us here," stated Wilson. "We have found one another again as brothers and comrades in arms, enemies no longer, generous friends rather, our battles long past, the quarrel forgotten—except that we shall not forget the splendid valour, the manly devotion of the men then arrayed against one another, now grasping hands and smiling into each

10. John B. Gordon, *Reminiscences of the Civil War* (New York: Charles B. Scribner's Sons, 1903), 464–65.

11. For photographs of the fiftieth and seventy-fifth reunions, see Jack McLaughlin, *Gettysburg: The Long Encampment* (New York: Appleton-Century, 1963), 213–30.

other's eyes." Roosevelt opted for virtually identical rhetoric: "Men who wore the blue and men who wore the gray are here together, a fragment spared by time. They are brought here by the memories of old divided loyalties, but they meet here in united loyalty to a united cause which the unfolding years have made it easier to see." Of the veterans present, "All of them we honor," said Roosevelt, "not asking under which flag they fought then—thankful that they stand together under one flag now."[12]

Countless speakers at other battlefields struck similar chords. A pair of widely separated ceremonies at Spotsylvania underscore this point. In May 1909, forty-five years after the horrific fighting at the "Bloody Angle," veterans of the 15th New Jersey Infantry returned to Spotsylvania to dedicate a regimental monument. Speakers from New Jersey and Virginia selected themes of sectional harmony, common valor, and American greatness. No one mentioned slavery or emancipation. Governor J. Franklin Fort of New Jersey stated that "all who fought here are now canonized as heroes," and a survivor from the 15th told the audience that "no braver nor better soldiers ever lived than those produced" by the Union and the Confederacy. "We respect a *good* soldier," the old veteran concluded, "no matter what flag he fought under." Fifty-five years later, on the centennial of the fighting at Spotsylvania, another set of speakers evoked similar images in rededicating the 15th's monument. A New Jersey man rhapsodized about "the symbols of our unity, our love of country, of our cry that we are all Americans, cherishing and protecting the same ideals conceived by our forefathers." A Virginian claimed that his grandfathers, both of whom had fought under Lee, came out of the war "without bitterness or hatred." "They were Americans," he said, "and so were the New Jersey soldiers who fought here on this field a century ago."[13]

As the turn of another century approaches, themes of reconciliation continue to galvanize those who would preserve battlefields. The president of a

---

12. "An Address at the Gettysburg Battlefield," July 4, 1913, in Woodrow Wilson, *The Papers of Woodrow Wilson*, ed. Arthur S. Link, 69 vols. (Princeton, N.J.: Princeton University Press, 1966–94), 28:23; "Address at the Dedication of the Memorial on the Gettysburg Battlefield, Gettysburg, Pennsylvania," July 3, 1938, in Franklin D. Roosevelt, *The Public Papers and Addresses of Franklin D. Roosevelt*, comp. Samuel I. Rosenman, 13 vols. (New York: various publishers, 1938–50), 6:420.

13. Peter S. Carmichael, "'We Respect a Good Soldier, No Matter What Flag He Fought Under': The 15th New Jersey Remembers Spotsylvania," in Gary W. Gallagher, ed., *The Spotsylvania Campaign* (Chapel Hill: University of North Carolina Press, 1998), 203–22.

July 4, 1913: Union and Confederate veterans clasp hands across the stone wall on Cemetery Ridge at a reunion marking the fiftieth anniversary of the Gettysburg battle.

Pennsylvania Commission, *Fiftieth Anniversary of the Battle of Gettysburg: Report of the Pennsylvania Commission, December 13, 1913* (Harrisburg: William Stanley Ray, State Printer, 1915)

leading preservation group recently challenged people interested in the Civil War to contribute money to protect "the fields of honor" on which the armies contested the war. Many unprotected sites, he cautioned, face an unknown future: "You know their past. You know the courage and spirit of the men who consecrated these fields with their blood. You know their valor and sacrifice is too precious to be scraped away by the bulldozer and hauled to the dump. You know you are their link—their only link—to a future that preserves their deeds and their memories." This man closed with a reference to the verdict of history. "Remember," he warned, "future historians will judge you on the decisions you make today."[14]

This implication that historians will judge harshly any Americans who do not support preservation brings us back to the first of my two questions. Does the Lost Cause taint the battlefields where Lee and his army fought? A number of historians, both academic and nonacademic, in effect answered no and affirmed the value of such sites by vigorously opposing construction of Disney's history theme park in northern Virginia. "Nearby is the Manassas Battlefield National Park, other Civil War battlefields, historic homes and communities dating from Colonial times," wrote several of them in an open letter directed at Disney chief Michael Eisner: "All will be endangered by the cancerous urban sprawl that proliferates in the wake of Disney projects." Elsewhere, C. Vann Woodward, one of the signers of the open letter, stated that Disney's park "would be an appalling commercialization and vulgarization of the scene of our most tragic history." James M. McPherson, another signer, insisted that battles such as Manassas helped reshape "the identity and destiny of the United States" and should be preserved so Americans could visit them "to study that terrible but triumphant trauma and to experience an emotional empathy with the brave men who fought and died there."[15]

14. Dennis E. Frye, "Preservation News," *Civil War News* 22 (December 1996):2. Frye was president of the Association for the Preservation of Civil War Sites, a national organization with a membership of more than 10,000.

15. *New York Times*, July 11, 1994, p. A15 (open letter headed "The Man Who Would Destroy American History"); Fredericksburg (Va.) *Free-Lance Star*, May 13, 1994 (Woodward quotation); James M. McPherson, "Civil War Sites Hanging On by Slenderest of Threads," *USA Today*, June 20, 1994, p. 15A. Protect Historic America, a coalition of historians and others concerned about the Disney development, placed the letter in the New York *Times*. A provocative quotation from Eisner ran across the top of the letter: "I sat through many history classes where I read some of their [historians'] stuff, and I didn't learn anything." Playing off Eisner's words, the signers responded, "Unfortunately, he means it. Michael Eisner wants to carve out a 3,000-acre

Other historians questioned both peers who took a stand against Disney and the wisdom of investing additional financial resources and emotional capital in battlefields. These scholars objected to a Lost Cause–tinged framework within which Confederate armies and leaders and the campaigns they waged could be examined without specific reference to the fact that they fought for a slave-based republic. "By celebrating the battle sites as the ultimate symbols of the Civil War," stated one academic, historians who opposed Disney lent "credence to a common but worrisome interpretation of the epochal event in our history—one that makes the sacrifices of war more important than the achievement of freedom." This scholar mentioned late-nineteenth-century reconciliation and its "sanctification of the battlefields" and portrayal of the war "as a time of universal bravery and tragedy . . . [when] all Americans, North and South, fought honorably for their beliefs." Lamentably absent, he argued, was a sense that "one side fought for freedom and the other to preserve slavery." White northerners and southerners at the time of the reconciliation movement—and by implication Civil War battlefield preservationists today—could derive a sense of unity from this interpretation, but "it excluded black Americans."

This critic pointed to battlefield preservation and Ken Burns's television documentary as evidence of a flawed popular understanding of the war. Here he joined the large group of primarily academic historians I discussed in the preceding essay on Burns's series. Like the individuals I quoted there, he accused Burns of treating the war "mainly as a military event and an American tragedy. . . . [W]hat was missed in the series and is being overlooked again in the fight over the historic sites is the war's larger significance—the struggle over the meaning of American nationalism and our concept of freedom."[16]

The deputy executive director of the American Historical Association made comparable points in opposing the creation of a Civil War Sites Advisory Commission during testimony given before Congress in September 1990. Claiming to speak "on behalf of the broad community of historians" represented by the AHA and scores of affiliated organizations (a ludicrous notion that provoked a pointed response from a number of members of those organi-

---

commercial development—hotels, offices, stores, houses, golf courses and an amusement park— right in the heart of historic America." In early 1997, Disney struck back at preservationists with a television advertisement dismissing Civil War battlefields as unworthy sites for tourists (Disney's theme parks in Florida, the commercial assured viewers, were ideal destinations).

16. Thomas Bender, "Disney Is an Easy Target," New York *Times*, July 25, 1994, p. A15.

President Woodrow Wilson, flanked by Union and Confederate veterans and the flags under which they fought, at the fiftieth-anniversary ceremonies at Gettysburg. Pennsylvania Commission, *Fiftieth Anniversary Report*

zations), this man opposed congressional support for additional Civil War battlefield preservation on the grounds that it would perpetuate "narrow, anti-quated views" of history that give undue emphasis to battles and generals. "Historians today have redefined the study of the Civil War," he stated, "shifting attention from military action to the diverse experiences of individual groups, the impact of emancipation," and the ways in which the war exacerbated old social divisions and created new ones. Acknowledging the "emotional appeal of 'hallowed ground,'" the AHA's spokesman deplored the "assumption of the special historical significance of Civil War battlefields."[17]

Historians skeptical about battlefield preservation have a point in asserting that perpetuation of the conciliatory movement has left much of Robert E. Lee and the Army of Northern Virginia and little of emancipation and the larger context of the conflict at many eastern sites. Jubal Early undoubtedly would find much to applaud if he took a tour of his old battlegrounds. On the imposing Virginia monument at Gettysburg, Lee sits astride Traveller looking toward Cemetery Ridge. At Manassas, an equestrian statue of Stonewall Jackson dominates the plateau where the general and his brigade won initial fame. Visitors to Chancellorsville can stand on the spots where Lee and Jackson held their last important meeting, where Stonewall fell victim to fire from his own troops, and where a triumphant Lee rode into the clearing near the Chancellor house amid his cheering, victorious troops. A few miles away at Guiney's Station, the small plantation office where Jackson died remains much as it was during his last days, preserved and interpreted by the National Park Service as the "Stonewall Jackson Shrine." The Widow Tapp's field in the Wilderness and the "Mule Shoe" at Spotsylvania, virtually unchanged since May 1864, conjure images of the famous "Lee to the Rear" scenes. Lee's Hill at Fredericksburg, the McLean House at Appomattox, and numerous

17. *Testimony of James B. Gardner, Deputy Executive Director American Historical Association, before the Subcommittee on National Parks and Public Lands, Committee on Interior and Insular Affairs of the U.S. House of Representatives, H.R. 3513 and S. 1770, September 4, 1990* (Washington, D.C.: American Historical Association, 1990), 2–3. In one response to Gardner's testimony, senior Civil War scholars Gabor S. Boritt, James M. McPherson, Mark E. Neely Jr., and John Y. Simon expressed shock that "the American Historical Association, without consulting its members, testified . . . against a measure to establish a national Civil War Sites Advisory Commission." (Copy of the statement from the four historians provided to the author by Gabor S. Boritt and Mark E. Neely Jr., March 19, 1991.)

The equestrian statue of Stonewall Jackson on the battlefield of First Manassas.
National Park Service

other sites similarly encourage continuing recognition of Lee and his campaigns.

Later Lost Cause spokesmen such as John B. Gordon would appreciate the fact that interpretation at most battlefields treats Confederate and Union courage and determination as equally praiseworthy. Living history exhibits at National Park Service sites and reenactments on or near historic ground invariably accord full respect to Confederates. People from the North "serve" as Confederate reenactors, and, if anything, "recruiting" for southern units proceeds more smoothly than for their northern counterparts.[18]

This brings me to the question of whether battlefields enhance or obstruct understanding of the Civil War. Contrary to the claims of some who cry "enough" at the prospect of more battlefield preservation, attention to Lee and other Confederates does not compromise the intrinsic historical importance of the eastern battle sites. Neither does the fact that most people who visit them probably conceive of the Civil War largely in terms of generals and military clashes. Gettysburg, Antietam, Chancellorsville, and all the other places where Lee and his army fought *should be* studied as important military sites; indeed, it is almost impossible to grasp the nuances of any Civil War battle without walking the ground over which it was fought. Moreover, the officers and men who struggled at them, Confederate and Union, *should be* remembered. The battlefields also should be used to get at more than the purely military dimensions of the war; that they often are not reflects a limited vision of how they can be interpreted rather than a problem with the sites. Most critics of preservation probably never have set foot on a battlefield with the intention of instructing anyone about the crucial issues of the war. Were they to use a battlefield as a teaching tool, I believe they might join the ranks of preservationists.

I say this based on fifteen years' experience of taking people of all ages and backgrounds to battlefields. These sites have the potential to bring a piece of the past vividly to life for Americans too often conditioned to rely on elec-

18. The phenomenon of reenactments with more Confederates than Federals has inspired spoofs. For example, one "advertisement" offered "Civil Ant Wars," featuring "a jar of 30,000 blue army ants and a jar of 20,000 gray army ants" that would "grapple like demons with unbridled ferocity." "When purchased below the Mason Dixon Line," read the ad, "you get 30,000 gray army ants and about 1000 blue army ants, just like the reenactments of today!" Undated advertisement from *Camp Chase Gazette* (ca. 1991), supplied to the author by T. Michael Parrish of Austin, Texas.

tronic images to stimulate their imaginations. Battlefields permit us literally to touch our past, and in that moment to make a connection to earlier Americans and their lives that cannot be duplicated in classrooms or any other forum. I am fortunate to live and work within easy reach of Antietam and Gettysburg, which I visit often with students from my classes. I will draw on these two battlefields, and on my use of them to teach students, to answer my second question. I believe firmly that battlefields enrich our understanding of the Civil War, and I see their preservation as a means toward the end of educating Americans about the conflict's full meaning.

I suspect that a poll of my academic peers would reveal a strong consensus that Civil War battlefields hold only limited value for anyone except military buffs who want to examine troop movements in excruciating detail or to evaluate the tactical decisions of generals and colonels. This attitude radically underestimates the value of Civil War battlefields as tools that can help us move well beyond any specific tactical story. Over the years that I have taken my classes to Antietam and Gettysburg, I have found these sites to be singularly effective in helping students place themselves in another time and in encouraging them to understand the people who lived and worked in that time.

I will start with Antietam, where I trace the battle chronologically during walking tours that last six or seven hours. Traversing the field on foot most obviously enables students to grasp what happened militarily at Antietam; more than that, it promotes their shifting mental gears so they sense the presence of the people who lived during the war. At various stops during the tour, we discuss the circumstances that sent men into the respective armies, the responses to the war in the different states represented by monuments on the field, the factors that led slave states such as Maryland to remain in the Union while others seceded, and postwar efforts to create a suitable public memory of the war that resulted in the erection of the monuments.

Because the battlefield constitutes a tangible link to one of the watershed events in our history, students easily move from specifics concerning what they see in the Sunken Road, or at the Dunker Church, or at Burnside's Bridge, to the larger questions of the era. Did the founding generation envision a true nation, or did they have in mind a collection of semiautonomous states? Why was emancipation added to restoration of the Union as a second great goal for northern armies? How did events on the battlefield influence morale behind the lines? Were the soldiers in the two armies more alike than different? How did women such as Clara Barton, who made her first major appearance at Antietam, overcome a range of obstacles to play a significant role in a conflict too often seen as exclusively the province of men?

At Antietam, especially, I explore the ways in which the battlefield and the home front intersected during the Civil War. For example, I talk about the battle's importance in allowing Abraham Lincoln to announce his preliminary proclamation of emancipation. I go on to discuss the nature of the proclamation, its relationship to earlier congressional actions such as the Second Confiscation Act, and the shift in historical analysis from a preoccupation with political events in Washington concerning emancipation to a broader interpretation that takes into account the actions of African Americans—both slave and free—that furthered the cause of black freedom during the war.

Antietam also provides a good place at which to discuss the diplomatic implications of military events. I point out the irony that on September 17, the day Antietam was fought, British foreign secretary Lord John Russell agreed with Prime Minister Viscount Palmerston that a victory by Lee's army in Maryland would open the door for Britain to attempt to arrange an end to the conflict. I next mention that England and France backed away from some type of mediation following Lee's retreat from Antietam in September 1862.

I use the battlefield at Antietam to examine internal rifts in northern and southern society. At the Dunker Church, which stood at the epicenter of the battle, we discuss conscientious objectors in the North and the fact that western Maryland contained few slaveholders and thus did not welcome the Confederate invaders. At the site of the North Woods (now gone) where the battle opened, I talk about the straggling and desertion that had depleted Lee's ranks and the factors within the Confederacy that sometimes promoted dissension. I use the postbattle meeting near Sharpsburg between Lincoln and George B. McClellan to explore the chasm that divided the two men politically, and to stress that millions of northerners shared McClellan's conservative ideas about what the war was about and what kind of reunified nation should emerge from it.

Gettysburg affords an equal number of opportunities to consider broad questions relating to the war. In the National Cemetery, where students are surrounded by the graves of roughly 4,000 Federal soldiers who died at Gettysburg, I talk about what the concept of Union meant to thousands of northerners in the mid-nineteenth century. In my experience, one of the hardest things to get across to students—or to adults interested in the Civil War—is some idea of why hundreds of thousands of Americans risked their lives to hold the

Union together. Historian Barbara Fields has labeled preservation of the Union "a goal too shallow to be worth the sacrifice of a single life,"[19] an observation that might seem to make sense to modern students. But Fields's comment overlooks the fact that untold northern men and women did believe the Union worth fighting to preserve, and we cannot understand them or the Civil War unless we try to grasp why. No one captured the war's essence more effectively than Lincoln in his address of fewer than 300 words delivered at the dedication of the cemetery in Gettysburg on November 19, 1863. My students and I read those words in the cemetery and discuss how the conflict evolved during its first two years.

The war had begun as a war for Union—a test to see if a republican government could withstand the threat of disunion. At Gettysburg, Lincoln spoke to the widely held belief that the United States was a beacon of democracy in a world where that form of government had yet to take firm root. If the Confederacy succeeded in winning its nationhood, believed Lincoln and other northerners reared on the rhetoric of Daniel Webster, the noble American experiment in democracy would have failed. When the students hear Lincoln's words in the setting of the cemetery, it brings home to them the awful price that thousands paid to keep the Union together. They see evidence of what Lincoln meant when he said the Federal dead gathered on that hilltop had "given the last full measure of devotion."[20]

Lincoln also touched on the North's second great war aim when he spoke at Gettysburg about the conflict's bringing "a new birth of freedom" to the United States. This opens the door to talk to students about the addition of emancipation to Union as a focus of northern efforts and to emphasize how controversial this was across much of the North. I talk about the viciously racist character of the New York City draft riots, which took place in the immediate aftermath of Gettysburg, and the grudging acceptance of black soldiers by many of the northern men who in 1861–1862 had enlisted to save the Union but in 1863 expressed a disinclination to die for emancipation.

The numerous monuments at Gettysburg constitute perfect props to use in following up on the theme of racial tension during the war. I explain that

19. Barbara J. Fields, "Who Freed the Slaves?" in Geoffrey C. Ward, Ric Burns, and Ken Burns, *The Civil War: An Illustrated History* (New York: Alfred A. Knopf, 1990), 178.

20. For this and the second quotation from Lincoln's address, see Abraham Lincoln, *The Collected Works of Abraham Lincoln*, ed. Roy P. Basler, 9 vols. (New Brunswick, N.J.: Rutgers University Press, 1953–55), 7:23.

most of the monuments were erected during the era of reconciliation, and that commemorations of Gettysburg and other battles often included scenes of former Union and Confederate soldiers in cheerful interaction. Absent were black veterans, a testament to the almost universal agreement North and South to slight or ignore entirely emancipation in favor of celebrating the war as an epochal event that made the nation a great world power. I allude to the late-nineteenth-century shift in Lost Cause emphasis from resolutely anti-Yankee rhetoric, typified by Jubal Early's writings and speeches, to the conciliatory tone adopted by what might be called the John B. Gordon School.

Another theme I develop at Gettysburg concerns civilians caught in the war's path. I discuss how all major battles overwhelmed local residents, who suffered catastrophic loss of property, had to help care for masses of wounded men, and cleaned up thousands of dead animals and untold material wreckage—all with very little or no government help. I make the point that Gettysburg's civilians were among the very few northerners who experienced the war the same way that scores of thousands of southern civilians did. Any consideration of the respective home fronts, I tell my students, must begin with acknowledgment of this difference. I use the example of Louisa May Alcott's *Little Women*. For most northerners, the war was much like that of the March girls. Their father is gone and they miss him, but otherwise their lives proceed very much as before the war. Few southerners, white or black, could claim as much.

Virtually all of my students are moved by standing on ground where Americans paid the ultimate price in a struggle over their differing beliefs. They look over countryside that evokes images of people trying to settle profound questions relating to slavery and freedom, to the nature of the Union, and to the relationship between segments of a population that had become increasingly estranged over the previous half century. In anonymous written evaluations of my class, students most frequently mention the trips to Antietam and Gettysburg, and many of them describe these trips as the most memorable part of their four years at the university. I believe such statements attest to the great value of battlefields as tools to help those of us who teach about the Civil War.

The Organization of American Historians has joined with the National Park Service in a joint program designed to review interpretation at Civil War parks. The program began at Antietam in October 1995 when three historians selected by the OAH spent two days at the park. They evaluated the park's current interpretive strategy, consulted with Park Service historians and other staff, and participated in a public forum. Much of the discussion between the OAH visitors and the Park Service historians centered on how the park can better convey to Antietam's visitors the ties between the battle and the Emancipation Proclamation, the experience of black and white residents of the area during the war, and the relationship between Antietam and the larger military history of the conflict. In reporting on the consultations, one OAH historian stated that "the site visit sparked good discussion and a stimulating exchange of ideas that will lend additional support for National Park Service efforts to provide the best possible experience for visitors." This kind of cooperation between the academic and the public spheres promises results that should go a long way toward silencing critics who question the importance of Civil War battlefields as historical resources.[21]

We need the battlefields because they can serve as gateways to a fuller appreciation of how the war shaped nineteenth-century America and continues to shape us today. Lincoln said at the dedication of Gettysburg's national cemetery that the world would never forget the Union soldiers who had given their lives on July 1–3, 1863. That cemetery and the fields that surround it, as well as scores of other Civil War battlegrounds, stand as wonderful reminders of what men and women, North and South, black and white, struggled for and against during our most profound crisis. They are wonderful stages for anyone who would coax out the subtle shadings of the conflict's rich story, and we should preserve and protect them as national treasures.

21. Barbara Franco, "Antietam National Battlefield Visit," *OAH Newsletter* 24 (May 1996):3. A second OAH team visited Richmond National Battlefield Park in 1997.

Index

Acton, Lord, 104
Adams, Richard, 218
Alabama, 246
Alcott, Louisa May, 282
Alexander, Bevin, 102, 112
Alexander, Edward P., 9, 35, 37, 41, 42,
  60, 61, 70–72, 74, 79, 87, 88, 90,
  111, 161, 167, 235, 237, 241
Alexandria, Va., 29, 122
Allan, William, 55, 61, 67, 83, 93, 154,
  165, 175, 181
Allegheny Mountains, 107, 188
Amelia Court House, 234
American Historical Association, 274,
  276
American Revolution, 4, 25, 249, 268
Anderson, Richard H., 65, 84, 96, 98,
  152, 169–71, 173, 174, 183
Anderson, William "Bloody Bill," 255
Annals of War, 235
Antietam, battle of, 24, 33–43, 80, 82,
  89, 108, 240, 254, 261, 278–80,
  282, 283. See also Maryland cam-
  paign, 1862
Antietam Creek, 37
Antioch Church, 152
Appalachians, 210, 251
Appomattox, 50, 158, 199, 200–202,
  204, 222, 228, 233, 234, 249, 276
Archer, James J., 172
Arkansas, 259

Arlington, Va., 212
Armistead, Lewis A., 132, 133, 228, 239,
  256
Army of Mississippi, 255
Army of Northern Virginia, xi, 3, 4, 5, 9,
  15, 19, 21, 27, 29, 30, 33, 35, 38, 42,
  43, 45. 47, 50, 52, 68, 71–74, 77, 78,
  80, 81, 87–89, 102, 105, 117, 118,
  135, 138–40, 151, 157, 162, 167,
  169, 172, 173, 181, 186, 187, 199,
  202, 204, 205, 208, 211, 215–17,
  222, 249, 251, 253, 261, 265, 276;
  as a rallying point and symbol, 14,
  20, 22, 108; casualties in, 15, 18, 35,
  41, 48, 98, 133; numerical strength
  of, 29, 30, 33; supply problems in,
  30, 32, 33, 34, 70, 78, 79, 98
Army of the Potomac, 10, 17, 28, 36, 43,
  50, 63, 65, 71, 73, 79, 88, 114, 118,
  124, 127, 131, 134, 158, 169, 170,
  188–90, 192, 212, 249, 261
Army of the Shenandoah, 191, 193
Army of the Valley, 126, 191, 193
Army of Tennessee, 83, 253, 255, 260
Army of Virginia, 23, 28, 111, 183
Arts & Entertainment Network, 103
Association for the Preservation of Civil
  War Sites, 273
Atlanta, Ga., 16, 17, 18, 254, 255, 260
Atlanta Southern Confederacy, 116
Augusta, Ga., 187

Badeau, Adam, 207
Baltimore, Md., 23, 26, 27, 69, 73, 120
Banks, Nathaniel P., 105, 107, 108, 188,
    189, 192, 255, 261
Barksdale, William, 52
Barton, Clara, 279
Battle, Lewis, 13, 14
Battlefields, as teaching tools, 278–83;
    Lost Cause interpretation at, 273–
    78; preservation of, 264, 265, 268–
    83
Battle Flag, 218
Battle Cry of Freedom, 249
Beasley, David, 265, 266
Beauregard, P. G. T., 259
Bemiss, Samuel M., 6
Berdan, Hiram, 132, 133
Bermuda Hundred, Va., 234
Berryville, Va., 190
Big Bethel, Va., skirmish at, 121, 122
Black Horse Tavern, 61
Bloody Angle (at Spotsylvania), 271
Blue and Gray Magazine, 221, 246
Blue Ridge Mountains, 188
Bonham, Luke, 174
Boritt, Gabor, 105, 222
Boteler's Ford, 41, 43
Bowers, John, 102
Bradford, Gamaliel, 143
Bragg, Braxton, 4, 22, 27, 80, 253, 254,
    259
Brandy Station, Va., 265
Brent, Joseph L., 126, 130, 133
Bristoe Station, Va., 82
Brock Road, 91
Brown, George Campbell, 69, 91, 94,
    176–78
Buell, Don C., 259
Buford, John, 170–72, 256
A Bullet for Stonewall, 218

Burns, Ken, xiii, 245–48, 250, 251, 253,
    256–63, 274
Burnside, Ambrose E., 16, 40, 51
Burnside's Bridge, 279
Butler, Benjamin F., 261

Campaigns of the Army of the Potomac,
    50, 141
Canada, 202
Cannae, battle of, 36
Carlisle Road, 67
Caroline County, Va., 119
Carter, Hodding, 216
Casdorph, Paul D., 102, 214
Cashtown, Pa., 170, 171, 175
Catoctin Mountains, 189
Cedar Creek, battle of, 191, 193, 194
Cedar Mountain, battle of, 109, 111,
    159
Cemetery Hill, 54, 65–68, 81, 112, 159,
    162, 163, 165, 168, 173, 176–80,
    229, 230, 235
Cemetery Ridge, 270, 276
Chamberlain, Joshua L., 219, 256, 269
Chamberlayne, John H., 39
Chambers, Lenoir, 1–3
Chambersburg, Pa., 72, 169, 170, 175,
    190, 240
Chancellor House, 276
Chancellorsville, campaign of, 13, 14,
    18, 57, 69, 73, 84, 101, 103, 108,
    109, 111, 113, 159, 168, 183, 185,
    214, 220, 262, 268, 276, 278
Chantilly, Va., 32
Charles City Road, 128
Chattanooga, battles around, 210, 253,
    254
Chesnut, Mary, 8
Chickahominy River, 124, 126–28
Chickamauga, campaign of, 80, 84

Chilton, Robert H., 136
Churchill, Winston, 217, 218
Cincinnati (Grant's horse), 220
The Civil War (documentary), xiii, 246–49, 253, 259, 261, 262
The Civil War: The Magazine of the Civil War Society, 103, 221
Civil War Journal (documentary) 103
Civil War Sites Advisory Commission, 274
Civil War Times Illustrated, 104, 221, 246
Clark's Mountain, Va., 88
Cobb, Thomas R. R., 135
Coddington, Edwin B., 63, 64, 162, 166, 172, 230
Cold Harbor, battle of, 98
Columbia, S. C., 266
Columbus, Ohio, 246
Company "Aytch," 262
Confederate Bureau of War, 43
Confederate flag, controversy surrounding, 265–66
Confederate monuments, controversy surrounding, 266–67
The Confederate Image: Prints of the Lost Cause, 105, 222
Confederate morale, scholarship on, 20
Confederate Veteran, 211, 227
Confederate War Department, 10
Confederates, 218
Connelly, Thomas L., xii, 15, 206, 213, 252, 257
Conolly, Thomas, 5
Conquering the Valley: Stonewall Jackson at Port Republic, 102
Conrad, Bryan, 63, 149, 150
Continental Army, 4
Cooper, Samuel, 74, 94, 136
Copperheads, 262

Cornwell, Bernard, 218
The Court Martial of Robert E. Lee, 218
The Crater, 220
Crisis at the Crossroads, 162
Cromwell, Oliver, 184
Crook, George, 193
Cross Keys, battle of, 108, 110, 188, 194
Culp's Hill, 69, 81, 112, 159, 162, 163, 165, 177, 178, 229, 256
Cumberland Valley, 72, 169
Curtin, Andrew G., 71, 72
Custer, George A., 193
Cyropaedia, 217

Dabney, Robert L., 103, 111
Daniel, Jonathan, 216
Darbytown Road, 129, 130
Davis, Jefferson, 9, 18, 25, 26, 29, 30, 33, 34, 38, 43, 45, 56, 78, 87, 105, 123, 126, 136, 151, 165, 168, 175, 260, 261, 268
Davis, Joseph, 172
Davis, Nicholas A., 38
Davis, William C., 103
Dawson, Francis, 91
Death of a Nation, 229
Democratic Party, 25, 27, 28, 45, 150, 261
Devil's Den, 256
Dictionary of American Biography, 119, 151
Disney Corporation, 265, 273, 274
Dorn, Earl Van, 260
Douglas, Henry K., 112, 163, 166
Douglass, Frederick, 212
Dowdey, Clifford, 62, 90, 149, 165, 215, 229, 230
Dudley, Thomas, 24
Dunker Church, 279, 280

Early, Jubal A., xi, xii, xiii, 17, 20, 39, 66, 68, 69, 71, 84, 90–92, 94–97, 112, 113, 149, 157, 163, 165, 166, 173, 175–80, 182–87, 189, 191–95, 261; and the Myth of the Lost Cause, 51, 52, 57, 61, 62, 114, 141, 143, 145, 146, 148, 150, 158, 167, 199–213, 215, 216, 218–22, 224, 249, 269, 276, 282

Eastern theater, importance of, 22, 23

Eckenrode, Hamilton J., 63, 149, 150

Edmondston, Catherine A. D., 4, 9, 43, 104

Edwards, Leroy S., 47

Eggleston, George C., 144

Eisner, Michael, 273

Eldridge, E. J., 135, 136

Eleventh Corps, 109, 173, 176

Emancipation, as northern war aim, 24, 25, 28, 43–44, 46, 281; ignored during reconciliation, 282

Emancipation Proclamation, 24, 25, 28, 43–46, 240, 261, 280, 283

Emmitsburg Road, 54

Eternal Peace Light Memorial, 270

Evans, Clement A., 15

Evans, Nathan "Shanks," 32

Ewell, Lizinka B., 94

Ewell, Richard S., xii, 32, 48, 52, 54, 58, 61, 62, 65–69, 83–85, 87, 88, 97, 107, 113, 159, 160, 162, 163, 165–69, 171–81, 188, 193; problems and removal from command, 81, 82, 89, 91–96

Fair Oaks, Va., 128

"Faithfully and Forever Your Soldier," 231

Farwell, Byron, 102

Field, Charles W., 84, 97

Fields, Barbara, 281

Fifth Corps, Army of the Potomac, 95, 154

1st Artillery (U.S.), 119

First Corps, Army of Northern Virginia, 3, 60, 66, 68, 80, 83, 84, 90, 91, 96, 98, 169

First Corps, Army of the Potomac, 172, 173, 176

Fisher's Hill, battle of, 191, 192, 194

Five Forks, battle of, 234

Foote, Shelby, 255, 257–59

For the Love of Robert E. Lee, 218

Forrest, Nathan B., 259, 260

Forrest Gump, 215

Fort, J. Franklin, 271

Fort Donelson, Tenn., 10, 17, 110, 253

Fort Henry, Tenn., 10, 110, 253

Fort Leavenworth, Va., 119

Fort Monroe, Va., 11

Fort Pillow, battle of, 260

Fort Sumter, S. C., 250

Foster, Gaines M., 201, 206

Four Years with General Lee, 52, 148

France, 25; and 1862 Maryland campaign, 23, 24, 44, 280

Franklin, William B., 42

Frayser's Farm. *See* Glendale

Frederick, Md., 30, 190

Fredericksburg, Va., 7, 11, 16, 40, 51, 57, 67, 105, 108, 109, 185, 188, 189, 234, 251, 254, 255, 261, 276

Fredericksburg, second battle of, 114

Freeman, Douglas S., 42, 58, 61, 62, 66, 85, 87, 95, 119, 129, 130, 132, 136, 144, 149, 151, 162, 165, 180, 192, 212, 213, 215–17, 228, 229

Fremantle, Arthur J. L., 8, 15, 48, 56, 67, 74, 116, 171, 173, 217, 262

Frémont, John C., 107, 108, 110, 188, 189, 192, 259, 261

From Cedar Mountain to Antietam, 149
From Manassas to Appomattox, 157
Front Royal, Va., 43, 107, 110, 188, 194
Frye, Dennis E., 273
Fuller, J. F. C., 15, 63, 217
Furgurson, Ernest B., 214

Gaines's Mill, battle of, 111, 127
Gainesville, Va., 152
Gallon, Dale, 103
Garnett, Richard, 228
General Lee: His Campaigns in Virginia, 1861–1865, p. 148
Georgia, 265
Georgia units: 16th Infantry Regiment, 14, 135; 22nd Infantry Regiment, 13
Gettysburg Address, 281
Gettysburg campaign, xii, 13, 14, 18, 35, 47–76, 79, 80–82, 91, 101, 111–13, 141, 145, 149–51, 158–81, 207, 215, 218–20, 227–30, 233, 235–37, 239–41, 253, 255–57, 262, 268, 269
Gettysburg, Pa., 52, 54, 65–67, 70, 114, 159, 161, 163, 169–71, 173–76, 178–80, 276, 278–81, 283; monuments at, 281; reunions at, 270
Gettysburg (motion picture), 219
Gettysburg (novel) 216
The Gettysburg Campaign, 230
Gladstone, William, 23, 44
Glendale, battle of, 130
God and Generals, 219
Gordon, John B., xi, 91, 92, 97, 101, 112, 163, 164, 166, 177–79, 193, 201, 262, 269, 270, 278, 282
Gordonsville, Va., 87
Goree, Thomas J., 57, 134
Grant, Ulysses S., 4, 20, 22, 77, 78, 79, 80, 85, 87, 88, 105, 120, 142, 189,
190, 192, 193, 195, 199, 207, 208, 210, 212, 214, 216–18, 220–22, 251–54, 256–262
Grant and Lee, 217
Grapevine Bridge, 128–30, 137
Great Britain, 217; and 1862 Maryland campaign, 23, 24, 28, 44, 280
Greencastle, Pa., 240
Groom, Winston, 214, 215
Groveton, Va., battle of, 32, 175
Guiney's Station, Va., 276
The Guns of the South, 218

Hairston, Peter W., 95
Halifax County, N. C., 43
Halleck, Henry W., 73, 259
Hampton, Wade, 49
Hancock, Winfield S., 89, 90, 95, 168, 176
Harper, M. A., 218
Harpers Ferry, [W.] Va., 37, 38, 41, 43, 72, 107, 108, 188
Harpers Ferry Road, 89
Harris, Joel Chandler, 239
Harris Farm, battle of, 93
Harrisburg, Pa., 169, 170, 175
Harrison, Walter H., 229, 233–35, 241
Harrison's Landing, Va., 134
Harrisonburg, Va., 107, 188
Haskell, Alexander C., 33, 35, 40
Hassler, Warren W., 162, 165
Hassler, William W., 174
Hattaway, Herman, 249
Havana, 202
Haymarket, Va., 152, 265
Hays, Harry, 163
The Heart of a Soldier, 227, 232–34, 237, 238, 240, 241
Heidlersburg, Pa., 175
Henderson, G. F. R., 103, 148, 217

Henry Hill, 109, 183

Herr's Ridge, 172

Heth, Henry, 56, 57, 65, 74, 84, 95, 97, 160–62, 169–75

High Tide at Gettysburg, 231

Hill, Ambrose P., xii, 14, 32, 33, 87–91, 97, 114, 124, 126, 127, 132, 234; during Gettysburg campaign, 54, 65, 66, 68, 69, 82, 83, 158–62, 165–78, 181; illnesses of, 95–6, 171

Hill, Daniel H., 41, 121, 124, 126, 127, 132–34, 136, 144, 175

Hoffbauer, Charles, 251

Holmes, Emma, 6

Holmes, Theophilus H., 110, 118, 130, 137

Holzer, Harold, 105, 222

Hood, John B., 32, 38, 54, 62, 83, 97, 121, 152–55, 234, 260

Hooker, Joseph, 13, 85, 87, 108, 109, 112

Hopewell Gap, 152

Hotchkiss, Jedediah, 69, 87, 108, 161, 179, 189, 194

Houghton Mifflin, 216, 238

House of Representatives, U.S., 45, 46

How the North Won, 249

Howard, Oliver O., 109, 168

Huger, Benjamin, 118, 126–34, 137

Humphreys, Benjamin G., 52

Hunter, David, 189, 192, 261

I Rode with Stonewall, 166

Illinois, 46

Imboden, John D., 55

Indiana, 46

Inman, Arthur C., 227, 230, 231, 233, 237, 238

Jackson, Julia, 105

Jackson, Mary Anna, 105, 221

Jackson, Thomas J. "Stonewall," xi, xii, 10, 15, 30, 32, 37, 41, 62, 63, 67, 72, 81, 82, 89, 96, 101–17, 126–34, 137, 139, 140, 142–44, 146, 149–55, 157, 159–66, 168, 169, 175, 180–89, 192–95, 202, 207, 220, 240, 255, 256, 276; as Confederate hero, 104, 105, 106, 108–13, 117, 121, 134, 199, 210, 212, 251; in popular history, 102–105, 214, 218, 221–23, 227, 268, 269; religious beliefs of, 117, 138, 184

Jackson and Lee, 103, 221

James River, 121, 127, 133, 188

Jamieson, Perry D., 250

Jenkins, Micah, 83, 84

Jericho Mills, Va., 95

Johnson, Edward A. "Allegheny," 84, 87, 97, 175, 177, 178, 180

Johnston, Albert S., 17, 150, 259

Johnston, Joseph E., 9, 18, 35, 49, 80, 118, 123, 124, 128, 255, 259; criticism of, 16, 17

Johnston, William P., 58, 150

Jones, Archer, 249, 252

Jones, Charles C., 117

Jones, David R., 32, 89, 136, 152

Jones, J. William, 141, 143, 157, 158

Jones, John B., 10, 134

Jones, John R., 34

Jones, Mary, 117

Jones, Robert H., 13

Joshua, 184

Julio, E. B. D., 222

Kantor, MacKinlay, 216

Kean, Robert G. H., 43, 49

Kemper, James L., 32, 152, 228

Keneally, Thomas, 218

Kentucky, 254; political sympathies in, 27

Kernstown, Va., first battle of, 107, 188, 194

Kernstown, Va., second battle of, 190, 194

Kershaw, Joseph B., 84, 97, 193

The Killer Angels, 219, 220, 256

Knoxville, Tenn., 80

Krick, Robert K., 101–103

Ku Klux Klan, 266

Kunstler, Mort, 103, 104, 221

Lacy, Beverly T., 94

Lamb, John, 134, 136

Lane, James H., 174

The Last Meeting of Lee and Jackson, 222, 223

Law, Evander M., 61, 80, 83, 84

Lawley, Francis C., 7, 217

Lea, Alber Miller, 119

League of American Pen-Women, 241

Lee, Custis, 58, 80

Lee, Fitzhugh, 141, 142, 158, 168, 176

Lee, Mary Custis, 74

Lee, Richard Henry "Light Horse Harry," 138

Lee, Robert E., xi, xii, xiii, 3–20, 105, 123, 144, 150, 175, 182–84, 187, 188, 191, 192, 195 ,199, 204–206, 210–12, 215, 217, 219, 224, 235, 240, 249, 252, 253, 256–62, 271; background of, 6; criticism of, 8, 9, 11, 48–52, 57, 60, 85–88, 114; and European recognition, 25, 29; and Gettysburg campaign, 47–76, 80, 82, 83, 158, 159, 161, 162, 165, 168, 169, 171–74, 176, 179–81, 219; and Maryland campaign, 22– 46, 254, 280; and Mine Run cam-

paign, 79; and northern politics, 26, 29; and Overland campaign, 77–98, 114; personal qualities, 6, 7, 8, 18, 19, 114, 117; physical problems of, 63, 80, 88; popularity among south-ern civilians, 4, 6, 12, 13, 16, 18, 108, 109, 140; popularity among southern soldiers, 3, 4, 6, 12, 13, 14, 48; as post–Civil War icon, 4, 20, 51, 52, 103, 141, 142, 158, 167, 199, 200, 202, 206–208, 211, 213, 214, 216–18, 220–25, 227, 251, 265, 268, 269, 273, 276, 278; pur-suit of strategic and tactical offen-sive, 15, 16, 36, 46, 47, 50, 54, 55, 62, 64, 67, 69, 73–75, 79, 88, 133, 153, 154; religious faith, 7, 8, 114, 137, 222; and Second Manassas campaign, 139, 140, 143, 146, 147, 149–57, 220; and Seven Days cam-paign, 11, 124–37, 250, 251; and slavery, 257; and southern civilian expectations, 10

Lee, Stephen D., 133, 146, 148

Lee, Thomas, 121

Lee and Grant at Appomattox, 216

Lee and Jackson, 102, 214

Lee and Longstreet at Gettysburg, 231

Lee Considered, 213, 257

Lee the American, 143

Lee Chapel, 141, 216

Lee's Hill, 276

Lee's Lieutenants, 165

Leesburg, Va., 21

Lewis, John H., 45

Lexington, Va., 105, 141, 216

Life and Campaigns of Robert E. Lee, 50

Light Division, 14, 33, 159, 169

Lincoln, Abraham, 25, 36, 37, 39, 43, 44, 46, 72, 104, 190, 210, 212, 221,

235, 236, 240, 253, 255, 259, 261, 280, 281, 283
Lincoln administration, 25
Little Round Top, 61, 229, 256, 268
Little Women, 282
Lomax, Elizabeth Lindsey, 138
London *Standard*, 208
London *Times*, 7, 23
Long, Armistead L., 9, 61, 67, 128, 129
Longacre, Edward G., 231
Longstreet, Augustus B., 49
Longstreet, James, xii, 3, 30, 32, 38, 41, 82, 84, 120, 124, 126, 127, 129–31, 168, 169, 186, 187, 220, 227, 234, 235, 237, 240, 241; at Second Manassas, 139–57; criticism of Lee, 49, 50, 55, 114, 158; in Gettysburg campaign, 49–52, 54, 57, 58, 60–72, 74, 80, 83, 159, 160, 169, 180, 207, 236, 256; in Overland campaign, 79, 80, 87–91, 95, 96; relationship with Lee, 38, 83, 143, 144, 151, 157; as scapegoat of Lost Cause advocates, 47, 114, 140–45, 148, 149, 150, 157, 206, 207, 213, 219
The Lost Cause, 39
Lost Cause interpretations, xi, xii, xiii, 20, 51, 52, 58, 61, 68, 79, 141–43, 146, 167, 200, 207–14, 215, 217–22, 224, 241, 249, 251, 257, 264, 265, 267–71, 273, 274, 276, 282
Lost Victories, 102, 112
Louisville, Ky., 211
Luray Valley, 107, 188
Lynchburg, Va., 93, 187, 189, 190, 192, 194, 204
Lynchburg *Virginian*, 18

Macon, Ga., 11
Magruder, Esther H. Von Kapff, 120
Magruder, John B., xii, 118–38; criticism

of, 134–37; health problems, 128, 130, 137
Mahone, William, 98
Maine unit: 20th Infantry Regiment, 256, 269
Malvern Hill, battle of, 118, 130–35
Manassas, battles of: First, 109–10, 111, 183, 194; Second, 23, 24, 30, 32, 36, 44, 46, 68, 72, 82, 84, 108, 111, 139–57 *passim*, 183, 218, 220, 261
Manassas, Va., 21, 153, 154, 276
Manassas National Battlefield Park, 265, 273
The Marble Man, 213, 257
March to the Sea, 258
Marshall, Charles, 155
Marye's Heights, 255
Maryland, 28, 29, 33, 34, 36, 41–46, 189, 190, 251, 265, 279; political sympathies in, 26, 27, 45
Maryland campaign, 1862, xii, 22–46, 108; and Confederate independence, 26, 35, 46; and European intervention, 23–25, 35, 44, 46; hardships in, 32–34; and northern politics, 25–28, 45, 46; plundering in, 34; southern civilians' opinions of, 43; southern soldiers' opinions of, 39–40; straggling and desertion in, 32–35. *See also* Sharpsburg, battle of
Massachusetts unit: 6th Infantry Regiment, 26
Massanutten Mountains, 107, 188
McCabe, James G. Jr., 50, 51
McCabe, William G., 58
McClellan, George B., 8, 10, 11, 35–42, 105, 109, 118, 123, 126–29, 132–34, 188, 189, 193, 208, 240, 249, 250, 256, 261, 280
McClure's Magazine, 235

McDowell, battle of, 107–10, 188, 194
McDowell, Irvin, 11, 105, 108, 188, 189, 194
McGuire, Judith, 110, 111, 135
McIntosh, David G., 70
McKim, Randolph H., 48
McLaws, Lafayette, 54, 62, 66, 80, 83, 84, 97, 124
McLean House, 276
McMurry, Richard M., 252
McPherson, James, 249, 253, 273
McWhiney, Grady, 15, 250
Meade, George G., 49–52, 58, 60, 61, 63–65, 70, 72, 73, 79, 161, 253
Mechanicsville, battle of, 11, 13, 111, 126, 169
Mechanicsville, Va., 87, 88
A Memoir of the Last Year of the War for Independence . . . , 205, 207
Memphis, Tenn., 10, 111
Mercier, Baron Henri, 24
Mexican War, 6, 119
Mexico, 24, 121, 202, 203
Middleburg, Pa., 170
Middletown, Va., 191
Military Historical Society of Massachusetts, 58
Militia Act of July 17, 1862, p. 25
Milroy, Robert H., 107, 192
Mine Run, Va., 79
Minie, Claude, 250
Mississippi, 169
Mississippi River, 111, 253, 255
Mississippi unit: 21st Infantry Regiment, 52
Monitor, 268
Missouri, 255, 259, 261
Monocacy, battle of, 190, 192, 194
Montgomery, Walter A., 93
Monument Avenue, 114
Morgan, John H., 260

Mosby, John S., 161, 162, 262
Moses, Raphael J., 66, 70, 143
Mule Shoe salient (Spotsylvania) 41, 85, 87, 89, 93, 97, 98, 276
Murfreesboro, Tenn., 254–55

Napoleon, 74, 79
Napoleon, Emperor Louis, 24
Nashville, Tenn. 110, 211
National Urban League, 267
Nazi Germany, 266
Neely, Mark, 105, 222
Newsweek, 246, 257, 265
New Jersey, 46
New Jersey unit: 15th Infantry Regiment, 271
New Market, Va., 107
New Market Gap, 107
New Market Road, 130
New Mexico, 255
New Orleans, 10, 110
New York, 46
New York City, 184; draft riots in, 281
New York unit: 44th Infantry Regiment, 268
Nineteenth Corps, 194
Nolan, Alan T., xii, 15, 63, 64, 79, 213, 257
Norfolk, Va., 11
North Anna River, 85, 88, 89, 95–97
North Carolina, 169
North Carolina units: 4th Infantry Regiment, 163; 12th Infantry Regiment, 93; 37th Infantry Regiment, 14
North Woods, 280

Oak Ridge (Gettysburg), 176
Old, William W., 87
Opequon, battle of the. *See* Winchester, third battle of
Opportunity, 267

Orange Court House, Va., 57
Orange Plank Road, 85, 91, 92, 114
Orange Turnpike, 85, 183
Ordeal by Fire, 249
Organization of American Historians, 282, 283
Orleans, Va., 152
Othello, 120
Overland campaign, xii, 4, 18, 111, 184, 204, 215, 218

Page Valley. *See* Luray Valley
Palmerston, Viscount (prime minister), 23, 24, 44, 280
Pamunkey River, 127
Peach Orchard (Gettysburg), 256
Pea Ridge, battle of, 255
Pender, Fanny, 40
Pender, William D., 33, 40, 161, 169–74, 178
Pendleton, Alexander S., 82, 94, 163
Pendleton, William N., 32, 110, 132, 141, 150, 157
Peninsula campaign, 17, 30, 80, 105, 118, 121–24, 126, 128, 129, 188, 256, 262
Pennsylvania, 29, 41, 47, 49, 62, 73, 77, 78, 80, 81, 159, 228, 240, 251, 253
Pennsylvania State University, 282
Pennsylvania unit: 26th Militia, 71
Perrin, Abner, 174
Perryville, battle of, 45
Petersburg, siege of, 17, 98, 111, 190, 220, 234
Pettigrew, James J., 170
Pfanz, Harry W., 63, 64
Philadelphia Weekly Times, 145
Phillipi, Va., 122
Pickett, George E., xii, 55, 56, 83, 227–31, 233–42, 256

Pickett, LaSalle C., xii, xiii, 227–42, 256
Pickett-Pettigrew Attack (at Gettysburg), 56, 133, 228, 229, 233–37, 256
Pickett and His Men, 235–38, 241
Pickett's Charge, 229
Pickett, Leader of the Charge . . ., 231
Pickett's Men, 229
Piston, William G., 35, 206
Pittsburgh, Pa., 267
Poague, William T., 89
Pollard, Edward A., 9, 13, 39, 50, 67, 121, 143
Pope, John, 23, 28, 36, 111, 118, 146, 149, 153, 155, 183, 259, 260
Port Republic, battle of, 108–10, 188, 189, 194
Port Royal, Va., 119
Porter, Fitz John, 42, 124, 126, 149, 150, 154
Potomac River, 11, 14, 21, 26, 28, 36, 38–43, 45, 46, 70, 72, 73, 107, 122, 169, 188, 189, 206, 253
Powhite Creek, 127
Price, Sterling, 255
Prussian army, 74
Putnam, Sallie B., 135

Quaker Road, 132

Raglan, Lord, 7
Ramseur, Stephen D., 48, 97, 98, 163, 193
Randolph, George W., 43, 123, 124, 136
Random House, 216
Ransom, Robert, 4
Rapidan River, 77, 85, 87, 88, 112
Rappahannock River, 13, 77, 109, 112, 152, 153, 169
Ratchford, J. W., 144

Red River campaign, 192, 255

Reminiscences of the Civil War, 262

Republican Party, 25, 26, 45, 46, 51, 72, 104, 142, 149

Reynolds, John F., 113, 114

Rheinhart, J. H., 14

Richmond, Va., 10, 23, 29, 40, 43, 88, 97, 98, 104, 105, 107, 108, 110, 111, 114, 118, 121, 124, 126, 128, 134, 140, 188–90, 195, 204, 207, 210, 211, 234, 250, 251

Richmond & York River Railroad, 128

Richmond *Dispatch,* 7, 8, 11

Richmond *Enquirer,* 6, 43

Richmond *Examiner,* 9, 39, 50

Ricketts, James B., 152

Robert E. Lee, A Biography, 42, 212, 228

Robert E. Lee and the Road of Honor, 216

Robertson, James I. Jr., 102, 103, 172, 221

Robertson, Jerome B., 80

Rockfish Gap, Va., 191

Rocky Mount, Va., 184

Rodes, Robert E., 48, 66, 84, 93, 94, 97, 112, 163, 173, 175–80, 183, 193

Roosevelt, Franklin D., 270, 271

Rosecrans, William S., 8, 253, 259

Russell, F. Stanley, 78

Russell, Lord John, 23, 24, 44, 280

Russia, 24, 44

Sailor's Creek, battle of, 234

Salem, Va., 152

Savage, Douglas, 218

Savage Station, battle of, 128, 129, 137

Scheibert, Justus, 74

Scotland, Pa., 175

Scott, Winfield, 5, 121, 246

Screven County, Ga., 267

Seasons of the Confederacy, 251

Second Confiscation Act, 280

Second Corps, Army of Northern Virginia, 48, 55, 58, 65, 67–70, 81, 82, 84, 93–96, 101, 112, 113, 159, 165, 166, 169, 173–75, 179, 180, 184, 187, 189

Second Manassas campaign, xii, 11, 23, 24, 30, 36, 44, 46, 68, 72, 82, 84, 89, 108, 111, 139–57, 168, 183, 218, 220, 261

Seddon, John, 55–57

Sedgwick, John, 113, 114, 185

Selcer, Richard F., 231

Seminary Ridge, 65, 72, 173, 174, 176, 177

Seven Days campaign, xii, 9, 11, 13, 23, 24, 44, 46, 67, 68, 79, 108, 109, 111, 113, 118, 126–37, 140, 144, 151, 159, 170, 215, 249, 250, 261

Seven Pines, battle of, 9, 10, 17, 118, 124, 228, 233

Shaara, Jeff, 219

Shaara, Michael, 219, 256

Sharpsburg, battle of. *See* Antietam, battle of; Maryland campaign, 1862

Shenandoah River, North Fork of, 191

Shenandoah Valley, 107, 134, 137, 187, 188, 191, 205, 251, 259

Shenandoah Valley campaign: of 1862, xi, xii, 10, 11, 29, 72, 105, 107–10, 117, 121, 126, 159, 182–84, 189, 190, 192–94, 256; of 1864, pp. 112, 182, 183, 189, 192–94, 202, 204, 258, 261

Shepherdstown, Va., 47

Sheridan, Philip H., 97, 112, 113, 187, 191–95, 202, 258, 259

Sherman, William T., 17, 22, 105, 214, 216, 253, 255–60

Shields, James, 107, 108, 110, 188, 192

Shiloh, battle of, 10, 110, 250, 251, 253, 259

Shrouds of Glory, 214, 215

Sibley, Henry H., 255

Sixth Corps, 190, 194

Skimin, Robert, 220

Slavery, 28, 43, 44, 46, 240, 245, 246, 257, 267, 269, 270, 280–82; George Pickett's view on, 240

Slotkin, Richard, 220

Smith, Edmund Kirby, 22, 27, 254

Smith, Gustavus W., 118, 124

Smith, James Power, 58, 66, 179

Smith, Martin L., 87

Smith, William "Extra Billy," 177, 178, 180

Snow, William P., 144

Soldier of the South, 228, 230, 238

Sons of Confederate Veterans, 266

Sorrel, G. Moxley, 66, 144, 186, 238, 239

South Africa, 218

South Carolina, 174, 265

South Carolina Survivors' Association, 208

South Carolina unit; 13th Infantry Regiment, 160

South Mountain, Md., 37, 41, 61, 71, 72, 169, 189, 246

Southern Bivouac, 211

Southern Historical Society, 211

Southern Historical Society *Papers*, 51, 143, 148, 167, 206, 211, 212, 219, 235

Southern Illustrated News, 5, 104

Special Orders No. 109, p. 42

Spotsylvania County, Va., 13

Spotsylvania Court House, Va., battle of, 41, 85, 87–89, 93, 95–97, 114, 271, 276

Springfield, Ill., 235

Stackpole, Edward J., 149

Stanton, Edwin, 71, 72

Staunton, Va., 107, 188

Stewart, George R., 229, 233

Stikeleather, J. A., 163

Stiles, Robert, 185, 206, 207

Stivers, Don, 103

Stone Mountain, Ga., 267, 268

Stonewall, 102

Stonewall Jackson, 216

Stonewall Jackson and the American Civil War, 217

Stonewall Jackson at Cedar Mountain, 102

Stonewall Jackson: Portrait of a Soldier, 102

Stonewall Jackson: The Soldier, the Legend, 102

Stonewall Brigade, 110, 193

Strasburg, Va., 107, 191

Strong, George T., 71

Stuart, James Ewell Brown "Jeb," 30, 55, 64, 83, 97, 114, 153, 154, 158, 161, 162, 165, 172, 173, 251

Suffolk, Va., campaign of, 151

Sunken Road (at Antietam), 279

Sunken Road (at Fredericksburg), 255

Swinton, William, 50, 51, 55, 141, 158

Sylvania, Ga., 266, 267

Tarbell, Ida, 236

Taylor, Richard, 116, 141, 193

Taylor, Walter H., xi, 39, 40, 52, 65, 67, 80, 111, 129, 148, 172, 179–81, 208

Taylor, Zachary, 120

Texas Brigade, 38, 89

Third Corps, Army of Northern Virginia, 84, 85, 95, 96, 159, 160, 169, 173, 174

Thomas, Edward L., 174

Thomas, George H., 22
Thoroughfare Gap, battle of, 152, 153
Thouvenel, Antoine Edouard, 24
Todd's Tavern, Va., 88
Trans-Mississippi Department, 118, 124,
    135–37, 202
Trans-Mississippi theater, 255
Traveller (Lee's horse), 3, 8, 218, 276
Trimble, Isaac R., 162, 163, 166, 177
Troiani, Don, 103
Tucker, Glen, 231–33, 240
Tullahoma campaign, 253, 254
Turtledove, Harry, 218
Tyneside, 44

*Ulysses: A Biographical Novel of U. S.
    Grant,* 220
United Confederate Veterans, 241
United Daughters of the Confederacy,
    241
U.S. Army, 250
U.S. Mint, 268
U.S. National Cemetery (at Gettys-
    burg), 280, 283
U.S. National Park Service, 276, 282,
    283
U.S. Postal Service, 268
U.S. Sanitary Commission, 71
U.S. War Department, 25
University of North Carolina, 170
University of Virginia, 119
Unto This Hour, 218

Vandiver, Frank E., 62, 103, 144
Vicksburg, Ms., 17, 111, 210, 253, 254
Virginia, 29, 38–41, 45, 61, 121, 161,
    207, 251, 255, 257, 271
Virginia (ironclad), 268
Virginia Historical Society, 251
Virginia units: 9th Infantry Regiment,
    45; 12th Infantry Regiment, 47,
    13th Infantry Regiment, 78; (Mexi-
    can War), 1st Volunteers, 184
Von Kapff, Esther H., 120

Wallace, Lew, 190, 192
Warrenton Turnpike, 139, 152–54
Washington, George, 4, 25
Washington and Lee University, 167,
    207, 215
Washington College, 150
Washington, D.C., 22, 23, 28, 29, 39,
    40, 49, 51, 61, 65, 69, 73, 112, 121,
    155, 189, 190, 193, 206, 251, 259,
    280
Washington *Daily Morning Chronicle,*
    104
Watkins, Samuel, 262
Waud, Alfred R., 113
Waynesboro, Va., 191
Webster, Daniel, 281
Weigley, Russell F., 15
Welch, Spencer G., 159, 173
Welles, Gideon, 72
West Point, N.Y., 6, 119, 120, 121,
    184, 235
Western Virginia campaign, 1861,
    pp. 8, 9
Wheatfield (at Gettysburg), 256
Whig Party, 201
White's Ford, Va., 21, 26
White Oak Swamp, Va., 111, 127, 130,
    137, 155
White Plains, Va., 152
Whiting, W. H. C., 118
Wicker, Tom, 218
Widow Tapp Farm, 41, 89, 114, 276
Wilcox, Cadmus M., 56, 84, 95, 97,
    152–54

Wilderness, battle of the, 41, 58, 85, 87, 88, 89, 93, 96, 97, 101, 187, 276
Williamsburg, Va., 17
Williamsburg Road, 128
Williamsport, Md., 72
Willis Church Road, 132
Willoughby Run, 172
Wilson, James H., 246
Wilson, Woodrow, 270
Wilson's Creek, battle of, 255
Winchester, Va., 48
Winchester, first battle of, 107, 109, 110, 188, 189, 194
Winchester, third battle of, 191–94

Wise, Jennings C., 151, 161
Wolseley, Viscount Garnet, 217
Women's National Press Association, 241
Woodward, C. Vann, 273
Wright, Horatio, 193

Xenophon, 217

Yellow Tavern, Va., engagement at, 97
York River, 121, 188
York Road, 178, 180
Yorktown, Va., 25, 123
Young, Louis G., 170, 171, 174